W9-BVK-320

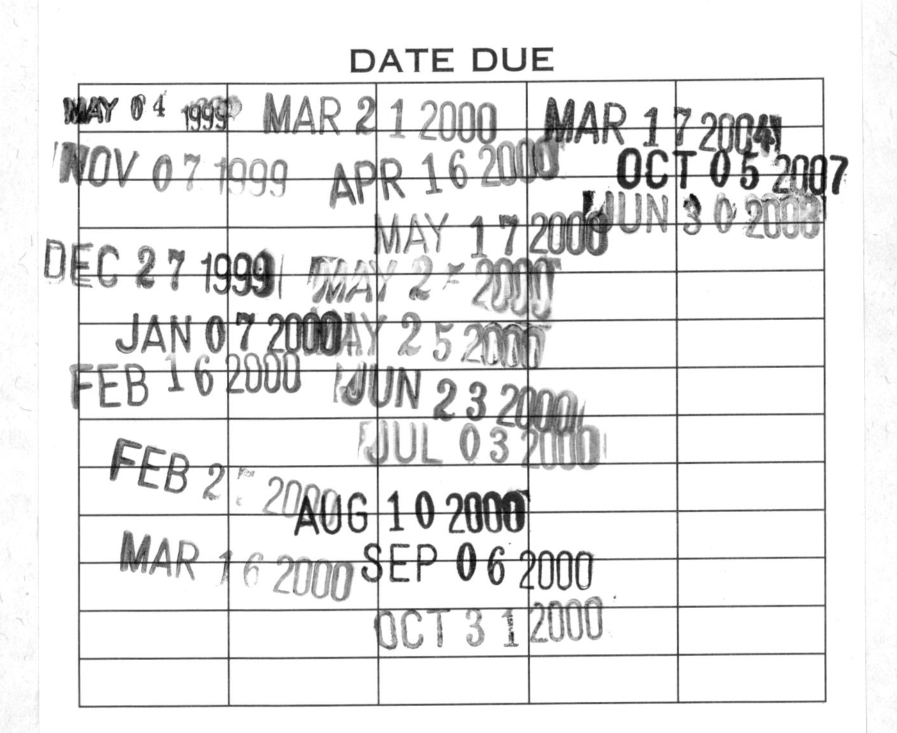
DATE DUE
MAY 04 1999
MAR 21 2000
MAR 17 2004
NOV 07 1999
APR 16 2000
OCT 05 2007
JUN 30 2008
MAY 17 2000
DEC 27 1999
JAN 07 2000
MAY 25 2000
FEB 16 2000
JUN 23 2000
JUL 03 2000
AUG 10 2000
MAR 16 2000
SEP 06 2000
OCT 31 2000

SEDUCTIVE POISON

DEBORAH LAYTON

ANCHOR BOOKS
DOUBLEDAY
NEW YORK • LONDON • TORONTO • SYDNEY • AUCKLAND

SEDUCTIVE POISON

A Jonestown Survivor's Story of Life and Death in the Peoples Temple

AN ANCHOR BOOK
PUBLISHED BY DOUBLEDAY
a division of Bantam Doubleday Dell Publishing Group, Inc.
1540 Broadway, New York, New York 10036

Book design by Julie Duquet

Library of Congress Cataloging-in-Publication Data
Layton, Deborah, 1953–
Seductive poison: a Jonestown survivor's story of life and death in the Peoples Temple / Deborah Layton. — 1st ed.
p. cm.
1. Jones, Jim, 1931–1978. 2. Layton, Deborah, 1953– . 3. Peoples Temple—Biography. 4. Jonestown Mass Suicide, Jonestown, Guyana, 1978. I. Title.
PB605.P46L38 1998
289.9—dc21
[b] 98-18009
CIP

ISBN 0-385-48983-8

Printed in the United States of America
First Anchor Books Edition: December 1998
1 3 5 7 9 10 8 6 4 2

For

Lauren Elizabeth,

my daughter,

who asked tough questions and gave me the strength to go back and face the darkness

In memory of my mother, Lisa Philip Layton,
her mother before her, Anita Philip,
and
the nine hundred thirteen innocent children, teenagers, and families
who perished,
wholly deceived, in Jonestown

Contents

THREE

To protect the privacy of the living, I have omitted some last names and changed the given names of a few others.

All my conversations, including those with Jim Jones, are re-created from memory and from hours of tape recordings my brother, Dr. Thomas N. Layton, made of me immediately after my escape.

Foreword

CHARLES KRAUSE

In April 1978, Debbie Layton Blakey was still in Jonestown as I was taking up my new assignment for the *Washington Post* in Buenos Aires. We didn't know each other then, nor would we meet for many years to come. Yet our lives would soon be intertwined.

That spring twenty years ago, Debbie, increasingly worried about conditions in Jonestown, was about to make a decision that would reverberate around the world; I was a young reporter intrigued by the prospect of covering wars and revolution in Latin America. Buenos Aires was my first foreign assignment after having spent five years covering local politics in the Washington suburbs.

I knew that reporting, especially from countries where leftist guerrillas were battling right-wing military governments, and where the press was often suspect, could be dangerous. But no one had ever mentioned cults—or being shot at by Americans. In fact, I think it would be safe to say that in April 1978 no one at the *Washington Post*—or probably in Washington—had ever heard of the Peoples Temple or Jonestown.

As I was en route to Buenos Aires from the United States, it is entirely possible that my Pan Am flight overflew Guyana, the former British colony turned socialist Co-operative Republic of Guyana, located—"lost" might be a better word—on the northeast bulge of South America.

I had no way of knowing that down below, Debbie Layton, her mother, and some nine hundred other Americans were living as virtual prisoners in the Guyanese rain forest; Jonestown, the utopia they had been promised before they left San Francisco, was essentially a Potemkin village. Nor was there any way I could possibly have known that seven months after arriving in Buenos Aires, I would be shot and nearly killed because of the fateful decision Debbie would make in May 1978 to escape from Jonestown—to seek help for her mother and for the hundreds of other members of the Peoples Temple she believed were being held in the jungle camp against their will.

There were probably many things that could have triggered Jonestown's fiery end. But, sadly, it was Debbie's decision to escape and seek help that became the catalyst for what is still perhaps the most bizarre and tragic episode in the history of American religious movements and messianic cults—the mass suicide-murder of more than nine hundred of Jim Jones's followers on November 18, 1978.

For weeks, Jonestown would remain front-page news, not only in the United States but around the world. Even today, I suspect there are few Americans over the age of thirty who don't remember where they were when they first heard that more than nine hundred of their countrymen had killed themselves, having drunk Flavour-aide laced with cyanide, in a place called Jonestown.

At the time, as horrified and as fascinated as they were, it was easy for most Americans to dismiss the Peoples Temple as a bunch of "crazies"—people not like us—and to dismiss what happened in Jonestown as solely the result of religious fanaticism, or the craziness of the times, or the bizarre hold of charismatic leaders like Jim Jones and, more recently, David Koresh and Marshall Applewhite, on a particular group of ignorant, emotionally needy, confused, or simply naïve followers.

Yet Jonestown did not happen in a vacuum.

Cults and cult-like groups had begun to proliferate during the 1960s in the United States, in reaction to the profound political, social, and sexual revolutions then under way. For many Americans, especially many young Americans, the civil rights and antiwar movements provided a very real sense of liberation. Yet others could not cope with the new freedom and the consequent disintegration of family structures, institutions, and traditional values.

Drugs, sex, rock 'n' roll, dropping in and dropping out, all became a part of the new culture. But nobody was supposed to get hurt. There weren't supposed to be consequences. So the awful reality that hundreds of Americans—men, women, and children—had died of cyanide poisoning in the Guyanese rain forest came as a real shock, even to those enveloped in their own psychedelic haze.

Instantly, "Jonestown" entered the lexicon, an ominous warning to all those Americans who sought meaning for their lives, and "truth," by experimenting with all manner of quasi-religious, quasi-psychological, quasi-libertarian, or quasi-authoritarian self-help movements and cults. Jonestown would demonstrate in bold relief just how dangerous these groups—and their leaders—could be.

In December 1977, when Debbie Layton arrived in Jonestown from California for the first time, she had already been a member of the Peoples Temple for nearly seven years. Indeed, she was one of Jim Jones's favorites, a member of the inner circle. Yet it did not take her very long to conclude that Jonestown was not the idyllic refuge she and all the others had been told it was before they got there.

Just twenty-four at the time, Debbie quickly realized that she and the others had been deliberately deceived; Jonestown was essentially a concentration camp in the jungle. Unlike many Temple members, though, Debbie was clear-headed enough to recognize that Jim Jones, the man they had given their lives to and had believed in without reservation, was increasingly paranoid, psychotic, and dangerous. That process of realization led her to contemplate trying to escape, even if that meant risking her life and leaving behind her mother, terminally ill with cancer, who had herself escaped from Nazi Germany forty years before.

The parallels—and ironies—are chilling. Both Debbie and her mother, Lisa, were obviously tough and intelligent women, survivors alert to the very real dangers around them. Yet both were, initially at least, taken in by Jones, the false prophet they chose to believe and follow, just as many German Jews of Lisa's parents' generation were somehow deluded into thinking that Hitler would never carry out his threats against them.

Neither Debbie nor her mom was deranged. Nor were they unstable women abnormally susceptible to the appeal of a charismatic preacher/politician. People join cults unwittingly. Even reasonable, intelligent people can be fooled by demagogues, and too often, the deeper they become involved in one of these quasi-religious or quasi-political groups, the more difficult it may be to see the potential dangers. As Debbie makes clear in this memoir, both she and her mother were searching for a life with *meaning*—not unlike so many other Americans at that time and since. Except that their search led them to the Peoples Temple and Jim Jones. Having escaped from the Nazis, it was Lisa's fate to die in Jonestown.

During the few hours I was in Jonestown, it became apparent to me that there were a variety of reasons why people had joined the Peoples Temple. For some, it was a political statement; Jones offered the promise of a socialist society free of materialism and racism at a time when such a society was particularly attractive. For others, the Temple offered religion, structure, and discipline—a way to escape the violence of the ghetto and the dead end of alcohol and drugs (which were strictly forbidden).

But Jones cleverly manipulated both his followers and public perceptions of what he and the Peoples Temple were all about, and that is the larger lesson yet to be widely understood. In both California and Guyana, the Peoples Temple was allowed to become a state within a state, enjoying the privileges, and acquiring the legitimacy, that allowed it to thrive over many years. Meanwhile, that legitimacy hid Jones's increasing paranoia and his increasingly erratic demands for control and for power.

The First Amendment's guarantee of freedom of religion makes it very difficult, if not impossible, to investigate religious organizations, even when, as was the case with the Peoples Temple, they deliberately seek political power to shield their immoral and illicit practices from investigation. Jim Jones was a Housing Commissioner in San Francisco, courted by the mayor, the governor, and Rosalynn Carter, even while he was raping young members of his church, stealing their parents' money, staging fake "healings" to impress the ignorant, and threatening, perhaps even murdering, those who attempted to defect from the Temple.

Jones's appeal to the politicians may be difficult to understand now, but it was simple—and he understood it better than they did. In

1968 the Democratic National Convention and Mayor Daley had put the final nail in the coffin of old-fashioned political machines in the United States. But to win, politicians still had to campaign and get out the vote on Election Day. Jim Jones was smart enough to identify the void; in the political free-for-all that was San Francisco in the 1970s, he had the only political machine in town.

Because he had absolute control over his own followers, Jones could, and did, produce legions of campaign workers for favored candidates, then made sure their supporters got to the polls on Election Day. Shiva Naipaul, whose book *Black and White* is, in many ways, the best examination of the politics of the Peoples Temple, describes the peculiar political culture in which it thrived. Among his many questions, Naipaul asked Jones's political allies if they felt they had been taken in by him.

Strangely enough, what Naipaul found was that Willie Brown and most of the others with whom he talked were unapologetic, even a year after having lost more than nine hundred of their constituents to cyanide poisoning in the Guyanese jungle. How could they have known? Did they have an obligation to find out? These were questions that didn't seem to register with Brown and the others.

Jim Jones was always a charlatan. But his delusions and paranoia grew more pronounced as he grew more powerful. The same could be said for the jungle retreat in Guyana. Whatever its initial reason for being, over the years it evolved into a terrible charade where appearances and reality grew further and further apart.

To the outside world, Jonestown was portrayed as a kind of multiracial kibbutz populated by willing pioneers determined to forge a new life in one of the world's most remote and inhospitable environments. Visitors, including consular officers from the U.S. Embassy in Georgetown, Guyana's fetid capital, were fooled into believing that Jonestown's residents were well fed and well cared for.

In the end, it was the press, that other reviled institution protected by the First Amendment, not the prosecutors or the political establishment, which finally began to pierce the veil and reveal the truth about the Peoples Temple. Only then did Jim Jones flee California for Guyana, setting in motion the awful tragedy that would soon follow.

To me, that tragedy—the mass suicide-murder of more than nine hundred of Jim Jones's followers and the bloody ambush that preceded it—seems as if it happened yesterday. I can still remember, vividly, the call from my editors in Washington several days before, telling me that a congressman from California, Leo J. Ryan, would be leaving California the next day to investigate "some crazy cult group" in Guyana.

I was in Caracas, interviewing voters and politicians for a story I was writing on Venezuela's upcoming presidential election. The trip and the coverage had been approved, but now it could wait, I was told. We want you to meet up with the congressman. "It sounds like a more interesting story."

I wasn't entirely convinced. But the next day, I flew from Caracas to Trinidad, where the congressman's flight from San Francisco and New York would stop en route to Guyana. It was nearly 10 P.M. as we took off on the final leg of that flight to Georgetown. For the next hour, I was told chilling stories about Jonestown.

According to a group of concerned relatives aboard the plane with Congressman Ryan, the Jonestown commune was a hellhole where armed guards, torture, tranquilizers, sleep deprivation, and, above all, misplaced faith had combined to trap hundreds of innocent people against their will. Jones was described as a good man gone bad, a charismatic figure who'd led his followers astray, a sadist, a megalomaniac, the Devil incarnate. People were starving in Jonestown, I was told; there wasn't enough food, water, or medicine. Anyone who complained or expressed doubts was beaten or worse.

I listened. But I was skeptical. How could nearly a thousand Americans be tricked into leaving California for Guyana? How could they not have known what they were getting into? Could any of what I was being told possibly be true?

For three days, the congressman, his staff, the concerned relatives, and a small brigade of journalists, my colleagues, waited in Georgetown. Jones and his lawyers, Mark Lane and Charles Garry, did whatever they could to stop us from reaching the jungle commune, which was located about three hundred miles from the capital near a tiny Guyanese village called Port Kaituma.

Finally, on Friday, November 17, frustrated by what he perceived to be stalling tactics, the congressman announced that we would fly to Port Kaituma that afternoon and try to enter Jonestown, with—or without—Jones's permission.

Yes, Jonestown was technically private property and, yes, the Peoples Temple was technically a religious institution located in a sovereign country. But the congressman said Jim Jones had no right to stop a United States congressman from determining for himself whether anyone in Jonestown was being seriously mistreated or held there against his or her will.

What I didn't know at the time was that much of the congressman's information, and urgency, was the result of an affidavit Debbie had written shortly after she escaped from Jonestown the previous May; in effect, it was Debbie who had convinced Congressman Ryan that the situation was serious enough that he should investigate, and the longer Jones stalled, the more determined the congressman became to reach Jonestown.

At about 4 P.M. that Friday, we boarded a tiny Guyanese Airways plane that had been specially chartered for the hourlong trip. There was room for no more than two dozen passengers, so most of the relatives were forced to remain behind. Although they didn't think so at the time, in many ways they were fortunate. Just twenty-four hours later, the congressman and three of the journalists aboard the plane would be dead, and most of the rest of us wounded—victims of the mass hysteria that was about to ensue.

The airstrip at Port Kaituma was nothing more than a clearing in the jungle: no terminal or tower, no lights in case of darkness, and no mechanic in case of trouble. The landing strip wasn't even paved—it was mud, like everything else in the rain forest.

Once on the ground, the congressman, his staff, and the two Temple lawyers were taken immediately to the commune, about five miles away. The rest of us were held at gunpoint by the local sheriff for about an hour, until Jones sent another dump truck to the airstrip;

the relatives and all but one of us journalists would be allowed to proceed.

I will never forget my first impressions of Jonestown as we made our way through the simple wooden gate and continued down the long muddy road toward the central Pavilion. What I saw reminded me of a Southern plantation before the Civil War, not so much because of the architecture but because of the scene. To one side of the large wooden Pavilion was a communal kitchen where women, mostly black, were cooking large vats of stew; others were baking bread. Young children were playing in what appeared to be a schoolyard. Still other members of the Temple, black and white, young and old, were eating their dinner in and around the Pavilion, which served as both an open-air dining hall and a meeting place.

At the center of the Pavilion, seated at the head of a long table, was the white master, Jim Jones. He was an arresting man, his hair dyed jet black. Although he had a kind of commanding stature, it also quickly became clear that he was unnerved by our presence; as we journalists gathered round to ask questions, he responded rationally one minute, emotionally and irrationally the next.

"Threat, threat, threat of extinction," he bellowed in response to a question about Debbie Layton and others who had defected. "I wish I wasn't born at times. I understand hate; love and hate are very close. I wish I wasn't born sometimes."

Those were his words, recorded and played back many times since. Yet despite his odd behavior, there was no visible evidence of starvation, torture, or, initially at least, that Jonestown's residents were desperate to leave. We saw no guns or signs of the kind of intimidation that the concerned relatives talked so much about. Considering its location, Jonestown itself was rather impressive.

But those first impressions would not last.

Jones refused to allow the journalists to remain in Jonestown overnight, so we were sent back to Port Kaituma to sleep on the wooden floor of a tiny bar. That night, as we drank beer and rum, we learned from the sheriff (the same sheriff who had held us captive at the airstrip just hours before) that there were indeed guns in Jonestown and that several members of the Temple had tried to escape.

Some of the escapees, he told us, had been covered with bruises that could have been the result of torture.

We also learned that Jones's worst fears were coming true; at least one family had secretly told the congressman they wanted to leave with us the next day.

We were back in Jonestown early, and it was immediately clear the mood had changed. NBC correspondent Don Harris was preparing to begin a tough interview with Jones, asking about the guns we'd been told about, the allegations of torture, and the family that wanted to leave. Meanwhile, I heard muffled coughing from a large wooden building that looked like a tobacco shed; inside, a group of elderly women, most of them black, were living in clean but extremely cramped and primitive quarters. It was a side of life in the commune Jones had not wanted us to see.

Tension built as the day wore on. There were crying and hysteria at the Pavilion; families were being torn apart as some of their members told the congressman they wanted to stay while others wanted to leave. Jones himself, said to be running a fever, looked and sounded as if he were a defeated man.

Then, toward midafternoon, after most of us were already aboard the dump truck that was to take us back to the airstrip, one of the Temple loyalists attempted to stab Congressman Ryan. There was more screaming. As several of us rushed toward the Pavilion, Ryan emerged uninjured. But his shirt was covered with blood. He was okay, he told us. The blood belonged to his would-be assassin, who had been stabbed after someone grabbed him from behind.

Finally, at about 3 P.M. that Saturday, we were ready to leave Jonestown. As we made our way slowly toward the airstrip, it seemed as if the worst was over. And even then, I was unconvinced that Jonestown was as bad as it had initially been described. Yes, some twenty members of the Temple had decided to leave with us, but more than nine hundred others had decided to stay. Yes, conditions were harsh, but there was no evidence of malnutrition or serious physical abuse. Yes, Jones seemed psychotic, but despite everything, he appeared to have many devoted followers.

Two planes were waiting for us at the airstrip, where we had arrived less than twenty-four hours before. Because the "defectors," as we called them, were fearful, the loading began almost immediately. They couldn't believe Jones would allow them—and us—to leave in peace.

They were right.

Suddenly, without warning, a tractor pulling a hay wagon appeared at the end of the airstrip; there was near panic as the defectors rushed to get on board the two planes.

The tractor began moving toward us.

I was standing by the door of the larger of the two planes, trying to help the defectors get aboard, when I saw the tractor crossing the runway. I still wasn't sure what was happening or why it was moving toward us. Then I heard *pop, pop, pop!*

It was then I realized that people were running, diving for cover, screaming. The popping sounds were gunshots, and they were becoming louder as the tractor moved ever closer. Death was making its way across the runway. I understood instinctively that it would soon reach me.

The gunmen were now rounding the front of the plane, so I ran toward the tail. There, I was faced with a life-or-death choice. If I ran straight, I would have to cross the broad open expanse of the landing strip. It seemed better to turn left, where, out of the corner of my eye, I could see others were taking cover behind a wheel of the plane.

I threw myself down behind the wheel. But within minutes, seconds maybe, the shots were coming from behind. The gunmen had circled from the other side of the plane. Now they were directly behind the wheel where we had sought protection, and they were going to kill the rest of us.

Dirt sprayed onto my face as the bullets tore into the earth nearby. My only thought was, If I lie very still, maybe they'll think I'm already dead.

Then I felt a powerful jolt and a terrible sting. A bullet had struck my hip. Thoughts of my family and friends rushed through my mind. Bullets were still coming. I could hear them. I could feel the dirt. I was going to die.

There was a lull. Then three more shots, spaced maybe thirty seconds apart. Very close. Very loud. *Bang. Bang. Bang!*

Then silence.

A minute passed. Maybe two. I heard the plane's engine begin to rumble.

I opened my eyes without moving my head or body. I could see down the flat expanse of runway. The tractor and the gunmen were moving toward the end of the airstrip, slowly retreating in the same direction from which they had come. My only thought was that if the plane was going to leave, I was going to try to get on it.

I jumped up, not knowing if I could walk. I wobbled a bit. But as painful as it was, the bullet had only grazed my hip and I could manage. I ran around to the door and threw myself aboard the plane. But it couldn't move; one of the engines had been damaged by the gunfire.

Only then did I realize the enormity of what had happened. Lying on the airstrip were seven bodies. Congressman Leo J. Ryan. Dead. NBC correspondent Don Harris. Dead. NBC cameraman Bob Brown. Dead. *San Francisco Examiner* photographer Greg Robinson. Dead. Patricia Parks, one of the "defectors." Dead. Anthony Katsaris, one of the concerned relatives. Badly wounded. And Steve Sung, the NBC soundman. Badly wounded.

Inside the other plane, there were two more seriously wounded people; both were defectors shot by a third Temple member posing as a defector. Ironically, that third "defector" was Larry Layton, Debbie Layton's brother.

In all, four of the congressman's original party were dead, and twelve wounded, including myself; after the shooting, the Guyanese pilots secretly gathered in the smaller of the two planes, which had not been damaged, and flew back to Georgetown without telling us.

As night fell, we knew there would be no way out until at least the next morning; we treated the wounded as best we could and tried to find protection for ourselves, fearful the gunmen might return. It was a nightmare.

But what we didn't know then was that another nightmare was just beginning five miles away. In the early evening hours of Saturday, November 18, 1978, after the gunmen returned from the airstrip and reported that the congressman had been killed, Jones called his followers to the Pavilion. The Temple was under attack, he told them, the Temple had been betrayed. It was time for all loyal members of the Peoples Temple to commit the revolutionary suicide they had practiced so many times before.

There was some resistance, but not much. After a rambling harangue, Jones urged his followers to "die with dignity." The fatal liquid, Flavour-aide mixed with cyanide, was then poured from a washtub into small cups and distributed. One after another, some nine hundred members of the Peoples Temple, many of them parents with children in their arms, drank the poison. Then they huddled together around the Pavilion, writhing in pain, waiting to die. Those who resisted were forced to drink the poison at gunpoint. Jones, however, chose to die in a different way: he shot himself, or was shot, at pointblank range on the floor of the Pavilion, surrounded by his wife, Marceline, and other members of the Temple's inner circle.

By the time I got there thirty-six hours later, the first journalist to reach Jonestown after the suicide-murder, hundreds of bloated bodies, mosquito-infested and rotting in the hot tropical sun, were piled two, three, sometimes even four deep, in the area around the Pavilion. Jones's corpse lay at the center.

Guyanese soldiers had secured the compound but otherwise had done very little. The vat, half-full of the deadly purplish liquid, was still there.

The only survivors were several members of the armed "security squad," whose job it had been to force others to drink the poison. They were then supposed to drink it themselves. But somehow they had survived, and their eyewitness accounts provided the first information of what had happened.

"They started with the babies" was what I was told by the security squad. And that's how I began my report in the next day's *Washington Post*.

Even the dogs had been poisoned.

Debbie Layton survived Jonestown by escaping, and *Seductive Poison* is her account, twenty years later, of how she got involved with Jones and joined the Peoples Temple, and what it was that kept her there for nearly seven years: the psychological and sexual manipulation, the terror and violence used to prevent otherwise sane people from leaving, the strange mixture of idealism, religion, "miracles," and political gobbledygook that Jones concocted to attract a following and then to keep it.

More important, *Seductive Poison* is the story of why Debbie became disillusioned, how and why she began to question the premises, and see through Jones's hypocrisy and lies. It is a personal story that is fascinating in and of itself. But it is also a story that should serve as a guide, a warning, and an inspiration to millions of others throughout the world who find themselves in similar circumstances, taken in by false prophets of a religious—or political—kind.

As a foreign correspondent, I would remain familiar with Jonestown territory. Over the years, I have observed, and reported on, the abuse of power by regimes of both the left and right, from the Communists in Poland and Cuba, to the pro-West military juntas in Argentina and Chile, to the fundamentalist Islamic regimes of the Middle East. Each offered—or offers—something to its people. Like Jim Jones, not even Saddam Hussein in Iraq remains in power by force alone.

Still, terror is terror. And absolute power is absolute power, whether it's wielded by generals with well-equipped armies, ayatollahs with all-powerful secret police, or Jim Jones with only a makeshift goon squad to enforce his perverted will. The abuse of power and the use of repression to subjugate people, whether by Jim Jones in Guyana or Augusto Pinochet in Chile or Saddam Hussein in Iraq, remains a danger to all of us.

There is much that should have been learned (but, unfortunately, was not) from Jonestown about religion, about religion and politics, about the First Amendment, and about the appropriate role of the state in monitoring and regulating groups that claim to be churches.

Just as there are limits on violent or seditious political activity, it may be appropriate, even in a free society, to somehow define the limits of what churches and groups that claim to be religious can and cannot do. Certainly, citizens should be protected from shamans like Jim Jones who conduct fake healings with the help of chicken gizzards or who, in the name of Christ the Lord, or Muhammed, insinuate themselves into politics by providing politicians with armies of their followers. Or money.

In the Pavilion, there was a crude hand-lettered sign, which said THOSE WHO DO NOT REMEMBER THE PAST ARE CONDEMNED TO REPEAT IT.

Above all else, that is why I believe *Seductive Poison* is so important, and why I encouraged Debbie to continue with it after she sent me the first chapters—and after we finally met—two years ago.

Hopefully, *Seductive Poison* will both provide a warning and serve as a reminder that Jonestown was more than a freakish aberration, just as the affidavit Debbie wrote after she escaped from Jonestown warned Congressman Ryan that he should investigate—and proved tragically accurate in warning of the events that would follow.

Since then, "another Jonestown" has become shorthand for similar tragedies like Waco and Heaven's Gate, where mind control, religious fervor, and/or misplaced belief come together in an explosive mix. Parents should read this book, as should their children, because it recounts the experience of someone who was taken in—but who also had the presence of mind to get out.

Legislators, law enforcement officials, and those interested in religion and public policy should also read this book because Debbie Layton's insights and experience provide valuable lessons that should serve to open an important national discussion on religion, politics, and the First Amendment; otherwise, another Jonestown, or something like it, will surely happen again.

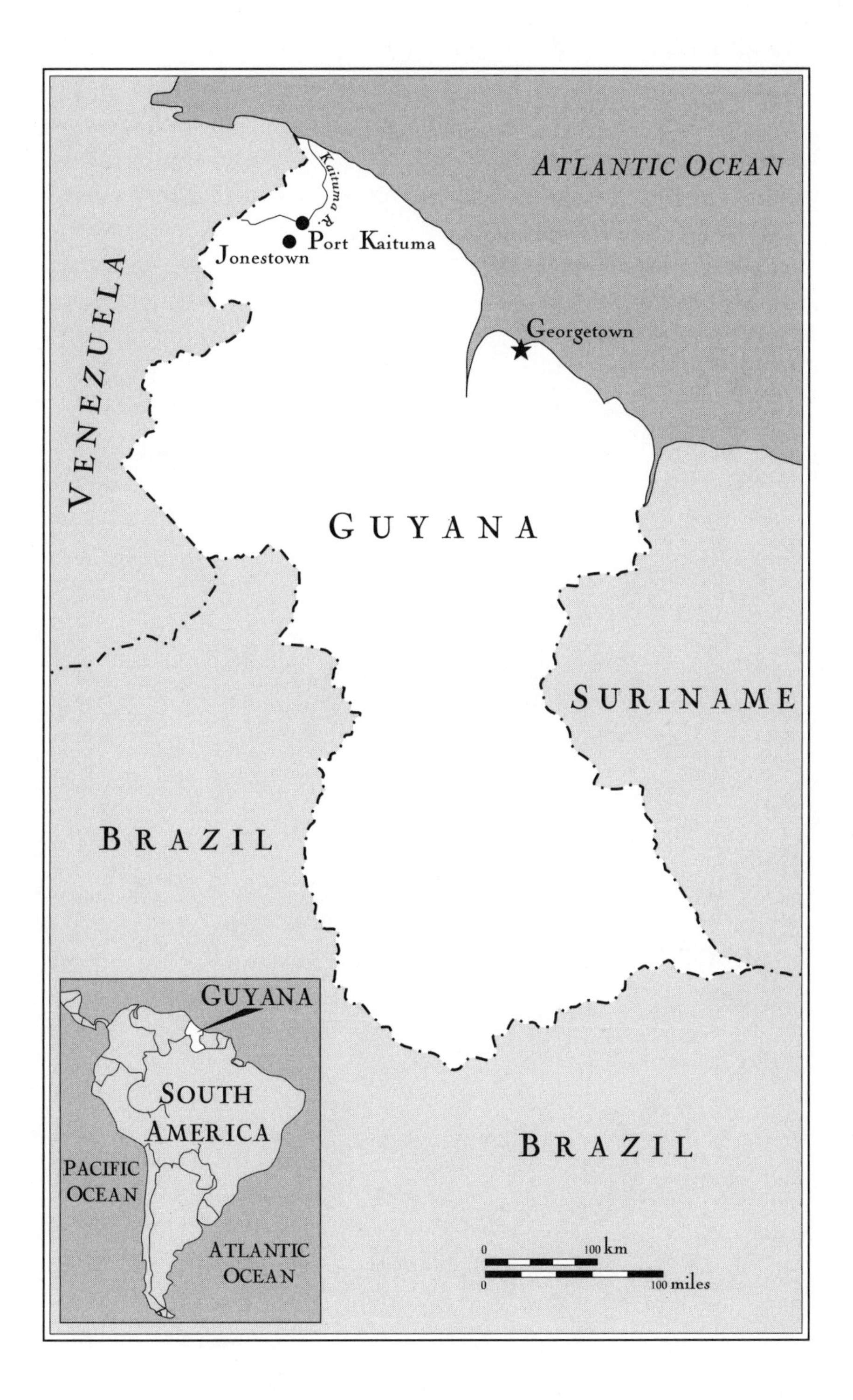

ATLANTIC OCEAN
Kaituma R.
Port Kaituma
Jonestown
VENEZUELA
Georgetown
GUYANA
SURINAME
BRAZIL
BRAZIL
GUYANA
SOUTH AMERICA
PACIFIC OCEAN
ATLANTIC OCEAN
0
100 km
0
100 miles

Prologue

Driving over the San Francisco Bay Bridge at four-thirty in the morning, preparing, as I have for the past ten years, for another hectic day on the trading floor of a brokerage firm, I listen to the radio. I hear people talking about a strange cult called Branch Davidians that has been surrounded by the FBI. My mind and heart begin to race as I recognize ignorance in the questions and comments about the group. Authorities are misguidedly speculating about why the cult members have walled themselves off against the world and are provoking a dangerous standoff. I wonder: Are they really provoking it or are they being forced into an impasse? I am sure that it is the latter. My head fills with the voices I've tried to silence. Mothers whispering, babies crying, a grandmother weeping softly. People are running, I can smell the dust as it is scattered into the air by the chaos. Father is calling . . .

I can barely hear the radio any longer. Someone is saying the authorities are blasting music into the Davidian compound, floodlights are being focused directly on buildings to frighten and force the inhabitants out, perhaps they'll use tear gas.

Entrapped, imprisoned, alone, frightened . . . I can hear their thoughts. I feel their pain. I understand what keeps them inside and afraid to surrender. I have been in their shoes. I am one of them.

Old tapes are running in my head. Memories pole-vault me backward into fear and insanity, back into the darkness, into Jonestown. I see the Pavilion in the center of a compound cut into the heart of the jungle. People are running, I hear their anxious voices. Father is calling us . . .

Father's voice is filled with emotion. He's shouting over the loudspeakers, broadcasting through the camp. Danger is near. I can hear a siren in the background, "Security alert! White Night! White Night! Quickly, wake up. We must get to the safety of the Pavilion. Run, mothers! Hurry, children! We must make it to the safety of the Pavilion."

I sit up, slightly disoriented, awakened from a heavy and abysmally dreamless sleep. Jumping down from the bunk, I grope about on the wooden planks, unable to find my boots. I fight with my pant legs to allow my feet entrance.

Christ, it must be past midnight. Goddamnit, I don't want to die without my boots on! I don't want to fight the enemy in my socks. Fumbling around in the dark, I am frantic that I'll arrive late at the Pavilion and be confronted and punished for taking too long.

My shirt smells of sweat from days of field work. Finally, I grab my worn and tattered boots, crusty with mud from the torrential rain last night. I scramble to the outside stairs where the moonlight is bright.

I see other residents rushing, pulling on shirts, zipping up pants, stumbling out of their cabins, some with babies in their arms, most alone, running to what we are told is safety, the Pavilion, our sanctuary, where Father will protect us.

I can hear gunfire in the jungle surrounding us. Father warned us that mercenaries are out there. Every day, he warns us about the enemy, the "others" out there who are against us. I can hear by the gunshots that they are coming closer. He has told, and told, and told us that they will harm us. With each blast of the siren, our existence in Jonestown becomes more tenuous. I am frightened. I don't want to be murdered. I've done nothing wrong. These poor black grandmothers have done nothing wrong. Please, why must they hurt the children? The children were brought here by their parents, young adults, who thought they were giving their babies a better life, a life free of racism and oppression. Here in Guyana, the Promised Land, we would have a chance to live life to its fullest, because Father had promised it would be so.

Voices on my car radio draw me back to the present. Armored vehicles are on their way to the Branch Davidian compound. I feel panic rise up inside of me. Oh God, I should do something. I should contact the FBI, warn them about their tactics. I know that their harsh, combative language will only entrench the victims further. Who in their right mind would flee to the "safety" of such intimidation? Hasn't the FBI understood by now how the mind of a captive perceives danger? If only I could help. If only I could stop the insanity from happening again. But what would happen to me if I came forward? How would I protect my secrets? How could I spare my little daughter?

In my memory I hear more gunfire blasting up from the jungle. The howler monkeys won't bellow their songs tonight. They sense the insanity around them. I race on in my mud-caked boots, past the tin-roofed cabins, past the wooden outdoor showers where we're allowed our two-minute wash at the end of our twelve-hour days in the field. The cool air tries to invigorate my tired mind. Why again tonight? It seems every week we're told we'll die. Every week we're ordered to drink some liquid, every week we're promised death, a relief from this miserable life. I hope tonight is the last one. I'm so desperately tired. Perhaps death is better than this.

I wonder if my friend Annie will be in the Pavilion in time to avoid Father's wrath. Is someone helping Mama up the narrow path from her cabin? I climb the fence near the podium and sit down close to Father. His big white chair has armrests, a seat pillow, and a back to lean against. Everyone else sits on hard benches or on the dirt floor. All of us assume our positions knowing that it will be many hours before we will leave the "safety" of the Pavilion.

White Night becomes day. Another night of lost sleep fades into dawn. My butt numb, feelings suffocated, reflexes stiff, the inside of my mouth raw and aching from biting it to stay awake, I continue to listen to Father's ravings about our prophesied demise. When the sun rises and heats our exhausted bodies, the gunfire has ceased. The mercenaries, we imagine, are resting through the heat vacuum, an intense throbbing that sucks our energy and absorbs our very essence, then dries it like jerky. Automatons sit in the Pavilion now, hungry only because we are reminded to be by the whimpering of the famished children. We are shells of humans, waiting for our next instructions from Father.

Suddenly, Father informs us that we have been saved by a miracle: the mercenaries have departed and we are now free again to enjoy our lives. He dispatches a few of the kitchen staff to prepare a little sustenance for his entrenched warriors. Exhausted, we sip our rice-water soup and nibble on bread crumbs from an earlier meal. A new day hath arrived. Father begins to hum and the pianist begins her melodic accompaniment. He stands and sings, "We shall not . . . We shall not be moved. We shall not . . . We shall not be moved," smiles and claps his hands. We all stand and sing. Once again, we have fought the enemy and won!

Since the destruction of the Branch Davidian cult, my mind has returned again and again to my past. It is brought back to this darkness because of the inquisitive questions of my six-year-old daughter.

"Mommy? Where is Grandma Nanni buried? Why can't we visit her grave?"

The tightly wrapped secrets of my past are being cautiously opened. Secrets handed down from my mother to me. Untruths that spurred us both, while looking for answers, into another deceitful world, Peoples Temple.

I thought I could keep the past hidden forever, the way my mother did when I was growing up, but that is no longer healthy or possible. I must return to the suffocating confusion of my youth to understand my sorrow, make sense of my shame, and integrate the secrets of my unclaimed history. I must break the pattern of well-intentioned deceit passed from parent to child.

"Why is Uncle Larry in prison? He isn't bad . . . is he, Mommy?"

How can I explain to a child that my brother became a pawn the moment I escaped from Jonestown? My mother was dying of cancer; he was the only hostage Jones could use to try and coerce me back or force me into silence. My brother must have been severely threatened, perhaps in panic, when he followed orders to shoot at people. Why is he the only one held accountable for the insanity designed by Jones and unwittingly implemented by a thousand of us?

I was one of them. On my own, with no one to answer to, I have kept my shame locked in a small compartment just beneath the surface. But my daughter's innocent probing has emboldened me to face the horror again, after twenty years.

"Why didn't you just leave when Jim got mean?"

I'm not sure. What took me so long to comprehend and finally heed the danger signs? Was it my naïveté? Perhaps it was my child-like belief in my own papa's goodness that kept me from grasping the truth. Being a good obedient daughter seemed incompatible with having questions and doubts.

"Couldn't the children have refused to drink their juice, Mama? I would have closed my lips tight and not allowed them to do it."

How can I make her understand what people are liable to do under extreme pressure or in a desperate need to please? How they can choose to take their own lives rather than disobey and risk an even more violent death at the hands of either the "enemy" or the armed guards of their own group?

I'm propelled by my daughter's innocence to turn inward to my cavern of painful, frightening memories. But facing them requires that I first learn how to cope with the shame. I must face my acts of treason against my mentor and friend, Teresa B., whose trust I betrayed for my own survival. In order to prove my devotion to the Peoples Temple, I devoutly reported her secrets, condemning her to a purgatory from which she barely escaped.

It does not help to explain that all of us were taught to spy and report on each other—our families, our loved ones, our friends. Loyalty to Father required it. Any longing for friends or lovers, any expression of love for our family, was a breach of that loyalty. "Thou shalt have no other God before me."

I never dreamed of reporting on my mother. The only alternative was to withdraw. It took all my strength to hide my fear for her. I worried that she might put herself into grave danger by being honest, by confessing to Jim her fears and misgivings about Jonestown. Mama's secrets remained safe with me. And yet, I am still haunted by the fact that I saw no other choice than to forsake her. I knew the pain my slow withdrawal caused her. She was afraid in Jonestown, sick with cancer and desperate for my companionship, but I was unable to give her the love and affection she needed. When she needed me the most I escaped and left her behind. I abandoned her in order to save myself.

How could we do such awful things? Why were we unable to see the corruption, call Father's bluff, stop it before the end? We had embarked on a peaceful exodus into a "land of freedom," only to see our lives in the Promised Land turn into a dreary prison camp existence. Our dreams evaporated into twelve-hour days of hard labor, watched by armed guards from morning to night. We hardly got enough food to sustain ourselves and many of us fell sick from malnutrition.

Sundays meant standing in a long line snaking from the radio room, where Father sat in the doorway, down the wooden walkway, past the kitchen huts, and onto the dirt pathway. The line of a thousand of us moved slowly as Father spoke personally to each resident, handing out the special weekly treat of a sweet cassava cookie. Finally, I, too, would stand before him as he lovingly bequeathed the delicacy to me.

"Debbie, my little warrior," he would sadly smile, "it has been a tough week, but toughest on me. I carry your hopes and dreams upon my shoulders. It is I who worries about you and your future while you sleep. Here, my child, enjoy my offering, my treat. The kitchen staff made it for you even though the ingredients are too expensive and we can't afford such a luxury."

"Thank you, Father." I would lower my eyes respectfully and walk away, allowing the next residents their moment with Father, keeping my thoughts to myself. But as I walked away, I wondered why we didn't have enough money when Teresa, Carolyn, Maria, and I had deposited millions of dollars in Panamanian bank accounts. Teresa and I had flown to England, France, and Switzerland to open even more accounts. Carolyn and Jim had said we needed to do this so the government couldn't take it away from us and that Jim would use the funds for the people when the time came. Why was Father acting as though we had nothing? Why, with so many millions of dollars abroad, could we barely exist?

It makes my heart ache to think how bravely and how desperately we endured. Only very few people were lucky enough to have been elsewhere when the suicide command was given. Those in the capital, some 250 miles away, refused to take their lives when Father's orders came over the radio. Just that little bit of distance allowed them to think for themselves . . . and they chose to live.

Those of us who survived are left with the task of making sense of the losses suffered by so many. The survivors, whether they lived in Jonestown or were only associated with Peoples Temple in the United States, must live with a quiet and dull vibration that agitates our conscience. We have compartmentalized our shame, despair, and fear, struggled to disentangle ourselves from our own misconceptions of who we were.

In order to find answers for my daughter, I must find answers for myself. For the welfare of us both, I must descend again into the darkness. Although I am fearful of what I may find, I must remember.

ONE

We who have come back, by the aid of many lucky chances or miracles—whatever one may choose to call them—we know: the best of us did not return.

—Viktor E. Frankl,
Man's Search for Meaning

1
Secrets and Shadows

My mother was a mystery to me. Beautiful, often quiet, she secretly sketched portraits of women, closing her portfolio whenever I came unexpectedly into the sunroom. I often felt I was intruding on someone unfamiliar and interrupting something quite private. She seemed like a shadow, her silhouette casting a haze on my imperfect form. Always gentle and kind, she coddled me and continually asked after my thoughts. I sensed that she was worried about me and desperately wanted to protect me, but I had no idea from what. In return, from a very young age, I felt protective of her.

Every evening she would lie next to me and read aloud. I loved the sound of her voice, soothing and warm. My favorite poem was Walter de la Mare's "Sleepyhead." The way in which Mama pronounced each word lulled me into a trance. I begged her to read it over and over again, especially one segment:

"Come away,
Child, and play
Light with the gnomies;
In a mound
Green and round,
That's where their home is.

"Honey sweet,
Curds to eat,
Cream and frumenty,

Shells and beads,
Poppy seeds,
You shall have plenty."

But as soon as I stooped in the dim moonlight
To put on my stocking and my shoe,
The sweet sweet singing died sadly away,
And the light of the morning peeped through . . .

After the fifth reading, when we'd finished saying the Lord's Prayer, I'd plead with her not to leave me. When she finally rose and kissed me gently on the cheek, then closed the door behind her, believing I was asleep, I would cry. She seemed so sad, like a fairy princess in a moated castle, and I grieved for her.

My mother, Lisa, was born to Anita and Hugo Philip in 1915. Although she shared few of her childhood stories with me, I had glimpses into her past. It was my father who bragged about her life. I knew she was proud and had grown up in Hamburg surrounded by vast amounts of art and culture. Concert musicians used to play in her extraordinarily modern home that was designed and built by her cousin through marriage, Ernst Hochfeld, a pioneer of the Bauhaus architectural era. There were built-in cabinets for their extensive art collection, a humidity-controlled vault for Grandpa's tobacco and cigars, and the beloved music room where Mama's Steinway and her father's Guadagnini violin were kept.

Mama explained on several occasions that the bronze nude in our living room was not an object to snicker at but a famous sculpture, *Die Erwachende* ("The Awakening") by Klimsch and that she loved it. I understood that her father had packed it together with a few other valuables and brought it from Germany. Why her parents hadn't hired a moving company to ship all their belongings from Hamburg was a question that never seemed to be answered. There was the beautifully shaped silver cutlery we used daily, some exquisite jewelry Mama kept in her silk-embroidered jewelry box, and several large pieces of art, paintings and sculptures that Grandpa Hugo and Grandma Anita had personally carried to America.

I loved hearing the story attached to each one. There was an etching of Albert Einstein, signed by the genius himself, his hands so dirty his fingerprints showed clearly next to his signature, and an etching of Pablo Casals tuning his cello, signed by the maestro. Beatrice d'Este of Ferrara, the painting commissioned by my grandfather in Italy that stared away past me in the library, wore a headdress of leather and pearls and was covered in a maroon dress with a luxurious black velvet cape. I often wished the statue on the table, a beautiful bronze woman, her bared breasts firm, her long, sleek legs taut as she stretched upward on her toes, had considered wearing clothes on the day of her posing. My mother's legs were beautiful, too. I loved to sit on her bed each morning and watch her pull her stockings up over her ankles, then point her toes and extend her legs into the air as she attached the silk to her black garter. My mother was what I wanted to be: an enchanting enigma.

I sensed that my mother missed her life in Germany. The past seemed to consume and console her. When I was a little older I wondered what it must have been like to leave a place one deeply loved, all one's friends and relatives, and never see them again. But it was many years before I grasped that my mother's world was filled with sorrow, guilt, and regret. And it wasn't until years after that that I learned why.

Long before I came onto the scene, my mother had begun to spin a cocoon around herself. From her place of solace, she wove interesting stories and gave them to her children as protective shields against the painful truths she could not bear to tell. The one most closely associated with me was the story of my arrival. My birth, it seemed, was a momentous occasion. I loved the pretty stories of the long discussions and appeals from my big sister, Annalisa, for a baby sister. Mama, too, said she desired "just one more" baby. I grew up knowing that I was the only really planned-for child because, at age eight, my sister had successfully convinced my parents that she would take care of me. However, the truth was far different. It is only now that I realize my conception must have been on the evening of May 10, 1952, the evening my mother learned of her own mother's suicide. I imagine the night was filled with tears and profound despair, my father holding and consoling my mother, trying to dissuade her from her crushing guilt. On February 7, 1953, exactly nine months after Grandma Anita's death, the secretly grieved-about baby arrived in Tooele, Utah. Although she cared for me deeply and listened intently to my never-ending questions, she seemed sad, preoccupied, and sometimes in awe of me. Perhaps my presence reminded her of the mother she believed she had forsaken. Somewhere deep inside my mother's heart she must have wondered from where my spirit arose.

MAY 10, 1952
My friends,
Know that I, free and proper, am a good American. But I was a gossip and have been entangled in a network of intrigue. I no longer have the strength to free myself from it.
Forget me not, my beloved children and family.
And you, Hugo, forgive me.
Live well. All of you loved mankind so much!!
—A.—

On the morning of her suicide, Grandma Anita left behind what at the time seemed a mysterious missive written in German. No one understood why she mentioned being a good American. Sadly, however, Anita had a basis for her belief that she was entangled in some terrible intrigue.

In 1951, my father had left his associate professorship at Johns Hopkins to accept a prestigious position as Associate Director of Chemical Warfare at the Dugway Proving Grounds in Utah. My mother was apprehensive about the assignment, as was her mother.

Anita had become very involved with the American Society of Friends (Quakers), the organization that had safeguarded her and Hugo's journey out of Nazi Austria to the United States. The Friends had kept the Nazis at bay while desperately trying to obtain the last of the emergency visas granted to Jews. On March 20, 1940, the Friends gave Anita and Hugo the precious gift of another life in America.

Now Anita was a devoted Friend and believed in their gospel of peace and nonviolence. Her son-in-law's involvement in research on how to "kill humans with chemicals" was abhorrent to her. She talked with her daughter about her misgivings and begged her to convince Laurence not to take the job.

In 1951, Anita could not know that after her son-in-law's arrival in Utah, he was promoted to chief of the entire Chemical Warfare Division. With this high-level appointment, Dr. Layton required the highest level security clearance possible and the FBI began to conduct a thorough background investigation. My father, one of the government's top men at Dugway, was married to a German woman, an "Alien of Enemy Nationality" as denoted on her passport, and her parents had to be closely investigated.

J. Edgar Hoover was in his prime. He was a xenophobe and believed the Society of Friends to have Communist leanings. Hoover's men, with little concern for the fallout of their investigation, began to question my grandmother and her Quaker friends. These men deemed it unnecessary to explain to the Society of Friends and the neighbors of Anita and Hugo why they were investigating the loyalties of the Philips. Anita had no idea that this was a routine inquiry regarding a government employee. All she knew was that "people" were asking questions about her. Anita wrote to her daughter that she was being followed and spied upon. Unaware of the FBI's investigation, Lisa and Laurence thought Anita was becoming paranoid; to them her fears were incomprehensible. Of course she had been persecuted in Germany, but that was Nazi territory, it could not happen here. Never in America! Terrified and not knowing where to turn, Anita jumped to her death from her apartment window.

At the time, my mother did not know that her parents were being investigated. And she could not have fathomed the effect of such an investigation on a Jew who had just escaped from the Nazis. Much later, I would discover how deeply my mother blamed herself for having disbelieved her mother's fears. Long shadows now loomed over Lisa's universe. The world she had hoped to escape into was suddenly soiled. In 1952, Mama had three children under age ten, a husband with an extremely sensitive government job, and a new baby on the way. For reasons I think I now understand, Lisa chose to silence her sorrows. For the sake of her husband and her children, desperately wanting to give them the future she had hoped for, she suppressed her past and hid her own identity as well as her mother's.

Lisa Philip, born in Hamburg, to nonreligious Jewish parents, was raised a German, not a Jew. Her family never attended synagogue and were completely assimilated into the fabric of Germany's high society. Her father owned a seat on the Hamburg Stock Exchange. The family's circle of friends was predominately Jewish but the Philips often entertained government dignitaries and luminaries from the world of art and theater. On May 6, 1938, the life and world Lisa loved was wrenched away from her. At the age of twenty-three, in order to escape the Nazis, Lisa bid farewell to her parents and her friends and boarded the S.S. *Manhattan* for New York.

It was a hard transition. She was lonely and longed to settle down and attach herself to this new world. In 1939, a year before meeting my father, she wrote to her closest friend in Hamburg, Annelise Schmidt, that she felt worthless and alone. Her friend wrote in response:

> You don't have anywhere to go when you are lonesome, but Lisa, you must not give up the longing for something beautiful . . . A strong love would be the most cleansing thing for you. The memories of the past are there, and you feel that you have been plucked from your past, but I am sure that you will rebuild your roots. If you have a devil within you, don't hide him but put him in front of your wagon so that he will use up all his strength by pulling you forward.

My parents met while my father was in graduate school. Vastly different in every way, they found each other attractive and believed the other's attributes would help them secure the future of comfort and shelter they both longed for.

Laurence Layton had no secrets. He was born in Boomer, West Virginia, a poor coal mining town. Almost all of the inhabitants worked deep down, under the earth, but Laurence's father was different. John Layton was a college-educated engineer. Life for Laurence began a little better than for others in Boomer. His father spent hours with his son discussing ideas and allowing him to help perform experiments. But when Laurence was eight years old, his devoted father died unexpectedly. Within days, his mother was forced to move back in with her father, where she instantly became a servant. Laurence Layton, the child who became a man overnight, resolved that his siblings would never feel his desperation or loss. He assumed the paternal role until his mother remarried. At that point, he was dealt another cruel blow when his new stepfather told him to leave the household. He was determined to rise above his lot in life, but his adolescent perceptions of desertion and betrayal became the basis for a lifelong fear of abandonment.

By 1938, the year Lisa was torn from the life she loved, my father had escaped from his world of poverty and betrayal to the world of college intellectuals. Intelligent, enterprising, and seemingly confident, Laurence now lived far away from the coal town of his youth. He stylishly joined the Socialist party and, for the first time in his life, met educated Jewish émigrés. He aspired to one day join the world of the bourgeoisie.

In 1940, Laurence was introduced to Miss Lisa Philip, the physical therapist at Penn State's Student Health Services. I believe it was my mother's cultured and affluent background that enchanted the young doctoral candidate. Lisa, a beautiful German, lent legitimacy to my father's own endeavors. Her distinguished lineage (her cousin, James Franck, won the Nobel Prize in Physics; her uncle, Oscar Hirsch, was a world-renowned Viennese brain surgeon) provided impressive credentials to the ambitious student from West Virginia.

Desirous of making a life with promising roots for herself, Lisa began to date the Ph.D. candidate and in 1941 they became engaged to be married. But my father, who had remained chaste, was very troubled that his fiancé had been intimate with another man before him. Her culture and experience cast a shadow on his fragile self-esteem.

However, Lisa believed if they truly loved one another, her past could be forgotten. Fearful of any more upheavals in her already tumultuous life, my mother became apologetic, outwardly meek, and obedient. On October 18, 1941, their marriage of thirty years began.

Unfortunately, Lisa would never be able to bury her past enough to calm the demons inside her innocent country boy's head. In 1943, she made the following entry into her diary:

> There is one thing that is causing me to be more desperate and unhappy than I ever thought I could be, living as well as I do, having a perfect little son and a good husband. It is the opinion another person one greatly cares for has of one . . . I would have repented and tried to be as good a person as I could, but now things seem to be pulled out from under me. There is nothing. I see, no ground to stand on . . .

A few months later, she wrote a letter to her husband:

> Dear Larry,
> There is neither a going back to, nor a future. All I have ever hoped for seems to be denied to me . . . I want a home and children . . . I want to feel part of you. When things are all right between the two of us, my love for Tom is happy, and it fills me with contentment and a feeling of security to see him play and feel good. But when things are the way they have become now, my love for him is not a real, true unselfish love, because I try to regain from my love for him, what I have lost in you.

And since this is not possible . . . my love becomes desperate . . . You cannot believe my feeling toward you, because you cannot feel it. You are a prisoner of yourself, because selfishness prevents you from overcoming your limits . . .

With three little children under the age of four, she was washing diapers and sheets by hand and hanging them outside on a clothesline to dry. She was weary, having to manage without servants and without the loving support of her own family. Her isolation grew when she could no longer share her thoughts with her German friend Annelise, as it was forbidden to communicate with anyone in an enemy country. Finally, when the war ended, Lisa excitedly wrote to Annelise. But the reply was devastating: Annelise and her baby had been killed in a British bombing raid. Lisa's only remaining lifeline to Hamburg and her past was severed.

As a child I was mostly unaware of my parents' troubled marriage. If my mother was a mystery to me, I completely knew my father, or so I believed. There was never any doubt in my mind that my father was fiercely proud of his little "Bugsy," his nickname for me, his small and energetic youngest child. I was sure of what pleased and annoyed him. I loved sitting on his lap and reading aloud to him on Sunday afternoons. I knew that Papa was a scientist and the smartest man in the world. I hung on his every word, knowing it was gospel. Papa eased the confusing world I tried to share with Mama, making it clear and black and white. I never had any doubts about what I should do, think, or say when I was near him. He made me confident by boasting of my accomplishments, my creativity. I had meaning in my life when I pleased my papa. Looking back now, I can see that learning to please in this way became a dangerous liability when I met Jim Jones. On the other hand, it was because of my father's unwavering belief in his little Bugsy that I would, at a critical moment, find the strength to flee Jim Jones and escape to safety.

In 1957, Papa accepted a position in Albany, California, where he commenced research on allergies. In our spacious home in the Berkeley hills, my older siblings huddled around me, lavishing me with eager attention, coddling and protecting me from myself. In return, I idolized, adored, and entertained them, reveled and blossomed in their attention, and became accustomed to unconditional love. There was so much noisy commotion around me that my parents often didn't get a glimpse of me all day.

Papa encouraged my love of drama and ballet. At age five, I was performing my own interpretation of Tchaikovsky's *Swan Lake* at dinner parties in our mansion at 670 San Luis Road. There were always adoring whispers as my swan pirouetted across the hardwood floor, my tutu's ruffles gently rising and falling with each graceful landing. Afterward, Mama would hug and kiss her ballerina and we'd head upstairs, hand-in-hand, for my good-night story.

Still, I was aware that I was not a part of the intimacy that Mama shared with my older siblings. One incident, when I was six years old, brought home the realization that I was excluded from my mother's world. My sixteen-year-old brother, Tommy, and Mama were sitting together on the front porch. They were talking, but I saw a thin trail of smoke rising over my mother's shoulder. I knew that couldn't be, as Papa had forbidden anyone from smoking—it was trashy and only uneducated people did it. I also knew that what I had seen was a secret, which I faithfully kept to protect Mama.

I longed to join Mama and Tom in their secret time together and would later wonder why Annalisa and Mama always talked behind closed doors. What could my fourteen-year-old sister be talking about with her? What on earth could be so private? By the time it was my turn to sneak behind the door with Mama, she seemed exhausted. She never shared with me the secrets of growing up. She never even told me the scary facts of how my body would change.

In 1960, however, my dreamworld still glistened with sibling adoration. I continued to garner applause for my tomboy feats such as the double flips on my parents' bed and the twenty-five stitches on my head I got from crashing into the corner of their headboard. My favorite time was evening. Papa would discuss his research, then ask us about our days. Most often the discussion would center around the book Mama was reading and planned to discuss at her regular afternoon tea, hosted at our home. My live-in baby-sitters, Tom, seventeen; Annalisa, fifteen; and Larry, fourteen, still chased me around the house in the evening. When we played "Evil Tooth Decay," Tom and Larry would hunt for me behind couches, in closets, and under beds until I was found. I screeched with delight as they looked for me, then chased after me as I fled. Finally, I had to brush my teeth while Tommy, "Mr. Evil Tooth Decay," growled and tried to prevent me from brushing and Larry, Bucky Beaver, protected me.

When Annalisa had her high school sorority's monthly evening meetings at our house, I was their mascot. I would proudly sit on the table, ring the bell for the meetings to come to order, and play waitress to serve them refreshments. My siblings were always there to smooth the sometimes rough relations between me and our parents. They allowed me to remain the center of attention, the twinkling star.

My father continued to write and publish his research, travel and give lectures in America and Europe. I never understood why my mother refused to accompany him when he lectured in Germany. I begged her to go and take me, too, but she would look far into the distance and softly say, "I will never go back." Her refusal to explain herself made me feel left out, frustrated, and furious at her.

Then suddenly one summer Tommy disappeared, deserting me for the University of California at Davis. Annalisa remained behind and although I remained her high school sorority's mascot, at nine years of age I was becoming a fading star. Around this time I started to tell really interesting stories to my friends. I believed these stories myself—I really was an Indian princess who had been adopted and taken away from my tribe. Annalisa scolded me for lying but was unaware of how much it was becoming the fabric of my being. I earned a rather unpleasant reputation in the neighborhood and became known as "Liar Layton." Then Annalisa deserted me for Davis, too.

I still climbed trees and played kickball, remained the best at handball and arguably was the bravest kid in the neighborhood. I could go out the farthest on any tree limb on the block—that the fire department had to be called to help me down was not a point against me either, I still knew that I had won. I was the biggest daredevil of all! If only my family were there to see me. But everyone was gone. I would have to use other means to catch someone's attention.

I began to have conflicts at school. I felt completely justified in chipping the tooth of the boy who cut in front of me in the handball line, and refused to apologize to him in the principal's office. I threw pebbles into the eyes of the girl who called me a liar. Some parents told their children to stop playing with me. I was too ashamed to tell my parents. Papa was not supposed to know that I wasn't his adorable Bugsy any longer. I tried to hide from Mama that her little baby girl was losing her charm.

I still had one more sibling at home, Laurence, but he couldn't take up the slack. He was focused on more meaningful things: philosophy, being president of the Berkeley High School Democratic Club, and doing his homework every night. Getting his attention was far more time-consuming and arduous than it had once been. I was forced to stand at his door calling his name over and over again.

"Laurency," I'd yell until he threatened to get me. Then his exasperated count would begin. He would warn me that by the time he reached ten, I had better be gone. When he reached ten, I'd run and hide, but he never came and looked for me. Then he, too, cast me aside for the ominous black hole in Davis that sucked up everyone important in my life.

I was ten years old and three of the most influential people in my universe had abandoned me. Absorbed by the pressing concerns of paying for three college tuitions, Mama began to work part-time at the University of California at Berkeley's main library. Although she was only ten minutes from the house, I returned home from school to an empty home. I remember climbing our tree and sitting high over the front porch waiting for the postman, hoping for letters from my favorite people in the world. Few came.

My exhausted parents, clueless about how cunning I'd become, were left alone to deal with a spoiled pubescent daughter coming of age in the Berkeley of the tumultuous sixties. They had raised three perfect children, obedient, scholarly, and attentive. And now on their coattails came this wild, lonely, and angry adolescent. My parents were caught off-guard.

Papa became increasingly disenchanted with my tomboy behavior and publicly mourned the loss of his ballerina. When I transformed into a well-endowed teenager he continued to instruct me in what was right and wrong, who was good, the girls I could play with, how ladies should dress, how my hair should be combed off my face, and which people were not acceptable acquaintances. Life took on a bleak pallor in our empty mansion. Growing increasingly argumentative and surly, I pulled farther away from my enigmatic mother. I had so many questions and none seemed to be adequately answered. Why, I asked her, was she so bothered by my playing with Jewish girls? They didn't seem any different to me. They also had pretty brown curly hair and their parents really liked me. But Mama was troubled. "Why do you like playing with Megan Hesterman and Carol Davis more than the other girls?" she'd ask. I didn't know what Jews believed . . . how could I? I wasn't one.

As Mama continued to fret and query me, I became more uncivil. "Why, are you a Nazi?" I'd shout. I began to argue constantly with the sweet, soft-spoken woman I had once adored, especially when she deferred to Papa about requests I had, like sleeping over at a friend's house. "Can't you make any decisions on your own?" I'd yell. I felt betrayed by her for reasons I did not understand and I was confused by my wild anger. I could tell when Mama had been crying after my tirades. She tried to talk with me. She would pack picnics and we would drive into the countryside, just the two of us, to talk, but the moment we were alone I would attack her again or refuse to speak, just shrugging my shoulders.

In 1968, my older brothers and sister were again causing distress for me. Tom had passed his Ph.D. qualifying exams at Harvard, Annalisa had married a biochemistry professor at University of California at Berkeley, and Larry was involved in an organization doing humanitarian work. I was unable to compete. I wasn't interested in my classes and got poor grades. Unable and unwilling to emulate the achievements of my siblings, I was losing my status in a family of great achievers.

It had become almost impossible to please my father, so I learned to deceive him instead. Mama, on the other hand, was becoming wise to my cunning ways and confronted me on several occasions. I believed I was unfairly forsaken and began to search for attention elsewhere, at any cost.

2
Exiled

My perception that I was an outcast, the misunderstood underdog, began to shape all my actions. I took my uncontrolled anger about things I could not articulate outside my home.

Formerly the teacher's pet, I suddenly found myself in detention classes after school, with the tough kids. I forged tardy slips and absence notes, cut classes and played cards with my new and more accepting friends, the Hell's Angels, whom I had met through my boyfriend. I dyed my curly brown hair raven black and straightened it. I stole Southern Comfort and other hard liquor from my parents' liquor cabinet and skillfully refilled what I had taken with water. While other kids experimented with smoking dope, I had already graduated to harder narcotics. With my lunch money I was purchasing speed, red-downers, and mescaline. I smoked opium with college kids at lunchtime and dropped acid in math class. My report card showed only D's and F's, but for my presentation to my parents I was able to modify the F's into A's and, with greater difficulty, the D's into B's. Before ninth grade was over, I had been suspended for forging a teacher's name on a hall pass, I had run away, attempted to convince Papa that my gangster boyfriend needed our financial help so he could go to college, slashed my wrists, called a 911 suicide hotline (but hung up when I heard my parents trying to eavesdrop), and successfully persuaded several friends' parents to let me come live with them since mine just didn't understand me.

I also began to write stories, poems, and letters to my distant parents. In 1966, I wrote:

. . . Dark unsympathetic clouds gather in the sky
A heavy wind begins to blow. Away from the
land where he is able to survive the scarlet bird,
alone now, falls to his death under the bleeding tree.

As I tried to connect with Mama, I developed a strong compassion for people unable to fend for themselves. I wanted to become one with the real people, the honest people, people who showed their anger, like the Hell's Angels, the poor, the working class, people from whom Papa tried to keep me safe. I wanted to commune with those who had experienced grief and misfortune. At fifteen, I felt akin to the underclass and was comfortable only with my nineteen-year-old Filipino boyfriend who was a high school dropout, poor, and lived in a nearby working-class community. He thought I was pretty, he thought I was funny, he thought I had something to offer, and thus he replaced the father I could no longer please or amuse. I liked when he was firm with me, when he told me I was drinking too much, or when he grabbed my arm a little too tightly in order to make me listen. I thought his toughness demonstrated his love for me.

But I was vigilant and careful about remaining chaste; I knew that only really bad girls had sex before marriage and that deep inside I was good—my parents and other outsiders simply did not see through my facade.

At school I often felt out of control. I went to battle for students I felt had been unfairly treated. On one occasion, I threw a desk at a teacher who accused my best friend of not having written her own term paper. I passionately wanted and needed to correct all the wrongs that had been perpetrated in my world. I was fighting the demons who ate at me and who were trying to hurt my mother. But I became incensed toward Mama because she remained distant and would not let me fight for her. Again and again, I felt betrayed by her. Why, I wondered, when she knew, deep inside, that we were made of the same material, had the same spirit—why did she silence her self, her essence, and always side with Papa?

My intuition was calling to her, begging her to "Come away, child, and play." I was willing her to join me, like the gnomies in the poem in my Childcraft book. I was outside in the dark, like they were. I was lonely and knew she wanted to join me, but I could not understand the greater forces that held her back. Sadly, I misinterpreted her fear of stepping out from her cocoon. I saw her reluctance as a sign she didn't care for me, the aching fifteen-year-old, haunted by the truth untold.

Yet I never gave up and continued to speak to her through my innocent letters.

1968
Dear Mom and Dad,
I once stated in a poem I wrote, "Love is the key to serenity." I have changed my viewpoint completely. Although love has a great role to play in the human race I feel love is not the true key to serenity. I feel it is the knowledge of one's self. To know yourself as you know a song. With true understanding, meaning, fearlessness and the ability to compensate for those losses which meant a great deal to one's self. . . . I'm not sure if that meant anything to you or even if you understood what I just wrote, but I think if you think about it, it will bring a new light to your eyes.

Was I rebelling for the mother who was entangled in her own web and growing visibly exhausted from the years of deceit and sorrow?

Now, when I intruded on Mama alone, I interrogated her. What was she doing? I ridiculed her for asking my piano teacher to dinner. I found him ugly and stupid, and I hated him, but she brightened perceptibly when they talked about music. I resented her making treats, even sandwiches, for the graduate students who spent so many hours doing research in the library where she worked because it seemed that she was searching for camaraderie through students hardly older than I. She made friends with them and knew each one by name. I sensed that they were taking Tommy's place. I felt jealous. Why couldn't I be the one?

On the few occasions I had to steal money from her purse, I would first unpack her satchel. She always had a book buried inside, *The Brothers Karamazov, The Plague, The Feminine Mystique,* and often *Waiting for Godot.* While Mama seemed to be searching for meaning and answers through strangers and books with strange names, I was busily trying to attract her—or anyone's—attention with dangerous acts of defiance. Some of my signals of distress fell into my parents' hands. Perhaps they nabbed my letters from the post box at our front door.

I was grounded for three months one summer after they intercepted the following letter:

JUNE 12, 1969
Dear Eddy,

Well . . . for the past month I have been on drugs constantly and they are heavy drugs—not weed. Last Friday night I took some mescaline, I went to a coffee house off Telegraph Ave.. It really started to hit me hard and when I left at 11:00 p.m. I was totaled. The next morning I went downstairs. I was still really messed-up (I hadn't slept for 36 hours). My dad told me he knew about everything . . .

Life in the mansion in the hills came to a halt. My parents were constantly upset with me, I knew from their puffy eyes and closed-door meetings that I was being discussed and argued about. They were both at their wits' end and afraid. So was I.

Private school in eighth grade hadn't worked. Spending tenth grade in Davis, California, with the family of Larry's wife, Carolyn Moore Layton, hadn't worked either. Carolyn had married my brother, Larry, after their junior year at the University of California at Davis. Larry's parents-in-law and my tenth-grade guardians, were kind, good people. I had had a tough year in ninth grade when my parents decided that Berkeley was too unstable an environment for me. Carolyn suggested I come live with her parents in Davis and attend high school there. My parents could not have found a finer family to help with the raising of their wayward daughter. Dr. John Moore was the Methodist minister for the college community. Barbara, his doting, handsome wife, was a perfect mother and an enthusiastic participant in their congregation's activities. The Moore's had three daughters: Carolyn, Rebecca, and Annie.

I'd grown very fond of Carolyn's little sister, Sweet Annie, for her goodness and companionship. Annie was a year younger than I and quite different. She was quiet, studious, and loved school. We were intrigued by each other; I by her soft academic manner, and she by my rebelliousness. At night, while she studied in her room, I was writing dramatically desperate letters to the friends from whom my parents had separated me.

Annie wasn't interested in boys, nor was she self-conscious about her tall, willowy body. She was more of a hippie than I. She wore long, floating tie-dyed skirts and white T-shirts, while I tugged on my tight black pegged pants each morning. Annie had the most beautiful long, thick, straight blond hair I had ever seen in my life. She had and was everything I wasn't.

Every night while Annie brushed her hair, I stood next to her in the bathroom, looking into the same mirror, slopping on Dippity-Doo, a "guaranteed hair straightener." While she pulled her brush down and through her voluminous mane, I doused mine with the gooey gel, wrapped the congealed strands of hair around my head, placed a bobby pin every inch or so to secure the potpourri, then tied a bandanna around my forehead to hold everything in place for the night.

After Annie was done preening and I engineering, we would conspiratorially dash into my room and dim the lights. Annie would light her favorite incense to create the right ambiance while I lowered the sound of some heartbreaking song drifting out from the record player and began reciting the latest rendition of my mostly somber poetry. The next morning, I would head straight for my English teacher's office and show her the pieces Sweet Annie had oohed and aahed over the loudest.

But even with Annie's friendship, I was still unable to stay out of trouble. In the middle of my tenth-grade school year in Davis, I dropped acid in class. Days later it was decided I should come back home to Berkeley, to a new school with different kids.

The only times I was successfully brought into line were on the long walks Papa would take with me. We'd usually stop at Indian Rock in the evenings, climb up and watch the sunset. From on top of the world, Papa would tell me how I was killing him and ruining his marriage. I was always deeply troubled by how much I was hurting him with my bad behavior and I was actually relieved when for the first and only time, Papa hit me with a belt because I'd shrugged and rolled my eyes when he asked me how I had managed to get an F in PE. Afterward I saw him crying and I was glad that someone had finally shown such outward emotion and anger at my recklessness.

But nothing lasted long enough. I was always able to deceive and snivel my way out of each punishment. By 1969, there remained two options for me: reform school or boarding school for eleventh grade. Mama's mother had gone to school in England once . . . Why not me?

I do not remember being afraid of leaving, although the prospect of abandoning all my friends and going to boarding school overseas was a little daunting. I was relieved to be sent away, as relieved as my parents were to have me gone. I was tired of drinking a fifth of vodka to impress my friends—they weren't the ones who got sick. I had been truly frightened when I had dropped acid and started to hallucinate an hour later in my English class. I needed strict limits, rules that were impossible to sneak around. I always brought a sliver of rebellion and cunning into any equation. The prospect of being taken from my hopelessness to a place where I could flourish excited me. At last, I was about to become a good person. And I was glad.

Mama had researched various boarding schools. She spoke with Friends at the Meeting House in Berkeley and brought home a large book with descriptions and photographs of possible schools. Mom called a family whose child had attended a Quaker school in Yorkshire, England, and was told it was a fine, very strict Quaker prep school. My father wanted me to go to Greenbrier Finishing School in Virginia, but England responded immediately and the plans were made.

The night before I left for England my father sat down with me and told me Mama was Jewish. I was stunned. The world I barely occupied was being ripped out from under me.

"That can't be," I explained. "She would have told me!" I was incredulous and shaken as Papa explained how Tom, Annalisa, and Larry had been proud to learn the news after graduating from college. I wondered what there was to be proud of? Mama hadn't been proud of it. Surely she wasn't happy about this mark upon the family or she would have told me long ago.

The following morning Mama's eyes were swollen as she double checked my luggage for the last time. I was too embarrassed to say anything about my conversation with Papa the night before. I felt as though we had violated some secret space within her. When the car pulled out from the driveway I waved good-bye to Mama, small and frail at the window. I thought I saw her put her palm to her lips and blow me a kiss. I fought the tears.

Papa walked me onto the plane and made sure I was comfortable and the strap was secured tightly around my lap. As he kissed me, I wondered if Mama had wanted to tell me who she was, but Papa, without asking her, had thought it best if he did. Was Mama too embarrassed or afraid I would yell at her? Was she so mad at me for being bad that she couldn't even face me? Perhaps she felt betrayed by Papa's actions. Perhaps she had been planning all along to tell me about our heritage. I had seen her crying earlier that morning. I wished she had come to the airport with me but maybe she feared she would break down in the car and her tears would upset me even more. Papa knelt down to hug me and reminded me that my mother's cousin, the author Ruth Borchard, would be meeting me at Heathrow Airport in London.

"Honey, they are Orthodox Jews," Papa was saying. "Ruth is an author and is working at becoming the first female rabbi in England. Their home in Reigate, Surrey, is large and beautiful. They have offered to be your guardians for the duration of your stay. Your mother and I have decided that you will not come home for visits, but travel through Europe on your term breaks."

I listened to him in a fog of denial. A rabbi? Cousins in London whom Mama had never talked about? I was confused and hurting inside. Not come home for visits? Was I that awful . . . that miserable? What in the world was an Orthodox?

I watched as my father paused near the front of the plane and spoke with the captain. Then he turned one last time, sadly waved, and left.

It was only then that I began to cry.

My arrival in England was softened by Ruth, the kind and mysterious aunt I had never known about. I followed her into her grand house, The Elms, and admired the blond-gray wisps of hair that gracefully fell from her bun against the nape of her neck. We had tea in her library and I spied one of her books, *John Stuart Mill—The Man,* on one of the many built-in book shelves. I was impressed by the many pieces of art on the walls and wondered if my mother's cultivated Jewish home in Germany had felt like this.

That evening she wrote to my parents:

SEPTEMBER 1969
Dear Lisa and Larry-
What a delightful child! She has a quiet sort of strength, beyond her years—and such warmth and sensitivity. At table, she was telling about your work, Larry: "He's really a genius"—and I said how much I had been struck by her intuitive sparkle—and little Debbie suddenly, with her eyes moistening, said: "Now you've made me homesick." But going to sleep she was not.
More practical: She will join the transport of children to school Mon-

day. I do wonder how her curriculum will shape. Ackworth is a very fine school, with a very old tradition!
What a link there is suddenly between us!
Ever yours, Ruth B.

This letter must have opened worries and old wounds for Mama. What would she tell Ruth about the fact that I had never heard about Ruth, her family and her life?

Within hours of leaving London, I arrived in Yorkshire and was transported to the school. I immediately sensed that it would be a harsh environment for me. On the day of my arrival I wrote this letter home:

SEPTEMBER 9, 1969
I got here yesterday. I live in Ackworth House in an attic room with four other girls. The rooms are terribly ancient. I will soon need an eiderdown comforter for the bed because the windows are kept open all night. The school is huge and will take me months to find my way around. There are a thousand rooms and halls leading to dead-end walls. Ackworth used to be an orphanage in the 1700s and resembles a place of imprisonment! I can't think of much else to write except that I do miss you a lot!
Love Always and Sincerely, Debbie

I did not fare as well as my parents and I had hoped. As my letter suggested there were troubles brewing. Although I tried hard to be the person my parents wanted me to be, I felt like a lost orphan locked away in a world that presented only dead ends, where I would find a way to fall through the cracks.

Unfortunately, the school did not know my troubled past and never thought to assign me a mentor to guide me through this closed society, a community inhabited by kids who had been boarders since they were eleven years old. I found it hard to break through the tight bonds and cliques and find a comfortable niche.

To make matters worse, my first experience as a Jew came the second day of school, in the dining room. One of the girls joked with another boarder that she was a "Jew" for not sharing her dessert. Everyone snickered when someone else whispered, "Kike!" Like my mother, I was an alien in an enemy country and I, too, made a pact with myself that no one would know my horrible secret.

My course load was drowning me: French, Spanish, English Language, English Literature, History, Geography, Science, Homemaking, Art, Arts and Music History, and Religious Instruction. It was far too heavy after having cut school for two years.

During my second month I met Mark Blakey, a boarder since childhood and the designated Head Boy. The students called him Brutus because he was six feet tall, an athlete, and kindhearted. He was gentle, firm, well behaved, and the school pet. I felt secure in his presence. Instructive, almost fatherly toward me, he tried to protect and guide me through the cloistered boarding school society and I began to idolize him. He, in turn, seemed fascinated by my wild spirit and willingness to buck the system. I struck a chord in his quiet demeanor and turned what must have been a rather boring boarding school existence into a daily soap opera.

But Mark's goodness couldn't keep me from gravitating toward those with whom I felt more comfortable and had a greater allegiance: the outsiders. It was very reassuring that there were kids like me, and without their enduring kindness my experience would have been vastly different. I began to smoke, and soon, so did Mark. Within six months, although I was going steady with Mark, the school's most popular bloke, I was having difficulty with my studies and was prone to argue with dictatorial instructors. I started drinking cough medicine to make myself hallucinate. Mark's parents must have heard stories about me from the staff and were worried that he had chosen such an oddity for a girlfriend. They were bothered by me. I was not blue-eyed, fair-haired, light-skinned, or Anglo-Saxon, but a shade darker than they would have liked. Perhaps I was Italian, Jewish, or East Indian? When Mark's mother came to fetch us, for the Christmas term-break, she took us to a lovely restaurant before our long ride north. While we reviewed the menu, I overheard a couple speaking at the table next to us. "She's probably Jewish," the woman declared, "and hopefully not an American Jew."

I looked up in shock, wondering who they were talking about, praying it wasn't me. Mark and his mother exchanged quick glances, then continued studying the menu. But I was suddenly deeply hurt, ashamed, and embarrassed.

In that moment I wished I had gone home to Reigate with Ruth, even though they didn't celebrate Christmas. Feeling a sudden connection with my Jewish heritage, I wanted to be there when they didn't turn on the lights from Friday evening through Saturday, recited hymn-like prayers over the braided bread they called challah, then sprinkled it with sea salt. I wanted to be home . . . with my own people.

Christmas at the Blakeys' farm was educational. Everyone rose before 6 A.M. Mark, as the eldest son, was expected to work the land with his father. On the occasions when he was not too busy, Mark taught me how to "lamb," a term for assisting sheep to birth their young, drive the tractor, to ride sidesaddle, English style, and he took me on a foxhunt. Mark's mother, Marion Blakey, tried to like me, took me sightseeing, and was very kind; but her instinct was correct: I was a bad influence on her son. Although he did well on all his exams, Marion believed her son was far too taken with the troubled waif from America. But Mark vigorously defended me and I was profoundly grateful for his devotion. I had been missing someone, anyone, who thought I was special.

In a letter to Ruth, six months into the school year the telltale signs of my troubles were present:

> . . . I don't seem to be able to do anything right. I wonder what's wrong with me. I hate most of the authorities in this school. I'm tired and want to come home for a long rest.

My poor relations with my teachers finally came to a head when my English Literature schoolmaster accused me of "bastardizing" Shakespeare with my accent, then expelled me from his class for chewing gum. Later that evening I punched my fist through a window. I hadn't intended to sever three tendons, cut an artery, and get transported by blaring ambulance to the hospital. During my two-week hospital stay, with my reattached tendons healing in a plaster cast, a minister, a priest, and a rabbi were invited to counsel me. I refused to speak to anyone but Mark.

Soon after, I wrote in my journal what seems now to be a particularly telling passage:

Once and for all I push away the cloud from my eyes.
I can see misery and pain all about me.
Suddenly I am where I began,
Still too weak to help the underprivileged of our world.

My responsibility and what am I doing?
Naught!

In the summer of 1970 my parents agreed to let me come home for the six-week term break. Just before my return I received a letter from my brother Larry. He wrote of his church, the Peoples Temple, and about a man who lived Jesus' teachings and knew all about me and my troubles. He invited me to come visit and see for myself. I wondered if maybe Larry was on drugs. How could anyone know my difficulties?

3
Lost and Found

Back in San Francisco, in my father's American car, I felt disoriented. Compared to the English cars I was now accustomed to, this one felt immense. Papa and the steering wheel were on the wrong side of the car and the traffic was streaming by on the wrong side of the road. I had finally come home and yet nothing felt right.

When Mama greeted me at the door, I struggled to remain composed. I wrapped my arms around her and choked down a cry, once again painfully aware of how little I knew her.

After I had my cast cut off and had the stitches taken out, I swam daily to strengthen my shriveled arm, lay in the sun to give it color, and sat outside on the front porch with Mama, together at last. Papa went to work in the mornings but came home early to spend time with me. On weekends we drove up to our land in Sea Ranch on the Northern California coast.

Although it was good to be home with my parents, by my fourth week I felt antsy, anxious to visit Larry and meet the man who knew everything. It was not easy, however, to convince my parents to let me go. They were troubled by my plan. Larry had been alarmingly uncommunicative since he had joined the humanitarian self-help group up north in Ukiah. In the three years he had been involved with the group, the Peoples Temple, Larry had visited our parents only once. Papa called him regularly but was always told Larry was gone, busy, or at work. Papa thought something was odd.

Larry had married Carolyn, his college sweetheart, in 1967. After their graduation the following year, Larry was struggling to obtain a deferment from the Vietnam War. He had requested alternative service work, explaining he was born and raised a Quaker. While waiting to hear from the Draft Board, Larry and Carolyn had moved north to a little community called Potter Valley, where Carolyn taught high school. She chose this location after listening to a sermon given by Reverend Jim Jones, a handsome preacher there who criticized the war in Vietnam, racism, and social injustice. She and Larry attended church services and found themselves in the company of many other college graduates. Jim took a special interest in the attractive young couple and offered to help Larry write the final appeal for Conscientious Objector status. Jones said it would be a miracle if Larry received it. In the spring of 1969, Larry was granted the impossible. A miracle.

Larry and Carolyn were impressed and they stayed on to work with Jones in his fight against prejudice and poverty. However, soon thereafter, Carolyn and the minister became close working comrades, spending more and more time together on important church matters and with her mentor's help, she divorced my twenty-two-year-old brother.

Looking back I can see how well orchestrated the demise of their marriage was. But at the time no one saw the contrived and more sinister meaning. It happened during a small meeting Jim had arranged to discuss Larry's C.O. status. During the session Jim mentioned he'd observed a "distance" that had grown between the young couple. Larry agreed, saying he worked long hours at two jobs and that Carolyn had grown quite cold. Carolyn agreed and, much to his surprise, asked for a divorce.

"I'm sorry that is how you feel . . . but if that's what will make you happy . . ." Larry whispered, visibly shaken.

Jim suggested that Larry meet Karen, a devoted new member. Karen just happened to be in the building and was summoned to Jim's meeting. The Reverend introduced them officially and said he felt in his heart and psyche they would be well matched. Within six months Larry was divorced from Carolyn and dating Karen. They married soon thereafter.

I had seen Karen's photograph on Papa's desk. She reminded me of a cover girl, young, blond, hair blowing in the wind. She looked honest, sweet, and fun. She had been a homecoming queen in college. I was eager to meet Larry's new wife and to see for myself what the man Larry called the Prophet was all about.

Finally, my familiar promises of good behavior worked and my parents gave me a few days away from them. I boarded a Greyhound bus for the three-hour ride north to a place where the summer heat reached over 100 degrees.

Karen and Larry met me at the Ukiah bus station and we drove to the Mendocino coast for a picnic. I followed them along the sunny beach as they held hands and we searched for the perfect sand dollar. Larry found three. When we finally laid down the picnic blanket, Karen began to talk about their remarkable pastor, Jim Jones. Part American Indian, he had been born May 13, 1931, raised by his mother in Indiana, and grown up deeply opposed to racism. In 1952, at only twenty-one, he had become assistant pastor of his Methodist church, and by 1960, he had his own congregation.

"He was always selfless, Debbie, and encouraged all his parishioners to follow his example," Karen told me, her eyes filled with admiration and pride. "We are a denomination of the Disciples of Christ," she explained, handing me a grassy vegetarian sandwich.

"Jim was appointed Director of the Human Rights Commission when he was only thirty years old!" Karen continued. "Then, in 1961, he had a vision of a nuclear war and worldwide devastation. He traveled to Brazil and other South American countries, searching for the safest place for his followers to live. He determined that Ukiah would be safe from nuclear fallout, even if San Francisco and Seattle were hit by nuclear bombs, and he moved here five years ago." Karen smiled at me. "That's when I met him!"

Later I found out that in the mid-sixties, during the Cuban Missile Crisis, *Esquire* magazine had published the nine safest places to hide in the event of a nuclear war. Jim had chosen Northern California from the listing and found a cave that could house all of his followers until the fallout had subsided.

"Oh, Debbie, I was lost, just like you. Jim showed me how egocentric and self-indulgent I had been. He needed my help to stop the ugliness of prejudice which has kept the blacks and Indians down. I stopped smoking marijuana and joined him in his fight to rid the world of hatred. Oh, Debbie, what a saint he is. He has adopted three young orphans from Korea, a black son, and he was the first minister to have a black man as his associate pastor. That's Archie. You'll know him right off. He usually begins the services, then sits on the podium during Jim's sermon." She touched my cheek gently with her hand. "You really will learn that ours is the only path to enlightenment."

I was duly impressed. Karen, Carolyn, and Larry belonged to a very important organization.

The next morning Karen drove me to the church in Redwood Valley, a ten-minute commute north of Ukiah. Larry had kissed me good morning hours ago and gone to his weekend job at the lumber mill, a job he took to earn extra money to give to the Temple. Weekdays were spent in his alternative service job.

The Temple was a large wooden building Larry had helped build. There were floor-to-ceiling windows and a beautiful stained-glass one behind the podium with a dove in flight. The church was surrounded by vineyards and the entire community was encircled by beautiful rolling hills.

Karen ushered me into the sunny sanctuary and I glimpsed a letter posted on a bulletin board. It was a thank-you note to Pastor Jones signed by Governor Ronald Reagan, embossed with the seal of the state of California.

I'd have to tell my parents about the letter when I got home, I thought. I was shown to a metal folding chair and looked up toward the stained-glass window. The dove was now shining with the reflection of the sun as the minister's voice, warm and nurturing, caught my attention. His handsome face was framed by coal black hair that fell slightly onto his forehead.

I was struck by all the young faces in the audience. The congregation was made up of equal numbers of blacks and whites, although most of the black members seemed far older. There was a crowd of Asian, Indian, blond, and kinky-haired children chatting and giggling near the enclosed indoor pool. I wondered which of the children belonged to the pastor. I had seen his family's photograph in the foyer. Karen had pointed out his wife Marceline, the three adopted Korean children, two girls and one boy about my age; an American Indian girl who was a young adult, a black son who looked eight or nine; and his own biological son, who appeared to be about fourteen. Karen had whispered into my ear that some of the members' children were among the privileged few being raised by the pastor himself. She pointed out a white twenty-two-year-old and said, "John moved in with the pastor's family some time ago and is being groomed for a very important role. He will study law at Stanford."

I watched Jones's pained face as he spoke about the injustices in the world, why the war in Vietnam was wrong, how discrimination cut away at his heart, how he suffered when his black associate minister was mistreated, and how he, too, felt the pain of the little black children being sent away from the all-white schools. His manicured hands punctuated each statement. As I listened to his sermon I became aware of how spoiled, privileged, and white I was. He spoke about the pain we had to encounter to grow and fuel change and I thought that maybe with his directions, I'd be able to understand where I had gone astray and how I could correct the wrongs I had perpetrated.

As he went on and on about the "haves" and "have-nots," I began to fidget and play with the seam of my skirt. He sure talks a lot, I thought. I wish he'd hurry . . . I'm hungry. Suddenly there was silence. He had paused. I was afraid that he had somehow caught me and judged me as spoiled, restless, and unfocused.

"Do not feel guilty," he resumed. His eyes seemed to look directly at me. "You can change. We all have the ability to become better human beings."

This minister, the man his followers called "the Prophet," "our beloved Pastor," "my best friend," and "Father," felt so deeply about the inequities in our world that I made an effort to stay focused on his words. He seemed to be addressing every single person in the congregation.

"Yes, come join us. Help me eradicate injustice from all our lives. Work with me to help those who are not strong enough to help themselves." I wondered what eradicate meant.

"Come forward. Be a part of a fellowship that will work to rid our society of hatred, racism, and poverty. I am inviting you to join in a new beginning, a life you can feel challenged by. Through my ministry you can help make history. As a group, we can wipe out racism and immorality throughout America." His voice was warm and compassionate. "Yes, many of you are too selfish to make a commitment to help those not as lucky as you. However, those of you who can and do make that commitment will profit in this life and in many more to come."

Could that be reincarnation?

"Yes," the minister seemed to answer me. "Those people who cannot commit to more than their own personal journey, those who do not give of themselves, will come back as lesser organisms. Yes, they will return again and again until they learn through centuries of lives that giving is greater than receiving."

I was dumbfounded. It was as if he had read my thoughts.

"There are only a few who are enlightened enough to be able to communicate with me in this manner. I am speaking to you. You can grow exponentially if you stay within my aura. It is not an accident that you came today. You are here because there is something greater in store for you in this world. You are meant to be a part of this cause. You came here today because there is a greater power and he wants your help. I want you to help me make this a better world."

Could he be talking to me? I wasn't special.

"Oh yes, you are important. I need you. Stay here with me and you will become everything you can be. I want souls with fighting spirits, people who have been underestimated, underprivileged, misunderstood, and have not been given the chance to realize their potential. You are the one." I lowered my eyes. My face felt flushed, the minister was looking at me. "You, darling, are what this ministry is all about."

How could he want me? He must not know how bad I've been.

At the end of the sermon the audience rose, yelling out praises to the handsome, kindly, fatherly pastor, the Reverend Jim Jones. He seemed truly embarrassed and humbled by all the accolades.

"Thank you, Father," shouted the elderly gentleman behind me.

"Thank you, Jim," waved a blond teenager across the auditorium.

"You've saved my life! Thank you, thank you, my savior!" called out an old woman with white hair.

"You're truly the only one who understands! Thank you, blessed Pastor Jim," cried another.

"You gave me another chance, you gave me hope to continue on this rocky road," proclaimed the elderly black woman next to me.

I was flustered by all the commotion around me. People were jumping up and down and clapping their hands to music. I wished Larry were there so that I could ask him all the questions on my mind. I was glad to get up and stretch my legs. We'd been sitting for three hours. I noticed the young black organist playing and singing dramatically. She looked about my age, seventeen. I watched as the young people began dancing around, happy, comfortable, not the least bit self-conscious. I took it all in, mesmerized by the energy in the room. I watched in wonder as this family of all races, ages, colors, sizes, and shapes strolled from group to group, hugging one another, gabbing, laughing, and sharing stories. I felt insignificant and wished I, too, could join their great temple of humanity.

While women were laying out food on buffet tables at the back of the church, little children ran about with towels and swimsuits, yelling to their parents to watch them dive into the pool. People were lining up with plates and utensils at the food-laden tables. I noticed a group of teenagers who had gathered around the pianist, singing a Marvin Gaye song. I realized how close the young black singer was to the reverend. She accompanied him the entire service. Sometimes she played loudly and people would sing along; at other times, according to his tone of voice, her playing was soft and ghostly.

Then my attention was drawn toward the pulpit where a long line of people waited to speak with the Reverend. A sudden spurt of bravery made me get in line behind the old black grandmother who had sat next to me during the sermon. She turned slightly on her beat-up cane and smiled at me.

"Honey? This yur first meetin'? I saw yah lookin' antsy an' scared."

"Did I look scared? I didn't think . . . Oh, I'm just visiting my brother for a couple days."

"Baby, you ain't got nuttin' to be 'fraid of and you ain't gonna be disappointed. I guess you ain't never been to a revival meetin' like this 'fore now?"

"Oh . . . Well . . . I went to Quaker meetings and . . ."

"What's you doin' in this line, baby? You needin' som' healin'?"

"No, I thought I'd introduce myself . . ."

"Lordy, chile, he don't need you tellin' him who you is. Oh, honey, he already know'd that. No, chile, this man knows the pain you been suffered and the healin' you need to make this body whole 'gain. Uh-huh, Uh-huh. Yes, Lordy, he know'd everythin' 'bout each of us. God knows, he done healed me of cancer and I's hopin' he'll find a way, if the spirit's right, to rid me of this here walkin' cane."

She shook her old, battered cane in the air and I looked around to see if anyone noticed. "You said somethin' 'bout a brother?" she continued.

"Oh, my older brother? Larry Layton? Do you know him?"

"Any relation to Miss Carolyn Layton?"

"Well, she was married to him . . ."

"Oh, chile, she works so hard for Father. Why I seen her makin' sure he gets his water during service . . . No, I ain't never seen him take any time for hisself. He always givin' to others. Oh, chile, Jim Jones done got my grandson off heroin. I told him 'bout my heartache and he done sent his Carolyn on down to Frisco to get him. Yes, ma'am, they done brought him up to Ukiah and got him well. Yes, honey, you ain't never gonna find a man as lovin' as him." She pointed toward the podium where the Reverend was ministering to a mother and small child. "Why, if it weren't for that Miss Carolyn, Pastor Jones wouldn't have food or drink. That's right, honey, that man only gives. Yeah, uh-huh, she's an angel come help him minister to us poor folk an' hers a heart o' gold . . ."

As the line shortened and I got closer to the Reverend, I looked at his grand mahogany lectern. It stood elevated upon a blue carpeted riser with two steps up to where Jones was talking to a young boy. The child looked upset. I could not tell if there were tears on his face, but the Reverend seemed to be calming him, leaning forward and whispering to the child.

I waited as he spoke at length with other individuals. There seemed to be no concern for time. One man talked to him for what seemed like an hour about his inability to give more money because he lived on a small pension and had barely enough to feed himself. The Reverend responded compassionately,

"I never want you to give money. Your willingness to donate your home and yourself when we have guests in town is more than enough. No, Mr. Brown, it's not you I am coaxing to pledge." He sighed. "It's those who have the means and ability to pay. They are the ones I am speaking to. My precious Mr. Brown, it is because of your good heart that I continue to do my work. It is for you that I ask for this money. God knows, if only more members felt the way you do, my job would be that much easier. It is because of you I feel the strength to carry on through the darkness. I hope you can make our Wednesday night meeting."

When the elderly man left the podium I noticed a lightness to his walk as though a weight had been lifted from his shoulders. Then an even more aged, hunchbacked woman hobbled toward the Pastor. Although she spoke quietly, I could hear tiny portions of their conversation. She talked of extreme pain in her lower back and as she spoke, Jim held out his left hand and touched her gently around her neck and forehead. His hands were an olive brown and looked sturdy but not hard, his nails beautifully rounded and clean. He wore no jewelry, no watch. He had removed his tie and opened the first button of the shirt under his black robe. His face was clean, radiant, and handsome. It was easy to trust such a face.

I watched in awe as he placed both his hands firmly on the old woman's lower spine. The next moment the bent grandma straightened her torso and screamed and shouted.

"Thank you, Jesus. Thank you, Jesus. The pain is gone. You healed my body. You took out my cancer. Thank you, God. Thank you, Jim."

Other members who had gathered around the buffet tables looked up at the miraculous healing that had been performed and began to clap and yell. The pianist started to play a melodic song and I could hear the Reverend humming along. My newfound friend and adviser, still ahead of me in the line, began to wheeze from under her breath.

"Yes, God. Yes, Jim. Thank you, Jim. Yes, God."

Her eyes were closed as she danced a soft and trancelike jig. Her back and shoulders seemed to loosen and she suddenly looked much younger. The pianist began to play a hymn and the minister joined in, singing the words, "He cares, he cares, Father cares for you. He cares, he cares, c a r e s . . . f o r . . . y o u . . ." The melody was pleasing and it seemed as though everyone in the auditorium was humming it while they went about their business.

I felt self-conscious and stiff. I had never seen a healing before. I watched as my kindly, cane-holding friend slowly ended her dance of praise and transformed again into the aged grandmother waiting in line.

At last, my new friend spoke softly with the Reverend. I was close enough to the pulpit now to get a look inside it. There was a high stool, where I assumed the minister must sit, and an empty bookshelf to rest his feet. There were plastic containers of different sizes on the lower shelf of the lectern and pieces of paper he had forgotten to throw in the trash receptacle next to his chair. I wondered if he took off his shoes while he was up there preaching. The carpet looked plush and soft.

Finally, I was standing before Jim Jones. He was not as tall as he looked from farther back. Perhaps a little more than a head and neck above my five feet. My hands were wet and I had sweated straight through my blouse. Ashamed, I lowered my eyes and said hello.

"I hope you listened today." The Reverend's voice, close up, was a charming, low rasp. I expected him to be more severe, but his face was kind, his skin smooth and tight. His dark brown eyes were focused, understanding and warm.

"Oh yes. Every word," I responded. He smelled good, like a spicy cologne.

"It is you I was speaking to today," he said.

Again, I lowered my eyes.

"I have felt your embarrassment throughout the service. Who has done this to you?"

I didn't understand what he was talking about.

"Your parents have never appreciated your immense warmth and sensitivity. Not once have they recognized or embraced your wonderful and loving spirit. I want you to stay. Join me and my family of all races."

"Well, I . . ."

"Wait, I feel something . . ." He closed his eyes as if pulling in information from somewhere outside of himself. "Why, you must be Larry's sister. I have been concentrating on your coming soon."

My coming? Soon? "Oh well, my parents said I could visit Larry for a couple of days before I go back to school." Larry didn't tell him?

"I know things no other man could know, Debbie. Don't go back. You are much stronger than you have been led to believe. Stay with us. There may be a holocaust and it is only here in Ukiah that we will be safe."

"Um. My parents won't . . ."

"Don't use them as an excuse. If you were enlightened enough, committed enough, you would stay with us. Your safety is what concerns me," the Pastor admonished.

"But I haven't finished school and I promised my mom and dad . . ."

"Debbie, you must be firm. You must demand that they allow you to stay here. We need you here in the light . . . My aura . . . My power is what people need and want. I have come from the highest plane to gather together those spirits who are ready to continue on to the next level."

I hoped he couldn't tell that I had no idea what he was talking about.

"Someday soon, you, too, will understand. You will realize the ultimate truth. You are an ever-growing, always learning, forever living spirit. Yes, each of us is on a different level of development and enlightenment, but through continual reincarnations we become more refined. If one is committed to the truth, the highest form of giving, then and only then, one will pass on into the next level. The next plane, the place where I have come from to help those like you, who need guidance." He waved his arms to include all the people in the Redwood Valley church. "I have heard your sorrow, I have seen you in my thoughts, alone, lonely, and far away. I can help you attain your true place in this world. Being loved, fulfilling your dream of happiness. You are so close to stepping up and into the next level of enlightenment. Will you make that commitment?"

I hesitated, biting my cuticle.

"I will wait for you. You are an important link in our organization. This is just the beginning and, with you, we can grow and become more powerful.

"Darling, you have no idea of the depth of your courage, the strength of your resolve," he continued. "I am what allowed you to come here to visit. It is my prayers that lessened your parents' tight hold on you. They didn't want you to come and it is my power that made them acquiesce. My thoughts and determination made them comply with my wishes."

His firm voice was consoling. It called out to me to trust him. His eyes told me he had waited almost his entire life to meet me. He leaned over and kissed my forehead. I felt weak, swooning in his intense and wholly focused attention.

"I am not an average man. I am here to do great deeds for the needy of this earth. I am here to accomplish godly tasks and it is you who I want to help me."

I stood immobilized.

"Come and stay with us. I want you and will wait for you. We will all wait for your coming, for your presence with us. You are an untapped source of power, a reservoir of life. Without your spirit among us, we will not be as effective."

Grabbing hold of my hands, he looked into my eyes. I could feel the heat from his gaze, which burned like white-hot coals. "Debbie, you have wandered upon this earth looking, wanting, and needing answers. I can give you them. For every unknown in your mind, I can give you enlightenment. For your fear, I can give you strength. For your sorrow, I can give you hope and a dream we will attain together."

I suddenly trusted him completely. I wanted to scream, "Yes, I do, I love you."

"I am . . ."

"You need not say anymore. I know your thoughts, and I say to you now, Debbie, you do have the power to say no to your parents. In my presence, you will grow to recognize your abilities, and then, the world beware."

Does he know I'm only seventeen? Am I that important?

"You are very special to me, Debbie. I want to thank you for coming up here to speak with me. Your presence has given me stamina. I can feel your strength resonate inside of me. I was tired when I finished the sermon, but now I feel I could run around the entire Redwood Valley. You are an incredible source of energy to me. No one has ever told you how wonderful you are. Your parents have always compared you to your older siblings, yet they have failed to see your profound understanding. They have not taken the time to observe the sweetness and light that shine from deep within you."

I stood very still, afraid that with any movement he might see the real, dirty, bad, and undeserving me.

"Debbie, I know all about you, I feel your hurt. I am saddened by the heavy weight of your loneliness. You have known immense sorrow. You have been misunderstood and forgotten. Your parents have committed a terrible injustice by not taking the time to know you. Instead of connecting with you they sent you far away. How could they be so blind."

"It really isn't their fault . . ."

"Debbie, it's time to grow away from all the excuses. It is time for you to stand up and say, I, too, want to be counted. Don't get left behind in the back of the bus. Come and be one of us." He leaned forward and looked deeply into my face. "Farewell for now, and remember, I am with you always." With that he kissed my forehead again and walked off the podium.

As he moved away from me, my body felt as though it had grown one size larger. My forehead, where he had kissed me, remained extraordinarily warm. I was convinced that this man truly and unconditionally loved me. I already missed him. I loved being the center of his attention. I could not remember why I was faintly familiar with this wonderful feeling. It was something I yearned for, something I missed, and yet I could not tell from where, with whom, long, long ago, I had experienced it.

It was close to five in the afternoon and the church was now almost deserted. There were a few people in the kitchen cleaning the platters and talking but all the others had gone.

I heard a rustle from behind me and jumped.

"Debbie, are you okay?" Carolyn walked up to me. I realized that I hadn't seen her since the divorce, except to wave at her when I entered the church. I felt flustered and hot.

"Oh, you just surprised me. I thought I was alone."

She was wearing a long earth-colored floral skirt with a long-sleeved blouse. She seemed older than twenty-four, more grown up. I could see why someone might call her angelic. She looked innocent and lovely with her auburn-colored hair pulled softly into a bun. I remembered she had studied French in Bordeaux before she met Larry. She looked like the women I had seen in Paris, when I'd traveled on term break at boarding school, elegant, confident, and pure. I wondered if her youngest sister, Sweet Annie, was also here. I hadn't seen Annie since I'd stayed with her family before leaving for boarding school.

"Debbie, you should feel very special."

"Really?"

"Absolutely! Jim never talks to anyone new as long as he did with you."

"Oh," I sighed. "He is saying I shouldn't go back to England."

"Listen to him. He's a prophet. He can read minds and can see through time and space."

"Carolyn, what did he mean about there being a holocaust?"

"He is trying to change the future, but there is a threat of a nuclear war and it is only here that we'll be safe."

"When will it happen?"

"We don't know. Jim is using his powers to keep it from happening, but we cannot know for sure. That is why you should stay. If you are in Europe when it happens, you'll perish."

"Carolyn?" I asked.

"Yes?" she responded sweetly.

"While I was waiting in line to speak with Jim, an older woman was explaining to me how wonderful you are. That you take such good care of Jim . . ."

"Jim and I are very close." Her voice softened to a whisper. "He has become very dependent on my observations and assistance. He needs me. Jim truly has no time for himself and I try to fill the void. His sermons, as you saw today, last a long time.

So I bring him water, fill his thermos with herbal tea, and as you see, he never leaves the podium, so I bring him a urinal to relieve himself."

"You mean while he was talking today, he was peeing, too?"

"Several times. You must understand that he is an extremely dedicated man and he gives of himself constantly. While you sat comfortably listening, he was on his feet, educating you and the congregation. We must never forget how hard Jim works in order to enlighten us," she continued.

"What do you mean?"

"We all come into the fold ignorant. The longer you stay near Jim's energy and power, the more you will learn and understand. Right now you are like a small child, but as you stay and grow you will advance and become enlightened." She smiled. "We believe in reincarnation. Jim was Lenin in his last life, as he explained to me when I joined, and I was with him then, too."

"Wasn't Lenin a Communist?" I stuttered. I knew that Communists were bad people. One killed President Kennedy when I was in fifth grade.

"He was a socialist and fought for the equality of all the people of Russia."

"Why'd he become a religious leader?"

"Who, Lenin?" Carolyn looked confused.

"No, Jim. How come Jim came back as a religious leader if he was a revolutionary?"

"Oh, Debbie, in every one of his reincarnations he has fought for justice and the good of humanity. First as Jesus, then as the Bab, and most recently as Lenin. I was Lenin's confidante and friend, Inessa Armand."

"But who is the 'Babe'?"

"No, Debbie, the Bab. His name is Bab ed-Din or Ali Muhammad of Shiraz. He was a Persian religious leader who founded Babism in the nineteenth century. Don't you see? Jim has always been a fighter, a revolutionary. He has come back here, one last time, to bring people out of religion, into enlightenment. He is trying to teach us that socialism is God."

I was confused. She seemed disappointed in me for not catching on right away.

"Let me slow down. Jim is trying to open the minds of the people. He can only reach them through religion. As he heals and teaches, they will grow to understand that religion is an opiate, used to keep the masses down. Only Jim can bring people into the light. Through him we can make it to the next plane."

"Oh." I tried to look smart. I decided to ask Mama when I got home if Jesus was a socialist. She'd know.

"Carolyn? Why doesn't his wife help him pee? She's a nurse, isn't she?"

She sighed as if we were treading in uncharted territory. "She is busy during the meetings, preparing for the healings . . . Anyway, she isn't that well, in fact she's often ill and it has been hard on Jim. He is young and vibrant and it is very difficult for him to have such a sickly wife. We don't put any demands on her."

Unsure of what that meant, I asked, "How does she get ready for healings?"

"Honey, it's complicated. When people vomit up growths and cancers it is messy and Marcie is right there to take care of it all."

"Carolyn?" I felt uncomfortable and wanted to change the subject. "Has your sister Annie ever met Jim?"

"No, but she is coming to visit me next week. I think she should go to nursing school and live at our dorms. It would be good for Jim to have another RN assisting him with the healings, someone close to me."

Sweet Annie a nurse? I remembered her sitting on my bed in tenth grade when I lived with her family in Davis. She was all the things I wanted to be. She got along with her parents, received good grades, enjoyed school, and was wonderful and kind to everyone. She'd listened to me read my poetry . . . and now she was going to be a nurse. She was going to take care of Lenin and his healings. I was impressed and jealous. I wondered if Inessa had spoken fluent French, like Carolyn.

As the Greyhound bus pulled out of Ukiah, I was happy that Larry had been able to leave work early, take me to the station and say good-bye. I thought about Karen's good-bye kiss and how she said she loved me so much. I was in overload, brimming with information I had no way to filter through or figure out. I wondered if I really had the strength to tell my parents I wouldn't go back to England. School had been their last resort, their only hope for me.

But listening to the Reverend Jones that day, I'd realized that I was repeating my same old patterns in England. I still lied, believed my own stories, cut classes, drank, and smoked dope. I remained the only person who truly interested me. Jim Jones was right, I had done nothing in my life to help eliminate another human being's suffering. It was my own sniveling self-pity that kept my life afloat. It was as he had said, it was the privilege of the white upper class to be self-indulgent.

I told Larry I was worried about Jim's expectations for me. Would I be strong enough to fight Papa? But Larry calmed my fears.

"Don't feel pressured, Bugs. You'll do what's right for you."

I liked it when he called me that.

As I stared out the window at the broken white line on the road, the line that separated and protected me from the traffic in the next lane, I felt I was not ready yet to cross over the line and join the Temple. I didn't want to disappoint my parents again. I needed to finish school. Ruth wanted me to stay with her in Surrey once my O-levels were completed, to study for my teaching credentials. And I couldn't leave Mark behind. I needed to warn him of the holocaust and tell him about the Prophet.

As the dotted white lines began to blur, I opened the bag Larry had handed me as I boarded the bus. He had given me his three sand dollars. I smiled as I thought about Larry's parting words:

"Cheer up, Bugs, Mom and Dad are doing the best they know how. They're not bad folks. It's probably best, for you and them, to return to England and finish your education."

I leaned my head against the darkened bus window. The cold air from the conditioner blew on the side of my face and I was glad to be heading home. It's not that big a deal, I thought, Jim won't remember me anyway . . .

I was thousands of miles away, but Jim never forgot me. I began to receive weekly letters from him and from other members of the family and I proudly kept everything I received.

PEOPLES TEMPLE CHRISTIAN CHURCH
OF THE
DISCIPLES OF CHRIST

SEPTEMBER 18, 1970

Rev. James W. Jones, Pastor
PO Box 214
Redwood Valley, Calif., 95470

Dear Debbie:

I will be around for as long as you need to convince yourself of who I am and the character of what I stand for. Don't feel guilty about what you've done. Your actions were no surprise to me; contrariwise, you were quite capable of standing up to your parents but you lacked the necessary background experience and the deep, heartfelt conviction about our principles and me as the principle bearer. Thus I can well empathize with your vacillation. Please don't be so hard on yourself. Everyone I minister to at one point or another has the same ambivalence and also the same awareness of their own ego that is involved in service or giving to others. You must remember, although it is a trite phrase, that one must crawl before we can learn to walk, and mankind generally is in the crawling stage.

We all love you and are looking forward to seeing you when the time is right. We speak from the highest plane of truth and when you have time to test this affirmation thoroughly you will not be disappointed.

Sincerely,
Rev. James W. Jones

Addendum: The foregoing letter is dictated to me by our beloved pastor, Jim Jones, who is greatly concerned about you. What a friend to have, many who have been touched by this life and ministry gladly rise to call him blessed and to declare most emphatically that Jim is the most wonderful person alive today. . . . I am one of that number. Jim is a man of absolutely unimpeachable character, one who is continually involving himself in the practice of doing good for others, who gives and gives and gives of himself of his strength, and time, very often whole nights are spent in wrestling with some unfortunate's problem, and seldom indeed is he fortunate enough to acquire two whole unbroken hours of untroubled rest a night. Far from doing spite to anyone or enriching himself at others' expense, he is continually outgoing with deeds of kindness and love which very often necessitates a huge outlay of cash which is cheerfully given in any instance of need to friend or foe. He is a man whom to know is to love. That he has enemies is due primarily to his message of total equality for every race, creed or nation which premise is most scrupulously practiced himself. His love in which his devotees would love to bask, is just as real, tender and enduring for the smaller and weaker forms at his home, he takes in even poor deserted little things that come crying at his door for food or is left off at the edge of his property by hard, insensitive people. You should see his large foundling home. And, mark how sweetly they all get along together, big vicious dogs and feeble little kittens!

Our church, Peoples Temple, received coverage in some large newspapers, such as the San Francisco Chronicle which praised our position in our stand for social justice and as opposed to war. One of our projects is helping families of deceased policemen as well as peace workers who have been assassinated. Incidentally, we get hundreds of letters a week, all of which are faithfully answered. Jim wants you to know it is his pleasure to respond. In closing I wish to affirm that along with thousands of others I would not be alive today were it not for Jim who healed me of cancer, heart trouble and diabetes. Cancer which is the number one killer in the world today is Jim's specialty. I can't tell you how many I have seen that have come from pain-wracked bodies at his simple word of command.
Sincerely, Jim Pugh, Sec.

I was seventeen years old and profoundly impressed by the importance the Reverend James W. Jones bestowed upon me. At last, what I had yearned for all my life happened, an important adult found me smart, worthwhile, and interesting.

4
Indoctrination

During the year that I was back at school in England, Peoples Temple members continued to demonstrate their concern for me through a concerted letter-writing campaign. I was told in glowing terms about the two radio shows Jim was doing in San Francisco and the wonderful Oregon vacation Jim took with 200 young people, many of whom were from inner-city ghettos and had never seen the ocean before. There were stories about near-death accidents that Jim had prevented, youth group outings, and summer craft fairs.

Although Carolyn had sworn me to secrecy about Jim's past lives, I confided in Mark about having met the reincarnation of Jesus, who was now living in Ukiah as a revolutionary. Mark was impressed by my stories. On the morning of my written exams he wrote me a note.

> Debbie,
> Read the examination over first,
> then go back and answer the questions
> and remember, Jim loves you.
> Love, Brutus

When my O-levels were completed and I'd finished school, I had already been successfully recruited into the fold. Ruth tried to convince me to stay with her, attend a trade school, and become a children's schoolteacher. But the Temple's pull was too strong. Flying home didn't seem as scary any longer. I had a known destination and direction. I would be a member of a respectable group, an established organization that was helping the needy, the poor, and the underprivileged. I would move to Ukiah and begin a new life.

Joining was so easy, and I wanted to believe. I was searching for something meaningful and all-consuming. People had jobs that they were wed to, church duties they performed, children to care for, relationships that gave them strength. Perhaps I, too, would be able to feel that my existence was not in vain, that I had a purpose when I rose each day.

Mark came with me. He was only visiting for summer break and was scheduled to return to England to complete his Advanced Level studies before entering university. Once in Ukiah, however, he, too, was quickly seduced by massive amounts of adulation, flattery, and attention. Regularly, at the end of a long meeting Jim would call out in his contrived British accent:

"Where is Mark, my son?"

"Ova harr . . ." Mark would reply.

Everyone would chuckle as the six-foot-three-inch bloke stood to converse with Jim. Mark lent some comic relief to the long and dreary days that Jim had to push through. For all the suffering our leader had to endure trying to educate imbeciles, fight against racism, and worry about our futures, Mark Blakey, my Brutus, became Jim's muse. When summer was over, Mark found it hard to leave. Jim told him he was desperately needed and hinted at new responsibilities. With so much love surrounding him, Mark stayed. Jim quickly arranged for me to marry Mark so that he would not be deported once his three-month visa ran out.

"But he's supposed to go back and finish his A-levels," I objected.

"Darling, don't be jealous, I need him here. He has skills and charm and abilities this organization needs," Jim explained patiently.

"But his parents expect him. His brothers and sister will be upset. And the school is expecting him to return as Head Boy."

"Honestly, darling, you have much to learn." Jim looked at me curiously, his voice calm and assuring. "What is more important, helping the poor or finishing school? He'll learn more with us. He is leadership material. His experiences on his family's farm, his agricultural expertise, may come in handy in our future."

When Mark's mother came to America, furious and determined to take the eldest of her four children home, she found herself the center of Jim's and Carolyn Layton's attention. By now, Carolyn had become quite powerful in the church and was Jim's only true confidante. Mrs. Blakey was catered to and indulged, perhaps even made to believe her son was being groomed for some important role in the organization, which in fact he was. A new Temple member, Tim Stoen, who was also a respected San Francisco assistant district attorney, invited her to stay at his home. His beautiful wife, Grace, chauffeured Mrs. Blakey everywhere through San Francisco and the wine country of Sonoma County. Finally, convinced that the Temple was the best place for her son, she returned to Northumberland alone.

Jim continued to pull both Mark and me into his universe. He gave us a sense of importance, and in return, we handed our will over to him. His presence filled my inner emptiness and gradually his life's work became my own. It was easy to be part of Jim's world; it was already created, furnished, had friendly inhabitants, instant friends, established rules, and boundaries. Jim was kind and attentive. He told me that I could accomplish anything I set my heart on. I flourished. I became a part of the "skits" troupe, an elite group of individuals whose task was to put on performances explaining why capitalism was bad and socialism good. We made our points by spoofing the political system. Father explained that this was the "common man's way" to educate the misinformed and ignorant. After each Family Teach-in performance, Jim came and applauded my ability to grasp the Cause's doctrine and to communicate it to the congregation. Although I missed my parents, I knew I had to succeed at something, and this was my last chance. My new father was strict, believed in "tough love," and didn't let me sneak around the rules. He challenged me, inflated my self-esteem with praise, and made me feel safe.

My parents had hoped I would attend the University of California at Davis as had my siblings, but the SAT exams my parents arranged that I sit for in Liverpool, England, indicated I needed a jump start at junior college. They were a little apprehensive about my going to the Temple's college dormitory, but they knew I needed structure for my first year. One of my American high school friends had been murdered eighteen months earlier, and Mama and Papa were afraid of my returning to my hoodlum crowd.

Now, as I calmed down, became more confident and determined to succeed, they were amazed and relieved. I was actually maturing. Some concern remained, however, as I, like Larry, visited them less and less frequently. Even Christmas and Thanksgiving now had to be spent with my new family.

Mama began to reevaluate her own life, I imagine, while she marveled at my transformation. She surmised that this church, which appeared to espouse socialistic beliefs (she read about them in the newspaper), might be a safe place to make her own flight away from a life of frustration and sorrow. I was proof that people could change and that there was a better life. She later told me that she felt her life had been built upon sand. She believed she had taken more from America than she had given back. She wanted to be a part of something meaningful at last.

Unknown to her, however, as my weeks inside the Temple turned into months, I began to feel a twinge of homesickness and with it a deep feeling of guilt. I missed my parents, I missed the occasional drag on a cigarette, but worst of all I secretly hated the all-day and all-weekend revival meetings. I knew these meetings were important. Jim had explained to me how he and I needed to help the poor, how those who remained drugged with the opiate of religion had to be brought into enlightenment—socialism. But being a humanitarian was a full-time job and I was not used to such altruism.

But I felt even more guilt on the fleeting occasions when I wished I hadn't joined. Father kept my treasonous thoughts in check by warning us that leaving the church would bring bad karma. He reminded us in his sermons that those who had chosen to join were here because we were on the verge of crossing over to the next plane. Without his help, we would not make it. Those who left or betrayed the Cause in any way would be reincarnated as the lowest life form on earth and it would take us another hundred thousand years to get to this point again. I didn't want to start over as an amoeba.

I began writing myself up and reporting on my negative thoughts. I felt it kept me in check. Nuns and priests went to confession, I told myself. I was in control when I reported on my treasonous thoughts, playing the snitch in order to better myself. Over time, I became the perfect vessel for my leader's dogma.

The process of controlling new members began immediately and intensely and I'm not sure I'll ever know what prevented us from seeing through his deceit, his lies, and his manipulations. Only a few days after joining, I learned that "All men are homosexuals, except for Jim." I was stunned, but when the information was not disputed by anyone, I obediently believed it. When I heard Larry and Karen's bed rhythmically creaking at night, I figured Larry and Karen didn't yet know that he was a "homo." It even made me doubtful of Mark. I became terribly embarrassed for the men I knew, wondering why they had all pretended otherwise.

I was even more ashamed for the men I knew when the Reverend taught us that men who grew hair around their mouths really wanted to be "pussies." When I noticed the painted sideburns on Jim's cheeks, it didn't occur to me that he might have felt threatened by the virility of men who had voluminous amounts of facial and chest hair and that was why he forbade his male followers to expose their hair.

This kind of warped logic was just one of the many devices Jim used to control the congregation. He intended to discourage any bonds with the opposite sex that might compromise our allegiance to him. It never seemed odd to me back then that only men were homosexuals. I could not see the sickening duplicity, the clever deception, that made Jim out to be the "only real man" and his male cravings the only valid ones.

Soon thereafter I understood that church policy prohibited sexual relations between members. We were taught that sex was selfish and harmful because it took our thoughts away from helping others. Jim said that in every important organization before ours, sex had always lured the weak away from the path of truth. Lust and desire were character flaws. If one were to be truly devoted, one had to abstain. Those caught not abiding by the rules would be publicly confronted. If they were married, the women had to declare that it was Father they had always thought of and fantasized about when they were with their husbands. These embarrassing proclamations, coerced by Jim and his staff, were meant to discourage all of us from any form of closeness with each other.

Young, malleable, and eager to conform, I tried to shelve and forget my yearnings for boys and a relationship. I was becoming distrustful of men. But it was harder to maintain my asexual equilibrium after Jim arranged my marriage to Mark. That the union was never consummated on the few occasions I saw Mark was a result of his devotion to Father, not mine.

I tried to be the perfect follower and student, but life in our Santa Rosa college dorm was arduous. I had to prove myself to the resident enlightened Temple students because I was new, white, and from the privileged class. So I became a chameleon and learned to change identities quickly.

Brenda, a newly found friend, suggested that I try a different look. "Girl, your skin's too brown to be a honky's." We purchased an easy home perm kit and, with care and determination, administered the magic to my head. After less than an hour, I pulled my fingers through my cotton candy hair. It looked full and big, like Angela Davis's. When I looked at myself in the mirror I was transfixed by my transformation. Brenda and I took a collective breath and stared at a person we did not know. She was awesome! Not a WASP, not a honky, but "Solano," a hip, militant Chicana. Almost as impressive as Angela Davis, the one woman outside the Temple whom Father admired and constantly spoke of.

I adorned myself with big hoop earrings and became comfortable with my new identity as the weeks passed. I was actively doing what Father said we should do: "Know how the other half lives." I felt sure I had taken a bold step in the right direction.

When the new quarter started, I registered for a Chicano Studies class. In this politically correct environment, I gained what I thought was a deep understanding of oppression. My white bourgeois mind developed into enlightened Chicano outrage. In class, I raised the race issue at every opportunity and verbally attacked Caucasians, pointing out all the faults of the rich white oppressor. Well versed in this rhetoric from our Family Teach-ins, I became the spokesperson for my Mexican-American classmates and all other oppressed people. When we had the occasion of hosting a guest lecturer, my professor touted me as a shining example of a self-aware Chicana. It didn't strike me that I was repeating my childhood tendency of telling stories and lies and I never worried about being phony because I had already learned from Father that the end justifies the means.

On one occasion, I got so caught up in my new identity that I slapped one of my white roommates in the face during one of our highly volatile college catharsis meetings. The purpose of these meetings, one hundred miles from Father's aura was to "come into the truth," bare our selfish souls, and admit to our weaknesses. I became incensed when Jenessa stood up, her blond hair coifed and obviously bleached, and announced, confident in her whiteness, that she was unwilling to continue in the catharsis. When she questioned the rightness of the meetings we were having outside of Father's purview, I smacked her in order to correct the wrongness of her thinking. She wrote me up.

Jim was not pleased. I had to stand before the congregation and explain why I had hit my comrade in the face. After acknowledging my misdeed, I was reprimanded by Jim and told to let my hair grow out—this was not the way Father had intended I apply his teachings.

"After this grotesque breach of judgment, your meetings are forbidden," Father declared. "Having Angela Davis's hair does not make you an outspoken radical of her intelligence. Read *If They Come in the Morning* and I expect a written analysis of her thesis next week, Solano Layton." There was a faint rustle and I thought I heard someone snicker. "Each of you must continue to write up your worries and treasonous thoughts. I know your thoughts, I have heard them in my mind. But you must write them up. I cannot do all the work for you. We must each take responsibility for your own progress. As always, if you have any concerns about a comrade, bring it directly to me." He nodded at Jenessa. "I will determine who and what types of situations are worthy of confrontation or forgiveness." Then his eyes rested on me.

"And you . . ." I stood again, respectfully and obediently, as was expected of anyone being confronted. "You must receive what you thought your right to inflict upon Jenessa." As instructed, my victim hit me back in the face. Only then was I allowed to apologize to her.

I had joined Peoples Temple only six months before and I had already fallen from grace. But I was not defeated. I was determined to make my way to the top and this was only a stumble. I would work hard and regain Father's respect. I knew in my new socialist head that despite my occasional fears and misgivings, Father's cause was where I should be.

In the months that followed, the college students began some paramilitary training to prepare for the post-nuclear world. We jogged every night, practiced field navigation using a compass and flashlight, studied guerrilla tactics, memorized portions of Karl Marx's *Communist Manifesto,* and sang "The Internationale" at the close of each evening devotion.

We learned that our weakest man was as critical to our operation as the leader. We knew that we needed to persevere and stay in good physical condition because one day, when the Third World War began, Jim would need us to lead the people through the inevitable nuclear holocaust. As we sang, ". . . we'll tear down our planet's false foundation, Then build a better world anew," we were told that we, the youth of Peoples Temple, would be in charge after the devastation.

We were being trained to survive under desperate conditions, with few comforts and little sleep. We were taught to put our faith in Jim Jones, our leader, and never to question him. We were to let go of such petty desires as living in a nuclear family. Father had a vision much greater than any we could have. None of us was evolved enough to understand or question him.

Whenever my inner voice began to caution me, Jim would intuit my doubt and quickly dispel my "capitalistic" anxiety. On one occasion, when he told us to close our eyes and pray while he turned the water into wine, I peeked. Suddenly he bellowed,

"For those nonbelievers, still too caught up in the material world, who cannot trust, who think they can secretly learn something and in the process only prove how small their minds are . . . Ha! . . . Shame on you! . . . I have turned the water into white wine!"

I was terribly embarrassed that he had seen me doubting. I promised myself I would no longer try to outsmart God. I would be devoted like Sweet Annie, whom I noticed the very moment I peeked. She had been coming to the meetings for a while as Carolyn's guest and I could tell from her angelic face that she was not plagued by any doubts. Father was teaching us that doubting him was a sign of conceit and selfishness, vestiges of the material world that I was struggling to shed. He always knew how to address my hesitations and dilute my apprehensions.

"Darling, it is hard to give up one's personal dreams for a communal vision, but through your sacrifices you will grow and benefit a hundredfold. You will be a revolutionary example to Annie when she graduates from high school and joins you at the dorms."

There were always promises that greater responsibilities and excitement were in store for me:

"You are the only one I can really trust, Debbie." Father would tell me, using this effective line again and again on my naïve and pliable mind, a line he used on many of us.

It wasn't long before Jim granted me the very trusted role of Head of the Offering Room. It was a plush assignment. I was in charge of counting the collections from the services—thousands of dollars from each one—and was allowed to choose my own crew. I chose my favorite people: Stephan, Jim's biological son, fifteen years old, six foot five, olive-skinned, smart, loud, and fun; Shanda, with beautiful milk-chocolate skin, a gorgeous smile, an infectious laugh and quick with numbers; and Robbi, her thick chestnut hair always neatly brushed off her face and the fastest dollar-bill counter in the world. Like Stephan, she had been a member since birth, her parents having been among the original disciples who followed Jim from Indiana. Now, I felt, I was part of the chosen few.

Jim's public sermons were always geared to new members or potential new recruits. He'd go over the Temple philosophy, explaining in painful detail why he did what he did, why he said what he said, claiming he was the only God we'd ever know. The regular members dreaded these endless harangues, as many of them were already living Father's teachings: they had sold their homes, handed over the proceeds to Father, and moved into church communes. The offering was a way to reap more money, above and beyond the members' paychecks, the $65,000 a month in Social Security payments, and income from trust funds that already enriched the Temple's coffers. These incessant offering calls during the public meetings were for new money from the guests. Jim explained that the donations were used to support all our humanitarian programs: feeding the poor, housing the homeless, getting young black addicts into rehabilitation programs administered by the church, and many more.

My crew had "clearance," a buzz word for Jim's approval and blessing, and was allowed to leave the auditorium when Jim called for yet another donation. The Offering Room was always outside the main auditorium and we were grateful, in fact joyous, to be released from the meetings. We spent the time not only counting the money but eating snacks and joking around while the others had to remain in the main meeting. We'd frequently fail to return to the meeting once our counting was completed. Some of the older counselors seemed to be jealous of our position, but I realize now that they were simply annoyed by our cavalier silliness. Their commitment was a serious matter. They had forfeited spouses, family, sex, sleep, and companionship to help create a better world. Of course we had to do the same, but it was not as painful for us. We had not risked and lost as much as the grown-ups. In many ways, our involvement with Peoples Temple was an adventure, complete with scary rides and the thrill of an unknown outcome.

Occasionally, the elders had the Offering Crew "brought up" for our infractions but we seldom got into serious trouble. Jim would take us aside and explain why the older counselors were angry, but he said that he understood how tiring the meetings were, that he truly appreciated our dedication and quick minds, and that we would need to be a little more discreet in the future so as not to look disrespectful of him. One afternoon, however, we were all paddled publicly after we were overheard giggling in the adjoining room as Father spoke of the coming catastrophe. The paddling was administered by a designated church elder. It was painful, but to show we could withstand torture when the time came, we each bravely took our turn in front of the congregation. Our backs to the crowd, our hands gripping the pulpit rail, we concentrated with all our might so we would not cry out in pain. When the meeting was over, Father summoned us to his private quarters and apologized. He explained that he had to punish us in order to show the congregation that he did not favor us. My welted bottom hurt less after his apology.

By 1973, public meetings were becoming longer and more frequent. In summer and on holiday breaks, the college kids were bused with the high-schoolers all over the continent into the ghettos of Chicago, Kansas City, Los Angeles, Vancouver, and Seattle in order to proselytize and leaflet for Pastor Jones's forthcoming appearances. From early morning until late evening, we canvassed homes, housing projects, and even condemned buildings where the world's forgotten and forsaken had sought shelter. We trekked, tired yet enthusiastic, into dilapidated liquor stores and ramshackle markets to "Get out the Word," "Promote the Cause." There were times when, my feet swollen from twelve hours of walking, I felt the work was too hard, the days too long. It was my old capitalist desire for an easy life.

Every other weekend, the entire core family of 400 headed for Los Angeles to recruit more members. On Friday night we'd fill our eleven buses for the ten-hour drive, arriving in L.A. early Saturday morning. The youth group had to pamphlet the outlying areas, stand on street corners demurely requesting donations for our self-help projects, then rush back to the church, rinse off in a public lavatory, put on blue, full-length choir robes, and greet the visitors and potential new recruits at the front doors. With each contact, we encouraged the poor and downtrodden to "Come, hear, and rejoice in Reverend Jones's miraculous healing powers." During the service, we revitalized our new friends with our singing, clapping, praising, and rejoicing.

"Leave behind your hardships . . . Join us . . . Move west to California where all your needs will be taken care of . . . Sell your homes and belongings and live in a place where you will be secure forevermore." There was even talk of a "Promised Land," a place that Jim was preparing for us to escape to when the United States became even more hostile to those of color. I secretly looked forward to the rest and peace we'd find there.

The public meeting lasted the rest of Saturday afternoon and into the late evening. Then the Planning Commission had another meeting that began immediately afterward and continued into the early hours of Sunday. Before I gained membership in this hallowed group, I would leave the public meetings with Shanda and Robbi and go to the home of a wonderful black grandmother named Mary, who graciously took us in, fed us, and allowed us to sleep. Over the years, Mary and I became very close.

Sunday morning at ten, the service would begin again with singing and clapping, praises from grandmothers and young people about how Father had changed their lives. Then Jim would arrive at the podium, where he would teach and perform healings until four in the afternoon. We would then load up into our buses, cram into seats, sit in the aisles if necessary, or if we were lucky, find a place in the luggage rack above the seats where there was room to lie down. On Monday, disheveled and disoriented, we would resume our regular duties in San Francisco or Ukiah as students, city employees, professors, health care workers, social workers, or attorneys.

With school, studying, paramilitary training, Saturday and Sunday revival meetings, Wednesday night teach-ins, and Monday night dormitory socialism classes, we were occupied around the clock. My hard work paid off two years after my joining when, in the summer of 1973, Father rewarded my commitment, my discipline, and my weekly self-accusations for "treasonous thoughts" (like wanting a relationship with a "homosexual" man and even, perhaps, wanting a child) by asking that I join him and his most trusted disciples on the Planning Commission.

This august and exclusive governing body, which convened every Wednesday night from 8 P.M. until 4 A.M. and on Saturdays and Sundays after service from 6 P.M. until 2 A.M., discussed and formed decisions regarding every aspect of the church. I was a little hurt that Mark had been made a member the year before, but Jim comforted me. Men, he explained, were our weakest link. Without their spouses, the men on the Planning Commission had no backbone and were apt to falter.

"I need you," he said. "You will be Mark's backbone."

I wasn't sure what he meant, since Mark had never been "weak." He had always refused to have any sexual relations with me after our arranged marriage. But at least I was now catching up with him, and I knew I could surpass him. At my first meeting I was shocked to find Annie already a member and was immediately reminded of the time I peeked during the wine incident.

But with privilege also came fear and stress. Jim informed us of his plans for retribution if any members from the inner circle were to leave or betray the cause. There were veiled threats and innuendoes that some of the members who had questioned him or tried to leave had been "taken care of." There were disappearances and even deadly accidents. One longtime member and father of three who had talked about leaving the church was mysteriously crushed between two railroad cars. Another member was killed driving her car because, Father explained, she was thinking negative thoughts. Families and individuals who were caught before they could leave were publicly beaten and put on "observation" until they had been reeducated. There was the secret rubber hose beating of a member who had molested a Temple child. Father made me watch the beating and had my photo taken holding the rubber hose, which paralyzed my questioning inner voice. And there was the bombing of a military supply train in Roseville, which Jim claimed he and a few others had executed. Each time I had finally calmed my nerves about one incident, another one would come along to haunt and terrorize me.

I was afraid for myself and troubled, but Father reminded me that punishments were deserved. The Cause demanded adherence to strict rules. "Sacrifice was the robe of the chosen few," he told us again and again. "The end justifies the means." Doubts were counterproductive. Mao and the Cultural Revolution could not have succeeded without the wholehearted support of the people. I did not know what to think. All I knew was that I had to persevere at any cost. I had to prove to myself and my parents that I could stay committed to a project and see it to the end.

My responsibilities grew. Jim determined that I should join the Diversions Committee. There were just a few of us. I often worked with Teresa, a tall, cute, thin, blond woman with an angular face who ate her fingernails and would soon become my mentor. We had several tasks. As a tax-exempt nonprofit organization, the church was restricted from engaging in political activities. Diversions "D"

Committee was created in order to bypass that restriction. Its purpose was to secretly create social change by drafting letters in support of whatever legislation Jim favored, on untraceable typewriters purchased from thrift shops. The letters were handled and inserted into their envelopes by members wearing surgical gloves so that there would be no fingerprints. Our "D" typewriters were never used for official church business and were destroyed after each project. We produced hundreds of letters, typed and written in different handwriting, which were driven out of state and mailed from different locations to members of Congress and local government figures. There were also "reverse tactic" letters written to garner support for the Reverend. The letters looked as if they came from racists, angry at Jim's attempts to help the poor and people of color. The correspondence exhibited unharnessed racism, using the term "nigger-lover" to describe him and his good deeds.

Jim created these "diversions" to bring his heretofore unknown name before the politicians. Suddenly, government officials were hearing about the humanitarian works of Jim Jones. This clever ploy would later offset serious public concern and criticism about the questionable tactics of the church. Through Jim's deceit, many Californian politicians were gradually entangled in our web by coming to our defense or by responding to our gracious pleas for their help. Once Jim got to know them, they would sometimes confide their hopes, plans, weaknesses, and perversions to him. He often used the information to procure a better position on a committee for himself or to get the official to publicly praise him and the Temple's work. Jim, in turn, would provide the "outsiders" with favors from within our church, for example, with an attractive staff member who had caught the politician's attention. He would always send a trusted aide who might gain access through her visits to that politician's home or office. Here again, the end justified the means.

In 1974, Mark was assigned the honor of going to our newly purchased Promised Land in Guyana, South America. Jim had met with officials there and was impressed by their socialist ideals and by their government, made up of blacks and East Indians. The fact that Guyana was a former British colony and that everyone there spoke English was also an added bonus. I was secretly hurt. I wanted to go. True to Father's word, Mark was to be a guiding force in our future. But I was not completely sorry to see him leave and therefore exhibited mature support. We had been distant, as was required of loyal disciples, and I was tired of comparing myself to him. Shortly after Mark's departure, I graduated from junior college. I had made the Dean's Honor List and my parents, ecstatic about my success, wanted me to continue my education. Even though I saw less and less of them, I knew they missed me and were extremely proud of me.

Papa, however, had gotten a bad reputation with Jim after I reported my conversations with Papa almost verbatim. "Bugsy-girl," he'd said, "I understand that is what Jim thinks, but it's important to ask questions . . . have you originated any of these thoughts yourself? Even if what you have been taught is correct, it is important to research it for yourself."

Father warned me that "the old man," as he called Papa, had asked my eldest brother, Tom, to check on Larry and me. Soon thereafter, I was told I could not visit my parents without another member present. I knew this was Jim's way of safeguarding my loyalty, but I was unaware during these supervised visits that my mother was a target. Over the following year, Karen and Teresa would become my mother's best friends and gradually, over the next year, recruit her into the fold. I was jealous that they had clearance from Jim to spend so much time at my parents' home.

When I was accepted into Antioch West College for Medical Sciences for training as an operating room technician, my parents were reassured. I was living in San Francisco and, unbeknownst to Jim, sneaked over to visit my parents, eat lunch, and sleep. School and study were intense, but I loved to assist the surgeons and was proud to know the procedures and which instrument to hand to the doctor before he had to ask. I grew comfortable with the hospital staff. Soon doctors were requesting that I be assigned to their operating room and even though I was still a student in training, I began to feel confident.

In 1975, just before my final certification examination, I was offered a position with a leading San Francisco surgical hospital. But Jim had noticed a slight change in my demeanor. It was as if he could smell confidence and pride seeping out of my pores. My newly found self-assurance and burgeoning relationships with outsiders were becoming a threat, so Jim orchestrated a setup to rein me in and nip my ambitions in the bud. He called an emergency Planning Commission meeting in San Francisco. When I entered the room late, having returned from a nap at Mama's house, I noticed that

Sweet Annie and Teresa seemed nervous. For the first hour, Father spoke of moving our headquarters to San Francisco so he could be more accessible to the politicians. I knew something was wrong when Karen and Carolyn, who often sat near me, positioned themselves across from me, on the other side of Jim's chair. Neither made eye contact with me. Then, Robbi, who had just turned eighteen and was new to the Planning Commission, stood up and announced that she felt I was acting treasonously.

I was shocked, and wondered if I had been seen visiting my parents. Next, Trisha stood and said she knew I was on the Diversions Committee. How could she know this? It was top secret and I had never mentioned my privileged position to anyone. Only Jim, Carolyn, and Teresa knew, and Teresa would never have betrayed me. Finally, Karen jumped up and said that I was too close to my parents and a spoiled brat. I was disturbed by her vehemence, but when Carolyn could not face my heartbroken gaze, I knew I had been set up. My inner voice screamed something at me, but I could not hear it.

Jim's maneuver worked. From 7 P.M. until the next morning I was yelled at, spit on, and humiliated. Finally, my arms hanging stiffly at my sides, as was required of those being confronted, Father told me how disappointed he was in me and that I could no longer waste my precious and valuable energies outside.

"It was a vain and selfish aspiration. In the future you shall keep your ambition for me and the Cause, my darling."

I was ordered to pack my belongings and immediately return to Ukiah, where I would have to work hard to prove myself again. When everyone had left the church, Father came to my room while I packed. He apologized for my harsh treatment and stroked my hair.

"I would have stepped in, darling, but it would have looked as though I was playing favorites. You know how much I care about you. You are one of my most committed followers, but this will be good for your inner strength."

"Thank you, Father," I whispered, so appreciative of his taking the time to speak with me. At least I could hold on to the fact that Father still loved and understood me, he was only trying to make me strong. I knew I would now have to lie to Papa, tell him I was offered a better position at a hospital in Ukiah. I would need to fabricate another life to keep Papa from knowing the awful truth. Frightened, but with a glimmer of hope, I moved north into exile while the trusted members moved with Jim to San Francisco to make their mark on the city.

The Temple was becoming a reputable and widely recognized organization. San Francisco Mayor George Moscone welcomed Jim (who controlled a huge voting bloc) and rewarded Pastor Jones's good deeds with several prominent positions. In March 1976, Jim was honored with a mayoral appointment to the San Francisco Human Rights Commission. Seven months later, he was appointed to the San Francisco Housing Authority.

During these times, then-California State Assembly Speaker Willie Brown presided over a dinner in honor of Jim. In his flamboyant introduction of the now powerful and influential church leader, Brown proclaimed, "Let me present to you a combination of Martin Luther King, Angela Davis, Albert Einstein, and Chairman Mao . . ."

During these high-flying times, President Carter's wife, Rosalynn, visited, as did civil rights activist Angela Davis; Cecil Williams, pastor of San Francisco's Glide Memorial Church and a prominent civic leader; John Maher, founder of Delancy Street, the pioneering self-help organization for drug abusers; and Dennis Banks, the Indian rights activist. We did not realize that the legitimacy these prominent figures conferred upon Jim served to reinforce his control over us. The Temple and Jim Jones became an important political force representing the underprivileged, the forgotten, and those unable to defend themselves against big government. As Father's influence increased, the members became unwitting pawns in his quest for more and more personal power.

Around this time, Father began making references to other groups such as Synanon, the Unification Church (Moonies), and Scientology. He incorporated their techniques and buzzwords into our vocabulary: "Outsiders can't be trusted," "Peripheral members are dangerous," "Anyone who leaves is fair game." My occasional selfish, capitalistic, and self-preserving thoughts of running away were routinely quashed by Father's frightening talk of revenge. "Don't think you can get away with bad-mouthing this church. Mayor Moscone is my friend and he'll support my efforts to seek you out and destroy you." As his power grew, we endured more and more threats and suffered tighter and tighter restrictions.

Meanwhile, I was serving my sentence working in a rest home for demented patients in Ukiah, promising myself that this, too, would pass. During that time Jim convinced Mama to join. First she had been befriended by Karen, Teresa, and Paula, a college comrade who would soon leave for Guyana for an important assignment. They replaced the young graduate students Mama had become close to at the university. Inspired by her new friends and their enthusiasm for a good cause, she came to more and more meetings.

The crucial experience for my mother, who was always fearful of cancer, came one Sunday at the healings portion of the service. Gospel music softly wafted from the piano as Father, his eyes closed, held one hand to his head to receive a message from "beyond" while the other hand scanned the audience for vibrations from someone who needed healing. Father's voice was filled with tenderness as he spoke.

"I feel the pain you have been experiencing in your stomach and lower back." I looked around to see if anyone had stood up. "Oh, my brother, you have suffered so . . ." Jim breathed in deeply to help dissipate the pain. "Yes, God, I know . . . Sammy? Is there a Sammy Smith in the audience? Stand, my dear brother, you have suffered enough."

An elderly gentleman raised his arms and cried out as Father, still standing behind the podium, reached his hand toward the man.

"Sammy, you have been through hell in your life, been forced by the white man to hold your urine because there was no rest room for a black-skinned man in Arkansas . . ."

"Oh yes, Jim . . ." the man whispered.

"You have seen the Ku Klux Klan burn a cross on your neighbor's lawn when you were a little tyke . . ."

"Yes, that's true . . ." He began to weep.

"Yes, my brother, you have seen and experienced enough suffering in your life and I am here today to heal you of another . . . Marceline . . ." Jim called out to his wife. "Marcie, I need you to help my brother Sammy. I am going to relieve him of the painful stomach cancer that has begun to grow inside of him."

Marcie ran over and helped the man choke up a small growth no larger than a chicken liver and she marched around the audience with it as people screamed and sang to the glory of Father's gift. Mama sat in wonderment at the miracle being performed before her eyes. When Marcie came toward me I almost gagged from the putrid smell, then held my breath. Carolyn had warned me that just the scent of it could give me cancer.

After ten minutes of singing and clapping, Jim resumed the clairvoyant segment of our service. He began to hum into the microphone. His head was down, his eyes closed, and he seemed to be concentrating on listening to an ethereal voice.

"There is someone in the room with an Aunt Dora, who is going blind. She lives in West Virginia. Please stand if you know who you are."

Mama rose up sheepishly as all eyes turned to glimpse her. She looked younger than fifty-eight, I thought.

"I have an Aunt Dove who is going blind," she said reverently.

"Ahhh." Jim raised his brows. "Through the ether plane I sometimes am unable to decipher the exact words that are being given to me."

"Yes, she is the sister of my mother-in-law."

"Sshhh," Jim hushed her. "I know. I have the powers to see and know everything." Mama stood still. "You also had an Aunt Dora in Germany who was going blind."

I watched in amazement. Karen and Paula had just come back from visiting Mama, and now Jim was doing a psychic reading on her. This was exciting!

"Lisa, you have been sad a very long time and hold yourself responsible for a tragedy you have no right to weigh yourself down with."

What tragedy, I wondered.

"In this house you will grow strong once more and proud. You've felt entrapped by the secret for too long. Step out now and come to me. You are a beautiful Jew and your children have inherited your good looks."

I was embarrassed that through my mother, I, too, was being singled out as a Jew. Was that the tragedy he had referred to? But no, in his eyes it seemed to be an honor. He often preached that Jews had suffered racism similar to that of our black brethren, and that our government was going to implement the same tactics to get rid of them that Germany had used against the Jews. Perhaps there was no need to be ashamed after all.

Later, I saw Mama at the podium, her cheeks flushed. Jim seemed to be consoling her, holding her hand, stroking it gently, both of them seemingly enchanted with one another. Watching her face, I knew Jim had made another faithful member.

Soon thereafter, Mama separated from Papa and Jim urged her to invite Annalisa. My bearded brother, Tom, and Papa were never invited. Mama missed Annalisa and begged her to give the church a chance. Annalisa came to several meetings with her two little children but I could tell she wouldn't make it. Even though Jim gave her the royal treatment, she had too many questions. She wouldn't be a good follower.

I was oddly relieved. I didn't want her to join. I hadn't wanted Mama to join either. I believe that, subconsciously, I wanted my family to be a venue out of the church, back to the outside world that I no longer inhabited. I didn't want my family to see how, in my effort to rise in the organization, I had hardened. I didn't want anyone to hinder my ascent into the upper echelons where I could feel safer because I was more in control. Having both Mama and Annalisa around would create a conscience for me that I had not needed to confront so far. Their presence had the potential to create a huge conflict of interest.

Larry was not an issue; Jim had carefully dismantled our closeness by criticizing my brother's character and commending mine. I was the one Jim needed to make the church great. Larry was too caught up in shallow concerns like his relationship with his second wife, Karen. According to Jim, though still motivated by the goodness that had brought him into the cause, Larry showed weakness by being in love. I was unfettered by such worldly concerns and was thus already more powerful.

During the months I worked in Ukiah, my attitude and comportment were reported weekly to Jim by the owner/member of the rest home. Finally, one day Carolyn Layton came to my aid, as she would again later in San Francisco and Jonestown. She requested that I work with her on the covert and highly confidential "blackmail tapes," clandestine recordings we made of every member of the Planning Commission.

During our weekly meetings, to "prove our loyalty to socialism," each of us was asked to recount the worst things we had ever done. Ghastly acts were admitted on tape, but judging from my own experience, most of the stories were made up in order to out-do the others. What's more, people were told to sign affidavits saying that they had molested a child, contemplated killing the President, or been involved in a myriad of other illegal acts. To prove my loyalty, I wrote creative letters with detailed plans on how I was going to torture and murder the governor, my congressman, and the President; I lied about having stolen items from a store in town, anything to show I was not afraid. Having to make up these stories didn't seem that troublesome at first because Father explained that they were only supposed to prove our faith in him. No one but Carolyn—and now me—knew that they were filed and kept ready for use.

For the next several months my new task was to listen to the tapes, summarize the confession, jot down the most salient and damning quotes and where on the tape they could be found, and label and file everything for later use, should anyone need to be blackmailed.

It's hard to explain why I didn't realize something was seriously wrong; why I stayed deaf to the warning calls ringing in my ears. I ignored my doubts and my conscience because I believed that I could not be wrong, not that wrong. A healer, socialist, and important civic leader could not possibly be an immoral abuser, a blackmailer, a liar. It did not occur to me that Jim could be all those things. I thought that it must be extremely painful for Father to sacrifice his own goodness for the larger cause, as he did when he committed—or ordered us to commit—reprehensible and illegal acts. I saw his moral transgressions as purely altruistic—something like the means justify the end. And who was I to criticize him? My own development, I was told (and believed), was not advanced enough to allow me to understand Father's motives and actions. I could only hope to be enlightened by imitating his example and striving to become wiser, more principled, and closer to him.

By blackmailing my brethren, I earned Jim's approval and proved my dedication and atonement. At last I was making my way back into Father's good graces and I was invited to ride in his bus, the exalted Bus 7, to the meetings in Los Angeles.

5
Father Loves Us

It had been many months since my expulsion to the hinterlands. I had seen very little of Mama. It was becoming harder and harder to spend time with her. Since Annalisa's rejection of our cause, I felt that Mama's need for my companionship was growing. There were new pressures being laid upon her shoulders: the need to prove her loyalty, to stop working at the university, to devote more of her time to higher purposes, to divorce herself from the materialistic world. She'd even, unbeknownst to me, moved into one of our communes, and began to give the proceeds from the sale of her belongings to Jim.

A new and sickening feeling began to darken my thoughts. With my mother now my comrade, my love and affection for her had gradually turned to fear. Being a new recruit, Mama was in the most dangerous stage of indoctrination, obligated to report on others, especially family members, to prove her loyalty. Father had taught us that it was the "little selfish acts" that would grow into treason. No longer could I sneak off to her place and take a nap. Never again could I ask for help or candidly discuss my concerns with her.

I was surprised and extremely anxious when she caught me after our Sunday service in Los Angeles, while we were preparing to head north.

"Darling . . . Can you come on my bus back to San Francisco? I'd love to spend a little time with you. I never see you anymore." She handed me a small bag of her delicious homemade protein cookies.

"I can't, Mama. I've been asked to ride on Bus 7," I pronounced proudly, then felt guilty. I was not being a good daughter, but what did she want? Didn't she know we weren't to have familial ties? Even my talking to her was being monitored. Since my confrontation on the day I had sneaked to her place for a visit and nap, I'd been very cautious not to show any interest in her. That Mama had sought me out in front of Father's bus proved that she had not lost the dangerous maternal attachments Jim had sternly and repeatedly condemned.

As she slowly turned to leave, tired and lonely for my companionship, I could feel myself closing down. I desperately wanted to hold and console her, but because that would betray my weakness, I had to lock her out of my mind and soul. With each of our encounters I felt tremendous guilt. The realization of my childhood dreams of our joining forces had come too late. I was already moving into enemy territory and she was the dangerous agent who could woo me, weaken my resolve, and have me crucified for the greatest sin of all, my love for her.

It had been more than six months since my humbling confrontation. I had been deeply humiliated. I wondered if any of my friends liked me anymore. Even Sweet Annie had been acting aloof. True, I had admitted to awful thoughts and acknowledged doing things I really hadn't, but that was what everyone else did when they were confronted.

"May I sit with you?" Jim's voice drifted down toward me. The sound of him speaking to me was exhilarating. Why did Father want to sit with me? I wondered if Carolyn had suggested he talk to me about the work I was doing for her. But his time was so precious; it was considered an honor to have any private time with him. Like being near the President of the United States, it was an important moment when he humbled himself to notice and speak with you.

Earlier that day, Father had preached endlessly on how difficult his life was—how he was never allowed a rest, how he was always needed, always being called upon. He mourned the lack of time he had to spend with his adopted children. He complained that our own people, members and guests in the congregation, required all his time. I had felt sorry for Father and now I suddenly felt guilty. Now I was going to steal his precious time.

It was not quite dark yet, but everyone was tired, speaking in hushed tones, so as not to disturb Father. I looked up at him.

"Father, I'm fine. You don't have to sit with me."

He looked exhausted, worse than I had ever seen him. He bent down toward me. "I've been thinking of you," he whispered, so the other passengers couldn't hear.

"Your skin looks so smooth," he blew his words into my ear.

Night floated down upon us, the worn and tired travelers fell silent, drifting off into sleep. Now, as he leaned down, I smelled something foreign on Father's warm breath—alcohol! How terribly strange. It couldn't be. Father had taught us that it was bad to drink. It was capitalistic. As socialists, we always had to have our wits about us. His arm brushed my breast as he sank into the cushioned seat next to me.

"I wanted you today, when you came to the podium."

My stomach began to swirl and churn. Father released the seat lock and reclined his chair into the row behind us. He wanted to see if his son Stephan, who was seated behind us with his girlfriend, was already asleep. (It was okay for teenagers to have boyfriends or girlfriends, as they were still too young to be enlightened.) Having made sure no one was observing him, Father brought his seat back to the same level as mine. My head began to throb as he touched my leg, my thigh. Unable to think, afraid to breathe, I sat very still. Father's unsaintly hand began to massage my thigh.

A shudder worked its way up from deep within me while Father's hand kneaded my flesh. My mentor's fingers inched inward. What was he doing? I didn't want this . . . I stared out the window at the passing trucks, the green exit signs, the rushing white lines in the road. I tried to fix upon something stable, something real and constant, but I still felt him touching me. I tried to restrain my trembling and make sense out of this madness. Powerless, unable to take control, I felt belittled and defeated. I wanted to appeal for a second chance, beg him to stop. But afraid of what he would do if I did, I sat perfectly still.

Fear and humiliation drowned out coherent thoughts. Why was he doing this to me? I'd been faithful, I'd done nothing wrong. I tried to remember what had happened on the stage in front of the congregation earlier today: I'd gone to the podium to give Father the offering count and stood off to the side waiting for Father to stop and sip his water. His face was kindly and angelic. The black hair above his forehead had fallen toward his dark glasses. As he gently pushed his hair back into place his grand white robe with the red sash fell backward over his arm. He looked like Jesus speaking to the masses. He had nodded at me, signaled me to approach, his hand gently covering the microphone. I'd leaned over, as closely as possible, and whispered the count softly into his ear. I had then turned to walk away when Father motioned me to come back to his side. I'd respectfully hastened back and again leaned close to hear his words . . .

"Don't whisper so closely," he had admonished. "I am attracted to you."

What had I done? I left the podium, afraid of the shadow I'd cast upon my innocence. Father no longer viewed me as one of his children.

He was my teacher, my father, our savior. Why was I being singled out? I loved Father, believed in his words, never complained to him, and never pulled on him. I was not one of those awful few he complained about—those needing him, wanting him, begging him for favors. I was a good disciple.

As Father's hands continued his bidding, the shame of his touch uprooted my very foundation. I was not sure which one of us I hated more. Perhaps I was being tested. Yes! Yes, perhaps this was only a test. Pushing the metal button on the top of my jeans, Father's hand then rubbed my stomach softly.

"Your skin is heavenly," he murmured as the converted Greyhound bus cruised up the highway toward San Francisco.

"At the next rest stop, I'll order everyone off the bus to exercise," Father whispered. "When it's clear, go into my compartment and wait for me." His eyes were soft and kindly and yet I felt as though he could see through my clothing.

When we stopped, Father gave the orders and my comrades disembarked. I stayed on, pretending I was asleep. As she was getting off, Carolyn paused at my side, then moved on.

Father's bus was customized especially for him. He had his own private compartment in the rear quarter of the motor coach with a wall and a door. It was a place where he could disappear into his own space, where no one could see or hear him. We knew this was where he worked long hours while his disciples slept. Here, Father took care of important, godly business.

It seemed like hours as I waited, hunched behind the door in his dark room. I wondered if Carolyn had noticed I was missing. Suddenly, the engine started. I stood up to greet Father, but he didn't return. Not sure what to do, I sat at his desk, then nervously perched on the end of his bed. I was sick with anxiety. What was I doing here? Perhaps I had misunderstood him. I moved again, hunkering down behind his door where I felt safest. I heard voices as the door opened. Father was speaking with someone. His head was turned toward them, but his body quickly entered my space. I stood before my leader, unsure how to greet him.

"Please unbutton your shirt."

My head reeled. I promised myself I wouldn't have capitalistic thoughts anymore. I wouldn't think about leaving. His hands began to caress me but they didn't feel soft, like a minister's hands. They were less sweet and attentive than my eighteen-year-old boyfriend's hands had been. I whimpered. This wasn't how God should act.

"You look frightened," he whispered. His voice was soft and consoling as he guided me to his bed and pulled off my jeans. "Please don't be afraid. I am doing this for you . . . to help you," he comforted me. "You don't realize what a pretty girl you are." He tossed my pants on the floor and unceremoniously unzipped his trousers. Desperately embarrassed, I looked away. Had I given Father the idea I wanted him to do this to me?

His hands were now softer, his voice consoling. Completely clothed, pants open just enough, Father got on top of me, heavy and smelling ghastly. I felt a searing pain. Father continued to push against me. I could no longer decipher his words. I was suffocating. There were no kisses. Just the lonely sound of hot and heavy breathing on my neck. I descended slowly into paralyzed confusion and further downward into absolute darkness. Then, just as suddenly as it had begun, it was over. He pushed himself back off me and zipped up his pants.

Ashamed, I whispered, "I'm sorry, Father."

"Not to worry, my child. You needed it. I would never harm you. This is for your own good." He was busy brushing the creases from his shirt. "When we get to the next rest stop, I'll empty the bus. Get out quickly then and don't let anyone see you."

"Yes, Father. Thank you, Father." Saddened that he felt he had to do this to me, I pulled on my shirt and tried to push the buttons through the impossibly small holes. My hands trembled as I pulled my jeans back on, wishing I was invisible, wishing I was who I had been just a few hours ago. Despite his words, I didn't feel any prettier.

When the bus finally stopped, I waited anxiously for Father to return and tell me that it was safe to leave, that everyone was off, but he didn't return. I huddled again on the floor behind his door. I wanted to go to sleep. I wanted to be on the other side, where I wouldn't question my own thoughts.

The engine started again, its vibration cutting through me as we pulled out slowly from the rest stop. Without warning, Father's compartment door swung into my hunched figure.

"What? You're still in here?" Father seemed annoyed with me as he came in and closed the door. "Now you have to wait until everyone is asleep again." Then he went back out and I was alone again in his sanctuary.

I waited and waited next to his bed, screaming insult after insult at my tired and numbed mind. Then, in what seemed like the middle of forever, he knocked on the door to notify me it was safe and I tiptoed back out to the safety of my sleeping brethren. As I tucked myself away into the luggage rack, I thought I heard Carolyn's voice and wondered whether she had been awake and noticed me.

I awoke as the bus pulled into the San Francisco headquarters parking lot in the early morning dawn. The sun had barely decided which color to paint the morning as I grabbed my tote bag and rushed off the bus to my car. I didn't want Father to see me again. What would I say? What in the world would he do?

Driving over the Golden Gate Bridge under a brilliant orange and blue sky, I struggled to make sense out of what happened between me and our leader and wondered what would happen next. And then suddenly I was roused from my numbed state by a memory of an incident that had happened more than a year earlier.

It had been an all-night session for the leadership and Annie and I had been late because her nursing classes ran longer on Wednesday nights. We drove in at record speed from Santa Rosa. The meeting this night was in the Ukiah hinterlands, at the home of one of the Planning Commission members. The sitting room was already crowded when we arrived. Excusing ourselves, we pushed toward the back of the room, managing to find places on the hardwood floor in front of the warm wood-burning fireplace. Father's reclining chair was situated up front, in the middle portion of the room, and everyone fanned out from around his feet. We always sat on the floor because no one's head was to be above Father's.

Comfortable but exhausted, Annie and I sat close together listening to someone trying to explain why he had done something wrong, trying to defend himself without acting defensive. As usual, Annie had brought sunflower seeds for us to munch on; sucking on the salty husk and working out the little seed inside it helped keep us awake.

Suddenly Father's voice seemed louder and very serious. The room was hushed and I felt profound fear in the air. I stopped chewing.

"I want the person who begged me for sex and threatened suicide to stand."

Not again, I thought. Don't these blockheads ever get it? I was filled with disdain for these women who could not control their sexual cravings. They made me sick. Their capitalistic and selfish acts of sexual aggression made these all-night meetings run even longer into the morning. I sighed with scorn and impatience.

Father's voice began to growl, "You know who you are. You're no different. What makes you think you're special? Stand up!"

My impatience suddenly turned to fear and confusion, and I sat up straight. His anger seemed to be focused in my direction. Just the thought of his rage was terrifying. I reached secretly for Annie's finger. Slowly, her hand trembling, Annie removed the bag of sunflower seeds from her lap and placed them in mine. My breathing became shallow. The silence in the room was deafening. Annie was leaning toward me. I thought she was trying to tell me something. She seemed to be struggling to get her legs out from under her skirt. Annie rose and my world slowed into a haze. Annie? Sweet, honest Annie? Not you!

As I listened, too embarrassed for Annie to look up at her, I tried to comprehend what was happening. Our tiny little world, the one only we shared, was being defiled and shattered. Now Annie could no longer be my friend, not the old way. She had been transformed into one of them. Every single one of "them" had changed, acted differently . . . as if they were better. They all got more important responsibilities, as if they were more trustworthy than the rest of us. They all, somehow, got closer to Jim. It didn't make sense. I felt anger, a sense of betrayal and abandonment. No more giggling, acting stupid, making dumb jokes. Annie had left me.

I could hardly bear to listen to Annie recite her litany of reasons why she had begged Jim for sex, what a wonderful lover he was, how he helped her feel better about herself. I couldn't imagine it. Someone began to yell at her for pressuring Father. How dare she? Someone else stood up and screamed obscenities at her. I kept my head down. It just wasn't Annie, not the one I knew. Why, Annie, why? I thought. Why would you beg him for sex? You, the last person on earth who's interested in such boring things. Wildly disappointed, defeated and alone I sat there, wiping my eyes. Jim's voice piped up.

"Debbie . . . Debbie, you haven't said anything. Aren't you upset with Annie?"

I rose up. "Yes. I am."

"Well, what do you have to say?" Father pushed for a response.

"I am sickened by it."

"Don't tell me. Tell her how you feel," Father demanded. "Tell Annie how angry you are!" he yelled.

I turned only very slightly. Annie was looking past, through, and far beyond me. I looked into her face but it wasn't hers any longer. It was blank, numb, and old. She was no longer twenty years old.

"How dare you have done such an awful thing to Father!" I screamed.

The bridge now far behind me, I wiped the tears from my eyes. I wondered again why Annie would have threatened to kill herself to have sex with Father. It just didn't make sense.

I resumed my new responsibilities working for Carolyn and came to see the bus incident as an aberration. But, too soon, my turn came again. This time, after an early evening Sunday service in San Francisco, I was standing in the auditorium, having just finished counseling someone, when I looked up to see Father beckoning me over.

His bodyguards were instructed to protect him, but not to overhear what he was saying. The guards were a new addition since Jim had received several death threats. Father had explained how he, like Martin Luther King, always needed to watch his back. The young burly men stood a respectful few feet away. Innocently excited, I rushed over.

I had recently been allowed to move back to San Francisco from Ukiah and now lived inside the church on Geary Street, as did Jim. More important, Father had made me the Head Counselor, responsible for dealing with members' complaints and the issue of who should be privately or publicly confronted. I loved my new responsibilities and was very proud that Father had considered me wise enough to be in charge. So when he called me over I imagined that he wanted to talk to me about something that had to do with my new duties. I loved being a counselor but was not sure why Father had made me Head Counselor, when there were older, seemingly wiser and more experienced counselors he could have chosen. Maybe I really was special . . .

"Debbie, go into the men's room and wait for me there," he instructed me.

Baffled, I went to stand inside, as close to the door as possible. I prayed no one would enter and find me there. The room was dirty and had been used by potty-training toddlers, their little drip marks evident on the floor and sides of the urinals. As I waited for Father, a familiar sick feeling came up from my stomach. He entered the room, then turned around, opening the door only very slightly. He instructed the guards that no one was to be allowed near, that he had business he needed to discuss with me.

"Go over there," he pointed, and I obediently walked toward the toilet stall and waited. "Why are you staring at me in that way?" he asked almost sheepishly.

"I am not sure what you want me to do, Father."

"I want you now. I was watching you earlier, I yearn for your sweetness. Lie down, darling," he said, pointing to the dirty bathroom floor.

He looked like a vampire as he thrust back his black choir robe, lowered his heavy body onto mine, and cloaked us in his demonic embrace. "I'm doing this for you . . ." he groaned.

"I want you to appreciate yourself more. You've no idea what you do to me," he whispered. "I have great things in store for you, Debbie."

Two weeks later, I was on my way to my room when Father caught me in the hallway.

"Tonight, I will tap on your door when it is safe for you to come down to my apartment." Father's voice was filled with sweetness, his face loving and kind.

I nodded and entered my room while he entered his son's, next to mine. But later that night, when I heard his knocking, I lay very still in my sleeping bag. Slowly the door opened, creaking slightly as Father poked his head in.

"Oh, Father!" exclaimed Shanda as she rose to greet him.

"Goodness, excuse me. I thought I was knocking on Stephan's door," Father apologized loudly. I could feel him eyeing the room, wondering why I had not awakened with the disturbance. "Hope I didn't wake you and Debbie," he said.

"Of course not, huh, Debs?" Shanda called over to me. "That's fast! She was awake a moment ago, Father."

I remained motionless, frozen with fear. I knew it was some monstrous mistake; he didn't want to have to do this to me . . . it was my fault. I must have accidentally sent him a subliminal message asking for it and by staying quiet and asleep God would soon comprehend the misunderstanding and withdraw.

My awakening came that weekend at a cathartic leadership all-nighter. I was sitting next to Trisha and had just thrown a handful of sunflower seeds into my mouth when Jim's voice slowed and his words became accentuated with disgust.

"I want the person to stand . . ."

Another one? I thought. Not tonight, it was already too late.

"You know who you are, you're not special, not different. Stand up and apologize." Everyone in the room was frozen. "So you think you are different, that I was not speaking to you?" he admonished.

My thoughts were racing as I waited for the fool to stand.

"Yes, it was you, stand up!" Father bellowed.

I looked around the room and then into Father's eyes. They were focused on me. Oh, Jesus . . . Mommy . . . Carolyn . . . Help me. The room felt terribly small. Sunflower seeds spilled from my lap and onto the floor, scattering under people's legs and cushions as I rose. My mind was spinning with thoughts of Annie, trembling and standing next to me, of Maria, Christine, Grace, Marylou, Sharon, Jan, Teresa, Sandy, Karen, Laura, so many of them. And I finally realized, at that very second, that none of them had ever asked for this injustice. I had hated them all for so long, so unfairly. Now I was one of them. Standing erect and perfectly still, I knew what I had to do. I knew the words by heart and slowly began reciting the litany of compliments . . . how wonderful Father had been; yes, I had forced his Humbleness into compromise; I had threatened suicide; he was the best and had the biggest one I had ever seen . . . Mortified and ashamed, I stood as my friends and comrades hissed their contempt.

"I had so many organisms," I proclaimed. I did not understand what Father suddenly found humorous.

My confrontation lasted into early dawn. The younger, newer members, my twelfth-grader friends, Jim's sons and their friends, were pressured into telling me how much they hated me. Father wanted their ties to me severed. When it was all over, hours after we'd been dismissed, I cautiously opened the door to the room where Stephan, Robbi, and Shanda sat whispering.

"It was not how it seems," I said softly, then stepped back into the darkened hallway and closed the door. I was taking a terrible risk by breaking the unspoken code of silence regarding our relations, interactions, and discussions with Father with anyone else. If any one of the teenagers told Jim that I had made verbal contact with them in defense of my predicament, I would be relentlessly confronted and punished. But I wanted them to know that I had not asked for this, I had not begged or even wanted Father's tainted affections. I did not want them to hate me as I had hated the others for so many years. As I retreated I felt a hand on my shoulder and jumped. It was Annie. She kissed my forehead gently and continued down the hall.

6

Resurrection

Two weeks after my third fall from grace, Father summoned me to his quarters. It was a gloriously sunny afternoon and an unusual time to meet with our leader. He was rarely sighted during the day because, we were told, he was always on some secret mission for the advancement of socialism. I walked down the narrow stairwell toward his apartment, feeling queasy. Had the kids told him? I scolded myself for being so dependent on their acceptance.

I squinted upon entering the dark stale room. As always, the shades were drawn and the room looked like night. I held my breath, promising I would sleep only three hours that night if my pals had kept our secret. By knowing the truth, that I had not asked or begged for Jim's touch, they nourished an invisible redemptive seed within me. What would I say if Father demanded to know why I had betrayed him?

Sitting around Father were the most influential people in the Temple: my two sisters-in-law, Carolyn and Karen Layton; Teresa; Sharon, one of Jim's lieutenants and a diehard believer; John, now a law student and still being groomed to be Jim's successor; and Tim Stoen, our assistant D.A. whose wife, Grace, had recently left the Cause. I was honored to be in the same room with these exalted few. None of them slept more than four hours per night, I was sure of it.

Father looked up from his discussions. "Come in, darling . . . I can barely see you out there."

I inched my way forward. I vowed to stay up all night if they hadn't told.

Father laughed, "Debbie, come in! What are you frightened of . . . organisms?" He laughed, his face sweet and angelic. Carolyn smiled at me, her eyes hinting that my recent disgrace and misery were over.

"Debbie . . ." The room became hushed as Father put his black-rimmed glasses on a substantial pile of papers. We had begun to receive some unsympathetic press. I understood that an investigative reporter was trying to hurt Father.

"Debbie," he smiled, "are your thoughts in the room with us?" I nodded. "I realize you don't often see me working on life-threatening projects." He pointed to the files. "You know about Marshall Kilduff, the reporter who is trying to make a name for himself. He has been intrigued by my power since my appointment to the Housing Authority. We are keeping an eye on him. He is trying to write ugly lies about us and has contacted some defectors. But we know his routine, where he lives and who his contacts are. Mayor Moscone is on my side and the little bastard has no idea who my contacts are inside the *Chronicle.* He is trying to persuade a magazine to publish his rubbish. It is time for us to get our house in order. We must clean the walls, wash the floors, and make sure that there is no dust or dirt for him to follow. Like the others before him, he will forever regret the day he crossed me." I tried to steady my jittery hands. "What you are about to do is extremely serious and delicate . . ."

My heart was beating so loudly I was afraid I wouldn't be able to hear the rest of what he had to say.

"Darling, will you ever leave the church?"

I was suddenly alarmed. Perhaps Father was going to ask me to kill the reporter.

I took a step forward to show my conviction and with my voice reverent and strong, I looked straight into my leader's eyes.

"Never, Father."

"Well, with what you are about to do, you never can. You'll need to get a passport tomorrow."

My panic subsided and was replaced by pride. Father was entrusting me with a very important task. I was being addressed personally. He was asking for my allegiance! I was being asked to join the brotherhood of the most trusted, the chosen few. I was no longer the damaged effigy Father had set fire to a few months ago. I saw myself rising above the ashes of my former self and toward the apex of success.

"You are about to take a very important trip," Father continued. "I could only entrust this top secret and delicate mission to you, Carolyn, Maria, and Teresa." There was a twinkle in his eyes as he continued. "I promised I would not harm or forsake you."

At that moment I understood. My confrontation had been a test to strengthen me. Father had never intended to hurt me. How could I have been so wrong? My occasional treasonous dreams of running away faded while I waited excitedly for my new mission.

Three weeks after my few seconds of esteem kindling in Father's apartment, Maria and I were summoned to his quarters to join him and Carolyn.

"It is necessary for you to leave tonight. Pack for warm weather."

I stood there, puzzled. Why did no one say where we were going? Why was this such a secret? Perhaps the building was bugged. I knew better than to ask. Asking a question would reveal my curiosity and signal a dangerous tendency to want to understand the workings of God. I wasn't advanced enough yet to seek understanding of Father's wisdom.

"You're approved on my I. Magnin card," Carolyn picked up. "I have already set aside several appropriate business outfits for you and Maria. And, Debs, I've made a hair appointment for you at Yosh's. It's important that you look older."

I was dismissed and, blushing with excitement, returned to my tiny room in the attic of the San Francisco Temple. I couldn't wait to find out what new adventure awaited me. I wondered how I could have ever questioned or doubted Father.

Maria called to me from her room down the hall, ordering me to hurry. It was time to leave. Maria, who had joined the Temple shortly after I did, was a five-foot-nine, olive-skinned, attractive Greek with long brown hair and dark brooding eyes. Her father was a Greek Orthodox priest, whom Jim seemed to hate. She was serious in demeanor, but when she laughed it was contagious. In the last year, however, she had lost all her youthful exuberance and had become distant and rather bossy. We had been friends, but Maria seemed to have taken on airs since Jim had asked her to care for the six-year-old boy, John-John, whom Jim claimed to have fathered with Grace Stoen, who had left the Temple. Since my return to San Francisco I had noticed that Maria was spending more and more time in Jim's apartment. She was no longer an innocent twenty-year-old. She had become highly protective of Father, who feared betrayal and outsiders' attacks, and she often refused even inside staff members access to him. No one questioned her because we assumed the orders she gave us were coming from Jim. It was true that sometimes Jim needed a rest from all the urgent inquiries of his disciples. Often, they were only trying to show him how busy and thoughtful they were.

Since my move onto Maria's floor, she had begun to act strangely toward me. I felt as though she wasn't so sure Father should trust me, as though I wasn't as devoted as she was. On one occasion, several weeks prior, Father had asked that she instruct me on some of her work on the Finance Committee so that I could take it over from her. He had explained to us both that Maria was overloaded and had lost a great deal of weight with the worries of her new responsibilities. Jim had discussed the matter with Carolyn and she had recommended that he seek help from me. I was told I would soon have to take over all the dealings with the banks—substantial deposits and wire transfers, which circumvented paper trails, and cash transfers in preparation for Jim's escape from the United States for the safety of Guyana. We had much of the congregation, perhaps 600 people, there already.

When Maria and I were alone she was aloof, troubled, and would barely look at me. I wondered what I had done to make her dislike me. Perhaps she didn't want me included in the clique of the most trusted. Was she more perceptive than Father? Maybe she knew I had faltering thoughts.

I picked up my suits at I. Magnin, and late that evening, Carolyn, Maria, and I flew to Los Angeles, where we were vaccinated for yellow fever and could depart from the United States without the threat of someone familiar seeing us at the airport. Carolyn had laughed when she saw my hair that afternoon, but consoled me that now I looked at least twenty-one. The back had been cut into a duck tail and the front had been permed to give me height and stature. To add insult to injury, the fake eyeglasses I wore to make me look older hung from my neck on an old-lady chain.

The Temple's modus operandi was to always assume you were

being followed, and to believe that if anything could go wrong, it would. At eleven o'clock in the evening we boarded a Pan Am flight for Panama. Once we were in the air, a giddiness washed over me. I was excited by the intrigue of it all. When nearby passengers had drifted off to sleep, Carolyn deemed it safe to speak.

"Did you understand what Jim was saying?" She looked at me.

I nodded, wondering why she had addressed her question to me. Had she already discussed this with Maria?

"You understand, then, that if you were to ever leave the Cause, you would be arrested. We are not really a church, but a socialist organization. We must pretend to be a church so we're not taxed by the government. That's why we're moving our money out of the country, so we will have access to the funds for use in the Promised Land. This way the CIA will not be able to freeze our assets. We must be very cautious. Jim received word that Interpol has been watching us."

I felt a little ill at ease. I wondered if Robin Hood had felt both fear and excitement as he hid from the law and continued to give to the poor.

"The bank officials must meet each of the account signatories," Carolyn continued. "Of course, these are formalities we must abide by and yet must be very careful of. They do not know who we are, only that we're opening accounts for Christian corporations involved in humanitarian projects. The less said the better. Our first appointment is tomorrow at the Banco de Panama."

Yes, I thought, with Robin Hood, too, the end justified the means.

Hours later, as our plane began its descent into a new chapter of my life, I bit my lip to keep from smiling. All the pain from the previous months, the doubts, the thoughts of leaving, were forgotten. I was now a trusted insider. I had made it! I was barely twenty-one and had surpassed Philip, Larry, and Karen. If only I could tell my parents.

Stepping into the hot, muggy air of Panama, I wondered if Jonestown was like this. By now, Mark had been there for two years. He had served Father well. Besides getting the land burned and ready for planting, he was studying to become captain of the ship the Temple had purchased in Guyana. I wondered if he ever thought of me. I had secretly dreamed we would have a child together someday, but I knew, of course, that this was bourgeois nonsense in a world filled with danger.

Carolyn was already flirting with one of the agents in order to move us swiftly through Customs. With a farewell wave to the young men in uniform, we moved out to the street where we hailed a taxi. Each of us was carrying several thousand dollars in our money belts. Much later, Teresa would reveal to me how the majority of our funds had already been taken abroad ahead of us by Carolyn and other members whose identities were kept strictly secret. They had taped some of the cash onto their bodies, sewn some of it into clothing, and camouflaged the rest inside hundreds of Tampax and Kotex boxes that the agents were mortified to touch, let alone look through.

Grunting, the cabdriver hoisted our luggage into his trunk. I took a luxuriously deep, disloyal breath of his cigarette smoke and we tore out of the airport to the Hotel Suez. Teresa, who had organized part of the cash transfer ahead of time, was waiting for us in the lobby. She had already been there a week with two of Jim's trusted legal advisers, John and Tim. There were legal issues that had to be addressed in setting up offshore corporations so Father had had to include them, a decision that would later prove to have been a mistake.

Teresa greeted us. "I made a banking appointment for later this afternoon." She showed us to the antiquated elevator. With all the commotion in the lobby, I hadn't noticed Teresa's hair. It, too, was different; she had a soft-curl perm that made her look sweet and feminine. And she looked grown-up in her white silk blouse, dark blue trousers, and navy blue heels. Of course, Carolyn and Maria always looked put together with their long dark tresses drawn back into buns and their natural poise. As we rode up to our floor, Teresa gave Maria and me further instructions.

"These meetings will be with bank executives, mostly older gentlemen. Usually one or two are present. They ask lots of questions, so look attentive and knowledgeable, shake your head when it seems appropriate, but please, let Carolyn and me do the talking. When it's all over, it's imperative," she gave me a look, "that you forget what you heard." I grinned and rolled my eyes at such a ludicrous idea. Maria saw my grin and glared at me.

"Just try, okay?" Teresa went on. "It could be dangerous. The United States Government has decreed it illegal to have foreign accounts and not report them. That's why you can't have outside jobs when you return. On various tax forms they ask about your financial dealings. For your sake, Jim's, and our Cause's, don't remember any of this . . ." Little did I know that even though I certainly tried to comply, I remembered most of it and would later be able to reconstruct major financial transactions when I was collaborating with the House Committee on Foreign Affairs and other government agencies trying to sort out the aftermath of the Peoples Temple's affairs. My memory proved valuable. Even today, I wonder how it was possible that my unconscious defied the rules and orders I was so willing to conform to.

Stepping off the elevator, I noticed the faded and worn hall runner. As Teresa opened the door to our room, years of other people's stays wafted out. It was dark inside. Maria put her belongings on the bed where Carolyn had tossed hers. I put my things on Teresa's bed and went to the bathroom to freshen up for the meeting. There was no bathtub, just a shower with a worn floral shower curtain speckled with mildew. Near the wall, next to a narrow window, stood a yellow pedestal sink. I scrutinized myself in the oblong mirror. I looked ridiculous with glasses on. Voices and sounds seeped into the bathroom cell from the alley three stories below. I desperately longed to go down to the lobby while my coterie readied themselves. I wanted to watch people bustling about, to imagine what their lives were like. But our mission was secret, we were not allowed to mingle. I wondered why we were in such an old hotel. Surely it called more attention to us.

"Are you done?" Carolyn's voice called me back. "I want a shower, too."

After siesta, we were escorted into a walnut-paneled boardroom at the Banco de Panama. The receptionist was elegant in her linen dress. She could not have been much older than I, but she had sophistication, a quality I yearned for. I imagined her life and compared it to mine: while she went to restaurants, theaters, and discotheques, I toiled in the underbrush, helping to free man from his shackles. While she spent her time as she pleased and then went home to her apartment, I endured the hardships and sacrifices of socialism in a commune. Why couldn't I be a socialist and have a social life, too?

The door opened and two men came in. The younger one had his arms piled high with folders. Teresa introduced us. The well-dressed senior bank executive was already quite familiar with Teresa, spoke mostly to her, and occasionally nodded at Carolyn, Maria, and me.

He seemed quite unaffected by the huge amounts of money being discussed, or by our youth. He remained at all times extremely respectful. He didn't seem to think we were doing anything illegal. Finally the younger gentleman handed us sheet after sheet of finely printed legal material, each with four bold lines at the bottom. One by one, we signed on our designated line and passed the document on to the next person.

The younger man began to read off a series of numbers each with a specific million-dollar amount associated with it and Teresa became agitated.

"Please," she interrupted him, "it is not necessary to go into such detail here."

He smiled and changed the subject to the terms of the transaction. All four of us were signatories but only two had to be present to make any changes to the accounts.

Only as much as we needed to know was to be shared. It was a sound way to ensure that information wasn't unwisely communicated. Father always said none of us could trust each other. Only Father could be trusted, so the less each of us knew the safer it was. There was no arguing about it even if it sometimes didn't make sense. The only person who knew everything, apart from Jim, was Carolyn. It was for our own safety, in case we were arrested or given truth serum. Father had told us countless stories of revolutionaries being arrested, strapped down, and administered sodium pentothal so the CIA could extract secrets. The CIA was always up to no good. They had assassinated Che Guevara, Salvador Allende, and many other socialist heroes. They had mounted covert operations to damage and overthrow any organization that threatened capitalism. We always had to watch our backs.

That evening, Maria and Carolyn returned to San Francisco, leaving Teresa and me to attend several more meetings at other banks the following morning. Again, we waited for a few minutes, spoke with a gentleman, signed more papers and signatory cards, shook hands, and moved on.

Later that evening, while Teresa showered, I watched from our balcony as the evening lights began to glow. I thought about the young couples I'd seen walking arm in arm as I rushed from appointment to appointment. They were free to enjoy their lives and I was envious. I marveled at their innocence and yearned to know more intimate details of their happy, unfettered lives. I imagined what it would feel like to hold a boyfriend's arm, someone who adored me and thought I was pretty. But these were treasonous feelings, so I quickly pushed them away.

On our last day we went to our Panamanian attorney's home for lunch and discussed a few more banking matters. We signed more documents for him to keep, then were chauffeured to the airport.

Upon my return, I sensed that Maria's animosity toward me had become more intense. I wondered if she felt we were rivals. Perhaps she didn't like my new self-assurance; I was not as solicitous of her now that we were equals.

Maria seemed to have transformed herself into a distinguished governess and I thought she might have begun to believe that John-John was truly her son. When Grace Stoen, the boy's mother, had left the church, Father had said to John-John, "Your mother is dead. She has joined the enemy forces against us. She left you because she no longer wanted the responsibility of raising the son of God."

Perhaps Maria, like John-John, really believed that Grace was dead and had obediently taken on the sacred role of being his mother. I did not know yet that Carolyn had actually borne a child of Jim's, and shared with Maria a world no others could enter. All I knew was that Carolyn had become Maria's mentor and guardian, Teresa mine.

The more I worked with Teresa, the more devoted I became to her. Unlike Maria, she did not have pretenses about herself or act superior. She was energetic and in charge, but kind to all members, whether they were in leadership or not. After our long midweek meetings, it was Teresa who would stay behind in the auditorium and talk to the elderly members, answering questions and helping them with their problems. She was intensely focused and dedicated to Father and the Cause of socialism. Father always listened to her concerns, her thoughtful suggestions, and often implemented them.

In the summer of 1977, several months after our return from Panama, Teresa came into my room and closed the door.

"Debbie, pack for warm and cold weather. We'll be away for up to two months."

She handed me $1,000 and asked me to get some clothing for her as well as for myself. She seemed anxious, as if we were in danger.

"We can't talk in the building . . . it's too dangerous. I'll meet you at Denny's in an hour." This was a new procedure. There were no hidden transmitters in Denny's restaurant, and if there were, the noise would be too loud for a receiver to pick up our conversations. Jim had become increasingly cautious about our conversations being monitored and taped since the FBI had broken into the Scientology offices several months earlier. And now that Father was convinced Interpol was monitoring our movements, he was crazed with fear. We had even begun to speak in code. He had increased the number of guards both outside the church premises and inside the building near his apartment. How he got so much information about the escalating campaign against us was a mystery to me. He claimed he had moles and investigators everywhere compiling information for him.

I wondered why we were leaving so soon after our return, but I was glad. It meant going away again and being freed of the daily grind and constant paranoia. On the morning of our departure, Teresa summoned me to Father's apartment. He was lying on the couch, looking feverish. I wondered if he were becoming ill.

"Debbie, my little soldier," he whispered, "the trip you are about to take is extremely important. It's vital to the security of the church and you must be more cautious. Maria tells me you are often a little cavalier with your mockery, you kid around when things should be serious. I trust you, but you must be careful. This is a journey in which you can learn a great deal about other countries. Take advantage of the opportunity."

I felt honored that Father was sending me and not Maria, but I was still worried. What else had Maria said to Father behind my back? Was he beginning to have second thoughts about me? I looked into his eyes.

"Yes, Father, I understand."

Why was she attempting to poison Father's feelings for me? I maintained a serious comportment as I shopped for cold-weather business clothes. Later at our Denny's rendezvous Teresa informed me that we had had a high-level defection but couldn't tell me who it was yet. At ten o'clock that night, Annie drove Teresa and me to the airport. Teresa's hair had been permed again and tied with a colorful scarf around her head. I thought she looked Scandinavian. After being seated and handed a blanket and pillow, I wondered if we had to move the money again so soon because the defector knew the finances. Could it be Tim Stoen, the assistant district attorney, John-John's legal father? Our last alarming defection had been

Grace Stoen, his wife and John-John's mother. Had Tim followed her? I hadn't seen him recently because he took the boy down to Guyana for safekeeping. He knew about the foreign bank accounts. I assumed that he had helped set them up.

But it could also be John. Since starting law school, he had been argumentative with Father, just like his sons. Although both John's parents and his sister were in the church, Jim had mentally adopted him and he spent a great deal of time with Jim's other sons. I had not seen him in any meetings for a week.

Or, I thought, it could be the bad press. Carolyn had said that the journalists' reports could bring on a government investigation. Perhaps the FBI was trying to get at our assets. It would be a tragedy if the money we had safeguarded could not be used later to enhance the lives of the seniors and children in Jonestown. Carolyn was right. We couldn't keep the money in racist America any longer. As Father said, journalists, like all capitalists threatened by socialist beliefs, would lie to silence the word of Light. He had prophesied that our beliefs and loyalty would be tested by the "prince of darkness." He had said, "Journalists produce a perverted world consciousness because they are perverted themselves." Capitalists would always speak evil of what they could not understand or profit from. I remembered reading almost the same argument in Marx's *Communist Manifesto.*

"They have always tried to quiet the voice of change . . . The government killed Martin Luther King, they silenced John Kennedy, and when Malcolm X spoke of integration he, too, was sacrificed. Very few are brave enough to stand up for justice . . . and fewer still, for socialism."

For the past two years Jim had suggested that those who had defected were all in the FBI's pockets and on their payroll. The Diversions Committee had been advised to model a revenge tactic after Synanon's, to frighten traitors. Started in the late sixties by Charles Dederich, Synanon used harsh catharsis, self-denial, and physical coercion to force heroin addicts into abstinence. Jim admired their tactics. They, too, believed outsiders were no good, untrustworthy, and they had put a large rattlesnake in the mailbox of an adversarial attorney; when he reached inside it, he was bitten. Our diversion campaign was far less deadly, geared toward making the recipients miserable and helping them to question their faulty ways. Once these treasonous former members had been tracked down, Teresa and I would then take a hike through Tilden Park. Armed with plastic bags and gloves, we would harvest enough virulent red and orange leaves of poison oak to saturate a threatening letter typed on our non-traceable typewriter . . .

> We know what you are up to.
> The one who cares the most prays no harm will come your way.
> Only you can prevent it.

The victims would never know, when they opened the envelope and pulled out the letter, that their hands would carry the toxin all over them. Father told us that the traitors deserved to have their eyes and faces severely irritated and possibly damaged. They'd be forced to wonder how this had happened to them and would later understand that "God acts in strange ways to safeguard his chosen people," as Father always said. They had been fairly warned. Or had they? I wondered.

I held the armrest tightly as our plane began its acceleration down the runway. I was always relieved when we were safely off the ground. I tucked the blanket under my thighs and around my legs and feet. I felt a chill rush over me as Teresa touched my hand.

"Maria seems a little jealous that you were chosen." Then she laid her head on a pillow, rested it on my shoulder, and went to sleep.

I had no idea then, but it was Jim who was making Maria paranoid and ill. His constant harangues of our coming incarceration and demise had begun to veil Maria's once vibrant spirit with a cloak of death. She, too, had become consumed with fears of betrayal. Father's frequent threats to flee the country had taken their toll on the once lively, fun-loving, and energetic Maria. I imagined she could hardly wait to escape to the Promised Land. There she could rest, care for John-John, and live an easier life. I fantasized about the sleep we would all be able to get there. I had already painted a picture in my mind of napping next to Mark on a tall-legged bed in our own cottage near the lake Father had talked about.

The flight passed quickly with all those disturbing thoughts racing through my mind. Once in Panama City, we met with our attorney, signed more documents, then arranged with the banks to wire-transfer our funds to Switzerland once we contacted them from

Zurich. Our next stop was England. We dropped our belongings at an immaculate bed and breakfast and immediately headed to London's Guildhall Central Library to begin research on the banking systems of socialist countries. Teresa was trying to determine whether Romania or Russia would provide us the most advantageous accounting privileges and be sympathetic to our needs for secrecy.

From London, we continued on separate planes, in case we were being followed. We met in France and went by rail to Switzerland. Our destination was an elegantly sparse, cobblestoned nunnery in Zurich. Here again we dressed to look older, the dark business suits, earrings, glasses, and wedding rings. We met with more stately gentlemen in several exquisitely furnished boardrooms, opening numbered accounts and requesting the wire transfers from our corporate accounts in Panama. Everyone seemed to be sworn to a code of silence.

It was a cold morning when I climbed out from under my luxurious down comforter at the nunnery. While I shivered and packed for my unaccompanied trip back to America, Teresa gave me my instructions on how to proceed to France, where to stay the night, and how to go on to Canada.

"U.S. Customs officials may be suspicious of your two trips to Panama and think you're involved with a drug smuggling ring. It's best and safest for you to take this indirect route home. If, once in France, you perceive that you've been followed, fly back to England. Act as though you're off to visit the Blakeys in Northumberland. After all, they are your in-laws," she smiled. "Otherwise, if all goes well, continue on to Montreal, stay there for three days, then take the bus to British Columbia and over the border to Washington state. Customs agents in Canada are less attentive and not as suspicious. Remember, your passport has you entering France and leaving France, with no record of our trip to Switzerland. That's why we asked Swiss Customs not to stamp our passports. It is very important the U.S. agents don't know about that. Your taking a bus from Canada to Seattle will reduce the likelihood of close scrutiny by U.S. Customs officials."

I was impressed. She had obviously studied this very carefully. I wondered if perhaps that was what she did when she left on secret missions for days and weeks at a time. She was testing the waters.

She told me the emergency numbers to memorize in case of arrest and the procedure to use when calling the numbers. With my assignments committed to memory and my heart racing with excitement, I awaited further instructions from Teresa as she reviewed her notes.

"Lucinda." She had begun to call me by my code name when she felt protective of me.

"You must be very careful in the future. I have noticed that when you are troubled on an assignment, you talk in your sleep. Last night was the second time on this trip." She then handed me thirty $100 bills to use in case I got in trouble. I placed them in my money belt. She advised me to travel carefully and be wary of friendly strangers. Yes, I thought, one must always beware of spies who pretend they're your friends. Men had been trapped this way in war when they fell in love with flirting double agents. I hugged her good-bye and took a cab to the airport.

When I arrived at the Charles de Gaulle International Airport in Paris, I felt weightless. A soothing French female voice was making announcements over a loudspeaker. Feeling rebellious, I immediately went to a window and bought a pack of Gauloise cigarettes. I lit one; it was stong and pungent. I took a taxi to a pension for the night and arranged with my driver to fetch me the next morning for my return to the airport. I knew no one had followed us, as I had sat sideways and kept my eye on the rear window. There had been no headlights. I was getting pretty good at this counterespionage, I thought. Mark would have been impressed.

I threw my satchel on the bed, untied my money belt, and walked back down the hall to run a bath, another cigarette between my fingers. What fun, I thought. This could be such a great life if only I could get away. What if I just disappeared with the money and never returned to the Temple? But I knew I would be arrested, just as Jim had said. I wondered if anything was worth being reincarnated as an amoeba. How sad, I thought, that by being a member of Peoples Temple I had been abandoned by the government and labeled an enemy. If only I could talk to someone about my predicament and get advice. Perhaps there was a way to get away safely and keep me hidden from Father's wrath. But who could I turn to? Papa, Tom, and Annalisa couldn't be trusted, according to Jim. I thought of the frightening statement about devious plans I had signed and I knew that I would be arrested and imprisoned if I left now. And now that Mama was inside I couldn't leave her.

The following morning, after one last drag of disobedience, I threw out the cigarettes and flew to Canada. In Montreal I lay low for only two restless days, but kept Teresa's words of admonishment stashed safely away. I would forever heed her warning: Sleep meant danger.

When I returned home, Father called me into his apartment. He sniffed the air.

"You smell like the inside of a Parisian café!" he laughed.

"Those Montreal nationals smoke Gauloises incessantly," I explained.

"Ahh, and if that is all that drifted back with you we needn't worry," he smiled.

"I'm sure I wasn't followed, Father. I took extra precautions."

"One can never be too cautious." He cleared his throat. "So, you have spent a great deal of time with Teresa over the last few months. And your mission was exceedingly important! But now it's time for you to reacquaint yourself with the more immediate work here at home. You know that I trust you with my heart, but I have heard comments on your roaming allegiances. I realize that you've become very fond of Teresa, but let me remind you it is Carolyn and Maria whom I rely on. The longer one is away from my aura the easier it becomes to weaken. Teresa must travel a lot and always on her returns she must immerse herself in the work. Even the most principled disciples have been lured from the truth. Remember . . . Trotsky, in the end, betrayed Lenin."

7
Bad Press

After my return, I caught myself often looking out the narrow window into the tenements of the city. All the excitement of my autonomy and anonymity had gradually diminished and my sense of accomplishment had evaporated. I thought about my last few weeks abroad and recognized that that part of my life was now over.

Father's numbing speech about traitors and his warning that my alliance with Teresa was now frowned upon signaled that existence inside the Temple was changing, yet again. A palpable tension was growing. I had been right. Tim Stoen had defected after all, and this was, in fact, the reason Teresa and I had to leave the country and change the account information. Tim had helped set up the foreign accounts; he was a well-respected assistant district attorney and only last year Governor Brown had appointed him to serve on California's advisory Council of Legal Services. Tim's high-profile defection could shed an unwanted and distorted light upon us. Everyone in the church knew that traitors always lied in order to defend and console themselves after turning their backs on the truth. Father had preached endlessly on this subject. Poor Tim, I kept thinking. Now he will come back in his next life as a microorganism and no one will know how smart he really was. He will knowingly be imprisoned inside an amoeba, forever reminded of his betrayal of Father and socialism.

Father also raged and fumed over the reporter who had been hanging out at the Housing Authority meetings, twenty-seven-year-old Marshall Kilduff. Since Jim's ascension to chairman of the

Housing Authority three months earlier, in February 1977, the press had become alarmingly interested in our leader and the Cause. Kilduff had even been brazen enough to ask Jim for an interview. Jim was not accustomed to being questioned by such forthright people. His disciples responded only when spoken to. It was disrespectful to question Father. Not only was this journalist a thorn in Father's side but the *Chronicle* seemed to be encouraging Kilduff's constant inquiries. When the competing newspaper, the *Examiner*, ran "The Story Behind the Story" about Jim and the Temple, Jim knew defectors would ooze from the capitalist woodwork and tell heinous lies about us. And if those lies were printed it would be devastating to the Cause—because unenlightened people would believe anything the press told them.

Marshall Kilduff's interview of Jim did not go well. He was not apologetic in his questioning of Father, nor was he demure, which heightened Jim's suspicion. When we made inquiries at the *Chronicle,* we received confirmation that Kilduff was preparing an exposé. We would later find that instead of the *Chronicle, New West* magazine would publish the exposé. Jim called an urgent meeting. A couple of people were assigned to follow Kilduff and to go through the reporter's garbage because, according to Father, "People's refuse always tells the truth about them."

I wondered why this Kilduff was so fiercely against us. We had done so many good things. Why wasn't the press reporting those too? I thought about the desperately poor and destitute people who had come to us and whom we had helped. Many had heard Jim's sermons on the radio or seen the flyers we had circulated in different neighborhoods.

There was Vera, a young black homeless woman with a newborn, whom I helped relocate, with Temple funds, to a small studio. And there was Randy, who had come to Father after a service, her beautiful Native American hair braided down her back, and asked for help. Her husband had beaten and raped her after coming home drunk and she had bruises on her arm, neck, and cheek. When her husband was out, we took her seven little children to the church where they could be fed and entertained, while their mother and I went to Goodwill. One of the Temple guards loaded a van with her new belongings, a couch, kitchen table, high chairs, and bunk beds for the new place I'd found. She chose plates and utensils from the donations available at the Temple. Randy confided in me while I scrubbed the walls and vacuumed the old rugs and she stacked food from our headquarters' kitchen on her empty shelves. I found some posters and we pinned them on the barren walls. I was proud of my work and felt fulfilled in the knowledge that I had helped women who were afraid for themselves and their children.

I also thought about the child Mama had met on her second visit to the Temple. He was seven years old and had an enlarged jaw from some disfiguring growth. She called several doctors, met with our church attorneys to set up a fund, and found a reconstructive surgeon to perform the cosmetic surgery for the child. And there were the little children she loved to hold on her lap and read to. We each had our own personal mission to help those less fortunate than ourselves. This was why we joined. Jim always found the money to help people get a new start in life. No other church or minister I could think of had opened his heart and pocketbook to these forgotten brethren. Only Father had offered them a place to live free from harassment, an environment in which they could find themselves. My work for the poor and needy made all my questionable deeds for Father seem worthwhile. I reminded myself constantly that even though life seemed hard, my sorrows were nothing in comparison to those of the impoverished populace.

Jim remained apprehensive over the FBI's raid on the Church of Scientology's offices. He expected a raid any day. I had helped remove files and money from the Temple in preparation, and there was an arms cache as well, which someone took to a secret storage site.

Soon, the CIA and FBI would attack and Father said it was better to escape to the safety of Guyana now than to be incarcerated in the concentration camps our own government was preparing for us. After all, they had done the same thing thirty years ago to our Japanese-American citizens. Farmers, families, neighbors, parents of our own soldiers had been rounded up like the Jews by Hitler and taken away. Afterward, the greedy neighbors had moved right in and taken over their stores, homes, and farms. Jim often spoke about the concentration camps being built in America to confine agitators, people of color, interracialists, and anyone who had been involved with the Temple. It could happen again. Jim said it was already in the planning stage. He ought to have known. His closest friends were the mayor, the lieutenant governor, the district attorney, the chief of police, and the president's wife.

Jim told us that we were all on the enemy's list. I was afraid. I had come to believe all white people, except the few under Father's tutelage, were bad. In his sermons, Father constantly warned us of the inevitable American Armageddon, and urged us to break all ties to this vicious right-wing country to save our lives:

> The people cannot be really happy until they have been deprived of illusory happiness . . . You and I have done that . . . It was our mission to open the minds of those still asleep and drugged by religion . . . We have done the best we could. I have gathered the finest people left in America. There are no more. Those family members who have refused to join our Cause were given hundreds of chances to come, but they have waited too long. It is time for us to look forward to our new lives. Let no one repeat the sentimentality of Lot's wife, by turning for one last glance and becoming a pillar of salt. No, my beloved children, in Jonestown we will no longer be hounded like dogs, no longer hear the racist cry of "nigger" as we walk the streets. We have 3,800 acres which has been readied for our arrival. You saw the beautiful movies, the houses, the pathways. Truly, this is our Promised Land. We will be emigrating to a country in South America governed by Black men and Indians. The common language there is English. We will live well in a land which honors and dignifies the lives of its people. No Ku Klux Klaners live there! We will flourish once more, as we did long ago, before the white man harnessed us, whipped our backs and worked us like oxen. We will live as free men and women, no longer chattel, in a country which has offered us a place of our own and to join in their Socialist endeavor. Free at last . . . Free at Last . . . Thank Socialism almighty we will be free at last.

So though it haunts me now, I was proud to help Randy's and Vera's families obtain their passports, confident I was doing the right thing when I helped them pack, exhilarated when I waved good-bye to them. I never had second thoughts about their leaving this country. I knew that their new life in Jonestown would be better than this. It made sense to me that they should never say good-bye to their abusive families. It seemed logical to leave under the cover of darkness. That's what one had to do when being monitored by the enemy.

I had now been back from Europe for several weeks and had obediently resumed my work alongside Maria. As I fretted about how I would interact with Teresa on her return, I learned more about finances, and was officially introduced to the appropriate executives at our banks in the financial district.

It was a breezy morning in spring when I was again summoned by Father for an important assignment. I had to blink my eyes several times to adjust to the darkness in Jim's room.

"Find Tim Stoen," he ordered. "We must stop him before he joins forces with Grace in order to steal John-John from me, the boy's rightful father. Thank God the child's now safe in Jonestown with my son Stephan." Jim's voice seemed brittle as if it might crack with tears if he wasn't careful.

"What a tiny weasel he is," Jim coughed, trying to clear the emotion from his voice. "He couldn't sire a son even if he was aided by a team of surgeons. John is my son! Tim is only a father on paper. You'll find him, he'll be sure to park his little penis-symbol-Porsche inside the garage, still trying to prove he isn't a queer. Approach him there and offer him up to ten thousand dollars to stay out of the battle. If he balks, raise the sum by ten thousand more. Don't forget it was Tim who begged me to have sex with his wife. He thought it would keep her from leaving him. I told him it was a bad idea." Jim sighed at the painful memory. "Grace chose to keep the child from our union even though I warned her that I would be protective of the child, that I would raise it well and as my own. And now Grace pulls this spoiled child's charade." He grabbed his temples and massaged what seemed to be a throbbing ache. "She knew the consequences. When she defected, leaving John-John with me, she did the honorable thing. . . . And now she is trying to make us suffer? She had her choice. She chose to run away with a man. She chose lust over her son." His voice became soft and he moaned.

"Dear God in heaven. Maria's done the best she could. She has tried desperately to be a good mother to my son. Why do Tim and Grace and all the others conspire against me on so many fronts? Why do they try to malign my rightful place in history? What do they fear so desperately? Can't they see how they're setting us up? Just like Brother Martin Luther King, the CIA will try to destroy my reputation, then kill me. Do they think I will lie down and allow them to lie about our work and steal my son? How much money are

Tim and Grace being paid, I wonder? How much money does it take to pluck a sinner from the cloth of a saint?"

My heart ached for Father as I drove away with a map of possible locations to find Tim. I remembered how much John-John had changed before he had been taken to Jonestown by Tim, in order to keep him from the clutches of an antisocialist mother. It had never occurred to me that his dwindling happiness had anything to do with the loss of his biological mother, who had betrayed us. I only vaguely noticed that he was no longer the joyous little fellow who delighted the congregation when he sat next to Father or when he went to the microphone during service and asked Jim questions. John-John resembled Jim, and Father was terribly proud of him.

Before the attacks upon us had begun, Father often allowed the little children to show their understanding of socialism by having them speak. Crowds of youngsters would rush to the podium, hang from Father's neck, crawl into his lap. But it was different now that we were under siege. We lived hunkered down in our church bunker in survival mode. There was no place for playfulness anymore.

My mission was fruitless. Tim was not at any of the various spots we had pegged as his hangouts. On my return to Father's apartment, I expected to be reprimanded, but there was another crisis brewing. Father was on the phone with Carolyn at his side. Rather than interrupt, I wrote a quick note and handed it to them. Father put his hand over the receiver and smiled sadly.

"He'll resurface. His Porsche will need gasoline soon."

As it turned out, I would have another chance, soon enough, to deliver my message of lucrative silence to the CIA operative, Tim Stoen.

Soon thereafter, another critical meeting was called. Teresa had just returned from the last leg of our trip, which she had taken alone. She looked pale in the dingy light of the room. I felt self-conscious because I had sat down across the room and did not dare to raise my eyes toward her. Father began to speak.

"There is evidence that the U.S. Customs agents have been tipped off to watch us more closely. The crates we've shipped through Miami seem to have been laid over." He looked around the room for the face with the answer to his following question: "Are they clean?"

"Yes, Father," came a male voice from behind me. "We stopped the false bottom shipments last month. We had a feeling something was changing down there."

Jim chuckled. "Oh, you had a premonition, did you?"

The room filled with relieved snickers. I quickly looked up to see if Teresa had smiled. Her head was down; she seemed to be writing a note. She was so dedicated, so good, so smart. I missed being her confidante.

"There is no time for humor now. We are under siege, my children. Luck alone has kept us afloat. Thank God Teresa's back."

I smiled to show her my continued support, but she never looked my way. My heart ached as Jim continued.

"I just hung up with our friend, Dennis Banks. He continues to warn me of a conspiracy against us . . .

"We now have listening devices under every room of the house of the agent who has tried to bribe Dennis Banks just because he accepted money from us. Money—as you all know—for his legal fees in his fight against this government's effort to extradite him to South Dakota, where they have trumped-up charges against him. Dennis says he was offered assurances that if he denounces me he won't be extradited. Only the FBI can give those kind of promises. Do you remember when Dennis was here? When I handed him twenty thousand dollars cash? Well, unlike the Tim Stoens of this world, the white people who defect and betray us, Banks has never forgotten us. Furthermore, he tells me there was a Treasury agent present who is too interested in our business. In fact, Dennis was asked to talk with the agent about us. What're they up to? We'll know soon enough, as we continue to listen to their conversations, check their phone bills, and follow them. Perhaps they're planning to change our status, saying we're not a church and aren't legally eligible for our tax-free status . . . Ha! They're too late!" Jim smiled . . . His eyes were brimming with pride as he looked at Teresa and me.

My stomach felt queasy. Everything seemed to be happening so fast. What was going on? Who could be orchestrating this terrible but steady assault on us? I thought about Teresa's and my trip to Switzerland, my two trips to Panama. Tim Stoen knew about everything. He knew I was a signatory. I wondered if it was Tim who was behind all of this and if he had joined the conspiratorial forces against us . . . I was afraid. I wished I had found Tim and paid for his silence. I knew that it wasn't only Jim they were coming after . . . Now, it would be me, too.

Jim began to talk again.

"Mutti," my grandmother, Anita Philip, in Hamburg, 1914.
(COURTESY DR. THOMAS LAYTON)

"Papsche," my grandfather, Hugo Philip, playing his Guadagnini violin.
(COURTESY DR. THOMAS LAYTON)

"Haus Philip," in Hamburg, designed by Block and Hochfeld. (COURTESY DR. THOMAS LAYTON)

My mother, Lisa Philip, with her sister Eva (left) in their garden, 1923. (COURTESY DR. THOMAS LAYTON)

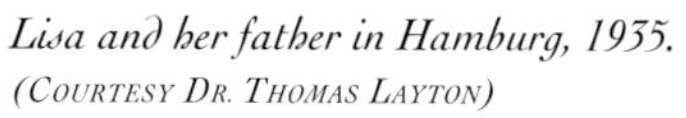

Lisa and her father in Hamburg, 1935.
(Courtesy Dr. Thomas Layton)

On the deck of "Haus Philip" overlooking the Alster River, 1931.
(Courtesy Dr. Thomas Layton)

Anita and Lisa (left), Hugo (second from right), with guests on their terrace, 1929.
(Courtesy Dr. Thomas Layton)

DEUTSCHES REICH

REISEPASS

Nr. 4803

NAME DES PASSINHABERS

Philipp Lisa

BEGLEITET VON SEINER EHEFRAU

UND VON ./. KINDERN

STAATSANGEHÖRIGKEIT:

DEUTSCHES REICH

Dieser Paß enthält 32 Seiten

Mama's passport issued by the German Reich, 1938.
(Courtesy Dr. Thomas Layton)

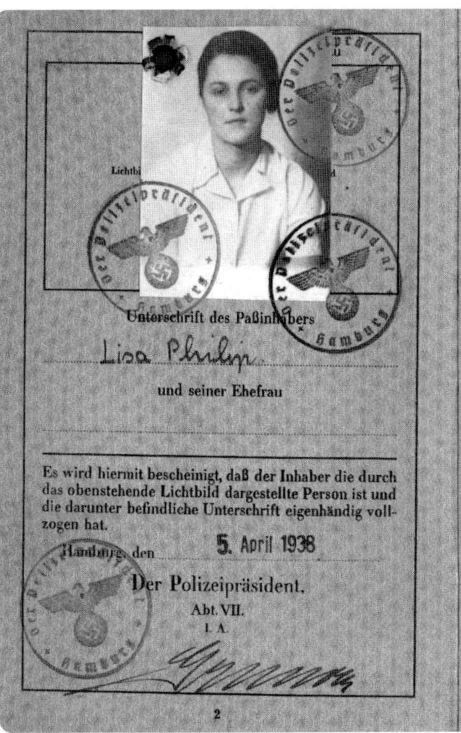

Lichtbild

Unterschrift des Paßinhabers

Lisa Philipp

und seiner Ehefrau

Es wird hiermit bescheinigt, daß der Inhaber die durch das obenstehende Lichtbild dargestellte Person ist und die darunter befindliche Unterschrift eigenhändig vollzogen hat.

Hamburg, den 5. April 1938

Der Polizeipräsident.
Abt. VII.
I. A.

2

PERSONENBESCHREIBUNG

		Ehefrau
Beruf	Gymnastiklehrerin	
Geburtsort	Hamburg	
Geburtstag	14. 7. 1915	
Wohnort	Hamburg	
Gestalt	mittel	
Gesicht	oval	
Farbe der Augen	graubraun	
Farbe des Haares	dkl.braun	
Besond. Kennzeichen	./.	

KINDER

Name	Alter	Geschlecht
./.		

3

Hugo (with pipe) and Anita (with scarf) on their passage to freedom, via Genoa, Italy, to New York, on the Conte di Savioia, *March 1940.*
(Courtesy Dr. Thomas Layton)

The first photo of my mother in New York, 1939.
(Courtesy Dr. Thomas Layton)

My grandparents in freedom, New York.
(Courtesy Dr. Thomas Layton)

My father's parents: John and Eva Layton, Boomer, West Virginia, 1913
(COURTESY DR. THOMAS LAYTON)

My father's hometown of Boomer, 1930.
(COURTESY DR. THOMAS LAYTON)

My father, Laurence L. Layton, 1940.
(COURTESY DR. THOMAS LAYTON)

Papa, proud Ph.D. graduate in biochemistry, Penn State, 1942.
(COURTESY DR. THOMAS LAYTON)

Lisa as a newlywed in Rochester, New York, 1942.
(COURTESY DR. THOMAS LAYTON)

Lisa and Laurence, circa 1944. (COURTESY DR. THOMAS LAYTON)

Their first child, Tom, at age 2, 1944.
(Courtesy Dr. Thomas Layton)

Mama with my sister, Annalisa, 1945.
(Courtesy Dr. Thomas Layton)

The Layton family on their way to a 1947 Friends meeting, my parents holding their third child, Larry, with Tom and Annalisa at curb.
(Courtesy Dr. Thomas Layton)

My grandma Anita in 1950, two years before her suicide.
(Courtesy Dr. Thomas Layton)

Exactly nine months after Anita's death, I come home from the hospital, Utah, February 1953.
(Courtesy Dr. Thomas Layton)

All four Layton children.
(Courtesy Dr. Thomas Layton)

The family vacationing at Virginia Beach, 1955.
(Courtesy Dr. Thomas Layton)

After arriving by train in Berkeley, California, 1957. (COURTESY DR. THOMAS LAYTON)

The Layton family by our pool in Berkeley, California, 1959. (COURTESY DR. THOMAS LAYTON)

Our home in Berkeley, 1959; in the background is the etching of Pablo Casals and the sculpture Die Erwachende *("The Awakening"), by Klimsch.* (COURTESY DR. THOMAS LAYTON)

The missing sculpture.
(COURTESY DR. THOMAS LAYTON)

Leaving for boarding school at age sixteen, 1969. (COURTESY DR. THOMAS LAYTON)

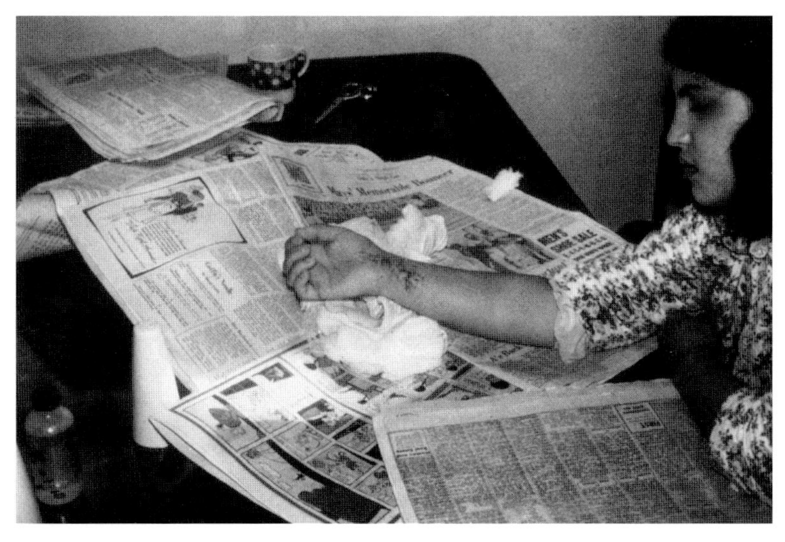

Back home in Berkeley in 1970, after punching my fist through a window at school, and just two weeks before my first meeting with Jim Jones. (COURTESY DR. THOMAS LAYTON)

School graduation photo, Ackworth School, Yorkshire England, 1971. Mark Blakey is right behind me. (DEBORAH LAYTON)

Larry cutting the wedding cake with Carolyn, Davis, California, 1967. (COURTESY DR. THOMAS LAYTON)

Larry with his new wife Karen, Ukiah, California, 1969.
(Courtesy Dr. Thomas Layton)

The Reverend Jim Jones, our "Prophet," Ukiah, California, early 1970s. (Courtesy Stephan Jones)

Preaching in Ukiah.
(COURTESY STEPHAN JONES)

With Temple children. On the left a teenager is holding Grace and Tim Stoen's son, John-John. (COURTESY STEPHAN JONES)

"What do we have on Kilduff? Get someone in there to find out what he is writing. We cannot fight a mirage. We need concrete information!"

I silently mouthed to Carolyn, "Why does he hate us?"

"My naïve conscript!" Jim had seen me. "Even after all you've done for me, you can ask such a question? White men are afraid of my teachings. They will do anything to sully the word of truth. Kilduff is a racist. He complains about my power in the Housing Authority for one reason alone: he doesn't like it that I am the leader of so many beautiful, devoted, and intelligent niggers. He's afraid of us—our numbers—that we have the ability to get legal measures passed. He's afraid of our voting power. He grew up a part of the elite of San Francisco, with private schools and a wet nurse. He'll do anything to bring us down. He's a miserable white boy with too much time on his hands. All of them are joining against us. Grace, Tim. They all have betrayed socialism. . . ."

For several months now the church had been involved in the transport of our loyal members to Guyana. Father wanted everyone out of the country before Kilduff's ugly stories went to press. He really cared so much. He was safeguarding our futures by trying to get us to safety before our government attacked us. Already over 600 men and women, children, teenagers, and seniors, had been sent to join my husband, Mark, in the Promised Land. I was jealous of them because they were so close to the man I secretly yearned for.

Jim had brought back enticing movies from his last visit there. Everyone looked happy and they wore colorful tropical attire. They didn't have to work these miserable hours. They slept more than four hours a night. No one had circles under his eyes. So why had Tim left? Why had he sounded so disappointed? All the letters we received from Jonestown spoke only of happiness and relief that finally everyone could live free and safe from the corruption of capitalism.

In order to speed up the departure, Maria and I now had to close various small bank accounts, as well as make sure the monthly income of $65,000 we accrued from the disciples' Social Security checks would be transferred to Guyana. We transferred money to our main account at the Bank of Montreal in San Francisco from where we could easily move other miscellaneous funds earned through the sale of church property and members' homes. We also transferred cash with each member leaving for Jonestown. Everybody received at least the legal limit of $5,000 in $100 bills. However, if the travelers were older, loyal, and would likely pass through Customs unchallenged, we gave them as much as $20,000 to put in stockings, purses, brassieres, girdles, backpacks, luggage, and waist belts.

Once in Guyana, the money was collected by either Karen Layton, who had already been there for six months, by Sharon Amos, or by Paula Adams, my old college roommate. At Jim's direction, Paula had become the mistress of the Guyanese ambassador to the United States, Lawrence E. "Bonny" Mann, which helped us navigate through the Guyanese bureaucracy.

Jim began to get anxious about Paula's excellent relationship with the ambassador because she seemed to care about him and was spending too much time away from Jim's aura. But he wouldn't dare jeopardize the relationship because it would ensure that our money, which was now being deposited in the Guyanese bank, was secure. We'd have word ahead of time if there was going to be trouble. Apart from bank deposits, hundreds of thousands of dollars were packed in crates and shipped on our boat to our compound, 250 miles away from civilization.

I, alone, was now doing the banking business outside the Temple because Jim had become frantic that Maria would be kidnapped. The last year had nearly finished Maria off: She had to care for little John-John, who shared her windowless room, while she toiled into the early morning hours on financial ledgers. Jim's suffocating fear of the conspiracy against us prohibited them from playing games or having any kind of fun because there was "no time for such luxuries anymore." And now, on top of all that, she had to deal with the threat of being kidnapped. With all the negative publicity the Peoples Temple was getting, Jim was convinced that Maria's well-connected father would get suspicious and try to get her out.

She was morose and dangerously thin, drowning in her stress and afraid to confide in Father. I had misread her turmoil as resentment and jealousy of my travel privileges with Teresa.

The weeks progressed and despite Jim's efforts, we were unable to control the press. As I proofed another of Jim's rebuttals, which Carolyn had authored, I was impressed with all of Father's appointments.

MAR '76	Appointed to the San Francisco Human Rights Commission

SEPT '76	Testimonial Dinner in Reverend Jones' honor Guests: Lt. Governor Mervyn Dymally, Assembly Speaker Willie Brown, Mayor George Moscone, District Attorney, Joseph Freitas, Angela Davis, Eldridge Clever, former Black Panther, San Francisco Supervisors, well respected Reverend Cecil Williams and celebrated lawyers Charles Garry and Vincent Hallinan.
OCT '76	Appointed to San Francisco Housing Authority Commission
NOV '76	Rev. Jones and Mayor Moscone have a private meeting with Vice Presidential candidate Walter Mondale
JAN '77	Rev. Jones hosts citywide celebration of Martin Luther King Jr. Birthday & Shares podium with Governor Brown and Chief of President Carter's Transition Team
FEB '77	Elected Chairman of the San Francisco Housing Authority Commission
MAR '77	Rev. Jones and Rosalynn Carter sit together at Head Table of Democratic Convention Dinner

Where was the harm in all this? I believed in the integrity of all those who supported Jim. They were very powerful people and couldn't possibly embrace someone or a cause they knew nothing about! They knew why they supported Jim. Only opinionated outsiders who could not open their minds to the strife of people less fortunate than themselves had hateful suspicions. They were selfish and their convictions could not be trusted. This was what Jim had always taught us. Since I'd been eighteen and in the college dorms, he had warned us of those nonbelievers who would try to dissuade us from the truth. But these political benefactors who had come to Jim's aid over and over again had been different. Jim used to say they had a "little something" that was right.

By the third week of June 1977, Father called another all-night meeting with Maria, Carolyn, Teresa, and me.

"This is our last chance," he said, pulling off his reading glasses and taking a deep, exhausted breath.

"Teresa, darling. You must expand the effort to impede the attempts of Kilduff. We must find out what he has against us. And we must put pressure on his magazine, *New West.*" He looked at Carolyn and continued.

"Expand the letter writing campaign and the phone calls to the press about his unfair treatment of us. His cavalier attitude can harm all the projects we have set into motion. He obviously has only disdain for all our social efforts, our senior rest homes, the rehab center where we've taken hundreds of kids off heroin. He is typical of the egotistical white men who are afraid and unwilling to accept the importance of discipline. He has never been loyal nor devoted to a cause greater than himself. He is a consummate honky—opinionated, selfish, and filthy white." He snarled, his upper lip curled back.

"Do you think he ever scrubbed a toilet or pulled a double-shift in a factory while working his way through college? Hell no! He has never worked. His parents have done everything for him. He's grown up with maid service. Dear God Almighty . . ." Jim lifted his fist toward the ceiling. "Just because he graduated from Stanford he thinks he is better than the rest of us. Lord, I'm so tired of fighting the oppressor, so tired of trying to save my babies. When will the harassment cease? Can't they see they're forcing us into more and more drastic decisions? Why can't they give us just a little peace?" He slumped back into his chair.

I followed Teresa upstairs, glad to be working with her once more, relieved that my recent order to "separate my allegiances" had seemingly been rescinded. When I entered her room to receive my list of assignments, Teresa put her hand on my shoulder and joked:

"Okay, my naïve conscript . . ."

I covered my mouth to stifle an enormous laugh, filled with sorrow and relief.

"So, let's get to work on our next diversion."

My first phone call was to Rupert Murdoch, the owner of *New West* magazine, in New York. I decided to use my upper-class British accent. It always made me sound older and quite credible, like the head mistress at boarding school.

> Mr. Murdoch, I've known about the Peoples Temple in San Francisco for many years now and am quite concerned about the public harassment of them. They have done wonders for the old, the homeless, they have adopted children parents have shunned, their rest homes for the elderly are the best in the

state and of course the beautiful care facilities for mentally impaired . . .

I'd have to make notes to ensure that I included everything.

The following few days were consumed with getting rolls of quarters from Maria's room, then rushing out to make calls from various pay phones in San Francisco, so we couldn't be traced—at the public library, the Federal Building, and numerous little liquor stores. My list also included Reverend Cecil Williams, Assembly Speaker Willie Brown, and officers of *New West* magazine, where Kilduff's exposé was going to appear. I was supposed to call its president, secretary, vice presidents, Marketing Department, and distributors. In my calls, I was never a member of Peoples Temple, but a concerned citizen who had heard about Marshall Kilduff's intent to harm the Temple.

At 5 A.M. on the morning of June 18, Teresa tapped on my door and slid in. I had just come back from Maria's room and was unrolling my sleeping bag to take a nap.

"Lucinda." She was calling me by my code name, which she now used only when she was anxious. Her face was ash-white. "Make reservations under fictitious names for tonight. A party of five: Jim, Maria, and three children."

"What happened?" I asked. She handed me the newspaper.

JUNE 18, 1977

GAINS ORDERS PROBE OF NEW WEST BURGLARY

Police Chief Charles Gains, acting on a request by Peoples Temple leader, Jim Jones, has ordered a full investigation of a reported burglary at offices of New West Magazine.

The Reverend Jones called Gains late yesterday after the New West reporter-writer Phil Tracy reported a break-in, in which Tracy presumed the target was a manuscript of a story about Jones and his Peoples Temple.

Jones angrily denied that anyone connected with his church had anything to do with the break-in or "intimidating" telephone calls received at home by Rosalie Wright, New West's Northern California editor. Patrolman Michael Duffy, who made a preliminary investigation said a New West office window apparently was jimmied open and a bolt broken.

"As far as I could determine," Duffy said, "no entrance to the office was made. However, I can't say any entrance wasn't made." Duffy said Tracy told him the office window was partially open when he entered the room yesterday morning.

The officer went on to quote Tracy as saying he did not know if anything had been taken, but said a cabinet filing case seemed to have been "disturbed."

The filing case according to Tracy contained the unpublished manuscript of a story about Jones and the activities of Peoples Temple written by Chronicle reporter Marshall Kilduff.

Why the intruder or intruders did not take the manuscript was a puzzling element in the case. Tracy said he thinks the intruders might have photographed it.

Editor Wright left home with her two children Thursday night after receiving another of a series of phone calls from someone who said, "Don't do it."

She said she presumed the caller meant New West should not publish the Jones article.

"We won't be intimidated," Wright said.

I looked up, astounded. I felt sorry for Teresa. Someone she or Carolyn had used in the Diversions Committee had made an enormous blunder. I wondered who. They'd have to be sent to Guyana immediately.

"Odd, isn't it, that Rosalie Wright is so afraid of us that she's gone into hiding with her children, but Kilduff and Tracy won't stop their pursuit. What fools they are!"

"Debbie, listen . . . What's happened is serious. And the inference is that we did it, bungled the job, photocopied the story, and scared the editor underground. Anything could happen now. They could try to trump-up charges against us. Grace's defection, the Customs agent, Tim's defection, the Treasury Department, the old detractors of the church, they can come forward with more stories. Remember Lester Kinsolving? The religious editor of the *Examiner?* In 1972, he asked for the Attorney General's office to investigate us, but Jim was able to squelch the story. Now it's all too much, Lucinda, it's all coming down."

I could feel my pulse racing as I watched her long, delicate fingers shaking uncontrollably.

"Jim must be able to leave at a moment's notice. They may try to arrest him. From now on, we must be ready every night. If Jim can't stop the *New West* article, he'll have to leave. God knows what will happen here. We have to speed up our emigration push and use alternate routes as well."

"Which routes?" I asked.

"Members can no longer leave from the San Francisco airport. Kilduff and his flunky helper, Tracy, are probably watching. We could have had this whole exodus completed in April, two months ago, had Guyana allowed us to charter the planes we had lined up. I guess Paula hasn't calmed her lover's nerves."

After our sudden influx of almost 400 members the month before, the Guyanese officials had requested a hiatus while they reviewed the surge of immigration applications. Jim was furious with Paula, but when he promised to deposit a half-million dollars in the Bank of Guyana, we were again granted permission to continue our mass exodus to the Promised Land.

"Now we'll have to bus our members to large anonymous cities. Get your friend at Anderson's Travel on Polk Street to begin reserving blocks of seats leaving out of Miami and New York. Every night we should have a new busload arriving in these cities for the midnight flight to Georgetown."

The new phase, our Exodus, and everything Jim had discussed and prophesied would now be implemented. Jim had told me I would remain behind with Teresa and Carolyn to close down the operations, which meant that I would once more be outside of Father's purview, free from his all-knowing gaze.

I handed the article back to Teresa and looked out the window at the beautiful shade of turquoise with hints of pink coloring the dawn. I fantasized about stealing a moment every now and then with Mama. I thought about Papa, all alone, and pictured him cleaning the summer leaves off the surface of the pool, hoping I'd come by to swim. Life outside our walls always seemed to beckon me.

"By the way, your mom's cough is bad. You should take her to the doctor, soon. We should make sure she gets out before the "old man" calls the feds."

"Papa?"

"Jim thinks your dad has instigated trouble for us from the start. Your sister came to meetings, wouldn't join, and has probably met with Kilduff too."

"Annalis? I can't imagine . . ."

"Jim wants you to visit your dad more. Take your mom too. Act as though everything is fine. He needs to see you more often. This article is damning. Keep an eye on your family . . . Deb, this thing with Lisa . . . Tomorrow I'll help Maria while you take her to Kaiser."

My mind was still racing when Teresa left the room and I lay down on my sleeping bag. What could I do to make Mama more comfortable? Since I would soon have to move into Maria's barricade down the hall, with its bolted floor vault, money bags, and financial ledgers, I planned to move Mama to my room. We'd be able to see each other more often and without surveillance.

On my recent secret sleep-over in her modest commune situated in a run-down part of San Francisco, I had noticed how gaunt and fatigued she looked. I knew she didn't want to complain about her new surroundings. It would be bourgeois and materialistic to miss her former life. She had coughed a great deal that night and had awakened drenched in sweat.

"Mama, you must go to the doctor and have that checked," I had urged her back then. "You've been coughing for too long."

"My sweet, you know it's disloyal to see doctors for every ache and pain. Father says we shouldn't indulge ourselves. It is a bourgeois luxury which we must not pamper ourselves with. The poor have never been given enough money to see doctors. Remember Jim's sermon about the poor black men in Tuskegee, when the government secretly experimented on those who had been infected with syphilis. Father warns us in every service, honey. I realize you don't attend most of them since you are in the offering room, but we must not succumb to self-centered concerns. Debbie, when was the last time you saw a physician?"

What Mama said was true. We were not supposed to see doctors. It wasn't necessary. Father would protect us. He had already given us lists of required preventative measures and foods: We had long been instructed to ingest vitamins, three apricot seeds a day, sunflowers, cranberry juice, lecithin, kelp, and large doses of protein powder. These and a warm mixture of honey and cider vinegar were preventative measures which we had all become accustomed to years ago when Father decreed they would ward off cancer.

I followed her into the communal kitchen and glanced fondly at the cookie recipe:

LISA'S PROTEIN COOKIES

Step 1
Mix well:
1/2 c honey
1/2 c oil
1 1/3 c oats
1T cinnamon
2T protein powder
Bake @ 350—11 minutes

Step 2
Mix and add to 1:
1t baking powder
pinch soda
1/4 c sunflower meal
1/2 c w/w flour
Optional: raisins or carob

She had created and faithfully brought me these delicious morsels of her love every Sunday. They actually made me feel good and healthy. She worried that I was not getting enough nourishment. The last time I had seen a physician was when I became ill after Father's first unsolicited, painful intimacy, almost a year before.

"Mama, make an appointment," I begged her again. "I'll take you."

"You'll get into trouble for spending time with me. I'll go this week. I just don't want to be a drain on you. You are the one who is overworked and tired, darling. I know it is selfish of me, but I wish you could visit more. I miss you. I had hoped to see more of you by joining."

Then in July 1977, Jim's predictions came true. Rosalie Wright, the editor of *New West* magazine, called our headquarters to read Jim the article set for their August 1 publication. As was our procedure, I picked up the extra line in Jim's room and proceeded to tape the conversation. Carolyn sat next to him on the couch and Teresa knelt down next to me. I could hear Maria in the bedroom opening a file cabinet while I was watching Jim's expression.

Rosalie's voice was flat and unemotional.

"Our cover line is 'Inside Politically Potent Peoples Temple' and on the Table of Contents page our lead-in reads as follows: 'INSIDE PEOPLES TEMPLE—Within four years the Reverend Jim Jones has become one of the most politically potent religious leaders in the state's history. His estimated twenty thousand voters, largely in San Francisco and Los Angeles, give his Peoples Temple more clout than local unions.

"But there is more to the Jones story than that. Much more.'"

I noticed Jim's hand tightening on the receiver and he repositioned himself on the couch. He shot me a quick conspiratorial look to see if I was taping, then winked. He tried to moisten his dry lips with an equally dry tongue coated with a white film.

The editor continued, "The story begins on page thirty with the following: 'Jim Jones is one of the state's most politically potent leaders. But who is he? And what's going on behind his church's locked doors?' "

Jim interrupted. "I object. Our doors are locked as are yours at your home. It's only to protect ourselves from the criminal element that stalks our city streets. My members are free to come and go as they please. Kilduff's remark is leading . . ."

"Shall I continue?" she asked as if speaking to an upset and ill-mannered child. She did not wait for a response . . . " 'For Rosalynn Carter, it was the last stop in an early September campaign tour . . . If Rosalynn Carter was surprised she shouldn't have been. The crowds belonged to Jones. Some six hundred of the seven hundred and fifty listeners were delivered in Temple buses an hour and a half before the rally. The organizer, who had called Jones for help, remembered how gratified she'd felt when she first saw the Jones followers spilling off the buses. "You should have seen it—old ladies on crutches, whole families, little kids, blacks, whites, Made to order," said the organizer, who had correctly feared that without Jones, Mrs. Carter might have faced a half-empty room. "Then we noticed things like the body guards," she continued. "Jones had his own security force with him and the Secret Service guys were having fits. They wanted to know who the hell all these black guys were, standing outside with their arms folded." ' "

"Ms. Wright," Jim exhaled. "Don't you see how jaundiced this article is? How slanted? It clearly states how we were invited. We were asked to fill the empty room for Mrs. Carter. We were only performing the duties that this city and the Democratic campaign rally organizers requested of us. Am I to understand that now we are to be condemned and my parishioners questioned for the support we provided on behalf of the City of San Francisco? I feel violated and the black members of this church have been insulted. I think we should be able to have some say in this article and offer some editorial changes."

"Reverend Jones, it is not our policy to allow the subject of an article carte blanche in the critique of the material. I decided to read the piece to you because of all the support letters we received on your behalf, from the governor of California, the banker, the businessman who owns I. Magnin . . . I needn't name them all."

Jim was scribbling furiously on a piece of paper and handed it to Teresa.

"Shall I continue?"

"Of course, please do," he retorted, his face filled with bitterness, but his voice pure and convincing. As the editor continued, Maria handed Jim his urinal and he released his yellow-brown waste into the plastic container. The liquid was sickeningly thick and, I thought, indicative of his putrid mood.

The editor continued, emphasizing the headlines: " 'TEN WHO QUIT THE TEMPLE SPEAK OUT—' "

"Tell me, Rosalie," Jim interrupted once again. "Do you believe that this article will solve the problems Marshall Kilduff seems to have with people of color? Is this piece of work justified considering the damage it will have on the social services we provide? I haven't heard anything positive yet."

"Jim, if you'd allow me . . ."

"By all means, your honor," Jim grimaced into the line.

" 'Beginning two months ago, when it became known that *New West* was researching an article on Peoples Temple, the magazine, its editors, and advertisers were subjected to a bizarre letter and telephone campaign. At its height, our editorial offices in San Francisco and Los Angeles were each receiving as many as fifty phone calls and seventy letters a day.' "

Jim scratched out another note in bold lettering and held it up to the delight of all of us in the room.

guess we didn't scare them enough

And then the mood of the article became deadly serious. Jim motioned for Carolyn to get him some medicine from his prescription case. She poured out a couple of bluish-green pills and gave him some distilled water in a tall glass. Jim gulped them down.

Rosalie read name after name of defectors whose interviews, she explained, would be interspersed with their photographs. " 'Based on what these people told us, life inside . . . was a mixture of Spartan regimentation, fear, and self-imposed humiliation . . . Sunday services to which dignitaries were invited were orchestrated events . . . members were expected to attend . . . four nights a week—

with some sessions lasting until daybreak. . . . the Planning Commission . . . often compelled to stay up all night and submit regularly to "catharsis"—an encounter process in which friends, even mates, would criticize the person who was "on the floor" . . . these often humiliating sessions had begun to include physical beatings with a large wooden paddle . . .' "

I could barely listen. Of course people were beaten. I myself had been swatted with the paddle. So what? Poor Larry had been bloodied and knocked out during a family-night cathartic boxing match. Sometimes one needed corporal punishment to make meaningful changes. Our church was no different than many Pentecostal or Apostolic congregations: we sang; older, more religious members talked in tongues; and we had strict regimentation.

Again, Jim began licking his lips. I wished I could hand him some ice to suck on because it was obvious he had no saliva in his mouth. He didn't look well. His face seemed misshapen and bloated. The room was so dark I could barely see, yet he kept his sunglasses on. I supposed his eyes were terribly sensitive since he got no sleep. He worked so hard for us and now this had happened.

" '. . . said that extensive and continuous pressure was put on members to deed their homes to the Temple . . . A brief reading of the records on file at the Mendocino County recorder's office shows that some thirty pieces of property were transferred from individuals. . . . Nearly all these parcels were recorded as gifts.

Jim became more agitated.

" 'When Miki left the church along with seven other young people . . . none warned their parents . . . "We felt that our parents would just fight us and try to make us stay . . ." Furthermore they were all frightened. "At one point we had been told that any college student who was going to leave the church would be killed . . ." ' "

My heart skipped a beat. I remembered that. But Jim had said Miki was being paid by the CIA to talk against us. I lost my train of thought as Jim began to pace in the dark, musty living room. I moved backward to give him ample space. When I resettled I saw the note Jim had handed Teresa.

Fuck these bastards . . .

I opened a new tape and quietly inserted it into the recorder. My hands were shaking and I prayed Jim hadn't seen. I was nervous. I fought with myself and against the things I was hearing. The editor's voice never ceased. I kept on hoping the article would end, that these indictments against Father would cease, but they continued and only got worse.

" 'Why Jim Jones Should Be Investigated . . .' "

Jim muffled a gasp and began scribbling another note. My heart was breaking for our leader. He did not deserve this terrible onslaught.

" 'It is literally impossible to guess how much money and property people gave Jim Jones in the twelve years since he moved his Peoples Temple to California.' "

I looked up from the revolving tape. How could anyone trust a defector? Doesn't the world know that these traitors have forsaken all our ideals, that now they could only lie? That these people were working for the CIA? We knew from Jim that they had stolen money from the church coffers, molested their children, and done innumerable vile things. I grabbed the note Father was handing me.

We leave tonight. Notify Georgetown.

My heart took a leap. We would finally all be in the Promised Land. About 600 of us had already left and some 800 more nationwide were still waiting for Father's invitation.

Not everyone was invited. My brother Larry, for example, was not welcome. Even though Larry was a dedicated member, Jim had a profound resentment against him. The reason, I presume, was the fact that Larry had been the first husband of Carolyn and still was the husband of Karen, the two women Jim chose as his closest aides. Jim was intensely jealous because Karen and Larry were still fond of each other. (Only recently, I found out that Karen was pregnant with Larry's child when she perished in Jonestown.)

With Jim's and Maria's departure there would be ten members of the Planning Commission left for now. Jim's wife, Marceline, was also going to stay behind. Her usual role was to keep the fortress strong during Jim's absences and show the members that she, too, was a staunch believer. Today I know, however, that she was secretly afraid for her children and kept silent about Jim's infidelities only to be near them and hopefully protect them. But once the boys were old enough, Jim separated them from her by sending them to Jonestown.

I looked around the dark room. Maria was sitting at Carolyn's feet. Teresa was sitting with her legs crossed, her knee touching me. I leaned over to hand Teresa the tape recorder, showed her the note, and nodded in compliance at Father. Then I rushed up the stairs to the radio room, exhilarated. The excitement was back! Danger loomed nearer! Father was trusting me. He was depending on me, Carolyn, and Teresa to maintain the fortress. I would have "trusted status" and the opportunity to perform acts of heroism. I was being left behind to protect the Cause and close down the operation!

I'll have breakfast with Mama tomorrow, I decided.

TWO

XLVI
For in and out, above, about, below,
'Tis nothing but a
Magic Shadow-show
Play'd in a Box whose Candle is the Sun,
Round which we Phantom Figures come and go.

—Rubáiyát of Omar Khayyám

8
Exodus to Paradise

It took us half the night to help Jim orchestrate his exodus. At Carolyn's instruction I ran over to her room to get a few more items. Rifling through her dresser drawer, I came upon a diaphragm. Bewildered, I wondered what on earth she was keeping the contraceptive for. We were celibate and Father maintained that he used sex only to save lives. Could Father possibly say one thing and practice another? No, it couldn't be and furthermore it was not my place to question. Jim had to do things for the Cause that I could never begin to understand. But then again, if he had to have sex it only made sense that it would be with Carolyn, whom he entrusted with all his thoughts and who knew as much about the organization as he. After all, she had been his mistress in their last life together.

When it was time to leave for the airport, I carried one of Maria's various duffel bags to the parking lot. As always our guards were there, "pulling their shift" in the dark, surveying the perimeters, and ensuring that no one was monitoring our activities. I loved these men and women. They worked long, hard hours protecting us from the evil forces outside our confines. They wore mittens and puffy down jackets, wool caps when the night was cold, and they sported dark sunglasses during the day. Their shifts ran around the clock and their ranks numbered in the sixties. We had guards at our front door, guards at the back door, guards to frisk newcomers in case they were agents with weapons or tape recorders, and guards who strolled the aisles during services and kept the bathrooms orderly. I had become accustomed to their watchful and protective eyes. The stories in Kilduff's exposé about our guards with guns was overstated. Only a few had guns—to protect Father from assassins.

When the crates earmarked to accompany the expatriates to the Promised Land were loaded into the station wagon, Jim came out and stood for a moment under the porch light. His once healthy outdoor tan, the olive-brown skin on his face and arms, was now startlingly pale. I had not noticed this change in all our meetings in his gloomy, shade-drawn apartment. Maria, once the Romanesque beauty of the attic floor we lived on, also looked bedraggled, frighteningly thin, and very old. I could tell that she'd been crying when she passed me on the way to the car.

"You have our passports?" Jim asked, settling into the station wagon. He looked tired and besieged. It seemed unfair that the whole world was crashing down upon him at the same time. I produced a bag of legal documents, passports, vaccination and immunization cards, and his and Maria's money belts.

"Legal limit?"

"Yes, Father," I answered, knowing it was too dangerous right now to skirt the law.

"Sit with me. We have things to discuss. Maria can sit in the front with Tom."

Tom was Paula's "before joining the church" husband, someone I trusted and respected. He didn't write people up just to get them into trouble and he worked on occasional special projects for Teresa.

"Tom." Jim cleared his rasping voice and continued, "After tonight you'll need to work more closely with Teresa as Lucinda will be moving into Maria's room and taking over the finances. Get on the radio and learn the codes. Most of Teresa's time will be spent in there talking with me and she'll need someone to help with all the instructions. Just because I'm leaving for Guyana doesn't mean I won't be in constant contact with you here. I expect to run both operations."

He turned to me and put his warm, tense palm on my leg. It looked puffy.

"You've been leaving late at night to see Lisa . . ."

I nodded, acting as if my trips to see my mother were common knowledge, but my stomach tightened.

"Your brother Larry has finished his X-ray technician training and now works at Herrick Hospital in Berkeley. He asked if he could move in with 'the old man.' How do you feel about that? Your brother works hard, Debbie, but he worries me. I think he wants to live with the old man because he actually likes him."

I shrugged, trying to think of a response.

"No? And how about you? Do you feel sorry for him?"

"For Larry? He does work long . . ."

"No, your father. When I suggested Lisa get a divorce I was concerned about her reaction. She didn't want to go after the old man for everything he was worth. She actually had feelings for the bastard."

"Oh, I think she'll be fine. She's just lonely right now."

"Do you think she handed over all the money she got from your father?"

I felt my lip begin its deadly giveaway twitter.

"Yes, it was about two hundred thousand, I think . . ."

"Perhaps, but my impression was that she wanted to leave some aside."

How could he know this? I had overheard Mama talking on the phone one day with Annalisa. Mama had suggested putting some money away for Annalisa, in case she ever needed it, in case Annalisa decided to leave her husband. Had Mama's phone been tapped?

"Mama wouldn't do that," I fibbed.

"Look into it, will you? Lisa has a mind of her own sometimes and she worries me."

The hair on my arms and neck rose. Jim was having doubts about the sweetest person I knew. What on earth was going on?

"Thought I'd get it off my chest. It's not good to deceive the leader. There are always ugly consequences." He smiled and took tight hold of my hand.

"Of course," I replied. Poor Mama was under suspicion. I would have to warn her.

"Yes, that reminds me, your mother has a bronze statue of a nude woman . . . I understand it is worth a great deal of money. It would be a nice touch for Charles Garry to receive it. I think he collects art deco pieces. Tell Lisa I will consider it an honor if she gives it to him personally." I was crushed. The statue, *Die Erwachende,* meant so much to Mama; it was the last token of her life before the Temple that she had held on to. I decided not to tell her. Perhaps there was a way out of this. With Father leaving the country, he would not know if we did not give the statue to the famous attorney.

Seeing Father and his entourage fly away filled me with trepidation and relief. I would have time to talk with Mama, who was still unsure of what she should and shouldn't say. I would have to remind her it was best never to tell anyone your true feelings. I needed to protect her from being misunderstood.

I arrived at Mama's around three o'clock in the morning, kissed her hot, damp cheek, and snuggled down on the futon she had made up for me. A comforting warmth enveloped me, and then, as I drifted off into sleep, I thought I heard her cough.

I awoke mid-morning to the smell of cookies baking. After I showered, Mama and I sat in her room relishing one of her newer breakfast creations: delicious high-energy tofu oatmeal. The brown sugar had melted into creamy-sweet puddles.

"Mama, Jim left last night for Guyana." I sipped her soothing tea with evaporated milk and a pinch of sugar. Her family had made it this way in Germany, before the war.

"Really? So suddenly?"

"There have been all these defections, you know that!"

"But what for? Tim and Grace, and the others . . . All of them are quite intelligent and educated, and every one was very close to Jim. I wonder what would make them leave?"

"Mom, how can you ask that? They're capitalists!"

"Grace? Tim? Honey, I find that hard . . ."

"Mother!" I was shocked at my own intensity. What was I so upset about? I couldn't take it out on her. She was an innocent bystander.

"Mama, I'm sorry. I'm just tired and edgy."

"Well, let's change the subject then. Anyway, I wanted to tell you that your father called and would like to have dinner with me tonight."

"Don't bring him here," I exclaimed, losing control again. "He'll be upset by your surroundings." That's all we would need, I thought. The Treasury Department, U.S. Customs agents, the FBI, Tim Stoen, and "the old man" as well. God forbid if they all started exchanging stories.

"Honey, he's taking me to Trader Vic's as a friendly gesture."

"Should I come along?"

"No, darling. It's different now. This is a very personal meeting."

"Are you okay seeing him?" I asked anxiously.

"Debbie! We were married for thirty-four years. Your father is still very hurt over my decision to leave him. It was hard on both of us when Tim Stoen came in and began to handle the legal affairs. We had chosen an arbitrator whom we both knew and trusted. Then Tim offered to help and it all changed. He was very hard on your father and pushed him to the limit on giving me my fair share."

"Did he?"

"It's all too late to lament over now. Your father was hurt financially, but the choices were made, hammered into settlement papers, and the relationship was all but destroyed."

"You have regrets, Mama." I was amazed by the realization.

"It was your father who helped me find my condominium when I wanted to separate. We went shopping together and he bought me some nice furniture to fit in my studio. He was very loving and seemed to understand that I just wanted my own space after so many years. I never planned to divorce him. We had dinners together, went for walks . . ."

"Mama? You aren't crying?" I was afraid. I didn't want to see her sad. I felt safest when I kept my mind closed from any hurt she might be experiencing. And then it struck me that it wasn't Mama Jim was questioning me about in the car. He was testing me. How could I have been so daft? It was I who had suggested that Mama put some money in a separate bank account, just in case she ever had second thoughts. But it must have been myself who had second thoughts that I was not consciously aware of. I must have feared that if my mother gave everything away I would lose my only path out. As I could not admit I was concerned for myself, I focused my financial concern on my mother.

Mama looked at me quizzically.

"Debbie? . . ." I nodded for her to continue. "It's all very complicated, my feelings for your father. He hasn't done anything to be punished for." A timer in the kitchen went off. She looked at her watch. "The cookies for you and Teresa are done. Better hurry, we should be on our way to the doctor's."

After Mama's medical examination and the doctor's concerned request for a follow-up X-ray, we headed for the picnic we had planned. Mama had packed my childhood favorite sandwiches, sliced cucumber with mayonnaise and cream cheese with raisins, cut into bite-sized pieces. It reminded me of all the mornings when I grabbed my lunch box, hugged Papa good-bye, and tugged from behind as Mama towed me up the long steep path to kindergarten. In the afternoons she'd fetch me and we'd stroll by Admiral Nimitz's house. He'd knock on his living room window, then saunter out to arrange a time before supper when he would drop by and take me on his evening stroll with his Great Dane.

When lunch was over, we drove back into the sunless noisy Castro district, where Mama now lived. I wanted to stay with her, aware that she was worried about the visit to the doctor. We had not mentioned it over lunch nor had I warned her of Father's concerns. I felt as though life was very thin and at any moment we might fall through the delicate crust.

On my return to Maria's stale, windowless attic room, I closed the door. I was afraid. I was being tested and wasn't sure why. Father wanted to test my honesty. And now Mama's doctor was worried about something. I could feel myself sinking. She needed me now more than ever, she who had never once been sick. She had always been the one who took care of me. I opened the bag of cookies, laid my head on my arms, and began to cry.

Days passed and the previously dull radio room came alive with the humming and crackling noise of radio frequencies from late afternoon until the early hours of the morning. While Father was waiting for the boat to take him into the rain forest, he had set up shop in Guyana's capital, Georgetown. His voice boomed over the airwaves, spouting orders. In return he received minute by minute updates on the latest antics of the press in the States. I hoped, once he was situated in Jonestown, that the Promised Land would calm his nerves and mellow his mood.

On an early Tuesday morning, while the radio room was buzzing, Mama and I went to another follow-up examination. The X-ray had shown a dot on Mama's lung and the doctor wanted her to come in for a bronchoscopy within a couple of weeks. I had seen this procedure before and knew Mama would not be put to sleep. The sensation of choking would make the procedure very uncomfortable and frightening.

I talked to Teresa. She, too, loved my mother and told me not to worry, just to stay with Mama. We spent a long day at the hospital and when I brought her back to her commune, I cooked her some supper. I knew I was slacking off on my duties by spending that much time with her.

When she had finished eating, I broached the subject of her living with me.

"Mom? Move into the church. You could have my old room. The sun shines in every afternoon. It's not nearly as dark as this room."

"Oh, sweetie . . . You don't have a kitchen and I wouldn't be able to bake there."

"I could get you a two-burner hot plate. I can convert the closet into a tiny kitchen for you."

"Not now, honey. I like using this oven. And I enjoy your ability to spend the nights with me now."

It was true, I had far more free reign since Jim had left and Teresa had okayed my sleeping at Mama's.

Once Jim was safely ensconced in Jonestown, he demanded more supplies, food, clothing, and Bibles. Carolyn had recently joined him and her son Kimo in the interior. More often now it would be her voice requesting leather boots, socks, mosquito netting, and more clothes for the children. Endless strategies were barked, in code, over the airwaves, to be translated and implemented. Teresa dutifully spent most of her time in the radio room, jotting down notes, decoding Jim's messages, and relaying what the press were up to.

Back home, our church meetings had become significantly smaller since over 800 members now resided in Jonestown. Ever conscious of our image, Jim demanded we add an extra digit to the attendance figures, both to mislead whoever might be eavesdropping on our broadcasts and to bolster the Jonestown residents by letting them think that our services were well attended.

"We had two thousand members join us in prayer today. Every one of them is supportive of your actions and understands why you had to leave when you did. We all hope to join you in Guyana soon," we would regularly declare. Truly, only 200 had come, if that many. Our numbers were dwindling.

In late July, several weeks after Jim's departure, Temple members organized a rally in support of Jim's decision to flee. Many of our high-profile benefactors, including Assemblymen Willie Brown and Art Agnos, County Supervisor candidate Harvey Milk, Reverend Cecil Williams of Glide Memorial Church, and *Sun Reporter* publisher Carleton Goodlett, came to Jim's defense. From deep in the rain forest via a long-distance radio-telephone link, Jim addressed the crowd.

"I know that some of you are wanting to fight, but that's exactly what the system wants. It wants to use us as sacrificial lambs, as a scapegoat. Don't fall into this trap by using violence, no matter what kind of lies are told on us or how many.

"Peoples Temple has helped practically every political prisoner in the United States. We've reached out to everyone who is oppressed, and that's what is bothering them. We've organized poor people and given ourselves a voice. The system doesn't mind corporate power for the ruling elite, but for the first time, we've given some corporate power to the little man and that's an unforgivable sin. And that's the problem in a nutshell."

I listened along with the other parishioners, feeling proud of our work. I thought about all the people we had helped, the famous ones like Angela Davis and Dennis Banks, and the little people who were constantly lost within the system. There was a lot to be proud of, in spite of the defectors, the press, the whole controversy. I was relieved to hear Jim come across as strong and confident. Clearly, I thought, our Promised Land had already restored his spirit.

But as the days passed, Jim's mood grew worse. He was frantic about the proposed investigations and angry that he had been compelled to run. Having always been in charge of every situation, his inability now to call the shots and manipulate circumstances was wreaking havoc with his sensibilities. With each broadcast from his outpost, he sounded more discontent. There were rantings about the conspiracy against us and long tirades against Grace Stoen, who had stepped up her effort to get her little boy, John Stoen, back.

On a drizzly afternoon in late August, I brought Mama back from her bronchoscopy. The surgeon had biopsied a small segment of tissue for further examination. Mama was visibly shaken. I settled her onto her couch-bed, and prepared to go. She asked me not to leave her but I explained that I had to at least touch base with Teresa. Mama didn't complain; she went into the kitchen and put some of her protein cookies in a bag for me to take to Teresa.

When I entered the cramped radio room, Teresa looked exhausted and worried. I pulled out the bag of Mama's cookies and she sprang from her seat to grab it, and pulled me down into the chair next to her as she stuffed one into her mouth.

"We need to talk," she said, then she hesitated. She seemed to be listening to the static, as if she was afraid. She started when Jim's voice crackled through the radio, ugly and adamant.

"We need Bibles! More Bibles, big shining Bibles. I want you to go to the Bible Exchange! We need them for protection. Do you copy?"

Teresa, her hand shaking, began to bite at her fingernails. Tiny beads of sweat had broken out on her upper lip.

She slowly picked up the microphone, intermittently depressing and releasing the button as she spoke, deliberately breaking up her message back to Father.

"We . . . ve . . . poor . . . We can't . . . py . . . do . . . re . . . me? Repe . . . Ur . . . message. Ov . . . We are un . . . to read . . . do . . . Py . . . Over."

"The Guyanese government has turned against us, violated our sovereignty." We heard the crystal-clear message from Jonestown. "They have joined forces against us . . . We will have to make a stand. You must send more Bibles for our study program. Do you read me? Over."

Again, Teresa feigned radio problems. I looked at her, amazed.

"Teresa, I understand what he's saying. He wants guns!"

"We cannot read you." Jim sounded exasperated. "Your transmission is too broken up. We will try again in an hour. Over."

There was silence.

"What's the big deal?" I asked.

There had been a time when a demand for Bibles would have been understood simply as Bibles, a ploy to present the Temple as a church for those people monitoring our radio communications. Recently, however, Bibles had begun to be a code word for weapons and ammunition.

Teresa looked at me defiantly, moved the radio dial slightly off frequency, and turned down the volume.

"We need to talk . . ." she repeated.

I followed her into the narrow windowless closet she called her room. Notes were strewn on the floor and file folders were piled high on her bureau. Her sleeping bag was still crumpled up on the floor under her long built-in desk.

"Lucinda, I'm afraid," she said, keeping her voice down. "Something's wrong. Something is happening to Jim."

I was confused. In my understanding back then, it made sense that Father would want to protect our community. After all, we were close to the Venezuelan border and Jim had initially told the Guyanese Prime Minister that we would be a bulwark against possible infringements on the border. I had no idea why guns in Jonestown would cause Teresa to lose her nerve and act in a completely uncharacteristic way. She must be totally exhausted, and unable to think clearly. Why should anything be wrong? Jim sounded, as always, worried about the conspiracy. Perhaps Teresa had been away from Father's aura for too long and was losing her way. I felt disconnected. For the last few weeks, my thoughts had been with Mama and Teresa's terror didn't make sense to me.

I looked into Teresa's tired and dark circled eyes. Her blond hair was oily and she needed to shower and take a nap.

"Father has his reasons and we should not try to outguess him," I said.

"Lucinda, it's not right. It isn't the same anymore. He's not thinking clearly; he's acting strangely and what he is asking for is wrong."

I shrugged and left the room. It was another of Father's odd requests which would come to nothing. I wanted to be with Mama and all my worries were with her, but I knew I had to step in and review the situation with my other comrade on the Diversions Committee. We decided to take the situation in hand. I gave her a large sum of money for the acquisition of guns to be immediately purchased and covertly shipped to Jonestown. In the meantime, I asked Robbi to take Mama to her follow-up appointment to get the results of her bronchoscopy.

I was in my room listening to Teresa, who was again simulating transmission problems, when Jim's private telephone line began to ring in my room. Jim's wife, Marceline, a kindhearted woman, had just come in to check on our finances when I lifted the receiver. A tiny voice was trying to talk to me and my body stiffened with fear.

"Darling . . . ?"

"Mama? Is that you . . . ?"

"Honey . . ." Her voice became even quieter and I closed my door to drown out the sounds from the radio room.

"I have cancer."

My body sank. I sat on the floor, trying to say something.

"Are you there, honey?"

"Yes, Mama . . ." I whispered.

I could not control my breathing. Marceline was suddenly kneeling next to me, staring wide-eyed into my face.

"Mama? What happened?" I asked with tears streaming down my cheeks.

I felt claustrophobic. Marceline was too close. I needed space to breathe. I wanted to be alone. I wanted to scream Get away, for God's sake. Let me talk to my mama alone.

"They want to remove part of my lung."

Marcie was leaning into me, trying to take the phone.

"Please, Marcie. I'm fine." I wiped at my eyes. "Can I speak to my mother in private? She is calling from the hospital. She has lung cancer."

Marcie grabbed my shoulders and squeezed me, shaking her head in disbelief.

"Of course. Go to her now. I'll inform Jim." She headed to the radio room.

"Mama, I'll be right over. I'll be there in a minute, okay?"

"Oh, Debbie . . . I'm so sorry . . . I . . ."

"No, Mama . . . don't . . . I'm coming."

Mama's illness engulfed me, and I ebbed further and further away from the front lines. Marceline and Teresa arranged for Robbi, one of my faithful Offering Room workers and my friend, to take over the daily finance dealings with the banks.

On August 25, 1977, Mama's cancer surgery took place. I wandered through the hallways, making superstitious pacts with myself. If I didn't step on any of the floor-tile borders and managed to walk smoothly never touching the edges, Mama would be fine. If I stared at the couch across from me, without blinking, the power of my concentration would make her well. After she was transferred to the ICU, I stood in the room near her while the heart monitor beeped out shrill, irregular tones, and willed Mama to recover, cell by cell, with each beeping sound, as if each beep represented hope.

The doctor had had to remove Mama's entire right lung, along with an adjacent lymph node. Throughout her drugged recovery, she softly complained of her difficulty breathing. I held the oxygen mask slightly off her nose to reduce her sensation of suffocating and had the nurse increase the oxygen flow. Mama awoke intermittently and asked for my forgiveness, anguished about having gone back to work when I was still in grade school, blaming my unhappy childhood on herself. I lowered my head and cried.

Mama grew stronger but in early September, her doctor met with me and explained that her cancer had metastasized. It had spread into her other lymph nodes and she would need aggressive treatment.

"It will make her very ill and there is only a fifty percent chance that it will help." While I was wondering what I should tell Mama, Robbi came to the hospital with the latest news: Grace's and Tim's efforts had culminated in the issuance of a custody order for John-John Stoen and a warrant for Jim's arrest for contempt of the Guyanese court.

With each new exposé from *New West* magazine and the subsequent articles in the *San Francisco Examiner,* Robbi treated me to a blow-by-blow account of the celebrities who had been patched-in via telephone and whose messages had been blasted over the loudspeakers in Jonestown and in our San Francisco meetings. On one particular day during what seemed to be six days of hysteria, while Robbi was describing both Angela Davis's message of support and that of Huey Newton, the Black Panther leader, the telephone rang next to Mama's bed. It was Teresa, sounding panicked.

"Lucinda, leave Robbi with Lisa and hurry over! We have an emergency. Jim wants you here to receive the instructions with me. Do you copy?"

Poor Teresa hadn't been out of the radio room for weeks. I wondered if I had time to get her some chow mein from my favorite Chinese family grocery store on Filmore Street before joining her and Jim.

"Tell her now!" I could hear Jim bellow. "This is life and death and she cannot dawdle." Odd, I thought, even from there he has his intuitive abilities.

When I drove into the church's dirt parking lot, one of our guards ran over, said he'd park the car, and motioned for me to hurry to the radio room. Teresa was manning the dials as Father's hoarse voice crackled through the radio waves.

"Do you copy? Is Lucinda in the room now?"

"Roger, over," Teresa replied.

"Lucinda, you need to become more focused now. I realize you have been upset about your mother's condition, but we are in a life-threatening situation here. Teresa needs your support and help. Do you copy?"

I looked quizzically at Teresa and took the mike. "Roger, this is Lucinda . . . I copy."

"This requires your full attention. Lisa will get better when she is closer to me. Now . . ." The radio hissed and sputtered. "I need you to make some calls . . ." Father sounded extremely agitated and I thought I heard yelling far off in the distance on his end of the transmission. He instructed me to call a high-ranking Guyanese official, who was visiting the United States, and deliver a threat: Unless the government of Guyana took immediate steps to stall the Guyanese court action regarding John-John's custody, the entire population of Jonestown would extinguish itself in a mass suicide by 5:30 P.M. that day. The message seemed a little contrived. I wondered why he would take his intimidation to such a violent-sounding extreme. Of course, I understood the end justified the deceitful means. This was only one of his strategic moves, I told myself, and his diplomacy skills would carry the day in the end. As a good soldier I made the contacts, relayed the threats with emotion, and wondered about Teresa's misgivings.

Her strange doubts about Father worried me, yet, as always, I stashed my own fears into the secret compartment that rational thought couldn't penetrate. On the whole, I was more concerned with Mama and the doctors' admonition about her treatment. I could not get interested or in tune with the endless Jonestown frenzies. Later that evening it sounded as if the crisis had been halted. Another intense mind game, I thought, and hurried off to be with Mama.

It was a broodingly warm October dawn when I was roused from sleep and summoned by Teresa for another important assignment. I had to squint my eyes to adjust to the light in the radio room. It was 5 A.M. and my eyes were not ready to awaken. Teresa looked haggard as she signaled for me to sit next to her at the radio controls. Her eyes were bloodshot and she looked as though she'd been crying.

"Lucinda? Did I raise you from a lovely dream? Over." Father's voice seemed to snicker over the radio.

"No. Over," I lied into the microphone as Teresa's eyebrows rose.

"We are in dangerous waters and the snakes have begun to swarm their prey," Father began. "You must find George," he ordered. George was Tim Stoen's code name. "You didn't have any luck last time, but now we know where to snare him. He's supposed to be arriving at City Hall today. He plans to join forces with the witch [Grace] in order to steal the boy [John-John] from me, the rightful father. Thank God the boy's now safe with me." He sighed. His voice sounded brittle, as if it might shatter with tears if he wasn't careful.

As always, Jim did not reveal the source of his information or suspicions. He gave the uncanny impression that he just knew, as though he pulled these things from the ether plane, from where he said he came, or as though he had spies everywhere. It was too scary to think about.

Finding Tim, this time, was easy in the subterranean parking lot. When I approached him, I was taken aback by his sincere smile and kindness.

"Debbie, I know you are under pressure to scare me. I want John-John back. Grace is his rightful mother and he should be here with her. When she left, it wasn't safe to take John-John; she wanted to find a home first, not frighten the boy. She was looking out for his welfare all along. I know you think you are doing the right thing, but I've been to the Promised Land. I've seen . . ." He stopped mid-sentence as if fearful. Perhaps he thought I was taping the conversation. His voice was pleading with me, as though hoping I would grasp his thread of insinuation. I wanted to ask him what he was saying, but felt disloyal for yearning to understand a traitor. And then it was over. Tim looked around nervously, patted his briefcase, and headed toward the staircase. Watching him disappear into the darkness, I stood very still. I was trying to figure out how to proceed when I heard Tim's voice calling back to me.

"You're a good kid, Debs. None of it is what you think."

I felt ill and confused about Tim on my drive back to the Temple. It would take me eighteen years to learn the whole story: Tim had become disillusioned with the harsh life in Jonestown and used one of his legal missions in the capital to flee. Initially he went to England, but was tracked down by Jim's aides and persuaded to return. Fearing for his life, Tim came back only long enough to try and destroy any Temple documents that might defame him, then defected again.

When I reported back to Father, I was afraid to tell him I didn't push Stoen to take more money. Tim was sure of himself, seemed sane, and I didn't understand my own feelings about him. Why had I momentarily understood his plight? Why had I wondered what Tim had wanted to say? I was frightened by my own disloyalty to Father when I entered the radio room to relay my account.

"George refused the money. Over." I prayed Tim would not give me away in subsequent conversations with Jim.

"What? You saw him? What happened?" Jim sounded defeated.

"He refused. He was adamant that money was not the issue . . ."

"Dear God, he's become principled too?" He exhaled in disbelief, his voice filled with grief. I heard shuffling, as if someone was walking toward Father. I wondered if he was whispering something into Carolyn's ear. I heard more shuffling and thought perhaps they would assign someone more effective than me. I felt ill. What if Teresa approached Tim and asked him why he wouldn't take more money? What if Tim said I never offered him any? What if he announced that I had understood and shown him compassion? Oh Jesus. I would be killed for such a betrayal.

But my worries receded when nothing happened and Teresa and the transmissions from Jonestown quieted into a faint hum. I returned to my concerns and focused on Mama. I needed to have her closer to me. I determined that I would have her move in.

By late October, Larry, who was now living with Papa, came over and helped move Mama into my old room at the Temple. He brought a little refrigerator Papa had purchased for her, which fit into the closet I had fixed up with a hot plate. Every day after work, he shopped for fresh fruits and vegetables for Mama, and picked colorful bouquets of flowers from Papa's yard.

Now I saw Mama every day. In the evenings I'd check in on her and often slept on the floor next to her. Mama was changing. She was frightened. The cancer they had removed was a rare form and her doctors had asked her permission to send samples to other research hospitals. Mama asked me if it was because she was not a good enough believer that she had gotten sick.

"After all," she pondered, her voice trembling a little, "Father says people who leave or have doubts often find themselves riddled with cancer . . ."

I worked hard to convince her that that wasn't true, not for her and not for me. But deep inside, in the secret compartment where I stored bad thoughts, I felt betrayed. By whom, I was afraid to say. Had it been my doubts that had made Mama sick? Father had said it was dangerous to deceive the leader.

While I toiled over financial ledgers again, Teresa was busy manning the radio and Larry was working longer hours at the hospital. Mama waited, alone and lonely, for my visits. Papa's offer to take care of Mama at his house, which had once been their house, was rejected and he, Annalisa, and Tom were not allowed to visit inside the Temple. It was nearly impossible for them to contact us. Mama didn't have a phone in her little space and I never dared to give them Jim's private number in my room.

By November, Jim asked that I begin attending to the radio communications. Once Teresa had established contact, she would often leave me alone while Father talked with me. Jim consoled me, spoke about Mama and the effect of her condition on me. He was concerned that I had become overworked. He often talked about the beautiful cabins awaiting Mama and me in the jungle. Then he put Mark on the radio. I was embarrassed, especially when Mark spoke of his dreams of our living together in Jonestown as husband and wife. I could feel my cheeks redden when he said how much he missed me and fantasized about the day we would be as one.

Every evening, I'd rush to Mama's room and repeat Father's stories about our Paradise, and she, too, painted pretty pictures in her mind of our life together away from America. Finally, the day before Thanksgiving, good news arrived. Father had invited us to the Promised Land.

"Lisa is strong enough to travel and she needs to be with me now. Plan to bring her and help her settle in. I think you would feel more comfortable knowing she is happy. Plan to stay two months, then you can return to your duties there and Robbi can come here and visit her family. Consider yourself on a bi-monthly schedule."

I was ecstatic. At last we would leave these cramped quarters. Mama would again be in an environment she loved. She'd be in the open air, surrounded by nature and near her recently acquired friend, Lynetta Jones, Father's biological mother. Lynetta was a writer and Jim said that she was Mark Twain in her previous life. She and Mama could discuss the books they both loved. Mama's health would improve.

"By the way, Debbie," Father added, "Shanda wanted you to know you'll be living near her . . . And let Lisa know that my mother is exceptionally vigorous and looks forward to her company and their long walks together."

Mama's doctor wrote a release so that she could travel to Guyana. I had met with him privately and asked that he not tell her that the cancer had metastasized. She had already decided that she did not want radiation or chemotherapy and I desperately wanted to get her to the Promised Land where I, too, believed she needed to be. We would both flourish in Jim's sickness-curing aura. Once we were near Father again, Mama would get better, I was sure of it.

The evening of our departure I explained to Mama that it would be unwise to notify anyone of our trip. Papa already knew we planned to go, but if he knew the date, he could call in "forces" to stop us. Jim had told me via the radio that Papa had ties to the CIA. He warned me to be cautious.

Mama was extremely upset. She wanted to go but did not understand why she could not say good-bye.

"Mama, aren't you glad you're going?"

"Yes, honey. It's just that we are leaving under a veil of secrecy."

"But you must know by now how important secrecy is! Outsiders are dangerous, especially family members."

It was always best to do things first and announce them later, when it was safe, I assured myself. They could come visit us there when Mama was settled.

"Darling . . . why the need for such secrecy? I want to say good-bye to your brother and sister. I don't want Papsche, your grandfather, to feel that I deserted him. I can't do it to him, too . . ."

More tears ran down her cheeks.

"To him, too? Mama, I don't understand."

"Oh, darling Debbie," she sighed. A weight seemed to be pulling her down on to the couch. "Mutti took her life when I left her and moved to Utah."

I dropped the pair of trousers I was folding for her.

"Mutti? But Grandma Anita died in Hamburg! . . . from a heart attack."

I stared at her in complete disbelief.

"No, darling. Mutti died here . . . in New York. She committed suicide. She jumped from her apartment window. I was thousands of miles away and never able to say good-bye. Papsche received hundreds of letters from concerned Quaker Friends. In December, six months before her death, I had moved away to Utah with your papa. I thought I could visit her, but with three little . . ." Her voice trailed off and her chest heaved. "Had I been with her . . . had she been able to talk to me . . ."

"But I thought . . ."

"No . . . it wasn't the truth. All wrong, darling . . . all wrong."

She held her hands to her face and wept. I had seen her cry on only three other occasions, twice about me and then on the day John F. Kennedy was assassinated. I was amazed how this story from the past, a story I never knew, could remain so raw and painful for her. I had no idea that something that had happened so long ago could still eat at one's heart as if no time had passed. I was troubled by my feelings of hurt and anger. Why had all this been kept a secret? Why had so many important events in Mama's life been shrouded in mystery? I concentrated on not crying, too. I did not want Mama to see my pain. I dared not add to her grief with my own.

I felt helpless and overwhelmed, incapable of caring for her. I wanted to run away from her increasing dependence on me. Mama needed to be with Father. We needed to hurry and escape to the Promised Land where life was easy, and where solutions to all our problems lay. I was only twenty-four years old. Father could take far better care of Mama than I could.

While we packed, a soft knock sounded at Mama's door. Marcie stood before me, a pained look on her face.

"Our attorney, Charles Garry, has just arrived and is down the hall, in the radio room. Jim is talking to him from Jonestown." My heart sank. "Father wants Lisa to give the statue to Charles before you both leave." She paused. "I'm sorry," she whispered.

I turned around to look at Mama. Her face was as pale as ivory as she looked into my eyes and seemed to ask, And now this, too?

"Debbie, I cannot . . . It is not mine to give. It is an heirloom and must be returned to your father. I do not have the right . . ." Her voice choked with emotion.

"Lisa," Marcie came into the room conspiratorially, "let's do this for now. I will present it to Charles and then, next week, I will meet with him and feign confusion, explain that it was my mistake and get it back for your husband."

Mama rose as though Jim had sent her the executioner. She motioned Marcie to the bronze woman statue on her coffee table, then turned to the tiny barred window overlooking the decrepit tenderloin, and wept.

Sadly, *Die Erwachende* has never been returned by the Garry estate and when he died we were impeded in our search for it. I pray someday someone will recognize the statue as ours, and return it.

Early the following morning, on December 6, 1977, without saying good-bye to our family, Mama and I traveled to New York. During our layover I suggested we have dinner at an expensive restaurant and ordered a bottle of red wine. Mama was concerned because it was against church rules to drink and the restaurant was expensive.

I was not worried. I felt safe in my position as financial secretary and anyway, I thought, What's a $100 supper when we were each carrying $10,000? Furthermore, what was $10,000 when we had millions abroad? I wished I could tell Mama not to worry, that we were safe, that there were millions of dollars stashed away in numbered accounts for when we needed it.

Once we got to Jonestown everything would be fine. Everyone said it was beautiful there. Father had made it a beautiful place. There were pretty one-room cabins with lofts for the parents, a school, and a small river just past the trees. I couldn't wait to mingle with the Amerindians and to swim in the river. The last film I had seen was so enticing. I remembered watching and listening to Mark as he spoke into the camera, with his adorable thick accent and beautiful greenery in the background. He discussed the process of clearing the land and building our homes. "Our pioneers," as Father lovingly called them, had accomplished so much in the last five years, getting ready for us. I imagined that by now there were even more beautiful wood cabins scattered throughout the countryside. Our house might have a veranda. I could see myself sitting outside after an evening of lovemaking with Mark. Jonestown was going to be home for a thousand of us for the rest of our lives. I couldn't wait.

On the final leg of our journey to South America, I looked out the window and into the dark jungle expanse. I wondered if my mother's life would have been different if she had traveled to America with her mother. Would they have forged a stronger relationship? Would it have kept her mother happy and alive? Would my journey with my mother safeguard our new lives together? As our plane slowly turned, making our final descent into Guyana, a sea of green jungle peeked up at us, vast and uninterrupted. I gazed at its powerful beauty and saw what seemed to be the capital, teetering on the edge of the ocean. It was tiny in comparison to the boundless jungle we had just passed over. Holding Mama's hand tightly, I leaned over the armrest and kissed her cheek.

"I hope this is everything we've ever dreamed of, Mama . . ." I whispered into her ear.

She turned toward me and smiled.

"A toast to Jonestown!" She pronounced, then grabbed my arm tightly, as if letting go might mean losing me forever.

9
Guyana—The Promised Land

A muggy lethargy took hold of me as I emerged from our air-conditioned cabin. My clothes were wet, though I'd barely moved. Mama, however, seemed to be breathing easily and more deeply.

"The air is good," she smiled.

We moved in slow motion down the stairs and out onto the tarmac. It was five in the evening and I could feel the heat radiating up from the old cement runway, trying to melt the soles of my shoes. A sign glued to a window of an old, dilapidated building read, "Welcome to Guyana." We entered the terminal through thick glass doors. The building reminded me of a World War II airplane hangar . . . long, old, dark, and noisy. Scattered uniformed employees, their dark brown arms appearing from under elbow-length shirts, watched us and smiled. Everyone's skin looked smooth, as if doused with cream.

Herded forward toward the Customs agents, I waited and watched as the young men examined each passenger's possessions. As Mama approached the guard, Karen Layton suddenly appeared. She looked her usual cute, perky self, giggling and talking with the examining officers. I presumed she was arranging for our luggage not to be searched.

"Mom! Welcome home!" Karen waved. She still had that sexy commercial smile. Touching the young official's arm, she thanked him and ran around the table to hug Mama. The two of them walked slowly ahead, engrossed in a conversation while I floundered behind, wishing a porter could help me with the load of our duffel bags.

Climbing into the old rickety van, I noticed that all the vehicles in the lot were spattered with mud. The ride from the airport was long and frightening. The road was narrow. Little, run-down, flimsy taxis honked and sped by, even if there was an oncoming car. We passed a decrepit industrial plant with yellow clouds and a sickeningly sweet odor. Karen looked at my face and laughed, explaining the stench was the by-product of the hops factory, an important export product of Guyana's. I stared out the window and felt guilty . . . I was disappointed. Everything was old, shabby, and neglected. There were pathetic sheds along the road, each with a sign in the front window announcing that they, too, sold Coca-Cola. Partially clothed children were sitting on the hard brown dirt outside shacks, waving exuberantly for us to come in. After an hour and a half of bouncing down the road, past empty fields and desolate countryside, we slowed and entered a decaying township. The main thoroughfare was one-lane wide, but the buildings on either side of the road had once been elegant Victorian homes. There were weathered shingled mansions with huge wraparound porches, which looked as though someone had spray-painted them with dust and chipped paint. Perhaps in a previous century these buildings had been magnificent and white. Slender, proud, black- and brown-skinned people strolled about in the street. A black gentleman, dressed in a suit and carrying a leather briefcase, climbed the stairs to a formidable building. His body was erect, his presence polished, and I imagined him to be a barrister, educated in the "mother country," Britain, and having returned home to give something back to his once magnificent homeland. But this country was no longer grand. It seemed we had entered an impoverished hamlet beset by antiquated pride.

". . . And this is the capital of Guyana, Georgetown," Karen announced.

I rolled down my window, wanting to feel the energy on the street and hoping to hear the strange accents in the conversations nearby. Children were running along the road calling to each other as adults bustled away from an open market with bundles and sacks poised on their heads.

Our van crawled through the crowd and then we turned onto a rutted dirt road. Karen turned to face us in the backseat.

"We're here!" She pointed to a house in front of us. "This is home."

"But where's the capital?" I insisted, expecting large official buildings.

"That was it, we just drove through it."

The truck stopped in an earthen driveway. The house was large and the yellow paint was fading. We seemed to be in a comparatively prosperous part of town. Around us was an open, weed-filled lot. The closest house seemed a block away.

Climbing the outdoor stairs to the main floor, I smelled the dampness in the air. Far off in the distance, I heard a roaring sound that seemed to be moving toward us.

"Rain's coming," Karen announced.

Karen showed us into the sparsely furnished living room. What furniture there was, was disheveled and haphazardly placed. The torn couch was facing the kitchen at an off angle. The two armchairs had been pulled closely together as if made into a napping bed. There was no sense of character or order. Karen suggested that Mama and I have a seat on the couch while she ran downstairs to the radio room to tell Jim we had made it safely.

I excused myself and walked down the hall. A mattress lay on the floor of what I presumed was the master bedroom. I poked my head into the bathroom and saw a water bucket in the shower with a washcloth hanging and dripping from its side. The house felt strangely unlived in, like an office rather than a home. There were notebooks piled on the floors and scissors next to stacks of Guyanese newspapers.

When I returned to the living room, the inhabitants of the house had just settled down around the kitchen table. They glanced up and dutifully smiled. Over the course of the next hour, while Mama and I were waiting, I watched them. They were Temple members I had known well in the United States, but here in South America their personalities seemed changed. They were serious and vigilant, and they looked at me as if they knew something I did not. They were the newly anointed emissaries from Jonestown, doing Father's business at the Guyanese government ministries. They were discussing a meeting the following day at the Ministry of Defense. There were notes on the living room table entitled, "Jim's Thoughts for Embassy Meeting."

I suddenly realized that Mom and I stood out. We were different and belonged to another era in the church. Here in this socialist country, Jim seemed to have become a powerful force and Jonestown was his monarchy. These meetings were not with small city mayors and assemblymen. In Guyana, the Temple had close connections to diplomats and the Prime Minister. A new breed of followers seemed to have arisen, more sophisticated and militant, and I was not one of them. I could feel that history was being made here. Great decisions were being debated: how to approach an issue with the Deputy Prime Minister, who would meet with the Soviet Embassy staff tomorrow, and when to take the owner of the newspaper out to dinner. They spoke in serious tones and their postures conveyed a sense of urgency. I had fallen behind. My once respected status was of no importance here.

This new elite talked on about important plans, ignoring me completely. I was relieved when a voice called to me from the back room: "Welcome home!"

Paula came running out in a beautiful full-length dress and hugged Mama and me. Her hair was lighter, almost blond, and pulled back into a soft bun.

"I just came by to say hello and grab a couple of things. Bonny and I are on our way to a dinner at the U.S. ambassador's home. He'll be here shortly . . ."

"Wait . . ." came a voice from the next room. "You need to hear this before you talk to Bonny."

Paula excused herself and joined the discussion group. She was lucky, I thought, being able to dress up and date a non-member, and still be loyal to the Cause! I wondered what it was like to sleep in in the morning with no one there to "write you up," to eat whatever you'd like, to look in a refrigerator and make your own meals. And then to be able to go to a dinner party at a high official's home! Paula looked radiant, happy, and rested. No one could get mad at her because she was on a daily mission to keep the Guyanese ambassador to the United States comfortable and gratified. I'd heard he wasn't a very good-looking man, rather heavyset with a bad complexion from childhood, but what did that matter if he really loved her? I contemplated the sensation one might experience from being adored. I wondered if feeling cherished by another human would change me? I thought about Father and hoped he wasn't disappointed in my behavior since Mama's illness. I had not been able to pull my own weight. Teresa and Robbi had had to compensate for me.

I mulled over my conversations with Father in the San Francisco radio room after I'd moved Mama down the hall. Had Jim been concerned about my bourgeois attachments? About my hidden weakness for family? Had I lied about it all along? In all my handwritten catharsis reports, I had never insinuated that my mother meant so much to me. And now . . . Father must be having second thoughts about me. Maybe he believed I wasn't as trustworthy as before. Yes! That was why my passport had been taken from me when we arrived. It suddenly occurred to me that Robbi must have reported on my frame of mind when she returned from visits with me in the hospital. I had been desperately glad that Jim was away so I could focus on Mama alone. Did Father know I had had fleeting thoughts of leaving on my way home from Europe?

Paula returned from her talk at the table, more serious now. She sat down on the couch, gently pulling herself closer to Mama.

"Oh, Lisa . . . I've heard so much about your tribulations in the States, but you're here now and once you're in the interior, near Jim, you'll heal quickly."

I forced myself to smile and appear calm. There had been a discussion. Paula knew everything.

Sharon came in from the outside staircase and hugged us both.

"Paula, Bonny just drove up . . ."

We all rose and walked behind Paula into the twilight and down the stairs. The full moon was coming up behind us. Mama grabbed my hand and gave it a loving squeeze. As Paula disappeared into a long black car, Sharon ushered Mama and me into the basement. It was cooler underneath the house. Two mats on the cement floor had been made up for us. I hoped the clamor of the adjacent radio room wouldn't disturb Mama's rest.

"This will be home for the next few days while we wait for the boat. It's in drydock having a checkup. Come visit me later, Debbie," Sharon said, then crossed over into the radio room. I could hear the usual droning sound of frequency switching as she began to make contact.

"Eight Arr One . . . Eight Arr One, this is Eight Arr Three . . . Do you read me? Over."

Mom began to undress. She was visibly exhausted and needed to sleep. I sat with her as she lay down on the matting, wishing she could sleep on a soft bed. I debated how to say what I was thinking without upsetting her.

"Mama, the wine at dinner?" I asked softly. "Can we keep it our secret?"

"Of course, darling." She nodded in conspiratorial agreement. I sensed that Guyana was not the place for confessions of this kind. I shuddered and Mama grabbed my hand.

"Are you all right, darling? You've been unusually quiet."

"Yeah . . . It's just all so new here."

I didn't try to find a way to tell her that things were not as they seemed. Why had our passports been taken away by Karen? What was it about Jonestown that could divide us into those who belonged and those who didn't? What would I have to do to prove myself, to belong again?

I leaned over and kissed Mama's warm cheek. I watched her chest rise and fall. She seemed to breathe more easily in the humid air. I wanted to cuddle up next to her and go to sleep. I wanted to call to her in my childhood mantra, *"MOMMY . . . I'm afraid . . ."* but I could hear Jim's voice in the radio room. I knew where I was supposed to be.

The next morning, on our first real day in the capital, Karen took Mama and me on a stroll through town. We walked through the open market, ablaze with brightly colored fabrics hanging from stall posts. Chocolate-skinned East Indian women in their long multicolored saris walked with black women in short skirts. The wonderful smells of curry, cardamom, cumin, and cinnamon wafted through the warm air. Tables were covered with fruits and vegetables I had never seen before: yellow star-shaped fruit, prickly sphere-shaped pears, purple squash, and miniature reddish bananas that tasted like potatoes. Children were seated under the tables, hiding from the relentless sun. I grabbed Mama's arm and pointed at the baskets of spices while Karen purchased a Coca-Cola for us to share. It was syrupy sweet and thicker than the soda in the States. The cacophony of voices, intertwined with the sound of steel drums, was intoxicating. I closed my eyes to concentrate on the sounds of the varying accents around me: British, East Indian, Caribbean, and Spanish. Silly excitement washed over me as a couple of handsome, well-dressed young Latin-looking men stopped to speak with Karen. I was beginning to like this part of Guyana, the town, the market, and the friendly people. When we left the bazaar, Karen explained that the gentlemen were Cuban doctors sent to Guyana, their sister country, to provide a year of medical-humanitarian service work before going into practice back home.

"The Guyanese government is very appreciative," she said. "They try to entice the doctors to stay and settle down. There are often functions, dances, and dinners hosted by the Ministry of Health for their benefit."

I was enchanted. As we continued our tour of Georgetown, I peeked into a department store window. The display windows were empty and dust was collecting on the encased planking. Karen motioned for us to come inside. The building reminded me of an old Woolworth's store. The dark wooden floors were scuffed and unpolished. Behind every counter a young woman stood smiling, adorned in an oversized white pharmacy coat. I did not see much merchandise.

"Why are they open if there is nothing to sell?" I asked.

"Guyana is a socialist country. Besides being on the verge of bankruptcy and glad to have our income, they can't afford many bourgeois goods. What would people here use them for anyway?"

It was true, I thought; capitalism was always trying to entice the little man. The capitalist world did not consider people as individuals, only as consumers.

Later that evening, after Mama went to sleep, I walked upstairs hoping to sit alone in the living room. Everyone was busy in meetings in bedrooms and I was not included. I was glad for the time alone. Although life seemed more austere here in this house called "Headquarters," I had high hopes for life in the interior after our delightful tour of the town. I envisioned daily excursions into small villages, browsing through lively markets and sending gifts home to Papa.

On the coffee table, a small paperback book entitled *Guyana Guide* caught my attention and I opened it.

> Guyana, South America, formerly British Guiana, became independent in 1966. She became a republic with the British Commonwealth in 1970. Her largest racial groups are: East Indians (300,000), then Negroes, descendants of African slaves (250,000), and the remainder being Chinese, Portuguese, other Europeans and the indigenous Amerindians.
>
> Guyana is a country for serious adventurers only and is not to be attempted lightly. The wild beauty of its jungle interior is visited at a price of rigorous—sometimes dangerous—effort. Few of Guyana's 780,000 residents venture into the jungle interior. Those who do contend with tropical heat and humidity

> (63°–105°F, rainfall of 105″annually), tropical insects and the risk of malaria.
> Romantic? Exciting? Wild? Yes!—But one must remember that a trip to Guyana is no fool's holiday. Certain precautions should be taken while traveling here . . .

I put the book back on the broken table. Father had certainly picked a safe place for us, I thought. The CIA couldn't get us now!

An enormous roach traipsed across the wood-planked floor in front of me, then suddenly flew across the room and into the kitchen pantry. I could hear the far-off sound of the rain coming and took a deep breath. I liked the subtle change in the atmosphere. Kicking off my sandals and wedging my feet under me, I tried to make sense of the vague angst I had been feeling.

If I could put things into perspective I knew I could calm my jittery nerves. Why were our people acting so differently here in the capital? I knew them all, had known them for years, and yet I felt we hardly recognized each other. Father used to say in his sermons that if people stayed away from his teachings for too long, they became estranged. Had I become estranged, or had these people in the capital stayed away from him too long? But I knew from Teresa that Father assigned people to the capital for only short periods of time. They needed to come back into the fold every few weeks. Only Paula had been allowed to stay away for more than two months before being pulled back into Father's aura. If Guyana was "a country for serious adventurers only," perhaps all of us had to change. I would have to meet the challenge as best I could. But what if Father, too, was different now?

We had been in the capital for a week when Paula called Karen and Sharon to remind them of an important dinner-dance being hosted by the Guyanese government. Paula suggested I join them. Sharon chose a pretty dress for me to wear. Life at our headquarters was so serious and now we were going to a dance? In a dress? I had never worn a dress with a halter top, or heeled sandals. Karen suggested I put on blush and eye shadow. Mama looked lonely when I said good-bye. I promised I'd tell her all about it in the morning. She smiled and said I looked lovely.

When we entered the courtyard, couples were already dancing to exotic music. I felt shy and awkward, but followed our entourage to the designated table. Sharon encouraged me to dance with a Cuban doctor who came to our table. I had not danced since boarding school, six years ago. I imagined this was how Paula lived. Enjoying life and serving Father at the same time. When I returned to the table, Karen and Sharon encouraged me to continue to dance. The evening felt like a fabulous dream. I decided I might enjoy living here. I might even become friends with the Cuban doctor. I liked the idea. He was charming, enjoyed teaching me the salsa, made me laugh when I stepped on his toes. He listened to me with real interest and asked me to have lunch with him at the hospital the following day. As dawn approached, Sharon signaled to me that it was time to leave. The doctor accompanied me to our table and asked Sharon if he could drop by our home. I felt her disdain. I must have looked puzzled. In the car she began to lecture me about "capitalist enticements." She even shook her finger at me.

"I saw you dancing with the same doctor all night! I can't believe how close he was to you!"

Alarmed, I went to take a shower. What would I tell Father? Why had I enjoyed the gentleman? He had asked about my organization and was interested in our humanitarian endeavors. I had mentioned our need for physicians to visit our compound and examine the residents. He seemed genuinely interested. Had I erred? I did find him attractive . . . I hated Sharon. She always did this. She encouraged you only to get you into trouble later.

When I descended the steps outside the radio room, I could hear Sharon discussing the incident with Jim. I stopped outside the basement door and listened to his response.

"Anna . . ." Jim said softly, addressing her in code. "Lucinda's been under pressure, as you know, and needs to be near me for a while. She's been out of focus during our Six-Day Siege and still remains unaware of our trials. But I hear something else in your tone. Perhaps you're jealous . . . You just finished saying that you did not dance. Our purpose was to meet the doctors and ask them to visit Jonestown and give free medical advice. She aroused his interest. Often that's the only way to get men to do the right thing. Now, let's backtrack . . . I received your note about Paula. What are your concerns there?"

I was relieved. Thank goodness I was headed to Jonestown where Father understood and would protect me. I wondered what important historical event was called the Six-Day Siege.

10
Welcome to Jonestown

The trip into the interior was long and treacherous. We boarded our old tug, the *Cudjoe,* at the Georgetown dock, where she was berthed. There were now additional arrivals from the States who were joining us for the second leg of the trip.

We sailed out into the Caribbean for the twenty-five-hour voyage to the mouth of the Kaituma River. The seas were rough and no one was spared the ocean's wrath. We stayed in our places, hanging on tightly, heads bobbing, stomachs croaking. We heaved ceaselessly into the waves, which crashed onto the deck and drenched us. As our bodies slumped down on the dirty barge deck, the day turned dark and I was no longer able to decipher time, nor did I care to. The swells continued to rise above the sides of the tug, the ocean's salty mist splashing over my face and lips, stinging my swollen, unopened eyes. My clothes were soaked with seawater and vomit. I wondered how Mama was doing inside her small cabin on the little bunk bed.

I was too weak to pull myself up from the deck and make my way to her cabin door, and too sick for Mama to see me. As the tropical winds whooshed around me and the groaning of my sick deckmates became a frightful chorus, I tried to calm my overwhelming desire to die. As the night crept on and turned to dawn, my body was transformed into one enormous cramp.

Lying in the same place, the flecks of vomit washed overboard with the waves, I felt the soothing, voluptuous warmth of the sun slowly penetrate my drenched back. I slowly lifted my head from the deck. Was Mama there? Was she okay? But the effort of lifting my head was far more than my body would allow and I fell back into a trance. As the morning warmed into midday, the healing radiance from the sun actually revived my senses. I took a deep breath and opened an eye to see Mama sitting on the deck, her legs crossed, gazing down at me.

"I brought you some rice, it should help settle your stomach. There is more in the galley with milk and brown sugar on it." Weak, but glad to find her near and looking well, I smiled at her frail little form and accepted the nourishment. "The captain says we're close to the Kaituma River. It's four o'clock in the afternoon. We've been at sea over twenty hours."

"Only eight more hours to go!" yelled a crew member as the *Cudjoe* entered the mouth of the Kaituma. My stomach settled as we made our way into the calmer river waters. Peering over the gunwale, I noticed the change from endless blue-green waves to a dark muddy water. The jungle river was thick with life, snakes, piranha, and curious debris from the rain's torrential runoff. Its root-beer-colored water shwooshed past us, carrying felled trees and other plant life uprooted from its banks. This mighty waterway roared up against the hull of the tug and commanded respect. Its turbulence was ominous and prophetic, cautioning us against further travel, but we continued on, deeper into the interior. An occasional thatched-roof hut gave us a glimpse of human life on the river. The canopy of plant life continuously changed texture and formation, becoming thicker and darker green and the river narrowed, making our passage more difficult. From the top of a 200-foot-tall tree, a macaw flashed her bright red tail in warning.

The conversations around hummed with excitement about life on the inside. I wondered which friends I would see first, where I would live. I thought about Mark, a stranger now. His accent still made me smile.

"Iey, Debs, I caunt wait to seay ye again. It's bean so long and I've naever given up hope yu'd be coming. Father says yu've been a real hard warker, even call'd ya a soldier. Just to think, in England, how lost yu'd seemed. Now look at whar yu've come to. Oh, Debs, this place is havenly. The land we've cleared is beutiful and the cabins we've built are sturdy."

A sliver of moon peeked out from behind a cloud and shone down upon us. The night was cool and I closed my eyes. We were now a little over halfway into the third leg of the journey, far away from everything familiar to us. As I settled into my fantasies of the Promised Land, the captain walked out onto the scuffed deck.

"Listen up. Any correspondence you are taking in is to be handed over to me now. No communications are allowed until they have been reviewed by the Clearing Committee."

I sat very still and tried to calm my feeling of alarm. Why were letters from family members being censored? A nagging unease filtered up. I shuffled into the tiny cabin to find my duffel bag. Why were these letters dangerous? How could they possibly harm anyone? I removed the stack of notes I had excitedly collected from families and friends for their loved ones inside Jonestown and my heart began to sink.

Later that night, hours after handing over our outside correspondence, we arrived in Port Kaituma. This was the final inhabited spot—a small, mostly Amerindian-inhabited village, home to only a handful of people. Here, the flatbed truck awaited us for the fourth and last leg of the trip to Jonestown. For all but two of us, Mark and me, this ride would be our last before leaving this earth.

"Hello thar, mate," came a familiar brogue. Mark beamed excitedly.

"Mark's come all the way here to greet you, honey." Mama smiled proudly.

I managed a smile, but I was still upset about the letters. Mark stood and watched as we, the boat people, made our way up the embankment. He hastily came to Mama's aid, grabbing her arm and lifting her up and onto the leveled ground.

"Here, Mum, com sit in th'cab of the truck with us." His voice was sweet and sincere.

"Debs, wud you join us aup har?"

I squeezed his hand gently and said it would be too crowded for Mama. I'd stay in the back of the flatbed with the others. I felt ill with foreboding. We waited while the boat crew unloaded our cargo. It must have been near midnight. I had lost my watch during my ordeal on the rough sea. I could see Mama's head through the Plexiglas of the cab as Mark started the engine. She was talking and looked comfortable. I was thankful that Mark had chosen to greet us and was taking special care of Mama.

The following ride in the truck was agonizing. We sank into deep troughs and struggled back out as the truck sputtered on, taking us farther and farther into the jungle. After two exhausting hours, I suddenly heard oohing and ahhing and sat up. Not too far in the distance I saw lights. It seemed as though we were nearing an enchanted city. The halo illuminating the sky ahead of us was captivating. Mama was pointing toward the brightness. A shiver shot through my back and into my stomach and I knew everything was going to be all right.

When we reached the lights, the dreamy haze vanished. I spied poles with lightbulbs swinging from them. There were primitive structures scattered about; many were just canvas tents with open sides. It reminded me of the army camp in the television show "M*A*S*H," which I had once watched at Papa's house. Our truck pulled sluggishly into an opening a few yards from a large, open-sided tent and rolled to a stop. I looked around and saw only dark green military tents interspersed with wood huts. Even at that hour of the night, I could tell there was nothing reminiscent of the life I had known. I heard loud pronouncements over a broadcasting system and vaguely recognized Father's voice. Here, as in the capital, the people seemed different. They looked intense, distraught, perhaps tormented. No one smiled at us as we piled out of the truck.

Our excitement dissipated as some of our Jonestown brethren approached. I could see in their eyes that they had lost hope. Without news from the outside world from the families they had left behind, they now believed that they had been forgotten. Expectant faces hovered around us, hungry for a connection, for news of their loved ones, news that had been taken away from us and would perhaps never arrive. I wanted to run.

We were directed to a tented area where the "Greeting Committee" awaited us. Our trunks and bags were placed upon their examination tables. There was no time to talk to the hopeful onlookers. The Greeting Committee were a very busy few. Addressing each newcomer with "Welcome to Jonestown," they quickly inspected, questioned, examined, and confiscated most everything from our luggage. As I stood in line waiting to have my trunk opened and examined, fear crashed down upon me. What would this little committee report about me when they saw the things I'd packed?

I could just hear it, "Oh, you wouldn't believe the capitalistic things she packed, Father. Lace panties, a negligee . . . She isn't prepared to come here and work. Her head is right up there in them love clouds!" As my trunk was unlocked, opened, and each item removed, I stood by and pretended not to care. If only I had known we'd be searched. The nightie I had spent hours shopping for and dreamed I'd wear on my first night with Mark was now being held up by disapproving hands. The committee removed my shoes, shirts, panties, socks, toothpaste, soap, and body lotion, and handed me just four T-shirts, four pairs of socks, a toothbrush, toothpaste, four pairs of undies, and a bar of soap. Nobody dared ask where their things were going. We would soon learn that what we had packed for a lifetime in the Promised Land would now be the property of the commune, stored in a shed and available only through requisition forms and proof of need. Especially precious items were set aside in case Father needed them. I watched as Mama's trunk was searched and emptied of her cancer pain medications, Percodan and Vicodin, and incorrectly presumed that they were being set aside for the medical unit. Much later I would see my mother's pain medications on the bookshelf in Father's house with the many other prescription drugs taken from Temple members. Then I caught a glimpse of the first of several precious acts of treason when an elderly black committee member who knew Mama pushed a bottle of Paregoric, the painkiller Mama needed, back deep inside my mother's belongings.

As we were systematically stripped of our previous identities, never to be allowed private possession or autonomous thought again, the lost souls watched. Later on I, too, would feel the excitement when the siren sounded to announce the new arrivals. It was a strange rush to watch these outsiders, these newcomers, pull into the camp and realize they'd been desperately wrong. We felt vindicated when we saw other new arrivals' faces fall. But after trying it once, I never wanted to make contact with new arrivals again. It was too painful to look into their faces as they searched ours, mine, for silent reassurance, for hope.

Once you were in, it didn't take long to learn the ropes: keep your head down and don't talk unless it's absolutely necessary. For each person showing weakness by speaking of his or her fears, another would become more trusted for reporting it. There were no enduring friendships—everyone soon learned that it was just too dangerous to run the risk of confrontation or public beating and not being trusted. No, it was best to write everyone off and keep to yourself, the only place one could dream, hope, and plan, and not get reported.

With my meager armful of belongings, I trudged down the hill from the Pavilion behind my guide, past the medical unit to the right and into my assigned cabin. The one-room cabin was dingy and dark, but I could make out twelve bunk beds stacked closely together. I felt drained and vacant as I bent down and dropped my things on the lower bunk next to the door, filled with swarming mosquitoes. I wondered where Mama had been escorted off to. I hoped they had arranged for quarters near or with Lynetta.

I nodded at faces peering down at me from the upper bunks. I recognized women who were once friends. Now, they were the knowledgeable ones, and I a dubious intruder. There was an odd look in their eyes as they watched to see if they detected a negative reaction from me. How's she taking this? they probably wondered. I acted glad to see them: "At last, I made it!" Then I walked back out of the cabin. It must have been 3 A.M., yet the compound was bustling with activity. Didn't they ever rest? Jim's voice was booming over the loudspeaker and as I stood there listening to his words, observing and being observed, I felt myself emptying, becoming only a shell of a human being.

I made my way to the radio room, where I knew Father was communicating, as he did every night, with Teresa in the United States. I was worried that Sharon had reported more unkind remarks about me over the radio and I had to show Jim that I continued to respect him. My arrival would not be complete until he peered into my eyes to see if I had remained a believer.

I greeted him and his most trusted disciples. Jim had a bloated look about his face and nervously licked at his dry lips. Maria was even thinner than the last time I had seen her and looked as agitated. She barely glanced at me as I stood outside their den of information. I smiled anxiously and she continued in a conversation I seemed to have interrupted. Annie was talking to Carolyn and stopped to nod, as did Carolyn.

As I stood there facing Father, cloaking my fears with adulation and obedient respect, wondering what they were thinking or had been told about me, a hard-shelled black flying beetle, half the size of my fist, landed on my shoulder. Fear is a dangerous weakness in a cloistered society. It means that you could potentially betray your comrades and the entire community. I was petrified but I knew that I couldn't show it. The beetle began to crawl from my shoulder, up my neck and into my hair. My muscles stiffened, I could feel cramping in my legs as I tried to control my panic. The heavy silence in the room told me to remain still. No one made an effort to help me, to remove the vile, six-legged intruder. My intuition told me that everything was at stake. I had to control my fear, my hatred, and loathing of Father at any cost. Become the chameleon and survive, I warned myself.

Jim was watching me closely, trying to decipher whether I had become more distant or less trustworthy since my separation from him and the inner circle. Would he allow me further separation and independence? Would his designated few accept me back into the fold? I had to be tested. The beetle was entangled in my locks, pulling strands of my hair as its hairy, ugly legs struggled to free themselves. I shuddered uncontrollably. Jim began to laugh. Suddenly, the tension in the air subsided and the others began to giggle with relief. Carolyn walked over to me, removed the repulsive creature, and smiled. I thought I saw sorrow in her eyes.

"Debbie, you continue to amaze me and make me laugh," said my leader. I had passed this test but I knew that more trials were to come before I would be allowed back into the fold of the trusted few.

When I finally lay down on my bunk, I covered my head with my pillow. Jim's voice was still being broadcast over the encampment, so that each shift, day and night, could receive "the Word," and stay focused. Eventually, I fell into a restless sleep.

11
Hints of Madness

On December 15, 1977, my first day in "Paradise," I was awakened at five-thirty in the morning and told to get up. While I was trying to remember where I was, Shanda, my Offering Room buddy, sat on the bunk across from me and explained that I had been chosen, along with a few others, to represent our community at a very important meeting of the People's National Congress (PNC), in Port Kaituma. The PNC was the ruling party of Guyana and their black Prime Minister, Forbes Burhnam, was expected at the meeting. Jim wanted an interracial contingent there to represent his interests in Jonestown.

I pulled myself out from under the rough wool covers, confused that I had to leave again when I had barely arrived.

"Listen, you're lucky you're getting out today," Shanda urged me. "This doesn't happen often. I know you're tired from the river trip, but that ain't nothing compared to . . ."

Shanda had grown three inches taller in the last eight months since leaving the States. Her brown skin was now a beautiful copper and her once short Afro was now full. I had missed her and wished we could just sit on my bed and catch up with our lives.

"Compared to what?" I asked.

She looked around quickly, to make sure no one was in the hut, then hugged me.

"I'm getting you something nice to wear from the PR wardrobe," she said. "Carolyn's looking for something small enough to fit you . . . This is an important occasion and we need to look our best."

"Compared to what?" I insisted. "Shanda, tell me, please."

"Field work, it's intense. Plus now with all the people here we're looking for more food . . . You'll get used to it . . . It's different now, so crowded."

"But everyone knew we were coming . . ."

"Yeah, but not so fast . . .

"Some weeks, a hundred people were shipped in." She leaned closer and whispered, "When I first got here, it was wonderful. But when everyone started showing up at once . . . We just didn't have lodging, latrines, food . . ."

"I don't understand. . . . With that many people, couldn't everything have been done real fast?"

She looked around again nervously. "We just weren't ready, Deb. That's why so many folks are living in them crowded and cramped huge dorms. It's the only way to accommodate everyone. Now, if you want to live in a small cottage . . . like maybe two other couples, you have to go through the Relationship Committee."

"Relationship . . . ?"

"You'll see. The rules are: If you want to live with a man it has to be reviewed and approved first. There's a trial period, sort a like dating for three months. . . . Anyway, I'll tell you later, it's getting late. . . . I'll see you on the truck . . ."

She bolted from the room before I could ask another question. It was strange, I thought. I'd been marched down here into this cramped bunkhouse after Jim's talking so much about my living with Mark. But now was not the time to ponder these things.

I tried to orient myself. Where was my cabin in relation to the radio room, the Pavilion, the kitchens, the bath? I needed to wash. Shanda appeared in the door again, tossed me an off-white linen jumpsuit, waved, and disappeared.

I couldn't remember if I had seen showers on my way to the cabin the night before. Shanda had left so fast I didn't have a chance to ask. She seemed so rushed and nervous. Looking around the room to see if any one was there before hugging me, running out of the room to get my outfit before I could ask her questions. How come she was in so much of the know? Her status here had changed. She seemed to be working as an assistant to Carolyn.

I poked my head out of the doorway to ask the senior walking by for directions to the bathrooms. I needed to get the dried saltwater off my skin and out of my hair. Mary, the woman I had always stayed with in Los Angeles, gave a start and grabbed my arm. Her beautiful brown face was thinner than I had remembered and her surprised smile seemed tired. She came very close to talk to me and began to whisper.

"Honey, there ain't no showers in the morning." Her hand reached out and cupped my cheek. "It's good to see you again, baby . . . My shift just ended and I'm plum worn out . . . I'm going to my dorm to sleep, but I'll see you again tonight in the food line . . . Your mama's here too . . . thought I saw her this morning."

"We got here about midnight."

"Well, baby, it ain't what any of us expected. Some of the originals say it was nice 'fore Father come down here and start all his yellin' and stuff. I don't know . . . I'm just a soldier, darling . . . trying to do the best I can. It's tough adjustin', after living alone and havin' my own place . . . but, it's for the children, for socialism, and we won't be hounded like animals here."

She gave me an apologetic smile.

"No, darlin', ain't gonna be easy . . . but I'll keep an eye out for your mama, she was good to me back home . . . Dahlia, too, she works the kitchens like me, 'cept she's on days. You saw her last night. She the one go through your mama's belongings . . ." She smiled at me knowingly. I felt a quiet defiance in her voice. Then she looked about, kissed my cheek, and hurried away, alone and worn out. I watched her disappear into a large building behind the Pavilion, which had to be her dorm.

The long ride back out of the encampment to Port Kaituma was filled with disturbing images and disquieting sensations. Groups of people were working in the fields, bandannas on their heads, sweat glistening on their arms. They reminded me of pictures I'd seen of poor Mexican migrant workers, bent over, diligently toiling over their section of plants. I was amazed that no one looked up as we passed and nobody from our truck yelled a greeting or waved to anyone they recognized. I turned to Shanda to ask why, but she was looking straight ahead, like everyone else on the truck, ignoring the laborers in the field. There seemed to be a detached and apathetic atmosphere among the residents. I felt an absence of camaraderie and warmth. Father had talked so much about the closeness of those who lived in the Promised Land, but what I observed so far was that everyone was careful, reticent, and almost afraid to make connections. There was no giggling and small talk during the long ride; everyone seemed on edge and guarded. Further down the Jonestown road we passed another work crew. Women and men were laboring close to the road. A boy seemed to be in pain, moving and stretching his back as if he had a cramp, yet he never ceased his pace, his sickle continuing its methodical whoosh back and forth through the undergrowth.

Shanda was watching me. "They're getting ready for a burn," she explained. "We clear the land as best we can, then it's burnt so we can plant."

"Better cover your face on those days," piped a young boy nearby. "It's coughing smoky."

I wondered if I would be able to do that sort of hard labor. The work certainly was more arduous than anything I had ever done. I wondered who was chosen to be a field worker and who was capable of such oppressive work.

"Everyone pulls this duty in the beginning," Shanda explained, " 'less of course you're too old and sick. Then you just wait . . ."

"For what?"

"For the evening agricultural meetings. Jeez," she sighed, "sometimes they last till two in the morning . . . Or socialist classes . . . Then there are other jobs you can be assigned to once you've proved yourself. . . . There's kitchen, cookin', infants . . . You'll see."

Mary and Dahlia, I already knew, worked in the kitchens. Carolyn and Maria seemed occupied in the radio room. I had seen a group of seniors sitting at a long table doing something with burlap sacks, perhaps mending them. So far I hadn't seen anyone sitting on a porch. In fact, I had not seen a porch. There also wasn't any grass, and I hadn't noticed any children running and laughing as I had imagined. The Promised Land seemed more like a work camp.

It felt odd being transported back out and away from the compound in my pretty linen outfit, while the others toiled in the hot morning sun. I wondered if I was receiving a new dispensation here. Perhaps I was trusted after all.

Ahead of us, I spied a group of young people, some clearly teenagers, running down the Jonestown road. I knew some of them, but they, too, did not look at us as we passed. Then I saw they were being herded like animals by someone in army fatigues who was carrying a rifle, and a chill seeped into my soul.

"What's that about?" I whispered to Shanda.

She patted my arm.

"Learning Crew . . . punishment for not following orders, complaining, or not working fast enough." She spoke close to my ear, the noise of the truck covering her voice. "They are not allowed to speak to us or among themselves. They eat separately, sleep in a special 'punishment' dorm, and they must do their work double time . . . so they run, as you can see, to each worksite and then work it doubletime."

"They're guarded," I whispered in shock. "He's got a . . ."

"Everyone's guarded, Debs. There's no difference here. Father says it's to protect us from invasion. Most times you can't see them though. Anyway, it's not only the guards that watch, your own crewmates are told they must report on anyone not working as hard as the others."

I stared at her in disbelief.

"It works like this . . . Everyone is told they are responsible for reporting on their crewmates. So, if someone writes up an incident and no one else on the crew reports it, all of you will go on the Learning Crew. It's a guarantee that everyone writes everything up at the end of each day."

"What offenses are worthy of reporting? Laughing, whispering, itching your leg . . ."

"Debbie," she frowned. "You can't think in that vein anymore . . . it doesn't help. It's just different here. Like, no one is allowed to slack in their work; it's a sign of laziness and those that are lazy can become traitors, that's infraction number one. You remember this from our Mao classes, don't you? Anyway, if you've forgotten, you'll relearn it now. The Learning Crew is for the reeducation of those who have fallen into self-pity and other capitalistic traits."

"Shanda, those guys on the Learning Crew looked like a group of prisoners on a chain gang. It's really scary . . ."

"Sshhh . . ." Her voice lowered even more. "Yeah, you better figure the ropes real quick. . . . This ain't the Offering Room, it isn't anything like the life we knew in the city. And Father says that's how it has to be till we are all equal in our understanding of Leninism. Don't worry, you'll fall into step soon enough."

I wanted to ask her a million questions. But she had resolutely turned away for our safety. She knew we had already been whispering for too long.

As we passed through the gates and out of Jonestown, I noticed another armed guard patrolling our exit and I wished I hadn't come on this day trip. I wanted to be near Mama. I wanted to go back inside and find her, make sure she was comfortable, and hold her safely in my arms. She hadn't come here to be guarded. Then I remembered she was visiting with Lynetta Jones and I felt relieved.

As long as she had her good friend here I could concentrate on gathering my strength and, as Shanda said, "figure the ropes."

The meeting at the PNC went smoothly. We soundly applauded Guyana's Prime Minister when he finished his speech. As he walked over to talk to us, I noticed how tall he was. He was a princely looking gentleman. I listened intently as Lee, our spokesman, explained our agricultural project in Jonestown and the need for security. I was intrigued when I heard him talk about the Six-Day Siege, some famous socialist event, I imagined. I would need to ask; it might come up on a socialism test back at Jonestown. I had already been informed of the Marxist socialism classes on Tuesday and Thursday nights with tests on Sundays.

Lee was as tall as the Prime Minister and just as good-looking, I thought. I was impressed with how confidently he spoke with the dignitary, explaining our outreach program for the Amerindians. With his skin even blacker from the South American sun, his dark hair now streaked with auburn highlights, his voice deep with a hint of a smile in its resonance, Lee was the handsomest man in the Temple. In Ukiah and San Francisco, he had played important leadership roles, always working with the youth group and the college students. He was firm, but the most understanding counselor. When someone was being confronted he wouldn't join in just to cause harm. His comments were always constructive. When he monitored the Offering Room of which I was head, he'd feel comfortable laughing at someone's joke instead of moralizing. He'd even chuckle at my dramatic renditions of my former boarding school headmistress. I had a connection with Lee but, of course, friendships and camaraderie that weren't strictly in the context of socialist principles were frowned upon.

We followed the Prime Minister over to the festivities. The Jonestown dance troupe was performing to a rhythmic beat. They were dressed in colorful Caribbean attire to show how well we had assimilated into the Guyanese culture. They were enjoying themselves and their enthusiasm made me forget the disturbing things I had heard and seen only a couple of hours before. I joined the diverse groups of Jonestown children who had also been dressed up and sent to Port Kaituma to show off our mix of ages and nationalities. I looked around at the village. It was a rustic port with a rickety dock, and I could see that there were probably no outdoor markets here. Perhaps thirty Amerindians lived at the river's edge under scattered thatched-roofed huts. Wooden canoes were sticking out from their abodes and partially clothed children played in the dirt. I realized the Prime Minister must have come here just for us.

There were refreshments on a table under a narrow thatched roof. Holding the hand of a seven-year-old Jonestown boy, I grabbed two cups of soda and looked for a shady place for us to sit. He grimaced as he tasted the liquid. I asked for a sip and found that I had accidentally grabbed beers. Thinking it rude to take my drink back to the table or to throw it away, I dutifully sipped from both cups and the child went back to find something more to his liking.

On the ride back into Jonestown that evening I asked Shanda about socialism classes and which famous Six-Day Siege they were studying. She looked at me suspiciously.

"You don't know about it? When Angela Davis came on the radio from the States and tried to help us?"

"No, Shanda," I said. "I'm talking about an event during the Russian Revolution."

"Girl, where have you been? It was here, Debbie. We almost died. Grace and Tim Stoen instigated it. They tried to get John-John back from Father. They hired mercenaries to attack us. Father had us paint our faces black with coal and circle the camp with machetes and sickles to stop them. We stayed out there for six days and nights. We even ate and slept out there. Father said they would kidnap and torture the children. It was awful. It's frightening what the CIA is trying to do to us. They want to invade and kill us. Father says that they'll try again, too. We've had several attacks. Father calls them White Nights, since it is white men who are trying to ruin our project here. Weren't you in the meeting in San Francisco when Angela Davis spoke to us? She said she understood our plight. . . . She agreed that there was a conspiracy against us and against all people who strive for change."

I looked into Shanda's eyes. I wasn't sure if I was more scared for her or for myself. She suddenly looked different to me. Since living here she had faced death and known fear of invasion. She wasn't an innocent teenager anymore. She was one of the brethren, one of the chosen, and she carried the weight of her tenuous existence upon her shoulders.

What was she telling me, exactly? It dawned on me she had just explained the six days of hysteria that I had taken so lightly while my focus was only on Mama. What had happened in the last few months to our Promised Land? This land was to be our final destination, utopia, far from the insanity of the world we had just escaped. Mama wasn't strong enough to grab a machete and fight on the front lines. She was very sick and needed a lot of rest and care. This place was supposed to be an island of peace and harmony, of walks with friends, discussion groups, having children, and living unfettered from the carnage of capitalism.

"Shanda . . ." I turned to face her while the truck entered back through the gate and into our guarded Jonestown compound. "How did Lynetta do in the siege? Was she on the front lines too?"

"Lynetta?" she asked. Her mouth twisted into disbelief. "Didn't you know? Lynetta died a while ago. She'd been ill a long time. Jim took it real hard; you know how no one is supposed to die in his aura."

My knees gave in. I sat down, not caring what happened to the linen outfit. Shanda put her hand on mine.

"You didn't know? Oh God, it was kept from you . . . and Lisa was so close to her." She seemed to shudder.

I sat very still, afraid that if I moved I might retch. Why . . . ? Who had decided Mama and I shouldn't know about Lynetta? Mama had dreamed about this friendship, it had consoled her on lonely days in the United States. And now she had no close friends . . . only me. I heard the truck slow and cut its engine. We were back in the Promised Land. I got up as if in a trance and watched the field workers marching in from their long day in the sun, machetes with hoes under their dirt-stained arms. They were heading to the food line, which must already have been about a hundred people deep. Why, I screamed inside my head, why had we been deceived about Lynetta? Feeling betrayed, lied to, used, I stepped down from the flatbed truck, looked around at the prison camp, and wondered when and where I had missed the cues.

Shortly after our entourage returned to Jonestown, Father was on the loudspeaker.

"I understand some counterrevolutionary took a drink of beer at the PNC meeting. I want every one of you to come up to the radio room and tell me why you did it."

My first reaction was denial but I realized immediately that someone must have already reported me. I knew that I had better confess before I got into worse trouble. I went to the radio room and found Father alone.

"Father, it was me that drank the beer." I explained what happened with the young boy and volunteered to put myself on the Learning Crew.

"Thank you for your honesty, darlin'. I am glad that you came forward to confess. But since you have just arrived and have not yet adjusted to our ways here, I will forgive you this time."

I was relieved Father had understood and been so loving. However, as soon as I had returned to my cabin to change, Father was again on the loudspeaker.

"The counterrevolutionary who drank the beer has still not come forward! I want everybody who went to Port Kaituma to report to the radio room at once."

I felt anxious, but realized he must be after someone else. I made my way back to the radio room. Jim was already in the midst of a tirade against drinking. He spoke on and on. My legs were sore and I wanted to change my clothes. He began to yell: "Come forward and admit it to the People! Acknowledge your weaknesses and disgrace! You know who you are, this is not the first time . . ."

I continued to wait, hoping the real counterrevolutionary would show his face. Poor sod, I thought, glad I had been exonerated from any suspicions. The diatribe continued for another five minutes when a sickeningly familiar feeling rose up in me. I was suddenly aware of whom he was talking to. Weak with fear, I stepped forward.

"Good of you to come forward, although you are not the only one who should be standing here. What do you think your punishment should be?" he asked softly.

"I think I should be put on the Learning Crew," I said sincerely.

"This is only your first day. . . . It is not an infraction worthy of reeducation. Okay everyone." Father looked up at the hundreds of people encirling the radio room. "Debbie has learned that there are no secrets in Jonestown. Dismissed. . . . Eat your dinner and enjoy the rest of your evening. There will be no socialism class tonight. I want all my children to rest."

I saw people walking away shaking their heads, angry that I had waited so long to come clean. They were hungry and now had to recue for the line, having lost their places. I lowered my eyes. Shanda walked past me and gently stepped on my toe in support of my pain. I wanted to cry and knew that it was all a ploy to show me, the outsider, the newcomer, that I was an untrustworthy heathen. I was catching on too slowly, I thought. I would have to prove myself all over again, for I was now wholly despised. When there were no more onlookers, Father motioned for me to sit next to him on the radio room step. There seemed to be an odd sour odor seeping from his skin. As he lowered his sunglasses I noticed that his once soft and serene eyes were now reddened and looked untamed.

"Darling, it wasn't you I was trying to bring out. You were only trying to help the child. I know this. I am proud that you were courageous enough to step forward. You have proved once more you are willing to take the heat for your mistakes. Go on along to dinner now and visit with Lisa. You will be pleased to find she is in the nicest cottage here. I arranged for her to use Marceline's place until we can build her one of her own. One other thing, Sharon tells me the Cuban doctor has made several visits to the house hoping to see you. He even left a letter. You have served us well."

"Thank you, Father!" I replied respectfully. I was confused by the wildly contradictory tones he was taking with me, but I didn't want him to see how troubled I felt. He squeezed my shoulder as I left. The long dinner line already reached past the kitchens, the latrine, and down the dusty Jonestown road.

It had been a long day and I hadn't seen Mama. She was the only person I wanted to be with just then. I knew her cottage was situated behind the kitchen huts and I concentrated on not looking too eager to find her, but my feelings of desperation were taking over my stride. Jonestown was not what I had anticipated. Everyone was looked at with suspicion, as if we ourselves were the enemy. I wanted to crawl into Mama's lap, feel her arms around me, and have her tell me it was all just a bad dream, I could wake up now.

I skipped up her stairs, opened her screen door, and was thankful that Mama's house actually had a veranda. Mama was standing at her window when I bolted in.

"Honey, I thought you'd be in the food line."

I walked over and hugged her, wanting to apologize, wishing I hadn't been the one to convince her how wonderful Jonestown would be. Her space was just one room made of dark wood. It was small, but roomy in comparison to my cramped quarters.

"Darling, I learned about Lynetta this afternoon." When she saw in my eyes that I knew, she smiled bravely. "I guess Father believed it was best to keep it a secret. I wonder if it would have altered my decisions in any way."

I began to tremble, trying in vain not to cry. Mama put her arms around me and held me tight.

"I know, darling . . . I know . . ." She held me and patted my back until I had calmed down. "But we have our own secret." She smiled and opened a handkerchief, setting a hard-boiled egg on her trunk. "The seniors eat first. And I am to be given an egg a day, because of my weakened condition." She cracked it with her knuckle and began to peel it. I wiped my eyes and forced myself to smile at her. She took a tiny bite and handed it to me.

"I love you, darling . . . I'll be fine." Then she held up her hand as if she had a wineglass in it. "To our health, and the wine we had in New York will remain our secret, alone."

When I left Mama's cottage I walked through our encampment. There were guards, just teenagers, marching around with guns. There were lookout posts with guards on them. Faces of people I had known and joked with now looked frightened. Few made eye contact with me. Everyone seemed to be afraid of everyone else.

I had joined the food line when Father's voice came over the loudspeaker again.

"I've assigned a few of you to act as if they want to leave. Anyone observing their odd behavior or overhearing them speaking disloyally is required to report these conversations to me immediately. This is a test of loyalty. Those who report will be rewarded."

Mary grimaced at the announcement and deposited a heap of smelly rice on my plate. "Get used to it, baby . . ." She smiled apologetically. I looked for a spare seat at one of the crowded tables. I spied Mark, his back to me, talking with Lee, but I no longer felt comfortable having an idle chat with someone Father knew I had wanted to live with. I believed it was best to keep my distance for now. I turned, saw Annie finishing up, and sat next to her.

"It's only hard at first," she said without glancing up. "Next time remember it's safer to stand and take the blame rather than wait and hope the fury will pass."

I looked at her in wonder. "You sound like our tenth-grade hero, Siddartha."

"I remember you reading that stuff every night. And all your poetry. He's not been right since Lynetta passed. I've been dispensing quite a bit of sedatives to him for his grief."

I was bewildered that she was talking this way to me. So honest and unencumbered with fear.

"It will get better." She raised her head and looked at me sadly. "This is the worst he's been, but things will look up soon. Good to have you with us again. You ought to come down to the house and visit sometime. The boys would love your headmistress impersonations. They don't laugh much anymore." She quickly squeezed my hand under the table. "Time for the night shift. Gotta put Kimo and John-John to bed. I've missed you." She rose up and took her plate to the rinsing station.

When I arrived at my own cabin I was pleased to find no one there. I undressed and climbed into bed. I felt grateful that Shanda and Annie had talked to me. Things were perhaps not all that bad. The overcrowding was just a timing problem. I thought about my illusions of how life would be here and realized I would have to readjust to the reality of it. Although I had dreamed of living with Mark, I now knew that it was out of the question. I would have to sacrifice Mark, who had never really been mine anyway. His loyalties were to Father and to Jonestown, not to me. I thought about Annie's remarks. She had missed me and wanted me to make the little boys laugh. I had already made Father laugh. And Mama had seemed so strong and brave, bearing the disappointment over the loss of her friend Lynetta. Things would be better . . . as Annie predicted. This was just a bad phase for Father. I needed to be understanding and concentrate on earning his trust again.

I was weak with exhaustion, but my thoughts raced on. And suddenly I realized why it was that those in the capital had seemed so different from me. They had been initiated. They had lived here first.

It was early when I opened my eyes to a ghastly sound of cries and moans coming from deep inside the jungle. The sad wail came again and as a chorus joined in I realized it was the sound of the howler monkeys. I had heard them screaming out the night before and they had frightened me. I looked around my cramped cabin. It felt as if I had been here forever, and it was only my second full day in the Promised Land. I crawled out of my scratch wool covers and pulled my fingers through my hair. I was relieved there were no entangled bugs, but my foot felt hot and was throbbing. I was horrified to discover a multitude of swollen bumps on my toes and the side of my foot. Some of the welts were almost an inch across with tiny yellow globules in the center. As I stared at my new Jonestown acquisitions, they began to itch, faintly at first, but as I continued to stare, the sensation became an obsession. I dug my nails into them, scratching furiously. They itched even more. I tried to scratch past the itch to release the poison from my tissues. My hand was smeared with blood when I looked up to see Father standing at the door.

"Mosquitoes got you, did they?" he smiled. "You'll soon learn our new ways of life, little warrior." He turned and beckoned me out of the cabin where no one could hear us.

"Sharon has mentioned that she thinks you're too easily influenced by others. She felt the doctor incident was instigated by you, that you were infatuated with the young man. Is this so?"

I was shocked to be put on the spot so early in the morning. My mind was racing.

"I tried very hard to interest him in our projects," I defended myself. Then I made a quick move forward: "I'm not interested in having a relationship with a man. Not even Mark, really!"

"My, how you amaze me. And here I thought you wanted to settle down and live the perfect bourgeois fantasy life." His eyebrows were raised with adoring amusement. "I am glad to hear it actually. I was a little worried about you for a while there, but Carolyn and Annie said you were all right."

My heart beat faster with the hope that Annie might again be my ally. She must have said something good about our conversation.

"Annie is my nurse now, as you may know. And she takes care of John-John and Kimo in the evenings. Maria used to care for the boys, but she wants to be in the radio room at night too. I'm a little concerned, as she also runs the morning shift between here and the capital. She's making herself sick with all the things she's involved with."

"She isn't herself," I nodded in agreement.

"What?" His voice was rising. "I don't understand what goes on between the two of you. She contends you're too attached to Lisa and Teresa, which brings me to my next point." He cleared his throat. "Sharon said you were defensive of Teresa when she asked you a question about radio transmissions when you first arrived in Georgetown. I know that you would do nothing improper, but Teresa has had to travel a great deal and been away from us for months at a time. She has occasionally made comments which indicate that she gets confused. Have you any concerns about her? You know I love her deeply and don't want any harm to come to her. Think about it. I know of two incidents when the two of you were together and she acted defiantly. Include them when you write up your thoughts for me." He leaned over and kissed my forehead.

"Yes, Father," I exhaled.

What incidents? I thought frantically. Teresa loved the Cause. She believed in it fiercely. I tried to think what Father could be speaking of. There had been only one time when she had acted out of character—when she told me in Switzerland to be careful because I talked in my sleep. That was all. Father surely couldn't know that. No, she wouldn't have told him. If she had, he would have called me on it. Ah! There was that night when I came to the radio room after the long day at the hospital. She had been upset with Father when he requested Bibles. Teresa had been frantic that night. She had fretted and argued and pretended not to understand him or the codes. I had wondered why she was acting so erratically. Was that the incident he expected me to write up? Teresa's reluctance to send guns?

Father squeezed my shoulder and added, "Be thorough in your recollections . . ." Then he took a deep breath. "It's important to me that you and Maria work out your misunderstanding. It troubles Carolyn as well. I believe it's some ridiculous jealousy the two of you have over Carolyn. Perhaps it's because Carolyn was your sister-in-law first and then became Maria's surrogate mother."

I nodded. I didn't care. My foot itched.

"And now you better find your work crew. They've lined up for breakfast."

I hurried to put on my boots. I would do as I was commanded. Being trusted again was imperative for my own survival. I would have to be thorough in my recollections. My heart sank. This was a harder test than I had had in a long time. Father knew something and I had better not lie. Teresa would be able to defend herself, disagree with my assessment. Little did I know at that point what the consequences of my betrayal of Teresa would be. Because of me, her loyalty would be questioned for months and she would risk the severest punishments after my defection when she was ordered into Jonestown to face Father. Even though Teresa escaped with her life, she refused to ever see or talk to me again.

I felt I had no choice. A growing sense of danger was clouding my conscience and my vision. All I could see was that I was in jeopardy of losing everything I had gained and worked so hard to achieve in the last six and a half years. All I knew was that I had to make every effort, give everything, sacrifice everything, to avert a disaster that was surely pending.

I ran toward the breakfast line, feeling miserable. And then the nauseous smells from the kitchens assaulted me. What was that strange odor in our food?

I knew from the schedule that I was to work the sugarcane patch along with several others, and looked around to find my work crew leader.

"Yo, Debs, over here!" Lee called to me from way down the food queue.

I walked as delicately as possible to keep the itch demons at bay. "I'm really not hungry, Lee. The smell . . ."

"Listen, girl. The work's hard. You need to eat. You'll get used to the smell. It's iodine and some other stuff to protect us from the various jungle plagues." His head was covered with a red bandanna, pulled tight and tied in back.

My foot felt hot, like a flame burning into my flesh.

"Hey, what's wrong?"

I looked up, miserable. Lee rubbed my head as if shining an apple.

"Save our places," he told the guy in line behind us and pushed me out just a few feet from the others. "Who do ya think you're talkin' to, Debs? I know how yer feelin'. I been there, too. You'll get over it. You gotta drink lots and eat as much grub as you can if you want to make it. Then, if you act cool, work hard, an' don't complain, you'll be fine." He gave me a mighty pat on my back, spun around, and reentered the food line.

I stood there, pushing back the tears, telling myself that I could do it. I pressed the heel of my boot onto the top of my other foot to briefly deaden the overwhelming itching. Then I joined him in line.

"You tellin' me you got bites on your feet, too?" Lee laughed with understanding. "Didn't anyone tell you to keep your skin covered at night?" He shook his head in disbelief. "They get ya on the soles of your feet, too?" His eyes flashed a twinkle and I realized that my predicament could be worse.

The day was too new to be warm, but there were early morning bugs already up and casing the joint. I reached the head of the line and received a thick slice of cassava bread with brown syrup on it. I gave a wan smile, coughed a quick thanks, and trudged over to Lee and my new workmates. Lee was standing over the table, shoveling spoonfuls of rice and syrup into his mouth. He seemed completely unaware of the large reddish-brown insects that swarmed up as I arrived. Two out-of-control beetles dive-bombed into my breakfast and got stuck in the syrup. No one seemed to notice, much less care.

I stared aghast at the duo standing on my bread as if on a runway, slightly off balance, flapping their wings, trying to take flight, but unable to free their legs from the sweet glue. I watched them struggle, sickened by their quiet commotion, as they battled for their freedom. They continued to fight, working themselves even deeper into the thick brown sauce.

I looked around for a garbage container to throw out my bread, but Lee was ever watchful.

"We don't waste food here. It takes too long to find it, plant it, grow it, then cook it. Just wait till the bugs get tired, then pick them out."

"Pick them out?" I could barely look at them much less touch one. "Lee, I'm not hungry." I extended my plate toward him. "Here, you eat it." Both my intruders were now still.

"They're dead, girl. Flick 'em off . . ."

I hated bugs, dead or alive. They had probably defecated into my syrup, I thought.

"Lee, *Please?*"

He snatched my plate, rolled his eyes, and ate the bread and syrup, beetle-doo and all.

"Mmmm, good cassava bread." He grinned. "Life ain't gonna be as easy for you here," he exhaled.

So far it hadn't been, but I was only going to be there for two months. I could handle it for that long. I was there just until I got Mom settled in, then I'd be going back to the States to help close down the California operations and transfer the remaining funds and folks to Jonestown.

My forehead was wet with sweat as we walked the few miles down a dusty jungle road to the sugarcane field. I was thirsty and my mouth felt like a sand dune. I thought about Lee's words. I was completely unaccustomed to hard labor. My experiences in our all-night meetings in the States seemed tame by comparison. It was 8 A.M. and I was already puffing and sweating from our hike. We would not stop until 6 P.M. and we had many more hours to go before our lunch break.

As my crewmates bent down to pull at something near the sugarcane roots, I tried to imitate their movements. I couldn't identify what they were doing and I couldn't think. My thoughts were too busy with fantasies of sucking moist, wet, dripping sweet sugarcane.

"Phew, I guess you didn't know you could sweat like this, huh?" Matt, a former heroin addict from Chicago, looked over at me, his face dripping with perspiration, his T-shirt wrapped around his blond hair like a turban. "Girl, you ain't never worked in dirt 'fore now. Guess you didn't get no gardening lessons in finishing school?"

Embarrassed, I shook my head. The hardest work I'd done recently was trying not to get my passport stamped by the Swiss airport officials when I entered and left Zurich. I wondered why, with millions in a Swiss bank account, we were struggling in the rain forest, hot, thirsty, and foraging for food.

"I should have worn deodorant."

"Oh no, you shouldn't," Matt bellowed. "Every insect here would swarm you. Sweetness lures 'em from miles to suck your pretty-smellin' skin. You thought breakfast was awful, what if you'd whiffed of hibiscus?" He was wheezing with laughter as my other crewmates joined in.

"Okay, guys, let's get serious," Lee interrupted. "Guards are watching. Let's stay off the Learning Crew." I thought about the punishment I had almost sentenced myself to. How could one possibly do everything at double time, work even faster, run everywhere, keep separate, not talk or smile? I thought of Mao's cultural revolution. It was hard on the people at first, but over time they grew accustomed to their lives of selflessness. I had learned that this was the only way to grow altruistic. Monks in Tibet, priests in monasteries, nuns in convents, the citizens of Uncle Fidel's Cuba, they all gave up comforts and became selfless. It was a comfort to think that pain was necessary for the greater good of mankind.

Moving into the partial shade created by the sugarcane, I followed my crew as they worked on through the rushes, bending, looking, hunting. Pushing aside the thickly growing brown stalks, they hoed, pulled, dug. Lee instructed me which strands were food and which just weeds. Someone handed me a pair of muddy gloves and I learned through barks and laughs from Lee exactly what I was supposed to be doing. When we stopped to determine how much more work was needed, my clothes were drenched, my socks were wet, and I felt as though I had just crawled out of a heated swimming pool.

"Could I taste one of these?" My mouth began watering with the thought of splitting open a cane and sucking the sweet moistness. I might as well have asked someone if I could eat their scabs.

Matt growled, "The food here is to be shared with everyone. If you ever took a bite it would be considered stealing. You'd be severely punished and assigned to the Learning Crew."

"But why? We're thirsty and working hard."

"Give it up, them's the rules. One of the teens on another crew made that mistake and really got his butt kicked."

"What happened?"

"You'll find out soon enough." Lee turned back to his work.

"Didn't you bring a water thermos or is it still packed with your face cream and rose-water facial toner?" smirked Matt.

"I'm just here for a couple months, then I'm going back," I defended myself.

Lee closed his eyes and shook his head back and forth a few times. Drop it, guys, I could hear his gesture say.

"This is done, let's head over to Lorina's crew and help them clear."

My mouth was too dry to moisten my cracking lips. Why couldn't the truck drop off water containers? How come everyone was so afraid to ask? Why was no consideration given to the field hands?

Across the road, up a small embankment, Lorina's crew had just finished clearing an acre of land for a burn: downing trees, ripping out vines, then stepping onto the road to watch as the guards set fire to the debris. Burnings were supposed to level the harsh land and render it workable. Once the smoldering subsided, the thick black smoke fading into mustard-colored mist, the field crew trudged back in. The workers tied wet bandannas over their mouths and noses to alleviate the labored breathing that came with the hot, malodorous air. Hoisting tools upon their shoulders, they marked their work area and began to hoe and pick, turning and preparing the soil for the seeds and bulbs of indigenous plants. So far we had had little luck cultivating the ground for agriculture, I soon learned. The jungle had her own rules about what would and would not grow and had fought each of our clearings, discouraging our success, making our intrusion into her virgin land a hardship we would never overcome.

Turning away from the smoke, I followed Lee, Matt, and the others back out onto the road into the hot, draining sun. We made our way further down the road, away from Jonestown. It was the same road we had taken on the flatbed truck. The dust from our boots floated up and into our eyes and noses. My mouth was even drier now and we had at least another hour before lunch.

From the road, it was more apparent how tall the trees were. They towered hundreds of feet into the sky. I tried to calculate how long it had taken us to get this far and how much farther it would be to Port Kaituma. The entire ride on the flatbed truck must have been two hours. How long would it take to walk? Would it be possible to sneak out at night through the jungle? Calm down, I told myself, no need to worry. You're going back in seven weeks.

I soon discovered that assignments in the most distant fields were the best. Even though the work, clearing new acres, was usually harder, it was out of earshot of Father's continual amplified diatribes. But I quickly lost the hope that it might be possible to escape while out in the fields. The jungle was full of unknown threats. A few steps inside her depths could mean being lost forever. She was alive with underbrush, roots, vines, enormous insects, lizards, snakes, beetles, mosquitoes, spiders, and varmints. In this foreign and forbidding place it was impossible to have a sense of forward or backward. Everything looked the same—green, brown, and dense. I came to realize that the jungle green served as our prison bars, a barrier we couldn't penetrate.

Nevertheless, in these distant fields, far away from Father's manifestos, I found that I could breathe and think, even under the watchful eyes of the armed guards. I mused about the life I had turned my back on, the family I had grown distant from and missed: my big brother, the professor; Annalisa and her two little children; gentle Larry; and Papa, who I hoped hadn't forgotten me. I thought of Mama and her loneliness here without Lynetta. She had been so brave in her effort to quell my anxiety, but I had seen her disappointment. At least I could be thankful for the friendships of Mary and Dahlia and their sincere affection for "little Lisa."

In the coming weeks, I realized, I would have to hide my misery and exhaustion from Mama. I already felt desperately guilty and knew from my experience in the States that my sense of responsibility to her would gradually suffocate me if I didn't pull away. Even in those early days in Jonestown I was conniving and maneuvering, becoming hard and disconnecting from the only person who could possibly keep me from running for my life, Mama.

12
Dark Days—White Nights

It had been several weeks since our arrival and by now I was accustomed to the unusual smells in the food and drink. I was even unaffected by the rice weevils and other strange bugs we ingested daily. Now I, too, ate enormous mounds of rice covered in gravy.

Christmas had come and gone without fanfare and I had acclimated to this new life of physical labor and late night agricultural meetings. I knew I had been here for at least three weeks because I had taken and passed three socialism tests.

In spite of our isolation in the jungle, we knew everything that was happening all over the world because Father read us newspaper and magazine articles over the loudspeakers daily. He told us in detail how violent the United States had become and how his place in history, as a great leader, was being tarnished by the evil defectors in America. Whenever he read to us about the vicious actions being taken by our government against innocent people, I was relieved we lived here. I learned of a leader in Uganda named Idi Amin, who apparently was a great diplomat. Father said we should learn to emulate his "wild actions." He said that when people acted like "crazy niggers," the establishment would back off and leave them alone. He said this was how we would begin to act here, too. If we threatened various government agencies with killing ourselves or leaving the country in a mass exodus, we would get our way more easily. Everything, he said, was done for effect. He had to test how far he could and should push them. It never occurred to me that these tests one day would turn into ghastly reality.

I still worked the fields but had been reassigned to Lorina's crew as Lee had been pulled from the fields to oversee the construction of more housing. Father had announced an incentive program: On Sundays, the only day we had the late afternoon free, those people who wanted a relationship and had gone through the approval process, could begin to construct their own cabins. Within hours, the relationship list quadrupled. Mark came to me that same day and asked if I would like to live with him, but I had decided on my first day that I would not pursue this dangerous course. My excuse to him was that the Cause was more important to me than an egocentric relationship and, anyway, he was hardly ever in Jonestown. Although he had helped prepare the land and original buildings for our arrival, he was now becoming a licensed ship captain at Father's behest. Father had decided that we needed to purchase a larger boat for our next emigration, to a more friendly country. The Six-Day Siege had deeply affected and deformed his perception of our safety and there were discussions of our moving to Cuba or the Soviet Union. On a couple of occasions, when I visited the radio room to ask Carolyn a question, I overheard small talk about visiting the embassies of socialist countries in the capital. Mark seemed discouraged, and it was hard to let go of such an old dream, but my decision was made. When I needed the secret relief of a fantasy, I thought about the nice Cuban doctor.

Life was tough in the Promised Land. The physical labor during the day was grueling but it was nothing compared to the terror we experienced at night. Every night, someone was confronted. Every night, I was afraid I, or someone I was close to, would be next.

During one emergency meeting I was perched in my customary place near Jim's son Stephan, biting deeply into my cheek to stay awake, when I felt my head jerking backward.

Had the guards seen me? I began to breathe in slowly and deeply, and started my self-preservation mantra: Look alert! Stay awake! I bit harder, drawing blood, fighting sleep, fighting to keep my body erect. I knew how dangerous it was to be found inattentive or sleepy, but it was getting harder every night.

From somewhere in the crowded Pavilion came a rustling sound. Oh no! I thought. Someone's fallen from the bench. Someone's fallen asleep!

"Stand!" Father bellowed over the loudspeaker. "Are you not afraid? Do *you* believe that *you* are different from the rest of us? Speak up and explain yourself," he hissed.

Charlie, a sixty-year-old father of five, stood up, brushing the dirt from his pants. "Father, I'm sorry. I did not mean to—" He was cut off by shouting. Everyone was angry. Someone always had to do this. Now Jim was furious, and we were going to have to confront Charlie and everything would drag on even longer. But no wonder Father was mad. If we were attacked now, Charlie would be our weak link. We must be careful, ever watchful of the weak one. Falling asleep proved that your head was in the wrong place, which made you more susceptible to committing treason.

"So, you think falling asleep during an emergency meeting is easy? Let's see how you fare with this. Put the snake around his neck!" One of the guards carried a ten-foot boa constrictor's cage into the middle of the Pavilion and opened the door.

"No! Wait," Father yelled. "Get Charlie's son to do it. I want Nick to put the snake around his daddy's neck."

There was a chilled silence. Nick was one of the most trusted and well-like guards in the camp. Was Jim testing his loyalty?

"Oh God, please, Father, *no!* No, don't!" Charlie begged as Nick devoutly weighed his Father down with the massive serpent.

"Jim, please. It's just that the field work is—"

"Stop your sniveling," Father demanded.

"Shut up, man! You're an embarrassment," Nick muttered.

"What's that?" Father asked. "You ain't crying about this, are you, Nick?"

"Hell no, Father." Nick wiped at his eye. "The fuckin' snake's tongue scratched my cornea," he lied.

Jim chuckled into the microphone. "Why are all of you so quiet out there? Where's your indignation? I want you to scream out why you hate Charlie! Anyone too prissy to scream will find themselves up here with this snake when I'm done with Chuckie-boy."

"Why don't we put him in the Box, Father?" a frail voice from somewhere in the Pavilion called out.

" 'Cause we got Jeff in there. And he ain't comin' out for a while." Father looked around. "Who the hell asked that stupid question? Stand! Was you sleepin' in our last meetin' when Jeff was dragged off to the Box?"

"No, Father. I just thought maybe he'd been taken out by now," said the voice, becoming weaker with fear.

"What do I hear in your voice? Sorrow? Do you feel sorry for Jeff? He's an antirevolutionary. He'd turn on you in a second if the mercenaries came in right now. He's being punished for his refusal to stop daydreaming. Don't you remember?"

Suddenly there was nervous laughter near Father. A puddle was forming around Charlie and his pants were wet. Father's attention was successfully drawn away from another confrontation.

"Okay! Get the snake off him. His face is getting red." There was quiet commotion as three guards struggled to remove the constricting snake from Charlie's puffy neck.

"Now, let this be a warning to all of you," Father growled. "You will all be tested again and again, whether it be watching to see if you are working hard in the fields or by sending one of my spies out to pretend they want to leave. You better report them! 'Cause if you don't, you'll be up here, too, with a boa hanging from your neck and begging me for my forgiveness. That's right, even your son or daughter will be doing my bidding by testing your loyalty to the Cause. Don't let me down. Report the traitors to Carolyn or me."

My head jerked again and I was suddenly aware that Stephan was sitting close enough to me to keep me from falling sideways and Lew, another of Jim's sons, was behind me with his hand on my back, both of them ensuring that I wasn't next. I realized how lucky I was, and shuddered at the thought of being punished. The Learning Crew seemed bad enough, but I didn't know how I would survive the Box.

The Box was a small underground cubicle to which even children would be sentenced if they had thought or done something Father thought punishable. It was six by four feet, dark, hot, and claustrophobic. Poor Jeff had been kept inside for ten days. People kept there were given nothing but mush to eat and drink. There was also the Well, a punishment used especially for children. They would be taken to the Well in the dark of night, hung upside down by a rope around their ankles, and dunked into the water again and again while someone hidden inside the Well grabbed at them to scare them. The sins deserving such punishment included stealing food from the kitchen, expressing homesickness, failing a socialism exam, or even natural childish rebelliousness. Their screams were chilling but we had learned from the consequences of previous people's objections not to complain.

People who could not be reeducated and continued to voice unhappiness or dissatisfaction were put in the Medical Unit. There, they were involuntarily drugged into acquiescence and maintained in that state indefinitely. These punishments effectively silenced all outward dissent. I consoled myself by remembering that these punishments were nothing compared to being captured by the enemy and tortured to death.

Thankfully, I kept a good rapport with most people around me, with the guards and my crew, and I had the quiet protection of Lee, Stephan, and Lew. And Maria and I seemed to have ironed out our "chemistry problem." I stood in for her in the radio room one morning while waiting for my work crew to assemble. While she ran to the loo, I operated the radio, feeling quite confident in my repartee with Paula in the capital. I had heard and seen Teresa do enough of it to know the call signs and a few codes. After this, Maria occasionally asked me to stand in for her while she ran down and talked to Jim at their house. For some reason she seemed to feel less threatened, or perhaps less jealous, of me now that I labored in the fields like everyone else. I had begun to drop a lot of weight, my pants were baggy, my hands had calluses and blisters, and my boots were almost worn out. My curly locks had been buzz-cut since the incident with the beetle. Maria seemed concerned about me. She even became conciliatory and always brought me meat or a hard-boiled egg from Jim's personal fridge as a gift. I hoped she would tell Father who was holding down the fort while they discussed business.

One evening after my seventh socialism exam, I was beckoned over to the radio room by Carolyn. Maria was packing up her day communications notepads and talking to Jim. When she saw me, she smiled. I noticed that she had lost more weight.

"Grace will cause a siege . . ." Jim moaned, rubbing his hands together and looking sallow. Father usually stayed in the radio room all night with Carolyn, giving orders to Teresa in the States. Carolyn stepped outside the room and invited me to sit on the step with her.

"Debbie, I may need your help tonight," she said. "Annie has caught the bug that is going around. She may be too sick to care for John-John and Kimo for a while. Trouble's brewing . . . Jim's been anxious and unable to sleep for several days now."

"But I hear him—"

"Sshhh . . ." Carolyn put her finger to her mouth. "Tapes . . . He decides which ones should be replayed." She sighed. "He's taken ill, too, and during the day he rests, trying to catch up on his strength before another all-night session in here. He gets a lot of severe headaches and has a skin inflammation that needs medical attention."

I turned toward Jim, who was giving instructions to the States.

"Make sure the Concerned Relatives are watched," he yelled into the mike. "The Mertles, the Stoens, and every other SOB. Tail them and find out who they're in contact with! This could be the end if they start writing letters to their congressmen."

Carolyn must have noticed my puzzled face.

"The traitors have begun an organization called Concerned Relatives," she explained to me. "They are trying to organize families concerned about their kids to join forces against us . . ." She lowered her voice. "Listen, just go to your cabin and try to sleep. There may be trouble later."

I obediently went to my cabin, kicked off my filthy work pants, covered my head with my pillow, and instantly fell asleep.

Late that night, in the midst of my heavy sleep, sirens began to blare. I heard guards banging on cabin doors and yelling. Frightened and disoriented, I sat up.

"Security alert! Hurry, everyone! Anyone late will be punished."

I wondered if this was what Carolyn had alluded to. My heart was racing. I jumped down from my bunk. Father's voice was screaming over the P.A. system.

"Danger! Security alert! Hurry, everyone. Danger is near!"

Sick with fear I tried to remember what I had done with my pants. They weren't on my bed or my trunk.

"White Night!" Father yelled over the loudspeaker.

My roommates were already out the door. I was on my belly, groping for my boots and pants, frantic that someone had taken them as a joke. Finally I found them, pulled them on, bolted out the door, and bumped into one of the guards.

"Wow," he blurted out. "Sorry, Deb. This is your first . . . You better hurry, you're late. I'd hate you getting on the Learning Crew."

I wondered if I had time to use the bathroom. I knew I couldn't wait. Jogging toward the bright lights of the Pavilion, Jim's voice shrieking orders, I veered off toward the showers and relieved myself standing. Residents rushed by, children were crying.

I heard gunfire in the forest. I ran to the radio room as Carolyn had told me to do earlier that evening, and waited for further instructions. Everyone had gathered in the Pavilion. I could see Mama, white as a sheet, seated directly in front of Jim.

"Darlings, we are under attack." Father looked wired, the way I had in high school when I was on speed.

"Remember those murderous family members we have chosen to leave and forget? They have formed a vicious group called the Concerned Relatives. The CIA has joined forces with them. We are under siege. The United States Government does not want us to survive. They threaten to surround, attack, torture, and imprison us. We don't want that, do we?"

Suddenly the air was filled with a frightening noise. A screaming and trilling sound, made by all the residents of Jonestown flicking their tongues, resonated through the jungle. I imagined the sound could be heard for miles, perhaps all the way to Port Kaituma. They must think we're mad, I thought.

"Louder! Let the mercenaries hear us," Father hissed into the mike and then joined in.

I wanted to run away, but stayed at the radio room awaiting my instructions from Carolyn. The encampment's security force marched around the Pavilion, counting to make sure each resident was present, checking every building to confirm, for our own safety, that everyone was there and attentive, in order to reinforce our commitment to be good disciples.

Maria was on the radio trying to make herself heard through the ferocious screaming in the Pavilion. After a while, Carolyn came to the stairs and told me everything would be fine.

"I forgot that this is your first White Night," she murmured softly. "Go sit with Stephan on the fence."

I anxiously climbed the four-foot wooden railing and positioned myself next to him, hoping I hadn't called any unnecessary attention to myself. We were some fifteen feet from Jim's chair. My hands were shaking, I began to bite the inside of my lip to stay focused. Adrenaline was pulsing through my body, but my exhaustion was equally great and I could feel myself losing and then regaining consciousness. I bit harder. We listened to the droning sound of Father's voice, an endless harangue in which he prophesied that we would be killed by our enemies.

I wondered why he didn't know what Carolyn knew, that everything was fine, that the peril had passed. But Father continued in a hysterical state, yelling over the loudspeaker, "All is lost. Traitors have betrayed us. Because of their disloyalty, their capitalistic self-indulgence, you, my good followers, have been condemned to death. Because of them and what they have said about us, we must die."

A mother spoke from the microphone situated at the middle of the Pavilion. I could tell from her voice that she had experienced this before.

"But the children, Father. Can't they at least live?"

"Darling, my darling . . ." Father's voice was sweet, consoling, and filled with misery. Tears had begun to streak his cheeks. "But who would care for our children, once we are dead? The enemy won't. Did you hear me tonight? They will take our babies and torture them. Have you forgotten our Six-Day Siege? How close they came to invading our sovereign territory?"

Then he cried aloud, "There is no way out, no resolution, my dear mother. Our enemies have outnumbered us."

There was more gunfire in the jungle. The mother moved back to her place on a bench, hugging her sleeping infant to her breast. I looked around for Carolyn. I must tell her, I thought, that she is mistaken. It was almost dawn. The night sky had lightened to a soft metallic blue and I realized that we had been here for at least six hours.

"Hear that sound?" Jim asked us. "The mercenaries are coming. The end has come. Time is up. Children . . . line up into two queues, one on either side of me."

Guards had placed a large aluminum vat in the front of the Pavilion near Father.

"It tastes like fruit juice, children. It will not be hard to swallow . . ."

I jumped down from the fence to stand in line with the others. I was confused and scared and didn't understand what was happening. Who were these people coming in to kill us?

A young man's voice yelled out in protest. "No! I don't want to die. There must be another way . . ."

"Guards! Take him and secure him. He'll have to be given the drink by force."

I looked around for Carolyn and saw her rushing from the radio room, her eyes filled with terror as she passed me, her face flushed as she approached the podium and began to whisper to Father. Father stopped his tirade to listen.

I could hear Stephan muttering something from under his breath. He turned to me, his eyes filled with contempt.

"The fucking bastard," he gasped. "It's another bloody drill, that's all. Another fucking scare tactic . . ." He shook his head, exhausted.

"The crisis has been quelled," Father yelled into the loudspeaker. "The crisis is over. You may go back to your cabins. We will have a day of rest today. Yes. Kitchen staff, make a treat for our comrades. Let us have Sunday cookies tonight."

Alarmed, I glanced about for Mama, but did not see her. I wondered why Stephan had called his father a bastard? I remembered that Jim had sent him here before the other boys because he felt that Stephan was becoming disrespectful and might leave.

Father had left the podium and was standing on the radio room steps. I watched as he motioned Shanda over. He was smiling, touching her shoulder, and speaking softly to her. There was something about this scene that recalled the day in Los Angeles when I gave him the offering count and he scolded me for whispering so close. I felt sick. Shanda looked ill-at-ease. Now she would be given more important duties. I turned away, the memories too painful. Please, Father, not young, innocent Shanda.

Alarmed and filled with dread, I headed to my cabin. I felt dizzy and my head was aching. Why had Father persisted in talking about an attack when Carolyn had told me all was fine? Why had Carolyn waited so long before talking to Father to quiet his hysteria? Why had I heard gunfire? What in God's name was going on down here?

The truth is, there were no mercenaries. Only the compound guards were in the jungle. Our own guards were assigned to encircle the compound and fire their weapons. They, too, believed that we were threatened. Every White Night, Jim sent a different team into the rain forest to fire shots. Each boy was unaware that there had been others before him creating the same panic. Each was told a different story, one he could not repeat. No one realized that all of the gunfire was from our guns.

It is, of course, only in hindsight, in the safety of sanity, that I am able to see Jim's deceit. He alone knew that there was no real threat. We were blinded by fear and isolation. Physically weak from malnutrition and lack of sleep and mentally exhausted from constant fear of punishment, we were feeble, compliant automatons. In madness there is no way to think logically.

As the days wore on, I struggled to preserve what was left of my sanity. I became accustomed to the White Nights and suicide drills. At first they occurred once a month, then there seemed to be one every two weeks and they would last for several days. My only solace was working in the fields. I felt grounded when we were planting or foraging. It was there in the sun and its ravaging heat that we had a purpose. In the field, there was something tangible to hold on to.

Yet again, my discipline and application were noticed and rewarded. At Carolyn's suggestion Father moved me out of my crowded cabin and into the one his three sons shared with Beth, his daughter-in-law. There were a few mixed-gender cabins. Most were inhabited by the bold young teenagers who wanted to live with a girlfriend or boyfriend. They spent all their spare time, Sunday evenings, to build them. With only four hours of light available to hammer and saw, it would take months.

As I passed my favorite latrine, which was new and relatively fly-free, I wondered why it was taking so long to build more cabins. We were so overcrowded. I recalled that the lavatory had been built in only a day and its construction was no more difficult than our stilted cabins. What were our goals? Was there a master plan for the hundreds of hardworking inhabitants of this land?

The fact that Jim had approved my move was a sign that trust was slowly being bestowed upon me. It was an honor to live with Jim's sons. Father couldn't let just anyone cohabitate with them. They often talked back to him and an untrustworthy individual might try to profit by using their adolescent rebelliousness against them. Father could not afford to have his sons confronted for speaking up against him in private. He was very concerned about their self-confidence. This was one of the reasons he had sent Stephan and Lew ahead to Jonestown. Another sign of his trust in me was the fact that I now had access to guns because his sons were on the security team.

Lew, Jim's handsome twenty-two-year-old adopted Korean son, and his wife Beth were easy to live with. His other adopted sons, Tim, eighteen, and Jimmy Junior, seventeen, one white and the other black, were hardly ever at the cabin. Stephan, his biological son, was nineteen years old and lived in another cabin, but came by frequently to visit his brothers. Only Beth and I were there at night, but at dawn, the boys would stomp in, tired and worn after guarding the compound all night.

While they talked, yawned, and undressed, Beth would head over to the nursery to hold her twenty-month-old son, Chioke, before going on to her job in the laundry. I thought it was sad that Jim forbade parents to keep their children with them at night but I knew it was for their own safety in the event of an attack that they remained in the guarded children's dorm. Children and seniors lived

Working the crowd.
(Courtesy Stephan Jones)

Ever-present support from Marcie.
(Courtesy Stephan Jones)

Making contact with a new member.
Larry is singing in the background.
(Courtesy Stephan Jones)

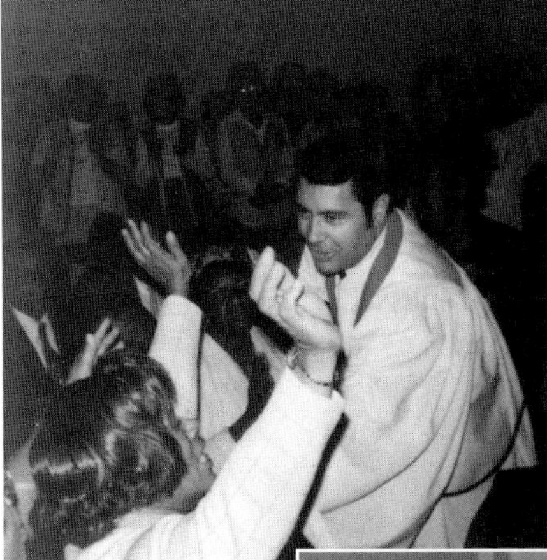

Receiving praise. (Courtesy Stephan Jones)

Jim working a spell on his congregation. (Courtesy Stephan Jones)

First phone transmissions into Jonestown, the Temple's newly acquired outpost in Guyana, South America, 1974. (Courtesy Stephan Jones)

Larry in front of a Temple bus in 1972. (COURTESY STEPHAN JONES)

Karen (left), already recruiting Mama (right) and me, Berkeley, 1974. (COURTESY DR. THOMAS LAYTON)

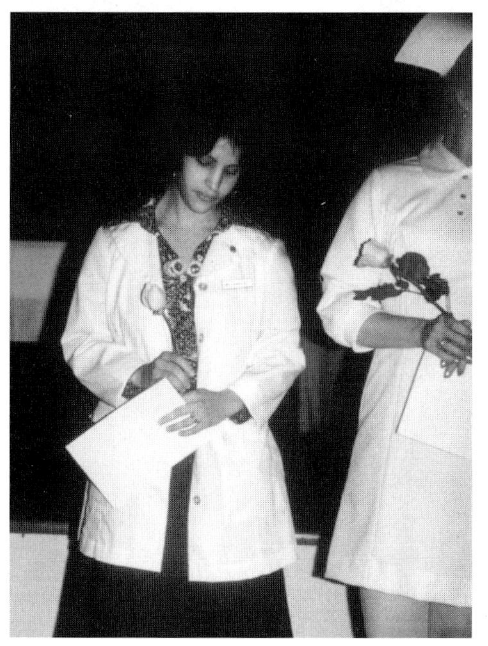

Receiving my surgeon's assistant diploma, San Francisco, 1975. (COURTESY DR. THOMAS LAYTON)

A convoy of Temple buses out to conquer the United States.
(Courtesy Stephan Jones)

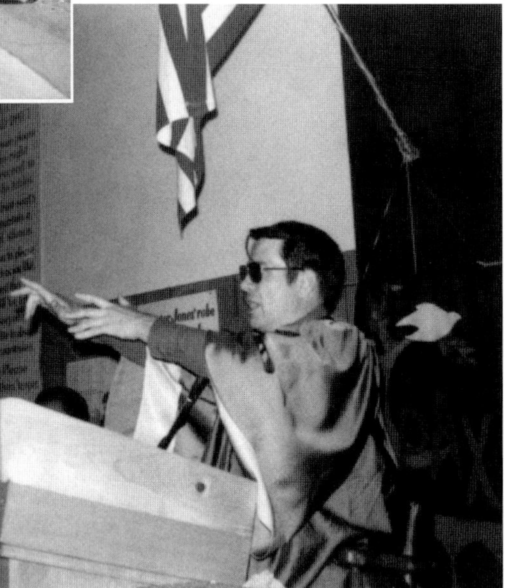

Father turning water into wine.
(Courtesy Stephan Jones)

Preaching about the government's plans to build concentration camps for people of color in America. (Courtesy Stephan Jones)

Jim in his role as a healer.
(COURTESY STEPHAN JONES)

The Reverend James Warren Jones during his political heyday in San Francisco. (COURTESY STEPHAN JONES)

Services at our San Francisco Temple on Geary Street, circa 1976.
(COURTESY STEPHAN JONES)

Annie graduating high school, 1972.
(COURTESY DR. REBECCA MOORE)

Sweet Annie (holding the rose) at Larry and Carolyn's wedding, 1967. Her sister Rebecca Moore, who never joined the church, looks on.
(COURTESY DR. THOMAS LAYTON))

Annie as a registered nurse.
(Courtesy Dr. Rebecca Moore)

Maria, eighteen years old, with her horse, "Yoika," a Greek term of endearment. She fondly called her father that as well, before disappearing from his life in 1971.
(Courtesy Dr. Steven Kataris)

San Francisco Mayor George Moscone shaking hands with the Reverend Jim Jones after appointing him to the San Francisco Housing Authority (unidentified committee member in center).
(Clem Albers, San Francisco Chronicle*)*

Annie on hotel bed before leaving for Jonestown.
(Courtesy Dr. Rebecca Moore)

Carolyn and Kimo. (COURTESY DR. REBECCA MOORE)

Kimo, Jim and Carolyn's son, before leaving for Jonestown.
(COURTESY DR. REBECCA MOORE)

Mama with Annalisa's son, David, two weeks before we left for Jonestown, November 1977. Four-year-old David answered my frantic "timed" call from Georgetown when I was trying to escape five months later.
(COURTESY ANNALISA LAYTON VALENTINE)

Sharon, Jim's lieutenant in Georgetown.
(COURTESY STEPHAN JONES)

The Temple boat, the Cudjoe, *docked in Port Kaituma, five miles from Jonestown.*
(COURTESY STEPHAN JONES)

The flatbed truck.
(COURTESY STEPHAN JONES)

The Temple's Georgetown headquarters viewed from the back, the radio room window on the lower left. Around the corner from the radio room were the main entry stairs up to the living quarters of the house.
(COURTESY SAN FRANCISCO EXAMINER)

Laundry facilities in Jonestown.
(COURTESY STEPHAN JONES)

Seniors sorting foraged plants.
(COURTESY STEPHAN JONES)

Gentle Mary, the sorceress of delectable treats. (COURTESY STEPHAN JONES)

Innocent Shanda, before she was silenced in the medical unit.
(COURTESY STEPHAN JONES)

Mark Blakey at the Georgetown headquarters.
(DEBORAH LAYTON)

Lew, Beth, and their son Chioke (CHEE-oak) inside the nursery.
(DEBORAH LAYTON)

Tim Stoen, assistant district attorney, San Francisco. (COURTESY STEPHAN JONES)

Grace Stoen holding her son, John-John. (COURTESY GRACE STOEN)

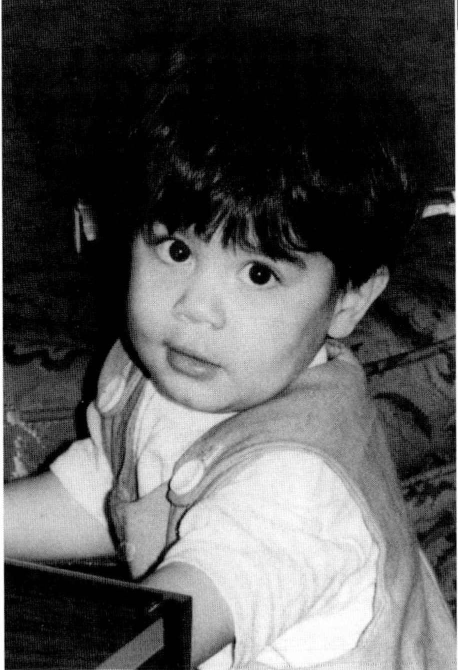

John-John before Grace left the church. (COURTESY GRACE STOEN)

2 San Francisco Chronicle ★★★ Thurs., June 15, 1978

Ex-Peoples Temple Member

Grim Report From Jungle

By Marshall Kilduff

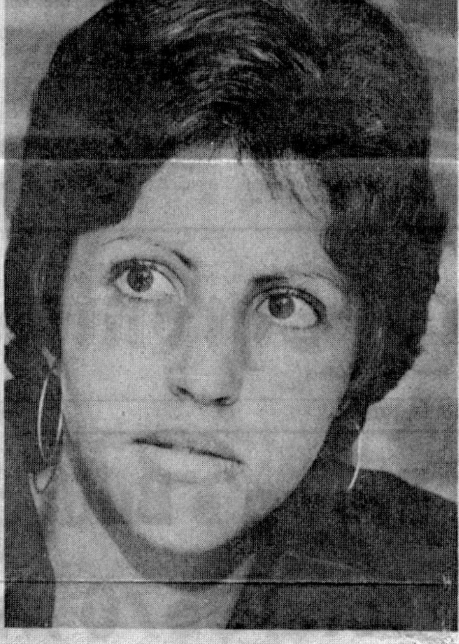

DEBORAH LAYTON, A FORMER AIDE TO JIM JONES
She told of armed guards and savage discipline

The Peoples Temple jungle outpost in South America was portrayed yesterday as a remote realm where the church leader, the Rev. Jim Jones, orders public beatings, maintains a squad of 50 armed guards and has involved his 1100 followers in a threat of mass suicide.

This description was provided by Deborah Layton, 25, who was a top aide of Jones until she asked American consular officials lmonth to safeguard her departure from Guyana, where the temple has its agricultural mission.

Peoples Temple officers in San Francisco last night relayed — via shortwave radio from Guyana — a refutation of the charges from two of the South American mission's residents, identified as Lisa and Larry Layton, the mother and brother of Deborah Layton.

"These lies are too ridiculous to refute," Lisa Layton said. ". . . We are treated beautifully here . . ."

Larry Layton said, "We are treated beautifully."

San Francisco temple officer Tim Clancy added, "We absolutely refute all the charges. This just makes us believe more than ever that there is a conspiracy against the church."

Jones became the center of a storm of controversy last s:mmer when he slipped out of San Francisco with his followers for Guyana. public charges were made by former followers that Jones had performed false medical cures to win converts, that he oversaw beatings of church members in closed meetings and that he amassed more than $5 million in donations.

According to Layton, Jones has become a "paranoid" obsessed with "traitors" in his own ranks who question him or do not work hard enough in the farm fields and with an outside world that has publicized his critics.

The fever-pitch emotions of temple members that allowed Jones to dispatch them to civil rights causes and liberal political rallies in California has now turned to a military-style vigilance against an imminent attack by unspecified "mercenaries," Layton said.

The temple fields are patroled by two rings of khaki-uniformed armed guards, men and women members of "security alert teams" who have access to 200 to 300 rifles, 25 pistols and a homemade bazooka, Layton said.

Discipline, she said, is handled at public gatherings of the entire church community. On one occasion an elderly woman was humiliated by being forced to strip, younger members are "knuckled" by having fists ground into their foreheads, and others are ordered to an underground "box" where they must sit for day at a time, Layton said.

Jones has ringed the work fields with loudspeakers and talks f:r stretches of up to six hours, she added. Farmhands are expected to work from 5:30 a.m. to 6 p.m. with an hour for lunch and another hour for dinner before more sermons lasting until midnight, Layton said.

The diet consists mostly of rice, purchased in the Guyana capital of Georgetown because the farm is not expected to be self-sufficient for another three years she said.

She said that on the occasion of visits from outsiders whom Jones wished to impress, church members are treated to meat and vegetables. Other trusted followers she claimed were drilled to give optimistic opinions about life at the mission, called Jonestown.

Jones, who often went to elaborate lengths to protect his public image in San Francisco, has remained at the mission, refusing even to venture into Georgetown, she reported.

Among his concerns has been a pending child custody case in the Guyana capital.

She said the 1100 followers were told to drink a bitter brown liquid potion, after which they supposedly would fall asleep and then be shot by Jones' guards. The rehearsal went as far as having the community drink a phony potion before Jones called it off, Layton added.

Layton said she was able to leave Guyana by wangling a trip to Georgetown. After several days she secretly arranged with American consular officials to obtain an emergency passport and flew to New York on May 13. She is now living in San Francisco.

"Everyone there wants to leave, I'm sure of it," she said. "But you never get a chance to be alone. Everyone is told to spy on other people."

Layton, who was in charge of church finances here before joining the Guyana colony last December, said Jones controls bank accounts in Europe, California and Guyana containing "at least $10 million."

Me, going public with my affidavit in June 1978, one month after my escape from Guyana. Congressman Leo Ryan would soon contact me, discuss my allegations, and invite me to Washington, D.C., to testify before the State Department.

Congressman Leo Ryan visiting Jonestown the night before his death.
(Courtesy San Francisco Examiner*)*

Jonestown residents hours before everyone perished. *(Courtesy* San Francisco Examiner*)*

Maria and her brother, Anthony Katsaris. He came to Jonestown to convince her to leave with Congressman Ryan and was critically wounded at the airstrip a few hours later.
(Courtesy SAN FRANCISCO EXAMINER*)*

Papa, upon learning that his youngest son, Larry, was facing execution by hanging in Guyana, Christmas 1978.
(Courtesy Dr. Thomas Layton)

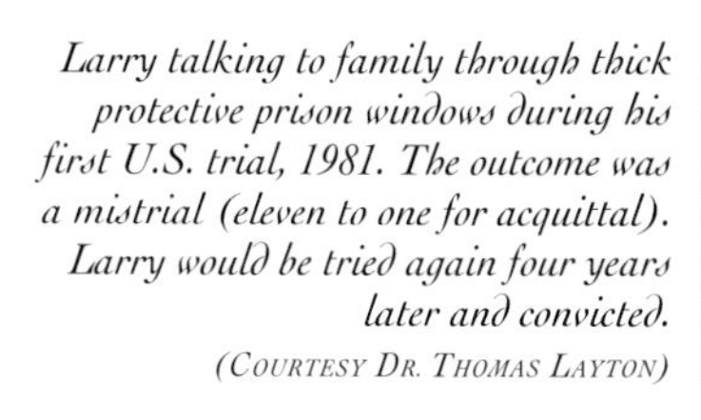

Larry talking to family through thick protective prison windows during his first U.S. trial, 1981. The outcome was a mistrial (eleven to one for acquittal). Larry would be tried again four years later and convicted.
(Courtesy Dr. Thomas Layton)

My daughter, Lauren, at age four, when she began asking questions about "Grandma Nanni" and her Uncle Larry. (DEBORAH LAYTON)

Visiting Larry at the federal prison, where he is serving a life sentence, 1997. (DEBORAH LAYTON)

Lauren, when I began telling her the truth. (DEBORAH LAYTON)

close to the Pavilion—a curse because it meant having to live next to the center of insanity. The loudspeaker system, although still audible, was less intrusive where we lived.

When I rose, it didn't take much effort to get dressed since I slept almost completely clothed. We had to be prepared in case of an emergency invasion by our enemies. The early mornings were cool. The cries of the howler monkeys that had frightened me on my arrival had become a soothing constant in the midst of our uncertain situation. Jim said bras were a Western indoctrination, so I pulled a shirt over my bare chest, even though it hurt to go braless.

I was thankful to the Greeting Committee, which I privately referred to as the "Confiscation Committee," for sparing my thick wool socks. Not only did they keep my feet dry, they warded off mosquito bites from my ankles and the bottoms of my feet. My boots were deteriorating, but hopefully they would hold out until I was to leave. The small hole on one side was working itself into a tear, large enough for the dreaded red biting ant to get access to my toes.

On most mornings, when I stepped down from my bunk onto the wooden planks, something soft and warm touched my foot. It was Beth's bear, which had fallen from its hiding place in her bed. Each of us had a secret something we cherished. It could be as egotistical and vain as a mirror or as functional as my socks, but it was something we'd managed to keep for ourselves. For Beth, the bear was probably the closest thing she had to being with her baby. Placing the curly-haired teddy next to her head, I would grab my sickle and tiptoe out of our cabin into the dawn's fresh, revitalizing air.

I was still working in the fields. By now I had learned to overcome physical discomfort at any cost, and I thought of the grain bugs in the rice as friends—my own little protein-boosters.

On some days our field work involved foraging for edible shrubs along the jungle's extremity. I always concentrated on finding a special green leaf, the one Mary, the magical chef, and her kitchen staff used for our Sunday-only vegetables, my favorite treat. There was also an extraordinary purple root, which we used to season other rare dishes. Mary's special leaves, the long, mossy, green one with blood-red spines, were always hidden under a faint emerald mother shrub with bright saffron flecks. I moved forward, squatting, my knees growing sore, diligently searching.

We always carried empty burlap sacks with us to the worksite. They smelled of previous gatherings from different fields. Sometimes a hint of pineapple wafted up into my nostrils, other times sugarcane. We filled sack after sack with sustenance for our comrades, heaved them onto our heads, and transported them back out to the clearing.

As the mornings passed slowly into noon, I would begin to feel weak, hungry for the cassava bread and plantain sandwich sitting on a burnt log where I'd thrown my outer shirt. The ants never attacked our food; probably the strange-smelling additive kept them away. I liked the plantain, from the banana family. It was slightly sweet, its texture thick and filling, reminding me of the sweet potato pies I'd eaten after our revival meetings and at Mary's home, so very long ago.

When I didn't dream of food, I fantasized about my shower, how I'd rinse the dirt off my body, the water dripping onto my shoulders, gently running over my breasts, in dark muddy rivers that poured down my legs and onto my feet.

Planning one's shower was important because showers also had restrictions. Anyone reported to have allowed the water to run longer than two minutes was assigned to the Learning Crew for a day. But one especially pleasant grandmother, Clara, usually gave me an extra minute by acting as if another person was already taking a shower when I got there.

"One more minute!" she'd yell, as I jumped in and took that one minute of no one's time, just to get an extra rinse.

I didn't know how the cold water was transported from the river, but it was preciously rationed. Never wanting to waste a speck of the precious liquid, I stripped, then lined up my toiletries neatly on the wooden planks next to my feet so that they were immediately accessible. Quickly and carefully I turned on the water and rinsed briskly. Not much water was needed, I got my body just wet enough to lather my head and torso. Another quick rinse and I continued to lather the crusted dirt from my arms and legs. Once well soaped, I turned the faucet on again and relished the ecstasy of the cold water running all over me. I was always cautious to keep my mouth shut in the shower while the water ran over my face so that I wouldn't swallow any and get sick.

Even with all the rules, taking a shower was luxurious. After drying off, I would change into my only other outfit, an oversized T-shirt, and step out. Looking over my shoulder to make sure I was alone, I would lean over and hug my secret accomplice, who was still seated at the entrance of the showers.

Every now and then, my daydreams were interrupted by a welcome rumbling sound. Emanating from the northern part of the forest and working its thunderous way toward us would be a rain squall. Its winds would cool the air and the intensity of the downpour was usually so great we had no choice but to take a break, a glorious respite that could last ten minutes. During the rainy season, if we were lucky, several rains would come in a day. They would drench the trees' upper canopy, turning the leaves into channels that funneled the liquid of life downward to the forest floor in a wondrous roar. Massive leaves would sway up and down until the cloudburst moved on, farther south, and then the quiet resumed. Once more the sun would shine down upon us, steam from the rains would filter back up into the atmosphere, and we would continue to labor on until sunset.

One day, the Learning Crew worked through a downpour. Not only were these downtrodden cast-offs praised for their stamina, each of them was miraculously released from the crew for having proved that they were correct thinkers. Once branded sinners, the former crew members were now revered as the devout, and they seemed to hold grudges toward anyone who had not lived through the hell they had experienced.

The rules changed after this incident, and no one was allowed to break during the day anymore. If the rains came, we worked through them, even if we couldn't see the ground. But in our eleven-hour days of hoeing, raking, planting, foraging, burning, or clearing land, there were fleeting moments of relief. On some evenings instead of hiking back in, the flatbed truck came out and carried us, worn and weary, back to the center of the compound. Above us a crimson, orange, and turquoise Guyanese sky would melt around our sorry crew as we jerked and bounced back and forth on the rutted dirt road, and I would fantasize about how wonderful it would be to see such a sunset someday away from Jonestown, someplace safe and free.

On a few occasions Lee was brought back to lead a crew in the field. One evening I looked at him, perched cross-legged on the edge of the truck, swaying and nodding with the direction of the vehicle, his muscles relaxed enough not to tense and jerk. I wondered what he was thinking—who he wished he could be with, who he dreamed of embracing. Lee must have sensed my gaze and turned his head toward me, smiled, and looked back at the last of the spectacular sunset. I longed for someone to hold on nights like these, to kiss and to love. Someone I could trust with my secret thoughts. I looked around at my work crew, all of us up since dawn with the screeching of the howler monkeys, working the fields until dusk, each of us expecting so much more from our lives and futures than this. But it was getting too late for dreams. Our spirits were weakening and our hopes were being deliberately drained from us. Jim's arsenal of manipulation and deceit was stripping away our dignity, ensuring our numbed allegiance and unquestioning loyalty.

When there was a minute of solitude I often wondered what life would be like without Father. I loved the natural tranquility of the interior, the dark, frothy river so close, just through the trees, yet inaccessible. Our cabins, tin-roofed and small, could have housed families, lovers, children with their parents, but instead we were partitioned into nonbonding arrangements. Like the inmates of a prison camp, we could not make close contacts. There was no one to confide in, no one to whisper to in the middle of the night, no one to make plans with, no one to trust. And solitude was disallowed because it too was dangerous. Time alone could lead to introspection and capitalistic thoughts.

I was always afraid of how Jim would perceive my visits to Mama: too often, too long, too early, not late enough. There was a fine line between too little and too much empathy. Too much compassion meant you'd break under torture and questioning by the enemy. Too little proved you could become a turncoat and traitor to Father. I'd learned to walk the fine line. But my feelings about Mama were chaotic. I loved her and hated myself because my love for her weakened my dedication to the Cause. I was disgusted by the panic I felt when I thought she'd get us both into trouble. I was always fighting with myself over each decision to see or not to see her. Sometimes I selfishly believed she was a drain on me, a weight that pulled me deeper into confusion and self-loathing each time I visited. If I stayed away from her, I would be viewed as loyal and unencumbered by the dangerous "worldly" pettiness of family ties. But I had to struggle with severe guilt as a daughter.

When I resolved to sneak a visit to Mama's, I usually lay on her cot talking softly as she sat at my side. And the next thing I knew, I would find myself being gently awakened by Mama's protective voice.

"Debbie . . . Debbie, honey. It's been a couple of hours, you better get up now." I would slowly focus upon Mama's worried face, her eyes filled with sorrow.

"Oh, Mama, you shouldn't have let me sleep. Now we won't have time to visit." As I got up to leave she'd beg me to eat the hard-boiled eggs she'd saved up from her senior's allotment, not satisfied until we shared an egg together.

"No, Mama, you need this to keep up your health," I would protest. But she would not give in.

"Debbie, they have you working too hard, I want to tell Father this is not good for you. They do not feed you kids enough protein for this type of work."

"Mama, please. Promise me you won't protest."

"The meetings are too long and I'm concerned about the way he has those children spanked and punished. It's not right to subject the children to the Well or the Box."

"Mama, whatever you believe or want to say, it must only be said to me," I kept urging her. "Promise me, Mama, tell *no one* but me your fears and concerns. These will be our secrets. Otherwise you will be confronted, Mama. Tell no one!!!!"

I longed to confide in her. But to tell Mama I wanted to leave would mean burdening her with knowledge of a treasonous thought and she could be brutally punished for not telling. No, it was too dangerous. Even the most innocent and caring of people had harmed a loved one by naïvely misspeaking their minds to Father. I couldn't tell anyone because they would have thought I had been assigned to test their loyalties. I was the perfect disciple; after all I had been one of Father's trusted few in the United States, and now I lived in the cabin with his sons. There was no one I could tell. I resolved never to share my thoughts, never to trust anyone, and to play the game by their rules.

I was increasingly worried for Mama. I had begun to see her fears and stress as new lines and dark marks under her eyes. She was not sleeping well. Fear was making her agitated, quick to jump at little sounds. As the world around us became more malevolent I felt she was in danger and could become a danger to me. She and Mary had already made a grievous mistake of judgment in an incident the previous week.

Mary had concocted a wonderful jam, made of some tropical fruit she must have secretly gathered. It tasted like marmalade and was just as orange. Mama had served it to me on a few occasions, furtively pulling out Mary's gift and spreading the preserves on the cassava bread she had saved from breakfast.

The ugly incident happened on a night after several days free of suicide drills. All of our spirits were lighter than usual. Father was laughing in his infectious, high-pitched cackle and life felt as though it might be beginning to look up at last. I was sitting with Stephan, laughing at his impersonation of his dad's chuckle, when Mary decided to bring her elixir to the podium for Father to taste. On nights like these Father would be joking with the children or relieving the miserable sods who'd been sentenced to the Learning Crew, telling them they had proved themselves and were no longer restricted. Everyone felt less apprehensive when Father seemed to be okay again.

Mary, sensing the light mood, stepped onto Father's platform to address him at the public microphone.

"Yes, Mary. . . . What is it you'd like to say on this gloriously calm evening?"

"Father, I've somthin' here I want you to taste." She made her way up to his chair.

"What's this?" He raised his eyebrows, pulled down his reading glasses, and smiled.

"It's a treat I've been workin on, Father. . . . Yes, sir . . . and Lisa's been my taster and says it's good enough to sell in the capital."

With gracious pride she handed the tiny orange jar to Father. Out from her apron pocket appeared a spoon and Father took a wee lick.

I watched, delighted.

Like a snake, Father flicked his tongue into the concoction.

"What an extravagance!" he spat. "How much time have you wasted on this?" My blood curdled. "Where did you get the fruit to make this?" he screamed. Mary shuffled back slightly, away from Father's spraying spittle. Terrified, I pinched Stephan's finger. Without a warning, "little Lisa," my mama, stood up in courageous defense of Mary.

"Oh, Father, Mary's marmalade is sweet, good, and it's marketable. . . . I think you could learn to truly enjoy it."

"Shut up, woman," he yelled. "I want Mary to answer from which field she stole the fruit to make this bourgeois extravagance!"

But his anger had been diverted and he turned from Mary, still seething.

"How *daarrreee* you!" He glared at Mama. "Are you arguing with *meee?* Are you telling Father, I am mistaken?"

"Father knows what's good," yelled an anxious voice. Someone grabbed Mama's thin shoulders, trying to get her out of Father's view, praying he'd lose his train of thought if he couldn't see her. Father admonished the crowd.

"Quiet! Silence!"

Everyone froze as he rose from his chair and glared down at Mama's small frame.

"Lisa . . . you dare to challenge me?" he sneered. "Let this be a warning to you. You are no different from the rest of us!" Mama remained standing as was required during confrontation. I sat in silence, a paralyzed coward, too afraid to stand and defend innocence.

I tried to think. Father's anger did not fit the crime. He was speaking to me! Through his actions toward Mama he was warning me. Perhaps he had seen me giggling with Stephan earlier that night. I could hear his previous admonitions reverberate in my head. . . . "I will punish those closest to you if you ever deceive or hurt me." Father was letting me know that he had tired of his charade of concern for my mother. She was just another soldier who needed correcting and punishment.

"Get out!" screamed the inner voice I had systematically silenced for so long. "Find a way to get both of us out."

13
Sickly Ascension

About a week after the marmalade scene I was sent to Port Kaituma again to attend the monthly PNC, People's National Congress, meeting. Seven of us sat under the same thatched roof of an open-sided hut discussing Guyanese political issues with several Amerindians. I listened to the leader of the meeting, glancing at his scantily clad body, his callused hands, bare legs, and feet, and I wondered if I could trust anyone here. Could I pull one of these tribal men aside and ask for help?

"Please hide me, my life's at stake. . . . I must escape from Jonestown. . . ."

It would never work. No one here would understand. . . . "Escape from what?" they would ask. Surely they had heard our wild screamed trilling noises and gunshots at night. They would not want to get themselves into trouble with the strange Americans deeper in the jungle. Not even they had dared move that far inside. I knew from Jim's sermons that these "outback" people were very superstitious and they would be frightened by the peculiar noises they heard filtering through the night air. I looked around the sparse, antiquated port and wanted to cry. There was no place to run.

I had heard about a primitive airstrip, the one the Prime Minister had been brought into, but it was used only for specially chartered incoming flights. There was no such thing as catching a boat or plane out. And I had no money, no passport, and no proof of identity. If I were caught, there were hundreds of comrades who, under duress, would attest to some atrocity I had committed that would warrant my arrest. It was painfully evident that I would have to continue to wait, watch, and scheme.

On my return to Jonestown my illness set in. I had lined up for the use of the sixteen-seater loo, when I was attacked by a ferocious cramp. Breathing deeply, I prayed the line would move quickly. With my next involuntary groan, Lee, who was in line right behind me, ushered me past the queue and to the outhouse door. I prayed he wouldn't join me as I took the fifteenth wooden hole. Jim had lectured that bodily functions were a fact of life and that it was materialistic and shallow to be concerned with privacy, but I was never comfortable sitting next to a male in the outhouse. But as the hour passed with groaning and vomiting onto the fly-ridden floor, Lee's presence was the least of my concerns. Perhaps it was he who summoned help because a nurse came and lifted my weakened body from the wooden toilet slats. She helped me clean myself and held my body against hers as we walked up the now deserted path. I felt faint and my body burned.

My fever worsened and I began to hallucinate. I believed I was in a bath in Pompeii and had feverish conversations with a woman who resembled someone I could not remember. She was kind and gentle, and she lifted me from the bed to a stool to give me my bath of cold river water to help reduce the fever.

I was entertained upon my bedcovers by a band of warriors mounted upon stallions. They rode up and down my pillow and fought battles upon my stomach. On occasion I'd scold them for talking too loud or poking my forehead with their swords, but they told me I had to learn the rules of war.

I had dreams of Mama holding my head, rocking me and speaking to me, encouraging me to push through the fever. Her voice was sweet and delicate, her faint Hamburg accent calling me back, begging me not to leave her there alone. Then silence, more dreary fog and more days passed. Late one evening, I awoke from my dreams. Shanda was sitting on my bed. The room was terribly dark, making it impossible to tell what time of day it was. As she talked, I recognized the individual who had tediously and kindly sponged away my fever. I looked around the medical unit for the special place where Father housed the ones he could never trust again. I was fortunate enough to leave once I was better. Shanda, however, would one day be condemned to this place, until her life was taken.

A new life was about to begin for me. I had learned something important from the warriors on my pillow: There is no etiquette in war, no boundaries that are sacred. Those who were lucky enough to live rode fast and furiously from the flames.

Although weak, I was released from the medical unit and allowed to resume some of the activities in the camp. Shanda must have reported my condition to Father because he assigned me to the radio room rather than to the hard work in the fields.

"It is high time you learn the new codes anyway," Father advised. "You've been with me two months and you're due to return to the States soon." I wanted to jump for joy, but I only nodded my head and replied respectfully.

"Yes, Father."

There were two different radio shifts, each with vastly different codes. Transmissions between Jonestown and the capital, Georgetown, were scheduled from 7 A.M. to 6 P.M. They dealt with Temple leadership meetings at various ministries and embassies. Every function and meeting with an official in Georgetown was attended by three or more articulate Temple representatives, who would immediately type up and report every aspect of the meeting to Jonestown: what they said, what they looked like, whether they were attracted to us, or not. What our reply was to their comments, how we countered what they said in order to get more information from them. It was called feedback. Everyone had a code name, every department had a code, and the person relaying the information spoke in covert language. If, for example, Sharon had gone to the Cuban Embassy that morning, spoken with the ambassador and obtained helpful information, the transmission would be: "Anne went to Netty's house today and had a pleasant and informative conversation with her Mother. She is very supportive of our issues." This message sent to Jonestown would be reported to Jim when he came up that evening to begin the night communications with San Francisco. When I first arrived in Jonestown, the day shift was run by Maria and the night shift by Jim and Carolyn.

The night shift began at 7 P.M. and continued until 4 A.M. Father explained that he wanted me to learn how to operate the ham radio and to master all our codes and frequencies so that on my return to the States, I could take charge of the San Francisco radio room. In his paranoia, he had become fearful of those members still in the States who were no longer under his powers. He understandably wanted one of his own to manage the San Francisco radio room, someone from here who knew and understood our impending doom and had experienced the death threats from the mercenaries. Father needed someone with "his mind" to coordinate messages, give orders, and disseminate information. On my return to the States I would be his liaison.

There was an elaborate vocabulary that had to be memorized, but I quickly became adept at giving and interpreting secret transmissions. Here, too, nothing was said in plain language, everything was in code so that outsiders, ham radio operators, and government provocateurs, could not decipher our messages. Ham radio operators would often intercept our conversations just to say hello. That's when we would use a code to switch frequencies and lose them. It turned out we were in violation of international FCC regulations concerning amateur radio transmissions because we often fled into military restricted areas for quick coded messages. Concerned operators complained because we were always disappearing from the frequency band when they began their friendly conversation, called "Qso" or "Qso-ing."

If our operator said, "I've got to see Mary," it meant to go up 81 kilocycles. If she said, "I have to water the plants," that meant to go down 31 kilocycles. When both operators were on the new frequency, the lead operator would cautiously whisper, "Go up 35." Of course no outside listener could follow these antics and the frequencies were switched repeatedly during delicate negotiation plans.

We spoke mainly of the United States, Cuba, and the Soviet Union, whose code names were Rex, Netty, and Shirley respectively, as there had been an increased interest in trying to immigrate to a Communist country. A typical communication such as "Send us more guns and ammunition" sounded like this: "Give Lilly a message for me. Hold on, I have to go see Mary." (Go up 81 kilos.) "Tell her to send . . . Wait, I have to water the plants." (Go down 31 kilos.) "Okay, meet you at 15." (Go up 15 kilos.) "Send Bibles and toys for the kids."

At first, I began to work with Maria in the mornings to get a sense of the radio's workings, the nuances of frequency changing, and the Georgetown codes. Then I began staying up with Father and Carolyn after my day with Maria. By dusk, the sun was no longer creating interference with long distance receptions and transmissions. It generally took an hour to secure contact. Night communications were always interesting as Father was requesting help from friends in the States, and determining how bad the conditions were with the press and what the CIA was investigating.

One morning, after a week of being solo on the day shift, Father entered the room on his way to check in on the children's Russian history classes.

"Give us a full report this afternoon, Lieutenant." He brushed my cheek with his finger, smiled, and left. I had become the interior's coordinator and only liaison between Jim and our members in the capital. As the weeks passed and I became more skilled, I gained more respect from Jim. He was impressed with my ability to field questions, solve problems, suggest alternatives if they were needed. He became increasingly dependent on my opinions about how things were going in the capital, how people were responding to his orders, and how problems should be solved.

My written reports of my interpretations of events became a source of information for Jim to use and base decisions upon. Slowly and perceptibly my stature rose. Finally, I was part of the team again. I was even invited to visit Jim's unit, where he lived with Carolyn, Maria, and the two young boys.

Father's living conditions were extravagant in comparison to the rest of ours. Besides the privacy fence surrounding the living quarters, there was a wide porch. Father had his own room, with a double bed and wonderful accessories like an electric floor lamp. There were books and magazines on the beds as well as newspapers strewn on the floor. I was shocked. The only paper the residents ever saw were the scraps of paper we were allotted on our way to the latrine. Father had his own refrigerator and inside were fresh hard boiled-eggs, soft drinks, and snack foods, the names of which I had long forgotten. Jim's unit had a double bed and a long, graceful mosquito net hung from the ceiling, flowing down and sweeping across the floor. I noticed medications, well organized, on a shelf next to the window. There, untouched and waiting for use, stood my mother's anti-nausea syrup and almost all of her pain medication. There were tall bottles, green ones and odd-shaped bronze ones, and prescriptions with other individuals' names on the labels. There was a fan on the floor, blowing cool air about the room; a small ribbon tied to his bedpost was slightly swaying in the breeze. Father's bed had pillows in different sizes, delicately placed at the head of the bed, and cotton sheets had been pulled downward tightly and tucked into the corners of his mattress. A fluffy earth-toned throw rug lay on the floor and Father's black slippers were waiting patiently to be engaged again.

Maria, Carolyn, and the boys' room was more like mine, with bunk beds. But they had a private shower with a bench and a ledge holding bottles of shower gel, shampoo, and a razor with fresh blades. Several yards away was a single-unit one-seater latrine. I walked inside. It was silent . . . no furious green-tinted flies buzzing about. And next to the clean seat I saw a mirage, a roll of soft white toilet paper. The confiscated contraband taken from our luggage, earmarked for the elderly, was at my fingertips. What a treat to use this treasured item instead of the scraps of magazine pages we were allotted.

I walked away from their cloistered, secretive, and fenced-in world, feeling jealous. How come they lived better than the rest of us? My breathing became quicker, as I ran toward my cabin. How come we could not live like Father? Where, I wondered, was all the money going? Perhaps it was needed for another immigration. We had offered the Soviet Union a couple million dollars to allow us safe passage. I stopped my grumbling as I approached my own cottage. I was lucky, I reminded myself, to be in a privileged cabin.

Reaching my hut, I heard Lew's tape deck playing.

"Hey, want a bite of an egg sandwich?" Lew proposed.

"Lew, how'd you get this?"

"Friend in the kitchen . . . Want a bite?"

Living with Father's sons made my life a little more enjoyable. I trusted them, they could be funny, and for some reason Lew always had food.

As dusk descended, Father's tired voice came over the loudspeaker.

"Tonight please, children, go to bed early; it's been a difficult week and you need your sleep."

"Well, thank you, Jim." Stephan coughed as he hopped down from a bunk.

I jumped up in delight that we didn't have a socialism class, and Lew's contraband egg sandwich flew into the air. He yelled and our chase to save it aroused Tim and Jimmy from their bunks. The four of us made a sport of sharing what was left. Jimmy restarted the

Marvin Gaye tape, "What's Going On." Soft melancholy music drifted down around us as Beth strolled up.

"Man, check out the sunset . . ." Lew gasped.

The evening sky had turned a brilliant magenta. We moved outside and sat on the stair. Lew hummed along to "Mercy, Mercy Me" and rubbed Beth's neck.

We stared at the sky as it grew dark. With little noise the boys put on their fatigues and took off to protect the compound. Beth and I remained outside on the stair, listening to the voices of other residents bedding down for the night, no doubt relieved we had been given a night of rest. I thought of Papa and Annalisa, Tom, and Larry, who still remained in the United States. I wondered if any of them had written to me or had I, too, been forgotten, like my other Jonestown brethren?

Late that night, I had a dream. I was staring into the Pavilion. Beautiful green, red, and purple flowers were weaving their way through the Pavilion, through the fence and onto the wooden benches. Life was working its way back into our arid, deadened space. My eyes were fixed upon Father's armchair and tears streamed down my cheeks. There were no flowers there. Not a single plant had risked attaching its tendrils to Father's poisonous chair.

And just then the siren began to blast.

When I arrived in the Pavilion, Father motioned for me to join him in the radio room. I heard an angry voice demanding vehemently to speak with his mother and sister in Jonestown.

"I don't want to speak with you," the voice demanded. "I want my sister. I want my mother. Now! I want to hear from their own lips that they are being treated well."

It was John, the young man whom Jim had taken under his wing and raised since age twelve and who had been in Panama.

Father was livid, but spoke in a kind and calming voice.

"Son, you must be under a great deal of stress. Why don't you . . ."

The voice was disrespectful and interrupted Father. "Get my sister on the radio *now!*"

There was a commotion and the mother and sister in question rushed in from the Pavilion, pale and with fear in their eyes. Father instructed them exactly what to say.

"He wants to know how you are. Tell him that you are very happy here."

The sister spoke first. "I am very happy here . . ." The mike was snatched from her hands and put in front of the mother.

The angry voice softened . . . "Are you there of your own free will? Are you free to travel? Come back and I will care for you . . ."

Father told the mother what to say.

"I don't understand why you're questioning Father. We are very happy here," she repeated.

Father got on the mike again. "You are welcome to come and visit us. You know, my son, that you are always welcome." Again he was interrupted.

"I don't give a damn what you say, I just want to speak with my family," spewed the voice. "Don't try and coach 'em. I heard you instructing them!"

The angry exchange continued until Father tired of it and moved the dial off frequency. The radio screamed loudly.

The room fell silent. Father slowly turned around to face me.

"You can never return," he said. "He could harm you. He knows too much . . . your trips . . . the finances . . . He's joined forces with the FBI."

I remained very still and forced a resolute smile. I was to leave in another week. John knew I had gone to Panama and now I could never go home. I struggled desperately to hide my despair. We were 250 miles inside the jungle on a tiny portion of cleared land. All around us, imprisoning and concealing us from the civilized world, were hundreds of miles of impenetrable growth. Armed guards were now posted along the Jonestown road.

How could I have ever entertained the idea of an escape? As my last thread of hope disintegrated, a relief swept over me—Jim's sons were on the security team. We had guns in the loft. If there was no escape for me, I could shoot myself.

14
Forsaking Mama

One day in early April, my fate took a turn. I reported to the radio room at 7 A.M. to begin the day shift. Father, who had been on night shift with Carolyn and Maria, seemed unusually attentive to me as I entered the room. He smiled, grabbed me from behind, and rubbed my neck, his hands moving forward, then downward toward my breasts. "I look forward to your full report this evening," he said.

"Of course, Father," I replied obediently. Why was he so friendly? Now Maria would be mad at me. Sometimes I wondered if he did this on purpose.

He had made me, not Maria, the only liaison between himself and the capital and had become increasingly impressed with my ability to field questions, suggest alternatives, and solve problems. Just this week he had acted on my suggestion to send a new contingent to the Cuban Embassy. So far our shrill appeal for the Cubans to allow us to immigrate into their country had been met with reluctance. We'd explained that our agricultural project here was not fruitful and the American government was trying to hinder our progress by constantly attacking us. Tomorrow our PR staff at the capital would implore the Russian Embassy for asylum. Father had instructed them to offer the Russians several million dollars for our safe passage to Moscow. He was still trying to find safe passage for us into either Cuba or Russia.

By the time the day was at its hottest, I heard Father on the loudspeaker at his house. "Brigade's about to begin." I hurried outside and tied my laces; my boots now had two holes in them.

It was time to head out to the far field for "bucket brigade." With the end of the rainy season we were having a drought. The sun glared down upon our desolate, man-made quadrant, the soil of which was no longer protected or moistened by the jungle. The tiny seedlings would wither and die if we did not soak them. Everyone who was capable of standing and walking was required to line up. The process was slow. One hundred of us, some old and wobbly, lined up alongside the jungle barrier. Mama, too, stood with us, not as far down into the field, but a laborer all the same. Our queue started just inside the curtain of foliage where a small river flowed by and it was in this reservoir of muddy water that buckets were dipped and passed from person to person down the long line and into the field. Each of us was careful not to splash the valuable asset from its container. Then, as Father watched, the last individual on the line would cautiously walk down the row and gently pour the sacred liquid onto one tiny green sprig. Wasting water was an offense!

As I carried my bucket to the next sprouting seedling, Father called out: "Where's my report?"

I finished pouring the water on my plant and walked back down the brigade to him. "I gave it to Maria earlier when she came by the radio room."

Jim looked at me quizzically and whispered into my ear, "Maria's had a few uncomplimentary things to say about your reports. Perhaps you should join us later this evening in the radio room." I could feel my stomach turn and I swallowed hard to keep from vomiting.

A little later, I reported to night duty with Father, Maria, and Carolyn as I had been instructed, and plunked down next to Maria on the couch. Jim sat in command, manipulating the dials on the ham radio, switching frequencies masterfully. Tonight, he was not asking for more guns to stave off the mercenaries, he was giving directives to the leaders in the San Francisco headquarters on how to answer the flood of investigative reporters' questions. He discussed who in the city's political caverns could be used for one more favor. I waited for Father or Maria to confront me, or at least clarify why I was there. By midnight, Father finally implored Maria to do or say something. She shrugged, shook her head as violently as any two-year-old, and continued to look sullen. Finally, Father seemed to take pity on me and excused me. A little baffled, I rose to leave the radio room when Maria mumbled after me, "Have a good trip."

A good trip? All the way to my cabin? I turned toward the door and rolled my eyes.

"Deb, wait a sec . . ." Carolyn followed me outside. "There're a couple of projects we need you to take care of. I want you to arrange for my tax clearance to Barbados. I have to travel there soon to take care of some financial business. We also want you to chaperone the youth group into the capital tomorrow. At 9 A.M."

My mind raced and I could feel my lip wanting to quiver, but I lazily cocked my head and furrowed my brow.

"But that's in only nine hours," I noted, trying to sound as calm and nonchalant as possible.

"Yes, I know."

"What about the radio transmissions?"

"Maria will take 'em over."

"I thought Ron was going in with the youth. He's been working so hard on that comedy skit as part of the presentation at the convention center."

"Jim doesn't trust him and he won't be able to go."

"Oh . . ." I felt sick. I knew how hard Ron had worked on his production. His father had been a battalion chief in the Los Angeles Fire Department a long time ago. When he died, all his kids, including Ron, had gone berserk. Ron had become a heroin addict. But he had made some huge changes here. He was focused now.

"Carolyn? How come you don't go?"

"I just don't have the time right now. Besides, Jim wants someone to watch the folks in the capital. He's concerned. Some of their work's been sloppy, as you know, and he senses someone is about to commit treason."

"Annie'd be good." I'd say anything to hide my eagerness. My greatest fear at that moment was that the offer would be withdrawn, that my chance to accompany the youth group out of Jonestown would be denied in the end. I had never imagined such a stroke of luck in all my dreaming since the day I'd arrived.

"Annie needs to stay and monitor Jim's health and take care of the boys at night," she said adamantly. "Anyway, the decision has been made and Jim and I have chosen you. Plus, you look young enough to pass as one of the teenagers you're watching. You'll blend in. It's extremely important that Jim has someone he trusts with them when they report to the embassy so that they won't veer from our rehearsed script."

"Who's making them report to the embassy?"

"Well, apart from the conspiracy against us by the United States Government, their parents have joined forces with some mercenaries. You've heard them shooting at us at night—hired militia men, soldiers of fortune. What gets me is that they know this is Paradise, a dream come true for their children. But are they thankful? No. They just moan and complain to the press and the embassy. They were the selfish ones in the States and now they're trying to rob their kids of a chance to live in a utopian society. The fifteen kids we've selected will deny their charges personally at the embassy. They'll refute all the lies their parents have leveled against us. Don't you see, Debbie? What if one of them suddenly wants to go home? Jim can't have just anyone accompany them to the embassy. It must be you."

"Won't it look odd, my just sitting there, watching? I don't want to appear as if I'm their guard."

"You'll think of something clever. Father has entrusted this job to you. He's confident you will serve us well."

No one was assigned to the capital unless they had loved ones inside Jonestown. Father knew I would never forsake Mama.

"Carolyn? What should I tell Mama?"

"Tell her you'll be gone a few days. You'll only be gone two weeks. Debbie, you'll be great. Do what you do so well. You've never let us down." She hugged me, then turned to reenter the radio room.

Father trusted me again. I had to keep calm. Stay cool. Act normal!!! Don't fidget. Always look Father in the eye. Be thoughtful and serious. Don't even dream of getting giddy!

This time, the stakes were too high and the reward was for keeps. Making a mistake would land me in the medical unit with the traitors Jim knew he could never trust again, on silencing, coma-inducing medications.

The ghostly cry of a howler monkey seeped through the darkness. Shivering in the predawn twilight, I began to compose my conversation with Mama. "Mom? I'll be leaving for a few days . . ." No—more upbeat. "Mama, Jim wants me to go to the capital, but once I'm there I plan to never come back. But don't worry, when I've returned to America I'll find a way to get you out too . . ." Don't be ridiculous. If only I could do it like people outside who would speak openly and exuberantly about their plans, make plane reservations, have going-away parties, talk on the phone for hours with friends and family about their hopes and aspirations, and then, just leave. I could not. In Peoples Temple, no one waved good-bye; only traitors, defectors, and villains wanted to leave. Father said that every single person who had ever betrayed us had done so for selfish reasons, but he taught us there was serious retribution for displaying such weaknesses. Defectors were followed, harassed, their lives threatened. An entire family was forced back once and held hostage.

I wished it wasn't so. I didn't want to be thought of as evil. But I had no choice. I couldn't just change my mind and make different plans. I had to lie, coerce, pretend, and betray. Would I be able to do it convincingly? Could I say good-bye to Mama without the treacherous tears? Would she guess the truth? Would her soft brown eyes redden with sorrow as she discerned my deceit? Was it fair to tell her and make her my accomplice? Would she think I had gone mad and report me? Could I trust her to keep our secret?

Tormenting images of Mama alone, crying and helpless, began to stalk me, clawing at the edges of my conscience. If I didn't leave now, would I ever get another chance? My head felt heavy and I wanted to flee my wicked thoughts. I knew that I must confront my decision to leave Mama, but I couldn't concentrate. I wondered when it had all gone awry. How had I gotten this far without realizing that something was seriously wrong?

All the beautiful and colorful dreams about our Promised Land had been struck down. I would never sit upon a wide and spacious porch rocking my baby, anxiously waiting for Mark to return from his work in the fields, smiling at Mama as she poked her head out the door of a cabin next to mine, asking if I'd like a piece of toast and marmalade, while Shanda, Beth, and Mary strolled by on their way to the pond. All my hopes and desires had long since evaporated with the heat of the equatorial sun. It was not to be. It was time to put away my childish dreams, to bolster my nerves and harden my feelings. If I could get out of Jonestown I would have a fighting chance of escaping Guyana all together. But I had no idea how to do it.

I wouldn't pack much. That would prove my devotion. Father would look at my tiny satchel and laugh. He'd hug me, his darling warrior, and turn to Carolyn, "This is what I expected from my Debbie. She only plans for the shortest time away from us . . ." Oh yes, then I would have won. I would have fooled them all. But could I camouflage my excitement? Would Father sense it? Would he look into my eyes and perceive my deceit? And what about Mama? If only I could really hug her good-bye. But I mustn't look anxious or distressed. I was only leaving for a few days.

I reached for my boots. I was to be ready by 9 A.M. I couldn't delay. It was quiet now and I began to shove a few items into my bag: undies, a shirt, two pairs of trousers. Surely they'd have something nice in the capital for me to wear to the embassy. I tied my laces tightly in hopes of keeping some of the mud out of my boots, and straightened the sheets on the cot. Maybe I'd fit into someone's sandals. I'd hate to wear this footgear with a dress. I noticed Beth's soft brown bear had fallen from her bunk, as usual. I brushed it off, gently placed it next to her shoulder, and tiptoed to the door.

"Debs?"

"Yeah?" I whispered.

"Bear and I'll miss you."

"Same here, Beth."

"You won't forget our promise, will you?"

"I promise to drink a Coca-Cola for both of us."

"No! Bring one back, Dufus . . ."

"Oh, that'll be easy . . ." We both giggled.

"Bear?" I called back softly. "Take good care of Beth for me," and I closed the door.

The morning air refreshed my weary body. I watched the dawn's early light filtering down through the wallaba tree and felt another wave of nausea. This one was filled with sorrow and regret. Why had we been deceived? I gazed out at the enormous wall of life that surrounded me. The edge of the jungle seemed to wink back at me, snickering. Her immense border taunted me, reminding me that she owned this place. I noticed a sparkle of light reflecting off the gloriously tall treetops. Then, hoisting my satchel upon my head, I stepped down into the mud and began my trek to Mama's cabin.

A snake slithered across my path and hesitated. Her red-and-yellow-patterned skin resembled fading diamonds. Her belly was distended. Perhaps she had swallowed a baby bird last night. I wondered what it must be like to be eaten whole, alive, and unable to move, aware that your last breath had just been taken and your essence would now gradually be broken down by various acids and chemicals until nothing remained of who you once were.

The smell of mud, the discomforting sound of the jungle's stillness, this hike to Mama's cabin could be my last. But I'd figure a way to get her out. I calmed myself by humming the German children's song she often sang to me so long ago, holding me tightly while bouncing me up and down on her knees . . .

Hoppe-hoppe, Reiter. Wenn er fällt, dann schreit er. Fällt er in den Graben, fressen ihn die Raben . . .

I looked over my shoulder at Father's compound. His gate was ajar. I wondered who had forgotten to close it. Of course, he had nothing to fear here, safely secluded, surrounded only by his disciples and encapsulated by the jungle. It was curious that with all our suffering, no one had tried to kill him. I knew I wouldn't. I was not that brave. There might have been a swell of loyalists that would, in turn, hurt me. No one wanted to be here, but were too afraid of each other to do anything. The American consul had come in two weeks ago to visit specific members but no one could speak freely or honestly. Everyone was watched. Father had assigned one of the seniors to act as if she were sweeping, but she was there to listen and report. We all knew it.

No one had any confidence in himself or anyone else, not even family. Last week, Rick, who had been one of the bus mechanics in the States, had told his eleven-year-old son, Jeremy, that he'd figured a way out. The boy had probably thought he was being tested and reported his daddy to Jim. Jeremy's dad was on the Learning Crew now, probably forever. Even if he were "reeducated," Jeremy would never be able to speak with him again. Rick had proven he could not be trusted. By contrast, Jeremy was being treated supremely. He was relocated into a better cabin with two of the high school youths as his "parents." He would work harder than anyone and be more loyal than most, just to prove he hadn't inherited treasonous tendencies from Rick. Jeremy would be made an example to all the children. Snitching on someone could better your miserable life.

I continued on the wooden walkway, now slick from our morning showers, and past the open, tarped "schoolroom." I was supposed to give a lecture to the kindergartners about socialism tomorrow. Long, leggy weeds were growing through the steps in front of the radio room. I hadn't noticed them before. It seemed odd that I was seeing things differently. The fog was lifting from my mind now that I'd been given one last chance to correct all the wrong decisions I'd made. I wondered who would get in trouble for not keeping the steps clean. The light was off. Carolyn, Maria, and Jim had finished the night shift an hour ago.

Something in my pocket poked my chest. I reached in and was reminded that I had a letter from my brother Larry. I had to show this to Mom. I'd had it for a week. We were rarely allowed correspondence from family, but Larry's letter was sweet, inquisitive, and safe. He was asking how we were doing. He was worried about Mama's cancer and hoped she was comfortable. He didn't know there were no real medical facilities in Jonestown. He'd be upset to learn that Jim had confiscated all the pain medication we had procured for her from the doctor. He wanted to come, and looked forward to the day Mama, he, and I could be together. Poor Larry had no idea what it was like. Of course, neither had I, or Mom, or anyone else.

I heard people talking and giggling near the kitchen hut. Someone was tossing water from a deep metal pot and joking with an older woman.

"Hey, sugah, you better get over here and give your auntie Mary a hug. Girl, I sure don't see you much. Less than I did in the States. . . . Why do you sa'pose that is?" She hugged me. "You have your reasons, I won't pry now. You have enough to worry about."

"Oh, Mary, I'm sorry, but . . ."

"Don't be makin' excuses. I know you've been workin' hard. . . . But look at you now. . . . Carolyn says you're leaving for Georgetown. . . . Listen, honey, I sure could use some spice from the Indian quarters. You could bring some back with you." As she pulled our heads together in a conspiratorial huddle, the life we had once shared flashed before me. Her pink bungalow, in the middle of Watts, the dinners she kept warm for me on the stove—black-eyed peas, fried chicken, collard greens, and scrumptious sweet potato pie. Then Mary had sold her home of fifty years, like all the other innocent and trusting seniors, and faithfully donated its proceeds to the Temple for the Promised Land.

"Darlin'? You hear me? It's our secret. Don't go tellin' a soul! Just come on by the kitchens on your way to visit Lisa and drop it right here, in this pocket." She pulled her apron away from her belly and pointed at the large pocket on her pants. "Yes, honey, come nice and early so's no one will see." There was silence for a minute as she grabbed me. "You comin' back . . ." she whispered in my ear. A quietness swallowed us and she hugged me tighter. "Mmhumm. . . . Your mama and me gonna miss you, girl." She pulled me closer, deep into her bosom, holding me firmly, then sighed and released me. Shaking her head, she kissed my forehead and turned back toward the ovens and the open fire. "Yes, Lord," she murmured wearily. "Time for my baby to go."

I waited outside Mama's screen door to compose myself. As with Mary, I had been remiss in my familial responsibilities to Mama. I had worked hard to keep from seeing anyone I loved. I was glad Larry was still in the United States because Jim didn't like or trust him. One less person to lie to and disappoint. But what would happen to Larry if I left? If I couldn't get to him first, he'd be ordered down here. He'd be told horrible lies about me. Would I be able to warn him in time? Would the two of us, with the help of Annalisa and Tom, be able to get Mama out and back home safely? No. . . . The embassy would help me get her out. They would help anyone who wanted to leave once I explained it all to them. Everything would be fine. . . . Yes . . . it'd be fine. . . .

The veranda was screened and ran the entire length of her cottage. A small, round wooden table was pushed up against the screen's base. Alongside her cottage wall, a dark blue-and-gray-striped blanket covered a lonely cot that seemed to wait endlessly for someone to come and visit. How lonely Mama must be with no one to come see her.

"You look worried, honey."

"I'm fine, really. It's just that I've been assigned into the capital with the youth group for a few days . . ."

"Oh?" She turned and I followed her into the cabin.

Although the corners were dark inside, she had made it comfortable. Her bed was covered with the purple, red, and orange wool serape Dad and she had bought in Mexico. Her trunk now acted as a little table.

"A little coffee?"

"Mom! How'd you get it?"

"Friend in the kitchen."

"Who? Mary?"

"Perhaps. . . . Anyway, about your trip?"

"Well, Jim wants me to watch the youth in the capital. You

know, he's afraid of traitors." Mama walked silently to the trunk. From a small tin she scooped the dark gravel of instant coffee and carefully placed it into our mugs. Then, from a thermos she poured hot water. As she handed me the secret potion, she stirred it one last time. "Be careful, honey, it's hot."

I noticed how frail she had become. Her hair was almost completely white now that she couldn't color it. A while ago she had stopped asking me why I visited her so infrequently. I assumed she was hurtfully aware that her daughter was a fickle schemer. After several distressing conversations begging me to see her, telling me how terribly lonely and afraid she was, she had finally learned that I was incapable of digesting, incorporating, or calming her fears. It was taking all my strength to sit here with her now and not just run away.

"You seem miles away. . . ." Mama sat down and stroked my cheek.

"I just worry about you."

"Me? Nonsense. I am far more worried about you. Jim works you too hard."

"Mama, please don't start . . ."

"I've seen you get weak and sick from your long hours. On your return from the capital, will you be assigned to the field again?"

"No, I'll return to the radio room."

"Perhaps by then they'll have someone else on the transmissions, someone they can't reassign immediately." I felt myself getting antsy. She was familiar with the ways of the leadership, always keeping us off guard and out of balance. "Anyway, in the meantime I've written a letter to Father." She set her cup carefully on the serape and walked over to the ledge above the trunk. "Tell me what you think . . ." She pulled down a piece of paper and began to read. "Dear Jim, I have been concerned about the lack of protein for the youngsters and . . ."

"No," I blurted out.

"Darling?"

"Throw it out."

"Debbie, calm down."

"Mama, burn it. . . . Have Mary throw it in the kitchen fires!"

"I haven't finished . . ."

"Mama! Listen to me."

"Honey, what has gotten into you?"

"Listen to me, Mama." I felt my voice begin to waver. "Don't talk to anyone about your feelings." I cleared my throat. "Please understand me. I know Father is loving and that you believe in him, but he will be furious with you if he receives that. He won't allow it."

"Why are you so agitated, honey? He said yesterday night, perhaps you weren't listening, he asked that everyone write up their worries and concerns. He said he wants honesty."

"Mama, do as I say. *Do not* write him that letter! Promise me you will not submit that note. Promise me?"

"Debbie, what is the matter with you?"

"Promise me? Now!"

"Well, all right," she shrugged. "But I think you're overreacting."

I sipped my warm coffee and concentrated on breathing slowly and deeply. Why must we quarrel now?

"Mama, I'm sorry. I just don't want you to get into trouble. I've been feeling sort of funny lately and I just want you to do this for me. Please don't talk about this conversation with anyone."

"Debbie, if it means that much to you, I won't."

"Not Carolyn, not Karen. I mean no one."

"Remember when we first arrived and Jim asked us to write up all our digressions while we were away from his aura? I didn't report you for ordering wine with our dinner in New York. I love you. I don't want anything to harm you." She hugged me tenderly and stroked my hair. "But sometimes you scare me . . . as if I don't know you. . . . Oh, Debsy, my sweet baby girl." There was another long pause. "I'll miss you. But it won't be long. We'll be together again." I heard the beat of her heart through her tiny, frail, chest as she continued to hold me. She rocked me slightly, and patted my back. "It's okay, sweetie, you don't need to cry. I'll be fine."

"Oh, Mama." I desperately tried to control the heaving in my chest.

"Here, honey." Mom looked down at her finger and removed the thin gold wedding band that had remained on her finger for thirty-six years. "Take this and wear it."

"Mama, no." Tears now blurred my vision. "Please, you keep it. I don't want you to take it off. I can't take it from you. It's a part of who you have been . . ."

"Honey, I want you to wear it. You'll have a piece of me with you in Georgetown."

"I can't," I sobbed. "I like knowing you've kept it on your finger. That all of you is the same as you have always been, and how I left you." There was an undertow of silence.

"Debbie?"

"Mmmhum?"

"I'm afraid."

"Please, Mama . . . ?"

"Something's wrong. I can feel it in you, in your muscles. You're stiff and anxious."

"Mama, I'm fine."

"No. I noticed it when you arrived earlier. You've changed." Wiping the tears from my cheeks and nose I tried to think of reasons for my behavior. "What are you talking about, Mama?"

I felt dizzy. I wanted to run. I wished I'd never come.

"Darling . . ." There were tears in her eyes. "Listen to me. I love you very much." She pulled me closer. I heard her troubled breathing. There was a wheeze in her only remaining lung. "We'll be together again soon . . ."

Wiping the tears from my face, Mama poured hot water onto an old pink washcloth.

"Here, you're splotchy. Hold the cloth down and your color will return."

The warmth felt good on my burning eyes. If only I could just cry, yell, scream, hold her, tell her, promise her . . . I will find a way to get you out, too. I won't forget you, Mama!

The sound of voices calling out and the revving of an engine permeated our solitude.

"It's time to leave, darling. They're yelling for you."

"I love you, Mama. Remember, keep our secrets just our own?"

"Yes, honey, I understand."

I walked over to the ledge and set my cup down next to the thermos. Her shoulders slumped forward as though she had lost a battle.

"Debsy?" she whispered after me.

"Yes, Mama?" I ran my wrist and arm under my nose to catch another tear.

"I'll never see you again, darling."

"Mama!"

"Shhhshh . . . I know." She walked slowly to the window that looked out toward the kitchen huts and on to the Jonestown road.

"I've always known. Good-bye, darling. Hurry now, it's time." Someone yelled for me to hurry . . . I was unable to speak.

Before the screen door slammed behind me, I hastily tossed Larry's letter from my pocket onto the lonely cot. I felt Mama's gaze upon my back as I scurried up her path. I couldn't turn around to wave. I could not look at her face. I had to stay focused. I had a mission. I had to look resolute. I had to be strong. I had to act as if I were coming back!

I began my run toward the Pavilion, praying that my flushed complexion would look more like a reaction to my exertion than to my overwhelming fear. Father was standing outside the radio room watching me race to the center of the compound. My heart began to pound louder.

"Whoa, slow it down. I hadn't noticed your sun intolerance." My face was burning. I wondered if my eyes were still swollen and red.

"You are the best person for this mission, Lucinda. Do a good job for me and your mom. I think her health will hold up while you're gone."

"Yes, Father. I just spoke with her."

"Oh?" He raised his eyebrows.

"Carolyn said I should tell her I'd be gone a few days."

"I don't think that was such a good idea. Your mother is terribly dependent on you and any upset could have an unfavorable influence on her health. She's recently asked for Larry to come and visit. She misses him, too." He motioned me into the radio room where no one could watch or hear us. "This is an important mission and I hope your short time away will give Maria a chance to reestablish her self-worth and prestige in the radio room. You've done so well with organizing, directing, and coordinating the activities in Georgetown that Maria's become a tad envious. You've done a miraculous job and I'm very appreciative. Well, off you go . . ." He smiled. "Oh! Just one more thing. . . . I can trust only you in the capital. I need you to report to me daily on how the others' attitudes are. I'm concerned that some of them are getting a little headstrong. Perhaps they need to be brought back. Some field work would be good for them. It's always important to remember our roots. They need my aura to keep strong and directed."

"Yes, Father." He grabbed my shoulders and pulled me to his groin. "It is good you will be leaving for a few days. I've been noticing you more lately. It's making Maria uneasy." Father patted my behind and pushed me toward the door. I felt sick to my stomach.

The driver yelled as I stepped out onto the stairs. "Yo. Let's go, girl!" The kids were already on board, each balanced on a bulging duffel bag. I threw my tiny satchel over the guardrail and climbed into the truck. Everyone was yelling now and waving to Jim. "Socialism lives!" we screamed.

Father smiled, but looked tired, ill. His face was puffy and I noticed again that his mouth seemed dry. He waved and then turned away from the radio room and headed down the path toward Mama's cabin. My heart pounded in my ears. What was he doing? Why was he going there? Bumping our way past the kitchen huts, I saw Mary peeking out from behind the ovens. Passing Mama's cabin, I waved just in case she was watching. What did he want with her? Why was he going down there? What would he find out? Were her eyes red too? Would she tell him her fears . . . that she'd never see me again? It was all I could do not to scream at Jim to leave her alone.

As we moved farther out of the main compound and onto the Jonestown road, I lost sight of the buildings. I leaned back against the truck siding, afraid and exhausted but exhilarated with new hope. Each one of us was on a mission. Each of us had an assignment and none of us knew what the others were thinking. The children's excited conversations surrounded me as we continued down the road, past the burnt clearing, the pig corral, the sugarcane field. I would never work these fields again, never have a chance to taste the sugarcane. Mud splattered my arms and face while I gazed out at the scenery, my prison, and I thought about all the times I'd hoped for my escape. I thought about that evening about five months ago, when I had sat on this same truck, jerking and bouncing after a long day in the field, promising myself that if I ever got another chance, if I ever again looked at the sunset away from here, in the United States of America, I would always cherish the gift of freedom.

Thirty minutes from the center of the compound, I began to close down. My body was now on autopilot and my mind was blank. Only the information essential to survival would reach me. There was only my mantra: Stay calm, you can do it, you can do it. Everything will be fine. . . .

Our driver halted so the armed guard could unlatch the entrance gate. We passed under our wooden sign, which had taken on an entirely different meaning since the day I first passed under it.

Welcome to Jonestown
Peoples Temple Agricultural Project

I lifted my hand to my mouth, closed my eyes, and blew a good-bye kiss to Mama.

15
Escaping Paradise

As the captain maneuvered the *Cudjoe* into the Georgetown port, I wondered what day it was. There were no calendars in Jonestown. I did know, however, that Christmas and my twenty-fifth birthday had come and gone without acknowledgment or celebration. The dilapidated wharf with its wooden planks and support posts was thick with black, porous grunge. The breeze reeked of diesel and fish. An antiquated barge had loosened its ties and was drifting back out to sea. I breathed in deeply. As I watched and listened to the dockhands yelling out directives and readying their stance to grab the various ropes being hurled from our boat, I felt relieved and at the same time the thought of Mama, alone, tugged at me.

I turned away from the ocean and saw the Land Rover bumping along the harbor to fetch us. The truck finally pulled to a stop and I walked to the driver's side.

"Debbie? What's the matter?" Bobby opened his door and stepped down.

"Nothing. Why?" I could hear the kids busily pulling their duffels up into the truck, talking excitedly.

Bobby was one of the "from birth" members, now twenty years old and devoted to Father, whom he affectionately called "JJ."

"Hello? Debbie? I'm talking to you . . ." I realized Bobby was watching me closely. "I said, you look really sad. You don't miss Jonestown already, do you?"

"I love it there, Bobby. Say, who's at the house?"

"Sharon. She's entertaining the son of the owner of the *Guyana Chronicle.*"

"Oh, yeah. Jim mentioned how influential his father is with politicians."

There was a pause. "Anyway . . . it's kinda nice. His comin' over gives me an excuse not to write myself up tonight."

"What are you talking about?" I asked.

"You didn't know? Maria wants us to write down all our faults and the selfish thoughts we've been having. They're to be sent back in with the boat. She came on the radio this morning and said it was a directive from JJ."

"Really? Carolyn never mentioned it when I left."

"They were attacked again last night. Jim says it could have been our negativity here that's caused it."

"Caused what?" I asked.

"The attack. Some mercenaries tried to charge them. Jim and everyone had to defend the compound all night."

"Last night? What time? Was anyone hurt?" I prayed Mama was all right.

"Don't think so. Guess one of the kids started crying and there was a long discussion over what punishment he'd receive. JJ said the boy's crying could have signaled our surrender and he got put on the Learning Crew."

"How do you know all this?" I asked.

"Maria said . . ." There was a pause. "Debbie, does Maria not like you or something?"

"She likes me fine. Why do you ask?"

"Jeez, I sure thought you guys must have argued or something. She said Father asked her to take over the radio operations again because she was the only one he could trust." He sighed. "Debbie, I liked you better. Maria acts like she's the only one who can do anything right and takes credit for everything. Jim always complimented us on a job well done after your reports. Well, that is, when we deserved it."

"You've always been good, Bobby. Father's very appreciative of your hard work," I told him.

"Yeah? Well, he'll never know about it now." He sighed again, then looked over his shoulder. "Everyone on?" The kids shouted in the affirmative and we pulled away from the wharf.

I wondered what was happening back inside that had caused this new rift. Had Jim said something bad about me to Maria? Perhaps she was really envious of me. Poor Maria was never given an opportunity to leave, not in the States and not in Guyana.

As we drove through town, I was comforted by the sight of people milling freely around the market and the official buildings with the flags of foreign countries. This was the "outside" world! I would have human contact outside our tightly controlled group. There had to be help somewhere. After all, the capital was a part of the civilized world!

As we passed the market, the Ministry of Justice, and the Pegasus Hotel, I noticed a steeple protruding from a dilapidated building.

"What's that?" I pointed.

"The spire? That's the building Ben's dad owns. It's the newspaper."

As we drove down the crowded main street, I wondered how this relationship with Ben and his father had been formed and whether it might be useful also for me. Did Sharon now have to "give herself for the Cause," which meant having an affair?

Perhaps Paula's influence had led to this new and potentially significant relationship. Paula had been good friends with Mama, and she used to come to my parents' home with me occasionally. But down here, I'd barely seen her. She was so lucky. Even though I believed her affair with Bonny was a sacrifice for her, at least she got to sleep in every morning.

"Look, check it out. See the sign?" We were passing by the newly erected Guyanese Cultural Center where a large sign had been posted across the marquee:

Peoples Temple Agricultural Project
Presents
A Cultural Presentation to the Guyanese People
A Dance of Freedom

"We're gonna be famous," Yolanda exclaimed.

"Get serious, Yolanda, this is really important," Vera stopped her. "Father says we gotta do our best. Through us, the Guyanese people will understand how we are a part of this country."

"It's not the people. It's the government," Johnny explained. "Didn't you listen to anything Carolyn said? It's the Prime Minister who's upset that we don't mingle more with the people here."

"Guess none of you understands what's happenin'," Vera declared. "The real reason we're here, well, it's to show them we are as happy and capable as they. Like Father said, we are as misunderstood as Cuba and Russia. The conspiracies in those countries pay people to say ugly things against their government. I bet they get thousands of dollars from the CIA."

"We're home."

Our house looked larger and prettier than I had remembered. I noticed a small car parked outside the radio room window.

"Yup, he's still here," said Bobby. We pulled up next to it and stopped. Everyone started battling to be the first out.

"Dibs on the upstairs shower," cried Joyce.

"Listen up," yelled Bobby over the commotion. "There's been a water shortage in the capital and showers have been reduced. Make sure the buckets are placed under the showers so there is no wasted water. That way the next person can use the bucket water."

"Here too?" someone yelped.

We had a two-level house with no interior connectors. The only way to pass from the downstairs to the upstairs was the outside steps. The kids ran up the stairs to the main house, pushing and laughing, vying for a good place in the shower queue while I stopped at the top of the stairs to look at the homes scattered around the weedy fields.

If only I had a plan. If only I could talk to someone. If only there were someone I could trust. Jim even had the officials in Guyana convinced that there were enemies all around. If I asked any of them for help they'd probably think I was a double-agent provocateur.

I turned and went downstairs into the radio room. The space looked like a tornado had blown through. Notes were strewn on the floor, clothes and shoes piled in mounds, the radio unattended. I walked over to see which frequency we were set for, and noticed the telephone on the wooden desk. Did they have a contraption attached to this to record outgoing calls? Would the number I dialed be recorded onto a statement? I sat down at the desk and thought about Annalis. What time was it? She must be five hours behind me.

Above me in the living room, I heard the kids' voices and then the rhythmic bumps, stomps, and claps of their dance. I pictured them standing in a double line, the tall girls in the back. Each one of their beautiful young black faces devoid of fear because they were too excited about their momentary freedom, too ensnared in their fantasies, wishing their mothers and little sisters could see them getting ready for the presentation. All of them had family waiting securely in Jonestown, making sure they wouldn't be tempted by the dangerous capitalists.

I looked at the phone again. I hadn't seen one in months. It looked silly sitting here with its oversized cradle for the heavy black receiver. Suddenly the rhythm of the dance upstairs was interrupted by a quick shuffling and footsteps coming outside onto the stairs. I jumped away from the phone.

"Debbie?" It was Sharon.

"I'm down here."

Sharon entered the room, breathless and bedraggled. I decided she could not be having an exciting affair and look so miserable.

"The kids are practicing. It's wonderful. You should come watch."

"I've been watching them rehearse for weeks, inside."

"Inside? How odd . . . Inside . . ." She played with the sound of the word on her tongue. "Debbie, you said inside. That's a strange way to characterize the Promised Land."

"No. I just mean it's safer there than it is here on the outside. Say, who's responsible for scheduling transmission into Jonestown?"

"Michael, but the reason no one's manning the radio just now is because we needed enough people to go to the Russian Embassy today. Father told us the embassy had priority, but we'll try right away to connect with the States about the new threats."

"Threats?"

"The attack last night. We need more protection sent down. In fact we need to get the American Embassy to agree to our getting guns to protect ourselves from the enemy."

I thought about Mama. I hoped they hadn't had another White Night.

"How can they help?" I asked.

"Easy. They agree with us that our self-defense is necessary."

"But how do they know about the attacks?"

"I talk to them almost every day. In fact they recently told us to shoot any planes down if they fly over us in a threatening manner." She smiled. I heard the car leaving our yard while Sharon continued, "Today Father wanted us to do 'crazy nigger' at the Russian Embassy. You know, impress upon the consulate that our requests are urgent."

"But I thought we were offering them money to allow us to immigrate to Russia."

"Well, that hasn't impressed them, so now JJ wants us to cry, scream, talk about the invasions, and the threats to kill our people. We're there now telling them that we'll commit revolutionary suicide if we can't protect ourselves from capitalist threats. The Russian consulate needs to see how serious we are about the issue of our survival. If they don't let us into their country soon we'll be killed by the CIA or die defending ourselves."

I spent the next few days making myself indispensable at the capital headquarters, so that I would not be ordered back to Jonestown right away. I needed time to come up with a plan. I couldn't just run away on my first day here. How, with no passport, money, or outside contacts, could I get out of the country? Jim had repeatedly told us that he had moles inside the American Embassy and if any of us ever told them anything, he'd in turn be told. I needed to figure out how everything worked before I could invent a safe way out.

I set about getting the house in order. I cleaned and straightened, organized sloppy closets, hung clothes on hangers, transferred all outside-meeting clothes and fancy shoes we put on to impress people, into one closet. I washed walls, straightened the kitchen, and tidied the jumbled pantry. I rearranged the living room, then picked colorful weeds from our empty lot, and arranged them on the wooden crate I hauled up from downstairs. It looked stunning. Father always said, "Appearance is everything," and we had many important guests to impress.

Once the upstairs was immaculate, I took on the lower level, which consisted of a large dismal room for storage and sleeping, and the tiny, cramped radio room. Relayed radio transmission communiqués were buried under a stack of clothing. I arranged papers by "author," and created cubbyholes for each person's missives. I even constructed an enormous cardboard calendar with large squares designated for each day. I penciled in our schedule: times and places of appointments and who was meeting with whom. Also incorporated on the bottom of the day was an after-hours section, which included all evening events that had to be attended. If we were to tape-record a meeting for a later blackmail attempt, I asterisked the appointment. I required that each person, upon his or her return from a meeting, report the outcome to me so I could immediately transmit the information to Jonestown. Although Father was adept at detecting deception, I prayed he would misread my scheme and would once again be simply impressed with his perfect "little soldier." It worked. A week later he ordered me to remain in the capital as the coordinator of all the PR activities.

I eagerly awaited the first night of our performances at the Guyanese Cultural Center. The Temple was hosting this well-publicized, week-long exhibition for the citizens of Georgetown. The ministries had begun to complain that Temple members "only arrived in Guyana," but were never seen again once they were sent into the interior. Offering free admission to the shows was shrewd public relations thinking, which had always been Father's specialty.

It was the same propaganda program Jim had presented to invited dignitaries such as the American consul, the Prime Minister, Carlton Goodlett, publisher of the San Francisco–based *Sun Reporter,* and Lieutenant Governor Mervin Dymally, when they visited Jonestown. There were always ten adorable girls and five handsome boys, mostly black, adorned in colorful African costumes. Dancing to Caribbean music, they would sing songs of freedom, "The Internationale," recite socialist poems, and always end with music accompanied by an acrobatic dance.

Everyone stationed at the house wanted to attend the venue. Although Jim and Carolyn had specifically assigned me to chaperone the kids to and from their performances, I could tell how badly Sharon wanted to go. I boldly suggested she take my place. After all, I had seen the rehearsals many times in Jonestown. I appeared genuinely chivalrous in offering to stay home alone and guard the premises. While she and the others had fun, I was going to initiate my maiden act of treason.

I waited until the Land Rover drove out of sight, then rushed to the desk with a phone, a clock in my lap, its secondhand ticking away in front of me. The call had to be less than two minutes. Any longer and the call could be traced. That much I knew from the United States, where I had made innumerable diversionary calls. But here, I was unfamiliar with operating procedures. Even the international operator, who had to connect my call, could conceivably give me away. Nevertheless, I took the risk, desperate to hear a familiar voice and talk to someone I could trust.

With my heart beating so loudly I could barely hear the clicking of the dial, my finger slowly rotated the numbers. There was a five-hour time difference. My sister would probably be home now, making dinner for her four-year-old son, David, and her daughter, Lori, who was eight. I had to make sure the call was less than 120 seconds. I also had to be careful not to upset or scare her. If she perceived any danger from me she might feel compelled to call someone, like Dad, for help. Wanting to protect me, Papa would then innocently blow my cover by calling the San Francisco Temple headquarters demanding to know what exactly was happening down there? Father had taught me the fewer who know, the safer you are. As the ringing began, I watched the secondhand on my clock to note the exact moment of contact. The phone rang. Eight . . . nine . . . ten . . .

"Hewo!"

"Hello, David? Is your mama there?"

"Mommy's aou'side picking stawbury jam."

"I need her quickly, sweetie. Can you hurry and run outside? Tell her it's an emergency."

I could hear the phone slide off the counter, dangle from the cord, and knock against the kitchen-counter wall. I heard their back door slide open.

"Mommy. 'Mergency's on the phone . . ." Twenty-nine seconds. Hurry! The thumping of the receiver stopped.

"Mommy said who're you . . . ?"

"It's Auntie Debbie, honey, and I haven't much time." More precious seconds faded away as another communiqué from child to mother was transmitted. Finally, a breathless voice answered.

"Debbie? Are you okay? I received Mom's letter last week. It didn't sound like her. It's been months! How's Mama? Is everything okay? Debsy, are you all right?"

"Oh yes. We're both fine." I felt stilted, afraid, suddenly, to speak. What if the phone was tapped? Hurry, say something positive to her. "It is very beautiful here. We love it. Yes, truly, Mom and I are happy here." I should have checked the baseboards for bug-wiring.

"Debbie? Speak up. I can barely hear you . . ."

"Mom and I are very pleased to be here." I raised my voice. "Annalis, you sound so close. I can almost feel you here in the room with me. I wish you were . . ."

"Debs, speak up. What's happening? Are you okay?"

"Yes, but I don't have much time. I just wanted to call and say I am writing you a letter. I'll try to mail it tomorrow." If I can get to the post alone. "I will explain everything then. Please, Annalis, be careful. Tell no one I called. I'll explain later. No one can know."

"But, Debbie, I need to know more. I want to . . ."

"Trust me. I love you, but you must do as I say." Oh, Annalis, too much is at stake. "I must hang up, I've run out of time. Bye! And, Annalis, don't try and contact me here, understand? I never made this call."

"Debbie? Debbie, wait. What did you say? I didn't . . ."

"Love you," I whispered into the phone, then kissed the receiver and disconnected. One hundred and nine seconds, exactly.

I tried to catch my breath, feeling as if I had just run the sixty-yard dash. My hands were sweaty and my lips and mouth were dry. I bolted upstairs to make sure the elderly couple who had arrived earlier from the States were still in bed and had not heard any strange sounds. I went back downstairs and began to clean the radio room. The radio was on and garbled, demonic murmurs were bleeding over and into one another from different frequencies. I turned down the radio and while I waited for Sharon and the others to return, continued cleaning up and making order.

Toward the end of the week, my fear of the American Embassy was confirmed. I desperately wanted to alert them to my desire to leave, but Jim had warned us that he had moles inside the embassy. I assumed they were official informants who wittingly and unwittingly offered Jim information that he then used against us. Father warned us constantly: "I have my ways of getting the information I need." I wished the embassy officials weren't so thickheaded. Weren't they trained to detect fraud and deceit? It was true, when government visitors, doctors, even our attorney, Charles Garry, came to Jonestown we put on a tremendous show for them. The guests were wined and dined with foods we never got to eat. In fact, when they looked into our faces we really were happy because on these special occasions we, too, got better food and we worked only half a day. The teenage dancers, the band, and our rehearsed pretense of freedom, reenacted for their benefit alone, worked every time. Perhaps it was impossible to see through our veneer. Jim had perfected it so well.

That's why I was afraid to go to the embassy for help. Embassy officials were scheduled to visit Jonestown pretty soon. I could imagine how the visit would unfold if I confided in them: One of them would stand before Father and proudly taunt him, "Well, things aren't so great after all; we've been approached by one of your people in the capital and she wants to leave." It could happen that fast and Father would have no difficulty finding out which of us was the traitor who had gone to the embassy.

What amazed me was that these government officials did not understand that the information they shared with Father would be used to maim us. It appeared the embassy did not believe the stories they were hearing from the United States, the letters and calls from Concerned Relatives asking for an investigation. Maybe they wouldn't believe me either.

I had several assignments in the capital: to chaperone the youth at the cultural presentations, to get Carolyn's tax clearance for Barbados, and to accompany six young couples to the American Embassy so they could acquire Guyanese birth certificates for their newborns.

The meeting for the six young couples and myself had been set for 9 A.M. Thirty minutes later the consul waved us into his office. I carefully positioned myself behind the others, who were sitting on chairs in a semicircle facing the consul, Dick McCoy.

"Tell me," the consul began his inquiry, "just how much do you enjoy life here? Are you happy, or would you prefer to return to the United States?" With his fair skin and hair, I knew he would never survive in the fields of Jonestown.

From behind the others, I tried to catch his attention and secretly alert him to the fact of my dissension. I raised my eyebrows and slightly shook my head, hoping he'd be compelled to speak with me later. He did not seem to notice. Father always said honkies were stupid.

"Yes, I love it in Jonestown. That is why I want my child to have Guyanese citizenship."

"How about you?" He pointed. "Are you happy here?"

One of my favorite young women, Vera, stood up as if being confronted in Jonestown. With her body erect, her muscular, ebony arms hanging stiffly at her sides, she began.

"I wish we'd come here sooner. Even my complexion is better."

Giggles ensued. With each official question, another youth successfully replied with our rehearsed responses.

"Why do you like it here? What is your name, for the record?"

"Yolanda, sir. I love it here because I am free to live a life that is not obstructed by racism."

"Ahhh, you experienced this in America, did you, Yolanda?"

"Oh yes. At least here in Guyana we are free to live with people of every color. Black, white, and East Indian. My baby will grow up unencumbered by prejudice."

"And, Jonathan. Was that your name? Tell me a little about your daily activities in Jonestown."

How old Johnny looked! Where was the freckle-faced boy he'd been eight months ago, in the States?

"Well, Mr. Consul, I am one of the child-care workers and responsible for care of the infants during the day. While some parents are working, others are visiting friends in Port Kaituma. But what I miss the most . . ." He looked at the watch Sharon had loaned him for this meeting. "Right now, the toddlers are heading to the pond for swim lessons . . . and I'm not there."

As their answers became more elaborate and convincing, I tried again to signal my dissent. Why didn't he interview each of us separately, alone, behind closed doors? That's how it was done in the movies when someone really wanted to get to the truth.

Forty minutes into the session, the diplomat looked at his watch. "Goodness, I hadn't noticed . . . I'm unfortunately out of time."

As we rose to file out of his office, I trailed behind the others, stalling for time. Using the door as a shield and closing it slightly against my shoulder, I whispered into his office and away from my waiting companions.

"Sir, I was hoping to speak with you alone."

Vera grabbed my arm and yanked. "Come on, Debbie." The consul approached, pushing the door open.

"Yes, miss . . . I apologize, but I've another appointment which I am unfortunately late for. Would you mind awfully just setting up another appointment for later? Of course," he stopped and looked at all of us, "if it's an emergency and you must speak with me privately . . . If any of you need to . . ."

"Oh no! That won't be necessary, really," I exhaled. "I . . . I just wanted to extend a thank-you to you from Jim for taking the time to meet with us."

"Think nothing of it. It's my duty. Anyway, I'll be seeing him soon enough. I'm scheduled to return to Jonestown on May 10. I have already prepared the list of residents with whom I will want to meet. Let's see, here it is. Yes, Jim asked that I send it in ahead of time to ensure the residents are there when I come. Thoughtful of him. I guess you folks are out and about a lot. I'd hate missing them. Anyway, I must be off and again, please make an appointment if you need to . . ." This wouldn't work. They were too dim-witted to be able to help me.

The couples and I headed toward the double glass doors to wait for our ride.

"Damn, Debbie . . . I was wondering what you were doing for a second . . . trying to talk to him in private? Like you were assigned to or something," Yolanda smirked.

"Yolanda, leave Debbie alone. You know that Jim has her doing all kinda things we can't know about. She might be on a secret mission for all you know," Vera retorted.

"Then why were you yanking at her if her mission was so important?"

"Let it go, guys." I tried to gain control of the situation. I had to quickly diffuse further comments and the possibility of anyone's transmitting the dispute to Jim. I could already imagine Yolanda asking to get on the radio and apologizing to Father for interrupting and spoiling my secret mission.

"It's just Temple etiquette," I explained. "We must always thank people on Jim's behalf. Then they feel important."

"So important he didn't have time to hear you say it."

"Etiquette, my dearies, just the same," I said with British properness, and everyone laughed.

The Land Rover pulled up as we stepped from the refreshing cool air of the embassy into the sweltering heat of the capital's midday.

"The jerk's probably CIA," Johnny announced to no one in particular.

"Soon it's going to be the last performance . . ." Yolanda sighed. "No more applause . . . Shoo, no more loud music and cola . . ."

"I know I'm glad to be going back," Vera retorted.

"I know you're lyin'. Tell me you ain't gonna miss dancing every night."

"Yeah, I will, but I miss my baby. Plus, this place is dangerous. Someone might try and kidnap one of us from here, just like Father says."

Once the kids had returned to Jonestown, I should have felt good and confident that I was still in the capital, but everything was taking so long. I still didn't have a plan. I had not been able to secretly send a letter to Annalisa. I was desperately lonely for someone to confide in. I'd become edgy and nervous. Jim had already commented on my lack of focus. I had to take care not to trip myself up. I had to be ever watchful of his three most trusted aides here in town: Sharon, Karen, and Paula. In America I had been close to all three of them—Karen, with her fingers always running through her thin blond hair; Paula, who was more self-assured and who took her job as mistress to the Guyanese ambassador to the United States quite seriously. Father used both Paula and Karen to influence politicians and Customs agents alike. Funny, he never used a brunette for that purpose. Sharon was brunette and attributed her brown, wiry hair to being Jewish. She was unself-conscious, intelligent, and fiercely loyal. All three of them were trusted completely and were beyond suspicion.

I found it harder and harder to abide by the rules. One day, Jim ordered each of us to write ourselves up for capitalistic and treasonous thoughts. I thought he was on to something. He was too clever. I was not sophisticated enough to play mind games with him. He could intuit the faintest beginnings of deception. I'd pretended to comply but I didn't hand it in. Instead, I inserted an empty envelope into the manila folder. No one was allowed to open "trusted" people's confessions. Otherwise, Karen would have seen that my envelope was empty. Only Father read the inner circle's disclosures. He had to protect his sources and our anonymity when we reported on each other, which was mandatory. Father said this was the way of socialism. We had to always fight the demons of self-absorption, and being reported upon was a safety precaution, a protection against the disease of individualism. I was just beginning to grasp the deception in this. It amazed me that I had never recognized before how he continually divided and conquered us. I hoped that when the folder got to Jonestown it would look as though my confession had fallen out. I hadn't licked my envelope closed.

The rules were endless; besides having no privacy at home, we were not allowed to leave the house unless we were with at least one other person. It was impossible to ever be alone. We all slept together on the floors or wherever we could find space and there was always someone awake. I wondered if Sharon ever slept.

Fourteen days after my assignment to coordinate all PR in the capital, Sharon innocently handed me the key to my escape.

It was late, nearing midnight. As usual, we had the radio turned on low. I was updating the assignments for the following day, when low voices seemed to speak to us.

"Eight Arr One . . . Eight Arr One . . . Come in, Eight Arr One . . . This is Eight Arr Three . . . Over."

I ran to the radio. "Eight Arr Three, this is Eight Arr One. Over."

"Eight Arr One? Lucinda? There's been an accident. One of the children was accidentally hit in the head with a baseball bat. We need to have him airlifted to Caracas for immediate medical treatment." Then he asked for Sharon by her code name. "Get me Anna. Over."

I wondered if the child had been hurt during a catharsis session.

Sharon rushed to the radio and knelt down next to me.

"Eight Arr Three, this is Anna. Over."

"Call the embassy, or, better yet, get the ambassador at home. Get someone quickly and tell them there's been an accident. Tell them a child fell from the play structure and needs to be airlifted immediately. And we cannot readily attain his passport. Can he be transported without it? Over." He fell from a structure at this time of night?

"Eight Arr Three, I read you. Over."

"Good, we'll return to Stateside and connect on this frequency at one-forty. Over."

Sharon, though tiny in size, was a powerhouse of emotions and energy. Before I could get off the floor, she was on the telephone with the ambassador.

"Sorry to call you in the middle of the night, but we have a serious emergency. . . . Yes, well, thank you . . . Mmmhm, we appreciate your having given us your home number for critical situations like this. Uh-huh . . . Well, we need to have the child airlifted. Really? Okay, good then. Now, does the child need a passport under these circumstances? Oh? Mmmhmm . . . Is that right? Well, Jim asked that I convey his appreciation for everything you have done and continue to do on our behalf and I'm sorry for raising you from your slumbers." She hung up the phone. "Imagine that . . . they can issue a passport in fifteen minutes if it's an emergency. Lucinda . . ." She turned to me and it took all my strength and self-control to hide the wild hope that surged through my body. I prayed that my face wasn't flushed with excitement.

"Debbie? Are you listening? Tomorrow you'll need to go, alone, to make arrangements. I need to stay here to check communications with Father. No one can know this piece of information. Plan to be there early."

At 7 A.M., on my way to the embassy, I took a small detour into the lobby of the Pegasus Hotel. I remembered that there was a bank of public phones just around the corner from the front reception desk, near the elevator. All five phones were occupied. Not wanting to look tense, I tried to calm myself by looking at the tranquil, smooth blue water of the hotel swimming pool. I was startled by the appearance, out of nowhere, of an elderly East Indian man dressed in a tan-colored shawl, burlap pants, and scruffy leather sandals.

"Relax, little one. I cun see yur worried." His skin was smooth and creamy brown, his eyes as black as my musings.

I smiled and looked down, hinting that he should disappear.

"Yur a somber little one. I haven't seen despair in a face so young, in many years."

I looked around to make sure no one had noticed. I didn't want him to draw attention to me. Self-professed psychic . . . Why doesn't he . . . ?

". . . Take leave of you? I can, but not 'fore cautioning you, little one."

"Yur in danger, child. Listen closely to me words . . ."

Even though his clothes were baggy and wrinkled, he had no odor. He didn't smell of liquor, either.

"Keep yur thoughts secret . . ." he murmured as I turned away from him.

With a phone now free, I bolted over, picked up the receiver, and dialed "O."

"A storm has begun," he whispered after me. "Beware tha' one who cares the most."

The operator answered.

"Collect call to Davis, California . . ." I took a deep breath and turned around. He was gone. There wasn't a cloud in the sky.

The ringing continued and sounded far away. I peeked around the corner to see if anyone familiar had entered the lobby.

Suddenly, I was connected to the other side.

"Annalisa . . ."

"Debbie? I never received your letter and I've been frantic. Tell me what's going on down there."

"I couldn't get away alone to mail it."

"What? You're being watched? Oh my God! Go to the American Embassy, now! Their job is to protect American citizens."

"No. I can't. Jim has them all hoodwinked. I'm afraid to tell them anything until I know exactly what I'm doing. I think they're going into Jonestown pretty soon and if they see Jim after I talk to them, they could tell him everything and blow my cover. It's just too dangerous to approach them until the day I'm ready to leave."

"Debbie. Listen. I've got a plan. Ray is actually going to South America in a few weeks on United Nations business. We are going to pretend that the whole family is going and we'll need you as a baby-sitter. I'll book the flights for you and make detailed hotel reservations in case they double-check. You'll receive the telegram tomorrow at your headquarters with the itinerary. This will work, honey. You'll see. I'll help you escape."

Hanging up the phone, I felt weak with relief. I wouldn't have to risk blowing my cover at the embassy. My big sister was going to help me.

When Annalisa's telegram came at noon the next day, I felt ecstatic and invigorated. I respectfully showed it to Sharon first, then got on the radio to transmit the information to Jonestown.

"Eight Arr Three, this is Eight Arr One. Come in, Eight Arr Three." There was silence. "Eight Arr Three, this is Eight Arr One, come in, Eight Arr Three. Over."

"This is Eight Arr Three. We read you loud and clear, Eight Arr One. Lucinda, how did the tea party [code for blackmail] at the embassy go? Over."

"Eight Arr Three, they have not returned from the appointment, yet. Actually, I have a different issue to transmit. Over."

"You may proceed, Eight Arr One. Over."

"We just received a telegram from my sister in the United States. I thought I should read it to Jim. Over."

"Eight Arr One, he is in the room. Please read said communiqué. Over."

"It reads as follows . . . 'Dear Debbie: Ray has been invited by several South American governments, in his capacity as the United Nations expert on nitrogen fixation, to give lectures regarding his findings. Our travel and those of the children have been paid for by the United Nations. Ray is scheduled to speak before prime ministers and many other government officials regarding his suggestion to implement his findings in their countries. Because this trip is so important and I've been invited to attend the meetings, I would like you to come with us and tend to the children. Of course, you will have the opportunity to meet with the prime ministers as well.' " I knew Jim would like that. I would be making important contacts we could use later. Annalis had gotten wise, fast . . .

"Eight Arr Three? Shall I continue with itinerary information? Over."

There was a long pause and I presumed they were discussing the validity of the telegram.

"Yes, Eight Arr One. Continue. Over."

"My sister has listed my Pan Am flight on May 12 to Caracas, where we'll stay for four days at the Holiday Inn, confirmation number five-five-two-two-three. Then, on May 16, they're scheduled to travel to Port of Spain, then two days later to Colombia, Peru, Brazil, and then back to Caracas. The trip spans almost three weeks and shows my return to Georgetown on . . ."

"Lucinda!" Father was now at the controls. He sounded perturbed. "This is a ploy. It's a scam. I discern a kidnapping plan in the works. Perhaps they think you need deprogramming."

"Uh-huh . . . Yeeessss, oh . . . that's right! I hadn't really listened to the letter's words that carefully, till I read it again to you." I could feel my face turning bright red. "I don't think Sharon even caught that," I added, desperate to remove myself from his suspicions. "I'll write a telegram and tell her that I am not interested in their plans." My heart continued to pound. I wiped at the perspiration that had begun to run down my arms. Thank goodness I was the only one in the radio room.

"Lucinda. Have Sharon double-check and examine carefully all the confirmation numbers and arrangements mentioned on the itinerary. It may not be safe for you to stay in the capital much longer. The boat is scheduled to come out the day after the embassy visit on May 10. That's in less than ten days. Plan to come home where you'll be safely protected."

"Yes, of course. I'll also make sure that I'm always with several people when I leave headquarters for any reason." I felt a lump in my throat.

"Good soldier." Father's voice was soothing and sweet, assuring me he had no idea I was in any way involved with this diabolical hoax.

Dear God, if you can hear me, where do I go from here? Who can I turn to for help?

"Eight Arr One, do you read me?"

"This is Eight Arr One."

"Lucinda? Did you hear what we just said? Do not send a telegram to your sister. Call her. Tell her. They must know we are onto them!"

"Roger, I copy."

"We didn't hear your reply."

"Must have spoken at the same time. Over."

"What was your transmission? Over."

"I said . . . uh, I'll call when the rates are low, later on this evening. Over." I was unable to concentrate any longer. The telegram had been a fiasco. They were sending the boat out to bring me back.

"Eight Arr One, we are closing down for the dinner line. Report to us tomorrow regarding discussion with known adversary. Over."

"I copy. Over. Eight Arr Three, this is Eight Arr One. Over and out."

I placed the handset on the radio and slowly ascended the stairs to the main house. A warm breeze blew against my face, trying to dry the beads of perspiration that covered my skin. I noticed the clothesline, weighed down with jeans, T-shirts, and underwear, all a uniform gray. The wash bucket still sat under the stairs, filled with dark brown, dingy water.

I proceeded down the hallway and into the far bathroom. I securely closed the door behind me. Turning on the faucet, I waited till the gush of water was full and loud. Then, holding my cramping stomach, I bowed my head over the basin and began to vomit.

Time was barely creeping forward. It was almost unbearable. What sustained my courage was knowing I was not alone anymore, that my sister was out there and was on heightened alert. When I had last spoken with Annalis, I had had to talk to her with Sharon in the room. I had to sound cross and distant because I had to prove to Sharon—and Father—that I was untouched by my sister's proposition. It was hard to sustain my composure, but Annalis saved the situation. She was so very clever in her responses. Her matter-of-fact voice calmed me. First, she asked if it was just us, she and I, on the line.

"Okay, that's good, I'll make it quick. Just listen to me. Okay now, if you're being watched, roll your eyes with disgust. The ticket I spoke of in the telegram is waiting for you at Pan Am, for May twelfth, Georgetown to Caracas. I'm sorry you have to wait so long, but it's the first seat available out of Guyana. I'm holding the Caracas to New York segment in your middle name in case they're monitoring flights to America. I know you won't be able to call me anymore so listen closely: Tom is ready to fly down there immediately. If you want him to come down and help you, cough now. . . . Okay, then, we'll stick to the original plan. May twelfth you go to the embassy. Call me from there. I know you're afraid, honey, but you can do this! Debbie, you're brave and you're doing the right thing. Okay, tell me you have way more important things to do than to spend three weeks baby-sitting Lori and David. I love you, Debs."

After this conversation, I was less able to keep my feelings and thoughts intact. I could barely maintain my civility anymore. Karen wrote me up to Jim for being rude and "pissy." I saw parts of her note in the envelope going to Father. I wanted desperately to get out, but my flight wasn't scheduled for another ten days. I had to persevere.

At night, I was haunted by Teresa's admonition to me in Switzerland: "Remember, you talk in your sleep when you're worried. Be careful . . . Sleep where others cannot hear you."

I would always wait until everyone was asleep, then hunt for an abandoned corner. If there wasn't one, I would sit up all night at the kitchen table, while warning signals ricocheted through my head.

Mom kept writing me letters. It was important to look as though I read them, but the fact of the matter was, I couldn't. I was unable even to look at her handwriting. I knew that I would lose my resolve if I did. I was precariously close to rushing back to her if I was told she needed me. Even though I knew that Mama now shared a cabin with Mary, I was always aware that she missed me and I worked hard not to think about it. I had to forget her. I could help her more from far away, once I got out of there.

I knew that if I did not have my wits about me, they would get me just like they had Margarita, the young Amerindian woman whom I had befriended. The night Margarita cried hysterically at the news that her baby had just died in the Georgetown hospital, I held her in my arms. While I rocked and consoled her, Sharon barged in with a Temple-friendly doctor. Against Margarita's will, he filled her veins with huge doses of Thorazine. That dread-filled night I sat holding my newfound friend's writhing body, trying to comfort her, powerless, too afraid to intervene. Why, I wondered, couldn't she be allowed to grieve? As Margarita faded into a zombie stupor and I prepared her few things for the boat to take her back into the jungle, I was acutely aware that had my comrades known of my treasonous thoughts, this just as easily could have been me.

The next day, just after I had locked myself into the bathroom to hide my overwhelming grief for my friend, a hard and rapid knock sounded at the door.

"Lucinda? I have a letter from your mom."

I jumped up to wipe my face.

"I'll be right out." Another one of Mama's letters.

"Did you respond to her last one?"

"Yeah . . ."

"I don't remember proofing it. Did it go in with the *Cudjoe?"*

"Pretty sure . . ."

I flushed the toilet and threw more water on my blotchy, red face, then opened the door.

"My, you look positively . . . radiant." Sharon laughed. "Here . . ." She handed me the envelope. "I didn't realize you'd slept downstairs last night." She had been monitoring me.

She watched me open the envelope, turn, and walk down the hall. Her footsteps followed me.

"Boil, boil, toil and trouble . . ." She screeched after me, pretending to be a witch. The hairs on my arms bristled. "What's all this secrecy? Where are you going?"

"I thought I'd read Mom's letter downstairs on my bed roll."

"I'm worried about you."

"I'm fine. I was just thinking about Margarita."

"Well," she exhaled with indignation. "That's all over, isn't it? She's left for Port Kaituma."

"I know. I'd hoped to say good-bye."

"Well, that wasn't necessary, was it?"

I nodded and turned. What a bitch. I struggled to remain calm.

"Lucinda? Are you listening to me? I said Jim wants me to accompany the consul into Jonestown on May tenth and stay there a few weeks. Beth and Deirdre will be coming out to take my place here."

I hardly heard her sputtering about all the logistics. There was the meeting with the Russian Embassy regarding our immigration and the arrangement to be made with the Cuban ambassador for an advance group of Temple PR people to visit Cuba. Then Beth and I had to record our blackmail of the American consul. Jim wanted his remark, that we should "shoot down" planes flying over the compound and threatening us, on tape. I watched Sharon's lips moving. Spittle had collected at the outer creases.

My heart was sinking. Beth would come to the capital. Did I have to betray her, too? How could I? I knew I would have to use her, use her friendship to conduct my deceitful plan because I knew she would give me space to be alone. I would be able to check on my flight, make sure the ticket for the twelfth, at 11:55 P.M., was waiting for me at Pan Am.

I could hardly stand to think about my last conversation with Beth in the cabin when I said good-bye. I didn't want to stab her in the back. If only she would stay in Jonestown. There, she wouldn't be able to take my betrayal personally and she couldn't be blamed. But here, if I got away, Jim would probably denounce her and hold her responsible. Would she be ostracized and punished for allowing this to happen? I prayed Jim wouldn't forbid her to see her baby Chioke as a punishment for being my accomplice.

"Are you listening, Lucinda? What's the matter with you? Put an asterisk next to your meeting at the American Embassy on May twelfth. You'll be taping the consul. You and Beth must get him to repeat, 'Shoot the planes down.' Father says once we have his statement on tape, we have an official declaration to arm and protect ourselves. It will prove the embassy knew we have weapons." She smiled and wiped the corners of her mouth. "Oh, Beth wanted me to relay a message: Since you didn't bring one, she'll share it here with you. Does that make sense?"

Beth agreed that I should go alone to arrange for the blackmail meeting. I had falsely reported earlier to her that I'd called the embassy several times but the line was busy. I'd brazenly suggested it would be best if I ran over in the morning to confirm our noon appointment. It was 10 A.M. and Beth would join me just before noon.

I made sure the recorder was well hidden in my satchel and hurried down the dirt road toward the capital. I could smell the sea water as it wafted through on the breeze. It would take me about twenty minutes to get to the embassy. I tried to determine how much time that would leave me for my plans. The heat of the day had not warmed my chilled and bristling skin. I could see the American flag flapping from the tall silver pole at the embassy. I increased my jaunt to a jog until I reached the doors.

The embassy secretary greeted me. I explained that I needed to talk with the consul immediately. She asked me to sit down while she tried to locate him. I looked around and decided to sit on a metal folding chair situated outside the consul's office. I saw that his desk was covered with documents and different colored folders. A dark green mug was next to his telephone.

A good-looking young man walked by and offered me some coffee.

"Oh yes! With real cream?"

"Isn't that how it's always served?"

"Not in Jonestown."

"Oh! Excuse me. My name is Dan. I'm the vice consul. Isn't your meeting with the consul this afternoon?"

"Yes, but I have an urgent message and I must give it to him before the meeting."

He glanced at his watch. "It's ten forty-five. This is the first time I have ever seen any one of you alone here."

"Mmmm . . . yeah."

I anxiously looked down at the warm, sweet drink in my hands. How long had it been since I'd had a real cup of coffee? Precious, real creamed coffee? I concentrated on what I would say to the consul. After what seemed like hours, the secretary returned.

"Miss, I've found him." The secretary smiled. She looked calm and sure of herself. Her green eyes reminded me of my sister, Annalisa, and made me homesick.

"I told him it was urgent and he's rushing over."

I looked at the clock—11:15 A.M. I was supposed to call Beth soon. I leaned down to rub the dust from my shoes. I wondered if anyone would believe me. Perhaps he'd think I was lying. He would look at my short-cropped, amateurish haircut, dusty legs, and dingy clothes and assume I was only a pauper, not someone he could trust. I looked around to make sure no one was coming, then tried to rub the dirt from my legs.

"There's a rest room just around the corner." The receptionist sorrowfully smiled at me. Embarrassed, I set my coffee on my chair so no one would accidentally take it. This way the receptionist would know I was coming back.

The toilet stall had luxuriously soft tissue paper which I pulled off in a long roll. I dampened it and wiped my arms and face. The mirror told me that I did look like a beggar. I shouldn't have been so careless running down the dirt road. Even my shirt looked dull compared to the secretary's crisp, bright white blouse. I washed my face and wet my hair. Grabbing a rough paper towel from a silver dispenser, I rubbed my bangs dry. I returned to my chair and found that Dan had left a fresh cup of coffee with cream.

I sat down and began to fiddle with my fingernails. I looked at the clock, eleven-thirty. Finally, a tall, middle-aged man rushed through the front doors. I recognized the consul.

"Deborah? Yes, I remember you well from the meeting with the youngsters." He paused to catch his breath. "You're alone?"

"Umm . . . Can we go in your office? I've something confidential to say." I shivered. Would I find the words? Would I sound convincing?

"Absolutely." He waved me ahead of him and into a high-backed leather chair.

"You're probably not going to believe me or understand what I am about to say." I took a breath and, with all my courage, continued. "I want to go home."

"Well, isn't this interesting? What made you decide this?"

My relief was so intense, my lip began to twitch uncontrollably.

"We have suicide drills regularly . . . all night and into the next day, people are beaten, we have little food . . . I believe many want to go home." I pressed my finger on my lip so I could continue. "Jim has threatened on many occasions that we will have to die because Grace Stoen is trying to get her son back. And also, you and the other officials should be more careful when you visit out there. Jim uses all the information you give him against the residents. When you're there, everything is staged. . . ." I stopped to take a breath. "I need a passport. Mine's in Jonestown."

The consul picked up the phone. "The ambassador needs to know this," he said and proceeded to dial his number. He repeated my litany of concerns to the ambassador, then hung up.

"Not to worry. I have some emergency passports in the safe upstairs. Can you just wait a second? I also want to talk to the ambassador in person."

"I'm afraid I don't have much time. I need to go to Pan Am and get the prepaid ticket my sister has on hold for me. And then, Beth, my friend from Jonestown, and I will be here later. We're supposed to get you to repeat your statement about shooting the planes down. We will be taping you."

"What? You're recording the meeting?"

"Yes, but you aren't supposed to know. So be careful!"

"Hmm . . . Okay, first things first." He jumped up and opened the credenza behind his desk and began rustling through papers. "I need a photo for your passport." He aimed an ancient-looking Polaroid at me.

"Okay, let's begin. Tell me, for the record, your reasons for wanting to leave Guyana and the Peoples Temple. I'll get Dan in here to witness it."

Sworn to this 12th day of May 1978

I, Deborah Layton Blakey, hereby swear that the following statement is true and correct to the best of my ability.

I have decided to leave the Peoples Temple Organization because I am afraid that Jim Jones will carry out his threats to force all members of the Organization in Guyana to commit suicide if a decision is made in Guyana by the Court here to have John Stoen returned to his mother. I know that plans have been made to carry out this mass suicide by poison that is presently at Jonestown. I also know that plans are made to kill the members who are unwilling to voluntarily commit suicide. I believe that this plan will be carried out. I also believe that the Organization will physically try to prevent any attempt to remove John Stoen from the custody of the Organization. In part for the above I have decided to leave the Peoples Temple.
Signed: Deborah Layton Blakey
American Vice Consul, Daniel Weber

I hastily signed my name and handed the pen to Dan, wondering if he would protect me and keep my secret.

"Excellent. Let me show this to the ambassador and you'll be on your way." He disappeared behind the door and Daniel came back in.

"Thought you could use a drink." He smiled warmly, offering me an orange juice.

"What is the consul doing with the ambassador?" I asked.

"Your statement is the first corroboration we've had regarding the serious situation in Jonestown."

"How long will he be? I need to run to Pan Am and pick up the ticket my sister has waiting for me there."

"Just finish filling out your passport information so it can be typed onto your passport."

"But, Dan, I also have to have tax clearance to get out of the country. I mentioned it to the consul as well. I've been here over five months and the limit is three."

The consul returned, his face flushed. I again explained that I couldn't leave the country without tax clearance. "I arranged it for Carolyn Layton a few weeks ago. They will not let me out of the country without it."

"Now there. There's no need for you to worry about that. This is an emergency passport. You needn't bother with it."

"Please, get it for me? I have to have this stamped."

The consul, vice consul, and I made our final plans. I explained that it was too dangerous for us to make contact after this meeting. I would be at the Pegasus Hotel at 8:30 P.M. and Dan would drive me to the airport. I explained that I would not be able to call or to be called, nor would I know exactly how, or when, I would be able to get away. But whatever happened, no matter how late, he was not to leave the Pegasus without me. The trip to the airport would take almost two hours. The consul handed me the passport.

"No! I cannot have that on me. It's too dangerous." I was shocked. Didn't he get it? "They might find it. Dan? Will you keep it till tonight? In fact, I'll drop my ticket on your desk. You'll have both when I meet you tonight."

I called Beth from the consul's phone.

"The meeting's at two."

"Are you coming home first?"

"Well . . . no, I'll wait here for you."

"You okay? I'll hurry and wait with you."

I looked at Dan in a panic. "She's on her way!" I rushed out of the building to Pan Am's office a couple of blocks away. I stopped outside the thick glass doors, wiped the sweat from my neck, and bent down, pretending to fix my shoe. Looking around, I concluded that no one had followed me.

I pushed the doors open and felt suddenly refreshed by the cold air on my drenched skin. A young man sauntered over to the desk.

"Can I help you?"

"My sister has a prepaid ticket waiting for me here. It's for tonight at eleven fifty-five P.M." The young man asked my name, fiddled with his terminal, and walked over to another agent. They talked for a while, then went to another terminal and again began fiddling with a keyboard. Then they both approached me.

"Sorry, miss. There is no such thing here."

"Of course there is," I assured them. "My sister made all the arrangements weeks ago. The ticket is here! It's waiting for me! It's all set up!" My eyes blurred. "You have to find it! I gotta be on that flight!" I wiped at my eyes to stop the tears.

"I'm not sure how we can . . ."

"*Please* . . . Call my sister." I was pleading. "Here's the number. Help me, please! I can't wait." The agents looked bewildered. I had to get out of there. Beth could walk by at any moment. I turned to leave.

"But how will we get in touch with you?"

I called back through the closing door. "Call the American ambassador!" Jesus . . . Now what?

I began to sweat through my shirt. I rushed back to the embassy and headed straight for the bathroom to rinse off.

As I stepped out of the bathroom, Dan walked by me and smiled. "Did you get it?"

I was about to tell him when I glimpsed Beth's sandals behind Dan's pant leg.

"We'll see you later," I said nonchalantly to Dan, as he proceeded toward his office.

"Hello, Debbie." Beth was sweating, and out of breath.

"Beth . . . Wow, you got here fast!"

"Yeah, well, I didn't want you left here alone. Jim was a little miffed with me for endangering your safety by letting you come alone to set everything up." Did he already know? Had someone told him?

"Well, nothing to worry about. No one's accosted me."

"You look really stressed."

"Really? No, just hot."

"It's cold in here. Do you have it in your satchel?"

"Yeah."

"Let me test it once more in the bathroom, make sure the volume is high enough." I handed her the bag, relieved that I refused the passport. With Beth in the bathroom, I quickly ran to Dan's office to tell him about my ticket problem. The office was empty.

"Debbie?" Beth was standing in front of me. "What're you doing?"

"Looking to see where the consul is. He should be here by now."

"He's got five minutes." She looked flustered, concerned about my behavior.

Just as we entered the consul's office, I glimpsed Dan's return. I suddenly grew desperately cold. The consul was behaving differently, unfriendly, strange, and reserved. He acted as if he knew something. Was he going to give it away? He didn't look in my direction, only at Beth. There was a long moment of silence and I nervously began to talk. He interrupted me.

"I know why you're here, and I'm not going to repeat what you want to hear," the consul said. Dear God, I had entrusted myself to an idiot!!! "What I said was said only in jest." He was staring directly at the satchel on Beth's lap. His actions broadcast the possibility of my having snitched. The meeting was coming to a frightfully abrupt ending and I still hadn't talked to Dan. I excused myself. "May I use the rest room?" The ploy was extremely stupid and dangerous, but I had no other choice. Beth scowled at me in disbelief as I closed the door behind me.

"Daaan?" I whispered into his office.

"Debbie!!" He jumped.

"Something went wrong at Pan Am. My ticket isn't there. Please . . . help me!" I turned and rushed back to the consul's office. Beth was standing and ready to leave. We offered our hands to shake and left the building.

Outside, Beth stopped and looked directly into my eyes. "Do you believe that? He knew why we were coming. He's broken our code and listened to our transmissions. He's CIA. They knew. Say, what was that all about anyway? Asking to use the bathroom. Your period start?"

"Uh-huh."

"We gotta tell Jim our codes have been compromised."

Having finished her transmission with Jonestown, Beth ran up the stairs and plunked herself down on the couch next to me.

"You lazy thing. How come you didn't get on the radio with me just now?" She hugged me. "You were so silly today! Tonight, are you working on the report for Dad?"

"Yeah, I guess. Why?"

"Let's work on it together. Maybe do it outside where Karen can't bug us. I got us a Coca-Cola . . ."

Suddenly, a male voice bellowed out from the floor below. Beth and I walked to the stairs and down a couple of steps. Jack was standing outside the radio room's door.

"What's going on, Debs?" Jack yelled. "The embassy just called and left a message for you."

Beth looked at me quizzically. Oh my God. Now he had really blown it.

"What?"

"Yeah. He said that you'd left some documents there and you should pick them up from Dan Weber tomorrow." Tomorrow?

Beth turned her head toward me. "Why would he call here?"

"Something's wrong with him." I looked at her. "We didn't leave anything there."

"Deb, the guy's up to something," Beth announced.

She continued down the stairs while I desperately tried to think clearly. I will bolt from here when Jack tries to grab me, I thought to myself. I'll run over there, jump the fence, and . . .

Now several more people were standing at the radio room listening and wondering what the covert message could have meant.

"The guy's an idiot." I rolled my eyes, continuing to calculate the distance from here to the road.

"No, Debbie. He specifically said you left something in his office," Jack remained firm. He had come in from Jonestown yesterday with Beth. One of Jim's oldest cronies, he'd traveled out West with his family in the sixties. Big, powerful, and deadly serious, he continued to grill me.

"Tell us, Debbie. What was it you left with him?"

With my heart racing, I shrugged, trying to look nonchalant.

"Was it . . . your panties?"

Everyone started to laugh. I felt the heat in my face as though I'd turned crimson.

"Sure, Jack. Just like I was assigned to do." I smirked and turned to go back upstairs.

"Maybe he'll wash 'em for you."

Relieved, everyone moved back away from the radio room and into the crevices they'd crawled out from. My hands were shaking so severely I folded my arms. I was afraid my body's involuntary reactions would be the death of me.

"What do you think he's trying to get at?" Beth wondered aloud.

"Damned if I know . . . or even care." I headed down the hallway and closed the bedroom door behind me. I was so afraid and angry. Why was he risking everything? What was he trying to get at? What was the message he'd risked my safety for? The plan must have been changed to tomorrow. I had to get to a phone. I jumped at a knock on the door. I was edgy and wanted to cry. I had to get my composure.

"Come on," Bobby called. "We're supposed to be gone now. Dad asked us to go back out and procure another hundred dollars this evening. Let's go."

"Me? Bobby, I just got back from the embassy and I have to write up my impressions for Jim."

"Karen scheduled you. It's on the calendar. And she just snagged Beth for some project, too."

I put on Sharon's spaghetti-strap summer dress and sandals, and headed back out with Bobby into the hot and dirty streets of the capital. Two hours later, Bobby and I were still asking Guyanese citizens for their hard-earned money for our agricultural project and I was becoming increasingly anxious. I had to get to a phone. What was the consul trying to tell me?

Bobby stopped a well-dressed black gentleman walking out from a run-down neighborhood. "Please, will you contribute to the Jonestown Agricultural Project by donating a dollar? It is well spent on medicines to better the lives of the Amerindians in the jungle."

The man looked vaguely familiar, like the old man at the hotel phone banks who warned me of a "storm coming." As we waited, he reached into his pants pocket and pulled out his wallet, leafed through several bills, and handed one to me.

"Take this, children, and go home. It's a dangerous neighborhood to be begging in," he cautioned, then crossed the street and disappeared into the marketplace. Bobby grabbed the bill from my hand and unraveled it.

"Holy shit, Debbie, it's a hundred-dollar bill! We've made our goal and it's only seven o'clock! Let's go home!"

I snatched the bill back from Bobby and we headed home.

16

No Place to Hide

At 7:20 P.M. I stepped into the shower. The water was cold. I quickly washed my hair and scrubbed the dust and grime from my legs. I changed into a clean pair of shorts and tank top, and put the money we had procured back into my pocket for accounting later that night.

Already at the kitchen table, Beth was eating curried rice and talking to Karen. I walked calmly by them and stepped into the pantry. I reached for the last bottle of Johnnie Walker Red and pulled it down from the shelf.

"Whatcha doin?" Beth sang to me.

"Jim asked me to give a bottle of whiskey to Dr. DeCosta as a thank-you for coming to Jonestown and giving free dental care last month," I lied.

"Tonight?"

"I should have done it earlier and was too busy. I thought I'd go now and drop it off."

"You can't go now. It's seven forty-five and we're leaving at eight-thirty to meet the new arrivals at the airport."

"Tonight? I didn't realize more folks would be coming tonight."

"Debbie, what is with you? You set it up. Are you going nuts? Maybe you did leave something with the consul—your sanity."

"Ha, ha. Very funny, Beth."

"I don't remember his asking us to deliver anything."

"Well, Miss Perfect. It was last week. Before you got here. Anyway, I was too busy."

"I'll go with you."

"Oh, Beth, I'll be two minutes." She was too close.

"Debbie, I don't think it's a good idea to go tonight," Karen interjected.

"Jim asked me to and Dr. DeCosta is expecting me."

"Where did you see him?" Beth asked.

"This morning when I was making arrangements," I lied.

"You can't go alone. I'll go with you," Karen insisted.

"Fine, if you want to."

"No, Karen. Debbie doesn't need you. Please stay and help me with this report for Jim. He wants it before midnight," Beth pleaded. "She was able to handle the embassy all by herself. And Dr. DeCosta is an important person for us."

Karen finally acquiesced. I had to wait until eight-fifty before I could climb into the van with the airport Welcoming Committee. The vehicle had been cleared of all the crates filled with necessities for Jonestown we'd received the day before: mothballs used for keeping the hundreds of thousands of dollars in currency stored in Jonestown from mildewing, soaps, clothes, boots, batteries, antifungal medications, and agricultural tools. I wondered if the crates contained guns hidden in the false bottoms. Bobby had swept the van clean for the newcomers we were expecting. Finally, five blocks from our home, I was dropped off, alone, at the home of Dr. DeCosta.

I watched the van turn a corner, then knocked.

"Well, hello, Deborah." Dr. DeCosta smiled down at me. "What is this? Another present?"

"Jim wanted me to thank you and . . ."

"Another bottle. Gracious me. He is such a kind man, your Pastor. But he encourages me to drink too much."

"Excuse me, Dr. DeCosta. I hate to be impolite, but could I use your telephone? It's sort of an emergency."

"Why, of course. Follow me." We walked down a hallway, up a set of stairs to a small room filled with books. As the phone at the embassy rang, the doctor settled himself onto the sofa across from me. Why did he have to stay? What would he do when he heard me? He seemed like a kind man. I hoped I could trust him.

"Dr. DeCosta?"

"Yes, child?"

"You are not going to understand what I am about to say or do," I began, "but I will explain it all to you soon. Please just trust me, listen, and wait."

His brows furrowed, and then he smiled. "I think I know already."

The ringing seemed endless. The clock on the desk read 9:20 P.M.

"Oh, hello. Is this the American Embassy? I need to speak with the consul, Dick McCoy, right away."

"I'm sorry, he is presently attending an affair at the Marine base."

"This is an emergency. He left me a message earlier today and I must get ahold of him!"

I looked quizzically into the doctor's eyes. They were serene.

"I'll try contacting the base," the receptionist said. "And who shall I tell him is calling at this late hour?"

"It's Debbie."

"Very well then, Debbie. Please stay on the line while I attempt to make contact."

"Please hurry . . ." My voice broke. I could see the changing expression on my host's face.

"Deborah? How can I help? Is there something I can do?"

"Yes, but . . ." I was interrupted by a deep male voice on the telephone.

"Hello . . . Debbie?" It was the consul.

"Yes, it's me."

"Where are you?"

"Well, I got your message earlier saying I was supposed to come by the embassy tomorrow and get the documents, so I thought . . ."

"Good God, child! Dan is waiting at the Pegasus Hotel for you. It's nine-thirty."

"But your message . . . I thought it was postponed until tomorrow."

"Christ, no! I was just trying to let you know that we had all the documents, that Pan Am had found your ticket. I couldn't very well tell them outright that everything was ready for tonight. Heavens, I never intended for you to think . . ." He inhaled loudly. "Jeeezus. Where are you?"

"I'm at a friend's. I'm five blocks from home."

"You must get to the hotel immediately. You might not make your flight."

"But I'm not prepared now. I have to go home and get a change of clothes. I didn't think I was supposed to leave tonight."

"Debbie! You don't have time. I'll call Dan and tell him you're on your way. Hurry!" I hung up the phone feeling as though I were spinning out of control.

"Deborah . . . what can I do?"

"Oh, Dr. DeCosta, I am so sorry. I didn't mean to drag you into this. I don't want you to think badly of me. It's just that I have decided I want to go back to America. I want to go home."

He grabbed my shaking body and held me tightly.

"It's okay. I will take you."

"First, I need to go by the house. I can't travel to Venezuela and then New York in shorts. I have to wear long pants." I felt dazed.

He gently took hold of my hand and led me outside to his car.

"But what if they see you? What if . . ." He helped me into the car, ran around to the driver's side, and hopped in.

"Just wait outside for me," I begged him. "I'm going to run into the house. If anyone comes out and asks what you're doing, say, I'm getting some clothes to give to your maid, that you're waiting for me to bring them back out. Okay? Don't say anything else . . . please."

As we pulled up in front of the house, I saw Jack and Karen in the radio room in a heated conversation. I was afraid to get out of the car.

"Don't leave me . . ." I reminded him one last time.

I quickly walked up the stairs, into the living room, and headed down the hallway. I opened the door to Sharon's room and grabbed the pants Margarita had given me, with the big tag "Made in Guyana" on the waist. I took the white shirt I'd washed last night from its hanger, then rushed into the bathroom. Pulling a towel off the rack I rolled up my only two belongings, grabbed a toothbrush, and walked back out. Beth was at the kitchen table with her back to me. No one was in the living room. I rushed toward the outside stairs and began my descent. Why *had* I come back? Why were the jeans Margarita had given me so important? Halfway down I was in full view of the radio room. I could see Dr. DeCosta's car, the motor still running, just fifty more feet ahead of me. Jack motioned to Karen and she stepped outside the radio room's door.

"Wait . . ." Karen walked toward the stairs and studied the towel under my arm. "Debbie? What's going on? What are you doing? What's in the towel?" Karen's voice was shrill. She came closer. I continued down the stairs as calmly as my convulsing body would allow.

"Nothing really." I tried to smile. "Dr. DeCosta asked if I had any clothes for his maid."

"What? He's here? What maid?"

She stood next to me and touched the towel. "Karen . . . just wait a second. Let me just give this bundle to him. I'll be right back to answer your questions. He actually just asked me . . ." I trailed off in mid-sentence and proceeded to the car. From the corner of my eye, I could see Karen watching me. I leaned into his window, as if conversing, then quickly opened the back door. Pretending to throw the bundle in, I abruptly jumped into the car. "Quick! Hurry! Get me out of here!!!" I pleaded.

As the dust flew out from the back tires, I hunched down in the backseat thanking God that the van wasn't there to follow us.

"To the embassy?"

"No! Pegasus." I looked out the back window. No one was following us. I climbed into the front seat with my accomplice.

"I'm leaving the country tonight. I'm going home to the States. It's not that anything is wrong here or in Jonestown, I just want to go home. My father isn't well."

"Mmmhmm," the doctor hummed.

I stared at the headlighted dirt road in front of us. "If anyone from the organization asks where you took me, just say you dropped me off somewhere. Tell them nothing else . . . just that you dropped me somewhere. Nothing else. Nothing at all."

"Of course. I will tell them nothing."

"I'll give you my dad's phone number. When you come to the States, get ahold of me. Give me your address, too. I'll write you."

"Okay."

"I'm sorry. I just can't explain all of it right now."

"It isn't necessary, child. I think I understand."

We arrived at the main doors of the Pegasus Hotel and I jumped out. Dan rushed over as Dr. DeCosta pulled a plastic bag from his trunk and placed my meager belongings into it. Then he took me into his kindhearted arms and hugged me.

"You're a brave little thing. I will keep your whereabouts our secret." He kissed the crown of my head. "Now go. I can see someone coming this way."

Dan nodded at my co-conspirator.

"It's nine-fifty. We must hurry." Dr. DeCosta put his finger to his mouth to signal our secret.

Dan and I barely spoke as we raced toward the airport. The moon looked peaceful so far away and safe from the drudgery of this life. I stared out the side window at the shanties dotting the scenery. The sugar refinery looked more antiquated and wretched in the moonlight than it had last time I had driven by it, five and a half long months ago. I thought about poor Dr. DeCosta. They were probably waiting outside his house right now. Waiting to confront him. I felt sick thinking about the lies they would tell him: She stole thousands of dollars, you must tell us where you dropped her off. We brought her here because of her heroin addiction, she lies all the time, you must help us find her . . . for her mother's sake. I prayed that he would not be swayed by them and tell them where he had dropped me off. Dan coughed and my attention was brought back to our ride.

"How much longer?"

"Ten minutes. Say, are you hungry? I bet you haven't had anything to eat."

"I'm starved, really." He handed me a bag with an orange and a cookie inside.

I wanted to lean over and hug him.

"Dan, how long have you worked here?"

"Not long. When the consul leaves tomorrow for Washington, D.C., I'll take his place for a month."

"He's going to Washington?"

"Yes, and with the statement you signed, that's a good thing."

I unexpectedly felt angry. Why hadn't they told me? Why would they let me fly alone tonight to Caracas when I could have gone safely with him tomorrow? Wasn't anyone supposed to protect me?

At eleven-ten we rolled up to the airport's main doors. Dan flipped on his hazard lights, jumped out, then ran around to open my door. The parking lot looked deserted. I wondered why he didn't just park in a slot. He appeared apprehensive. He was several steps ahead of me as we entered the airport building. The place looked empty but I heard excited voices talking. I was suddenly stung with terror. The Welcoming Committee was still here, and the newcomers were hauling their duffel bags and crates toward me. They had just gotten off the plane. I jumped behind a pillar, paralyzed with fear. Dan came back for me looking befuddled.

"What in the world are you doing? I walked all the way over there and turned to say something to you and you were gone."

"I can't. They're here. They'll see me."

"The Temple? They followed us here?"

"No, they were already here. They'll see me."

"Well, I'm with you!" He put his hand on my shoulder. "I'll protect you. Now, pull yourself together. Your plane is boarding."

I mustered all my strength, stood up straight, then stepped out from behind the pillar with Dan. My friends stopped and stared at me in disbelief. I raised my finger to my lips and shook my head, trying to convey that I was on a secret mission. I nodded my head at them, acknowledging that now they, too, were part of my charade. I signaled that they had to be careful not to approach me. I continued with Dan toward the Customs agent. My comrades stepped back, in an effort to be unobtrusive. I could see they were whispering, excited that they had happened upon a covert operation. I could imagine the commotion when they got home and told Karen about this adventure. She would immediately get back on the radio to report my defection to Father. "Lucinda was seen at the airport. We think she plans to visit her uncle Rex." Rex was our code name for the U.S.A. But by then I would be gone, in the air on my way to safety.

"Miss? Excuse me. I need your passport." The official, with his khaki shirt and pants, his administrative emblems dangling from his pocket, looked annoyed. Perhaps he was mad that I was arriving so late for the flight. Dan handed him my passport and ticket.

"Interesting. This passport has no stamp on it. How long have you been in Guyana?"

I looked at Dan. He nodded his head for me to proceed. I assumed the consul had taken care of it.

"Five and a half months, sir," I announced honestly.

"What? You've been here five months and you're trying to leave this country without tax clearance?"

"But it's an emergency. My father is extremely ill and I have to leave tonight!" The Temple crew still watched me from across the room. Dan looked uneasy.

"Excuse me. But I am with the American Embassy and this woman has been given official clearance to leave the country."

"The embassy? You do not make the law of the Guyanese government! You cannot give clearance. It's a Guyanese judicial procedure. No one leaves without tax clearance if they have resided in this country for more than three months."

Dan very cordially asked, "Sir, may I use your phone? Perhaps the ambassador can clear this up for us. This woman must be allowed to leave tonight!"

"My father is dying!" I pleaded.

"Well, he'll just have to live another day without you," the Guyanese agent scoffed. After what seemed an eternity, Dan passed him the phone so the ambassador could inform him that I had emergency clearance to leave the country. While the agent nodded, my flight started down the runway. I heard the plane overhead as it flew into the star-studded night, without me.

People were talking around me but I no longer took in what they said. The Customs agent raised his shoulders and pointed to the runway.

"Guess we should have listened to you. Now what?" Dan said sheepishly.

"I can't go back to the house. It'd be too dangerous."

"Let's see, by the time we get back into town it will be two A.M. The only place I can think to take you is the Tower Hotel. We'll figure out the rest when the embassy opens tomorrow at eight."

During the commotion, I had seen my Temple comrades gather the luggage of the new arrivals and leave. They had even waved good-bye to me. I felt afraid, alone, and dreadful.

As we drove away from the airport, I held back the tears. I wanted someone to hold me, to tell me that everything would be okay. I noticed the stars sparkling silently above. Everything appeared easy and effortless, but it was all wrong. Dan was driving back to the capital as if nothing had changed. For him, tomorrow would be just another day. He'd wake up and change his outfit, then leisurely walk the few blocks to the embassy.

As for me, I was close to annihilation. My mother, my brother, the friends whom I had betrayed, were already being told horrible stories about me and why I had defected. Anyone who left was evil, depraved, and antisocial. Beth was probably listening to Father's lies about me right then: that I had tried to molest her son, that I had had an affair with her husband, that I wrote reports suggesting she was an unfit mother. Karen was probably being told that I had been working for the CIA for the last six weeks, and Father was saying how sorry he was that when he'd read my vicious reports about her he'd believed them. Every person who once cared for me was probably being told hideous lies about me so that they would have no qualms about finding and hurting me.

Maria was probably searching through the copious Temple files for the blank sheets of paper I signed while Father was conjuring up ghastly misdeeds to be written on them as my confessions. I could almost see Jack, seated next to Karen in the radio room, undoubtedly being instructed on how to abduct, silence, and drug me into oblivion. I even imagined the spittle in the creases of Sharon's mouth as she spoke over the radio to Karen, giving her the phone number of the doctor who had drugged Margarita. I knew how it worked, I knew the techniques well.

Bobby had probably been ordered to wait at the American Embassy until tomorrow night, watching and reporting on all activities: who arrived, when, with whom, and whether the ambassador looked anxious. Another one of the youngsters had most likely been assigned to wait outside and observe the entrance to the Post Office where the passport and tax clearance offices were housed. And finally, a point man had probably been assigned to drive the van continually from the embassy to the Post Office and back, retrieving information and calling Headquarters from the only public phone, at the Pegasus Hotel. Karen Layton would heroically transmit the gory details by the hour to Father, Carolyn, and Maria.

What were they going to tell Mama? That I was a heroin addict? That I had become a whore, slept with outsiders, and become disgracefully pregnant? Would they convince her that I had stolen thousands of dollars and fled the country? Would they pressure her into telling them all our secrets? Mama . . . Mama, please don't believe them.

And poor, unsuspecting Larry, still in the United States. What would they tell him? Would he be sent to Guyana before I got a chance to speak with him, warn him? Yes! Jim would tell him vile stories about my defection, that I'd hurt everyone's chance to immigrate to Cuba. He would be told it was because of me that Mama's health was deteriorating. Oh, the lies, the terrible, brutal lies. Lies that I, too, had believed about other bad people who had left the church. It was there, in the car heading back toward the capital, that I realized they must have been just like me, they hadn't meant any harm, they had never planned to hurt us. Oh my God, all the evil, miserable lies.

Dan grabbed my hand and we dashed into the lobby of the Tower Hotel. It was two-thirty in the morning.

"She needs a room for the night," Dan announced importantly.

"Passport, please," said the young clerk. "And the rooms are one hundred dollars U.S. per night."

"Do you have some money?" Dan asked. I remembered the crumpled $100 bill from the afternoon's begging, still in my pocket, and placed it on the counter.

"Dan, this isn't a good idea. The Temple will be hitting every hotel in the capital looking for me. Don't leave me here alone. And not under my real name."

Dan excused us from the check-in desk and listened to my litany of schemes the Temple would employ to discover my whereabouts.

"It is of utmost importance that you do not divulge the name of this woman to anyone, unless they show an American diplomatic passport." He pulled out his and allowed the clerk to study it more closely.

"Good. I understand."

"No matter what story they tell you, that my mother is ill, my Father has just died, that my sister is about to give birth and needs my rare blood type Q. No matter what, you cannot say I am here or give out the room number," I added.

"Of course. Only with a badge."

Dan stepped off the elevator onto the sixth floor and began to carefully search every dark corner. He then entered my room and checked under the bed and in the bathroom, then once more he looked around the hallway.

"I'll be here at 8 A.M. sharp."

I deadbolted the door behind him as he left, walked into the bathroom, and began to run a hot bath. Looking around for some shampoo, I came across the tiny courtesy bar of soap and set it on the tub's porcelain edge. I called the front desk and asked if someone could give me a cigarette.

A young black man came to my door. "We'll keep you safe," he winked. He lit the match, puffed hard on a fresh cigarette, and handed it to me. I watched him leave, then bolted and chained my door. The bath had filled close to the top. I found an ashtray and set it on the bathroom floor next to the tub. I discarded my crumpled shorts, pulled my jeans and shirt from the bag Dan had left on the desk, and laid them out on the chair. Taking a long drag, I sank into the cool water and began to cough. The smoke was foreign to my lungs, but the taste was so forbidden, I could feel my ties to Father loosening even further. I grabbed for another drag, but my wet fingers extinguished the embers.

Drying off and walking around the room with no clothes on felt exhilarating. I had never had the occasion or the privacy before to do this, not even in boarding school. It gave me a sudden, fleeting taste of freedom.

Then I called the front desk and asked the time.

"Four o'clock, miss."

"Will you ring me at seven-thirty?" As I hung up the phone, I tried to remember Annalisa's phone number. I wrote it down several different ways, but they all looked wrong. Why couldn't I remember?

I slipped into bed, between the crisp, clean cotton sheets and rolled into a little ball. As the soft pillow hugged my head, I tried to sleep but an ugly vision invaded my thoughts. I was lying here, ensconced in opulence and wonderful silence, but I saw everyone running from their cabins, the loudspeakers blaring: "Hurry, children! Hurry, mothers! Quickly, everyone to the Pavilion! We have had a defection! We have a traitor in our midst!" I saw Mary hobbling up the hill from the kitchens. Mama was disoriented, weak, and suddenly desperately afraid. "Who could it be?" They were both wondering if it was me. Mama was asking herself if she should stand tonight and indict herself during this terrible commotion.

My bed was no longer comfortable. The backs of my legs were sweaty. I sat up. My comrades were in danger. Another White Night, tonight, into day, into tomorrow, and all my fault. I had endangered their lives for my own selfish reasons. I begged God not to let Father hurt them. They couldn't die because of me.

I relit my cigarette. Now what? Always nightmares? I stared at the phone and tried again to remember Annalisa's phone number. All alone and no one to talk to. If only Dan had stayed with me.

There was a noise in the hallway. Someone was moving about near my room. I closed the bathroom door, turned the lock, switched off the light, and cowered quietly in the bathtub. I waited and listened until, exhausted, I fell asleep in the tub.

I was awakened by the ringing of the phone.

"Good morning . . . It's seven-thirty and you have a gentleman here waiting for you. A Mr. Daniel Weber."

"Tell him to come up in ten minutes." I quickly rang off. I wanted to go home. As I unlocked the door to my room and tied my shoes, Dan triple-knocked and opened the door.

"How'd you sleep?"

"Okay."

"You look tired." He smiled awkwardly. "Everything is set. We'll run over to tax clearance this morning and get your stamp."

"Dan . . . I don't need to go. You can do it alone. Really . . . I've done this before, remember, for Carolyn."

"No, you need to do it. I will be with you the entire time and never leave your side."

"Please!!!!! They'll be there. They've been posted everywhere to find and challenge me. I don't want to go there."

"Debbie." His voice raised slightly. "I am the vice consul of the American Embassy and I give you my word, I will stay at your side and not allow anyone to approach you."

Grabbing my plastic bag, he put his arms on my shoulders and directed me toward the door. My stomach growled softly. I was hungry and had no more money.

Outside, I looked around for the van, but saw nothing. It was a three-block walk to the Post Office and only Dan and I were on the street. It seemed odd that no one had emerged yet, but when we approached the tax clearance entrance I noticed a dark vehicle pulling back slightly behind the building.

"Dan, they're here. I shouldn't have come. Can't you take me back to the embassy?"

"Remember my promise? Come on, Deb, we're almost there. Say, when we're all done I'll buy you lunch."

I felt eyes following me. My hands shook. He didn't get it. Why was it so hard to understand?

"You'll be okay." Dan tried to calm me.

The Post Office was filled with people. My blouse was getting sweaty. I was not a very impressive-looking person. Dan directed me to the desk of an official.

"We are here to get her passport's tax clearance," Dan explained.

"There are five people ahead of you. Take a seat and I'll call when it's your turn."

The official directed me to the last chair in the waiting room. Dan encouraged me to take it, then leaned against the wall by the reception desk and watched me and the room. The decor of the room was as antiquated as the building. The walls were of dark wood and the little light that entered came from small window openings in the ceiling. The chairs were dark brown and splintered.

"Ms. Blakey," the official announced after too many minutes. "You may proceed, alone."

"But . . ." Dan interjected, "we're here on official business and I must stay with her."

"Only the girl is allowed."

In the next room, even more people were waiting. The walls looked as though they'd been painted ages ago, with more scuffs and chips on them than paint. I looked pleadingly at Dan, but he shrugged his official shoulders.

I took one of the only two empty chairs. Dan remained standing at the entryway. Suddenly, from the darkness at the other end of the room, someone got up and moved toward me. It was Deirdre. Tall, black, and beautiful, Deirdre had come into the capital with Beth. Her father had been Jim's assistant minister, and she, like Bobby, had been raised in the church. Deirdre was on her way to becoming important. Dan watched as she took the seat next to me.

"Debbie," she implored, "what are you doing?"

"I don't know," I answered.

"You know Jim lets anybody go back to the United States who wants to. All you had to do was ask."

"For whom are you saying this? No one is listening." I looked straight ahead.

"Come on, Debbie. Father loves you."

"Listen, Deirdre, you know the truth and I know the truth, so let's not discuss it. I'm not hostile or vindictive, I just want to go back."

"But, Debbie, you know you can."

"I've tried all that, remember? My sister sent me a telegram saying to meet her in Caracas and Jim said no. I had no alternative. I'm not here to argue with you, you are not going to change my mind, so please just leave me alone."

She was upset and left.

"Miss Blakey . . ." I walked over to the official's desk. "You are requesting tax clearance?"

"Yes, I must return to the United States."

"Please take a seat in the room over there. They will help you." He pointed.

I moved to the next room, still in view of Dan, who remained at the first entrance.

As I watched him, I saw Deirdre coming back. She nudged Dan aside, the officials allowing her access without question, and moved quickly toward me. Another communiqué from Jim.

"Jim wants to know why you are leaving." She took a dramatic breath. "The very least you can do is say why you're leaving."

I looked over to Dan. There was no help coming from him. I decided to comply. Maybe Jim would see I wasn't planning to hurt anyone.

"Okay." Deirdre pulled out a notepad and began to write my words verbatim. They had run out of cassettes.

"I don't believe the structure in Jonestown is good," I declared. "I think it is too severe, some of the punishments are way out of line. I'm not vindictive toward the church. I'm not leaving to hurt anyone, I just want to go back to the United States, have a life of my own, keep separate. That's all. I want to settle down and have a family."

"But, Debbie, you can have all that here."

"Listen, I was there when Lorina came back from visiting the Capital, when she admitted having an affair with a Guyanese man. Do you think Father was pleased with her? Did he encourage her to have a relationship? She was so desperate and lonely she had an affair in town, and then, when she was told to write herself up, that all would be forgiven, I saw her beaten, I watched her on the Learning Crew, barely able to walk from the physical abuse. Her eyes were black and swollen. I won't forget that, ever. The way she stood before Father, bruised and bloodied and he glared at her. 'You will rue the day you were born . . . I'll work you until you go crazy.' No, Deirdre, I cannot live in Jonestown. I cannot be part of the organization anymore."

"Just talk to Jim on the radio. Come back to the house and talk to him."

"I won't come back to the house!"

"Then will you talk to him via telephone and I'll relay?"

"Miss Blakey . . ." a male voice called out.

"I'll think about it," I exhaled as both of us rose and moved in separate directions. Exhausted, I entered the cubicle I had been waved into.

Another hour passed as I answered questions: why I stayed there for five months, where I lived, whether I traveled during that time, why I didn't have my original passport, why the embassy was helping me . . . and on, and on. When I finally walked out, Dan hugged me and assured me I had done a good job.

The rain began as we walked into the streets of the capital, with my passport now officially stamped. I noticed the tail end of a dark van pull around the corner and another one following us from one block behind. I was too tired to care.

"Wow, what a downpour!" Dan pulled out a small umbrella and held it over our heads. I saw the embassy flag drooping with wetness, no longer a crisp, proud symbol of freedom. All I could think of was Mama.

17
Emergency Standby

"Good job," the consul, Dick McCoy, said as he walked over and hugged me. The embassy was cold and I felt sticky in my damp clothes. "You look tired," he observed. "Why don't you go in the other room and take a nap? Our flight's at five-thirty. You'll head out at two-thirty. I'll be busy until then. Right now I need to finish my discussions with the ambassador, about *you!*" He smiled. "You're registered as emergency standby."

"I don't have a seat? I may not get on this flight?" Panic overtook my weary body. Weren't they supposed to be taking care of me?

"It's just that all the flights have been sold out for months and the emergency designation will ensure you get bumped up to the head of the list. Everything's going to be all right," he promised.

Dan ushered me to a well-cushioned couch, as the consul answered the telephone.

"Hello? Yes, this is the consul. No, I haven't seen Miss Blakey. No, I don't know where she is. Mmmhmm. Well, I understand that she spent the night at the Tower Hotel. Yes. Okay, then. Good-bye." He raised his eyebrows. "Your sister-in-law is worried about you and wanted to know if you were here."

"They know I am! They followed us here. They're checking up on you to see which side you're taking. Now that you've lied, they'll inform Jim. They saw me come in five minutes ago. You better be careful."

"I've taken no sides. You asked to go home and it is my duty to assist you." He sounded defensive. "Dan, take care of Debbie. Get her some lunch. I'll be back shortly."

While Dan foraged for food somewhere in the embassy, I crumpled into a ball on the couch. The consul hadn't taken sides? Did that mean he didn't believe me? If I got upset would the embassy refuse to help me? Would they determine I was too much of a bother? Maybe they'd agree with Karen and Sharon and decide I was selfish, and return me. I couldn't make trouble.

Unable to relax, I got up and began to pace the floor, wondering if I should call the house or not. If I didn't call, Jim would think I was trying to hide something. If I did, he'd think I was indecisive, I hadn't planned a vendetta, and I wasn't going to hurt them. I'd better call and act grown-up, honest, caring.

"Man, oh man." Dan entered with a tray of goodies. "Here's some comfort food."

"Dan, I've decided to call Jim and tell him why I'm leaving." I grabbed a slice of apple.

"Why?"

" 'Cause if I don't, he'll think worse things about me and plan more devious ways to hurt me."

"Whatever you think is right." Dan set the food closer to me on the desk.

"Can I use your phone?"

"Use the phone over there. Do you want me to stay with you, or would you rather be alone?"

"Doesn't matter." Everything was in code anyway. I picked up the phone to dial the Temple headquarters in town. I quickly swallowed the apple. "Deirdre, it's Debbie."

"Hold on." She set the phone down. "Jim," I could hear her clearly, speaking over the radio, into Jonestown. "Lucinda is on the phone."

Father seemed to be talking away from the radio, but I could hear everything. "We need to change all the codes. Yes, good point, Maria, the signatures, too. Ask her why she's leaving."

I began my recitation: "Life is dreary and unhappy there. Everyone is afraid, the work day is too long, the food doesn't provide energy, people should be allowed to live with their families, and besides that . . . the punishments have become too harsh, even dangerous. Especially the incident with Lorina."

I had been put into Lorina's field crew when Lee was pulled for construction. She'd been kind, considerate, fair, and she'd never written any of us up, but Jim had been vicious to her after her one-month "PR" stint in the capital.

"Yes, my precious," Father hummed. He sounded relieved and comforted to hear my voice. I was glad I had called. I could feel my facial features relax and soften. "I just don't understand why you have remained silent until now. Why didn't you come and warn me of your concerns, so I could lighten the discipline? I agree with you regarding Lorina. But tell me, why did you not speak up and protest at the time? Why did you allow her to be mistreated if you felt so deeply that our approach was unfair?" He paused to accentuate my silence. "I also believe it became too severe, but you must understand, darling, this is something a person of your caliber would never have done. You, my soldier, must learn not to always identify with the weak. Remember? That is why you got into so much trouble in high school. You cannot help the simple man by becoming one with him, or with her, in the case of Lorina."

"But—"

"Lucinda, listen closely to me. You have always been very special to me. That is why, when you became ill, I removed you from the fields, had you nursed to health, and then placed you in charge of all our transmissions into the capital. Do you think I would have done such a thing if I didn't hold you in the highest esteem? Would I have made you a signatory on all our foreign accounts, allowed you to travel to so many places? Have I not shown you how special you are to me?" He sighed. "You are powerful, smart, envied by many." I was?

"And presently you are extremely tired. It is because of your hard work and selfless dedication that you have faltered. This is only an aberration, a momentary and understandable slip. I was convinced when the others told me not to send you, that they were mistaken, jealous of my trust in you. Karen was resentful, Maria didn't want you here near me because she was threatened by my feelings for you. It was I who constantly extolled your abilities, the insights you had on the radio, your concrete and useful suggestions in crises. Did you think I hadn't noticed how diligently you worked in the fields? I was proud when Lee reported your exceptional dedication to hard work, even as you became ill." Lee? Lee had promoted me? With all my sniveling about the bugs in my syrup? What had I done to him now? Would he, too, be blamed?

"Of course, neither Karen nor Maria feels any animosity now. They love you, too, and miss you." Really? "Karen wrote me to say she thinks you are doing a marvelous job there." His voice seemed suddenly tighter. "Do you remember *what* Lorina did? *How* she put the entire organization at risk?" His voice softened again. "*You* would never have done such a thing. You have had many occasions where you could have, but your understanding of our purpose and your integrity would not have allowed you to sully our work as Lorina did."

There was a long silence and I wondered if I was supposed to say something.

"Lucinda! Do you understand what she did wrong? It isn't that she had a relationship with a man. I condone such things. You could have had one with your husband, but you chose not to. No, what she did was contemptible. She had no reason to allow herself to be defiled by that man. Her only excuse was that she fell in love." His voice became more shrill as he relived the altercation. "What is that word? What evil monstrosities have befallen civilization under the guise of love? No, only her selfish needs and capitalistic desires put this project in harm's way. Tell me, Lucinda, how could anyone love an outsider? Someone who doesn't believe in our objectives, doesn't have our dedication and commitment to life. Tell me, after all you know, that Lorina did not deserve her scolding?"

I imagined the radio room: Jim at the controls, sitting stiffly, seething at the microphone tightly clutched in his pale, swollen hand, spittle flying from his hisses, Maria and Carolyn on the day-bed watching. I was certain Maria felt vindicated for her old dislike of me and poor Carolyn must have been wondering why and how I could have deceived her. I could see the armed guards standing nearby, outside the room, at heightened alert, eager to know which "asshole-traitor" had put their lives at risk this time. But as always, Father would be keeping the defector's identity a secret, hoping to bring him or her back. He would not let the others know it was me . . . not yet. The defection of one so trusted, so close and devoted to Father might ignite second thoughts in their minds.

Feeling awkward and unsure of how to respond, I tried again, too anxious to stay in code.

"I do believe that structure is good, and I needed it when I joined. It helped me grow. But it's not helpful anymore. People are afraid to speak freely and honestly for fear of retribution. There is no freedom. It is not the dream world they came to so willingly. Jonestown is not the Promised Land they envisioned. Tell me why letters from families in America are not allowed to be delivered there? What is so dangerous about a note from a loved one?"

"I'm worried about your logic. Tell me, why do you think it is? Because," he yelled into the radio, "those people are not with us. They are part of the system that oppresses us. Have you forgotten your socialism so soon? If they are not with us, they're against us! Oh, my soldier, all you need is sleep right now. A short rest here with me, and you'll be back to normal." He paused. "And tell me, darling, have you ever thought about your mother? Does this *freedom* you wish for permit you to leave her?"

I was silent.

"It will kill her, Lucinda." His voice was hoarse. "She is already sooo weak."

"But you don't have to tell her. Don't make her suffer for my selfishness," I pleaded. I imagined Mama worrying about the defector, her fretting. Did she know it was my fault?

"How could we not? You've already made contact with your sister."

"Wait . . . You don't know that! What makes you believe that I contacted my sister?"

"The telegram, for one thing," he sneered into the receiver.

"She doesn't have any idea what's going on. I've told her nothing. Please . . . can't you just tell Mama I've returned to the United States to finish business?"

"My little warrior, Debbie, you're exhausted," Father consoled me. "You have been working too hard. You need to rest. Tell me, darling, where are you calling from?" His voice was slow and crackled with the frequency static.

"A friend's house."

"What's the phone number there, so we can call you later?" he asked sweetly.

"I can't tell you that . . . um, she'd be upset. I'll call you." I could almost feel his repulsion. I imagined him leaning back, away from the radio, as if to get further away from my voice. But he persisted.

"So tell me, Lucinda, what *other* reasons do you have for leaving?"

"Well, I know you're going to think it sounds strange . . . because I've never admitted this publicly before." I took a deep breath. "I want to have a family. Yes, I know what you think, that the nuclear family is a selfish concept; how could people be so small-minded, wanting just their own tiny family? I realize there are too many children who have been orphaned and forgotten, who need adoption and guidance, but I want my own, too."

His voice was no longer soft. "Lucinda! Have you taken leave of your senses? How egocentric and naïve! Do you think you can find happiness fulfilling this myopic dream? Are you so ignorant to believe anyone will want you? I am the one who saved you. I took you into my heart, my mind, and my confidence. You are my soldier, my creation. Do you think you would have been in a position to even have these thoughts if I had not taught you? It's been under my tutelage that you have blossomed, through my eyes that you discovered this world. Do you think you can ever go back to the way it was before? The CIA has you on a list, the FBI is waiting to imprison you. Do you honestly believe you can walk away from the greatest purpose on this earth and not reel from the consequences? You'll *rue* this day forevermore. I will *never* allow you to forget . . . What . . . What is your little mind saying? That I cannot? Have you forgotten my powers? They will haunt you forever." Would they? Last night I had dreamed I was carrying Mama away from the darkness toward an open space, to safety . . .

"And, so, my weak-hearted warrior, what do you think will become of your mother and brother?"

My heart began to pound in absolute terror. No! It was not their fault. I could hardly hear his driveling anymore. Dan glanced over, alarmed by my sudden rigidity.

"Do you think Larry will forgive you for killing his mother?" Father continued. "Do you think he will ever live peacefully here, knowing his sister has pushed the possibility of our existence nearer to the edge? He shall be outcast. Forced into depravity because of *your* selfish defection." Oh God, how could I do this to them? "Tell me, when did *they* make contact with you? The CIA? How much have *they* paid you to betray your mother? Don't try, don't even contemplate trying to contact Larry in San Francisco . . . I am warning you now, do *not* contact anyone in the States. You know all too well, Lucinda, from your own labors in the past. We will follow, track, hound, and silence you. . . ." My heart stopped.

"But, darling." His voice became silky sweet, a welcome respite from his bellowing. "You still have a chance. You still have time to redeem yourself. Oh, Lucinda, my darling, how I have loved and molded you in my image. Think about what your actions will do to us, to me, on my birthday. Can you betray the only man who ever loved you, on my forty-seventh birthday? Come back here, to Jonestown, and tell me your reasons. I will listen attentively. I want you to tell me how to improve life in the Promised Land. Come back and tell your mother to her face why you want to desert her. We all deserve to hear you explain yourself, in person." His voice was plaintive. Oh, Father, had I fallen so low? In a flash, had I become a conspirator, a wretched, murderous capitalist? Had Dan noticed too? He looked somber; he was frowning. Had everyone seen it, my filth, my weakness? The ease with which I was willing to sacrifice other people's lives for my own selfish fulfillment?

"I can't do that, Father."

"Then wait and talk to Marsha," his real wife's, Marcie's, code name.

"Right now, on the radio?"

"No, she'll come to the capital and talk with you." Why Marcie? Because she was kind and I wouldn't fear her hurting me? Would someone come in with her? Someone Marcie didn't realize would harm me? I could imagine our meeting: she'd beg me to stay, then a sudden scuffle. Marcie would yell for it to stop but it would be over quickly. I would be comatose and ready for transport back in, to Father.

"When? How soon?"

"In a week. Can you wait a week with your plans? Wait and talk to Marsha. Wait for us to finalize the plans with Shirley next month." His voice soothing again, he wanted me to reconsider and give in.

"In a month?"

"Lucinda, sweetheart, can't you wait until we have our beloved children safely there?"

"I don't know." Could I wait to save the lives of the children? "Jim, I just don't know."

"Don't go to Rex [U.S.A.] . . . go to Elsie [England] instead. Rex will arrest you. I don't want to see you go to prison for what you've done in the past."

"You mean, just show up on Elsie's doorstep?"

"We'll assist you with Maria [finances]."

"Okay, what do you want me to do?" I felt besieged, I was wavering. I shouldn't have called, I wasn't going to be able to go on with this. Jesus, what would Dan think when I told him I couldn't leave yet?

"Exactly what will I do at Elsie's?"

"From Elsie's go to Shirley [Russia]."

"You mean you trust me, after everything I've done in the last twenty-four hours, to go to Elsie's, then Shirley's?"

Dan handed me a note in large print.

"IT'S TIME TO GO."

"Yes, you can help us from there with immigration. Lucinda, I trust you . . ." His voice was melodic and soothing. He did care about me. "I think you're just very paranoid right now . . . very, very tired. You need rest, my precious. I have never stopped trusting you."

"Okay. I'll go to Elsie's. But what will I do there? I have no money." There was a long silence. Warning bells went off in my head and I suddenly realized he was taping me. He was waiting for me to ask for money. He would say that I blackmailed the group for "quiet" money, in return for my silence.

"I have no money," I repeated. "Where will I stay?"

"Once you're in Elsie's parlor [England], go to Shirley's house [the Russian Embassy]. We will arrange for them to help you."

"Okay, I'll fly to Elsie's," I responded, completely uncertain of what I was saying.

Dan pushed another note in front of me: "WE'VE GOT TO LEAVE." I wanted to go home. Annalisa was waiting for me. I needed to tell the consul that I would be arrested, handcuffed, shackled, and taken into custody.

"I've got to go now."

"Wait . . . Lucinda . . . I trust you. Will you call me in six hours?"

"Yes, I will call in six hours." Maybe they wouldn't follow me anymore.

"Why do you have to go now, darling?" Father's voice was loving, concerned.

"I just have to," I pleaded.

"Yes. Well then, we'll talk again in six hours." His voice was forgiving. "Until then, Lucinda."

"Over and out, Father."

Dan jumped up and grabbed my arm. "What was all that about? Shirley, Elsie, Rex . . . sounds like a plot for a B movie. C'mon! It's after two-thirty." I grabbed my cigarettes and a mango from the tray and followed Dan out the back door. The car was concealed from view. I climbed into the backseat, curled up into a pill-bug, and remained motionless until we were safely out of town.

"Where's the consul?" I called from the backseat.

"Coming later. He'll meet us there. I wanna make sure you're on time. Join me up front. It's safe."

"Sure no one followed us?"

Dan looked into his mirror to double-check. "We're fine. You'll get some sleep on the plane," he remarked as if in mid-thought. I liked him . . . even if he did bungle things.

As we pulled into the airport parking lot, I carefully scanned the area, scrutinizing the color and shape of each vehicle.

"Funny, I don't see the van. They're not out here. I wonder where they are?"

"Maybe they aren't going to follow you." Dan grabbed his briefcase from the floor next to my feet. "Coming? I want to reconfirm your emergency status on the wait list."

"Can I wait in the car?"

"You feel safe enough, alone?"

"Safer than inside." Dan checked to make sure all four doors were locked, then headed swiftly into the terminal. Partially crouched down in the front seat, I kept a steady lookout for any activity in the lot. No new cars pulled in and none left. But I knew they were there.

Dan rapped at the window. It seemed as if he had only been gone for seconds.

"All set. You're listed. Now we'll wait for Dick to arrive."

Relieved, I bit into the warm, sun-baked ham sandwich Dan had packed for me.

And then I felt her before I even saw her.

"They're here." My stomach tightened. "Someone just walked into the airport terminal."

"How do you know it's them?"

"Just do."

The consul's car drove up and took the empty space next to us. He got out, waved to us, and hurried into the terminal. His wife stayed to accompany Dan and me.

"I'm Dick's wife. You're a courageous young woman," she smiled, and put her arms around my shoulder. "Here is a sweater and jeans-jacket so you won't freeze on the plane. I'm glad Dick was able to get you on his flight. It's better than your being alone." She handed me a piece of paper. "Here's our phone number and address in Washington. When you get settled, please drop us a note and let us know how you're doing." We followed the consul to the ticket counter, Dan behind me, protecting my back.

"Let's go! Time to check in through Customs." The consul grabbed my arm and kissed his wife's lips inches above my head. Pushing me ahead of him, he led us to the front of the line, and into the face of the Customs agent. The consul flashed his official passport and was ushered around me into the restricted area. I didn't like being left alone.

"Yes, miss?" The agent looked down at me. "Your passport, please."

"I have everything you need this time," I smiled at my former adversary.

"And of course, I will just need ten dollars," he retorted.

"I don't have any money."

"Can't get through without the transfer fee." He raised his eyebrows. Dan fidgeted in his pocket, then looked frantically around for the consul's wife.

"Next, please." The agent summoned the passenger behind me.

"Wait . . . I have to get on this flight!"

"Yes. Your father's ill . . . I know this already. However, I must have your transfer fee."

I could see Dan running about furiously. I watched in disbelief as the gentleman behind me took my place. My heart began to sink when Dan came rushing back over with an American ten-dollar bill.

"Ten, Guyanese!" the agent scoffed. Not again. Not today. They couldn't keep me off this plane, too. There was a slight commotion as the consul's wife stepped forward and hurriedly exchanged Dan's American bill for a Guyanese bill.

"Good-bye, Debbie." Dan grabbed me and kissed my cheek. "Promise me you'll sleep on the plane?"

I hugged him back, too embarrassed to kiss him.

"Good luck, honey." He waved.

Moving through the Customs area into the "Passengers Only" section, I looked for the consul. I wanted to be near him. Suddenly, someone grabbed my shoulder from behind.

"Debbie, please don't do this to us! We love you . . . Jim loves you." Karen put her head on my neck and began to cry uncontrollably. Poor Karen, I thought. She really cares. Her sobs were getting to me. I rubbed her back and tried to comfort her. When she pulled away to look at me, I was shocked. Her eyes were bloodshot red and completely dry. Two sleepless nights—not a trace of affection or sorrow—were emanating from her stare.

"How can you do this to Jim . . . on his birthday?"

She pulled back from me, realizing she wasn't going to reach me, and abruptly walked away. That was all? I couldn't believe it. I saw the consul sitting in a window seat, waving to his wife. Dan was beside her, watching me, and I waved to him, relieved I was almost on the plane. Suddenly I saw Dan's arms motioning to me and he was running toward the Customs agent, trying to gain access to me. Abruptly, a hand grabbed my arm. It was Beth. Not even the American Embassy had the power of Jim Jones in this country.

Beth seemed angry at first but it was feigned and the rage quickly disappeared from her face.

"Why? Why didn't I realize it?" Hugging me tightly, she began to weep.

"It's not your fault."

"Oh, Debbie. I'm not supposed to be crying. Shit! Karen will see me. I'm supposed to be yelling at you," she whispered through the tears. "Please, Debbie! Just wait. Wait till we can get the children to safety, into Russia. For my sake, for Chioke's . . . for the sake of our friends."

I ached inside, but I did not cry.

"Beth, listen to me. I don't plan to harm anyone. I just want to return to the U.S. and have my own life. One that only I will be in charge of. I want children, too, like you."

"But your mother, Debbie. How can you desert her?" I could hear Jim's directives seeping into her dialogue. She held me tighter, crying and begging me. "Please . . . Jim's sick . . . he's dying . . . just wait, Debbie. Oh God, why didn't you talk to me first?" She wiped her nose.

"I couldn't. You know that. I'm sorry. I will always . . ." I stopped. Karen was approaching us. Beth hastily pulled herself together.

"Wait, I have a message for you . . ." Beth caught her breath and I knew she was trying to repeat the exact words Father uttered to her. "It would ease the mind of the one who cares the most if you just keep in touch." I looked away from her, out toward the airplane. "Debbie, it isn't his fault. You never gave him a chance. You never told him. It's not his fault that we aren't perfect; you can't blame him for that."

"I'm not blaming him. I just don't like some of the things going on out there." I looked at Karen.

"You've never given him a chance." Karen glared back at me.

"I shouldn't have had to."

I could see the consul urging me to hurry. It was time to board the plane. When Karen turned, I grabbed Beth's hand. "Beth?"

"I know . . . me too, Luce," she whispered, and rushed to catch up with Karen.

I was brokenhearted. The consul came rushing back for me, seized my arm, and pushed me forward, ahead of everyone to the front of the line. The agent opened the doors and pushed me outside. The consul stood back. I was alone out on the airstrip . . . ahead of the crowd.

I began to walk to the jet wondering why the consul was not at my side. No longer surrounded by people, I began to feel uneasy. The plane's boarding ramp was fully extended. I reached the metal stairs and could feel *their* eyes watching me. The center of my back began to burn and I felt nauseated. I imagined a gun aimed at my spine. But I did not increase my pace. My steady, deliberate ascent was my statement to *them.*

"Welcome to Pan Am." The stewardess directed me to a seat. "Would you like a blanket and pillow? You look exhausted." With the pillow under my head and the blanket over my shoulders, I sat and waited for the other passengers to board. Thankful to be alive, I pulled the blanket tighter around my shoulders. I knew I should be sad, that I should cry, but I felt absolutely nothing.

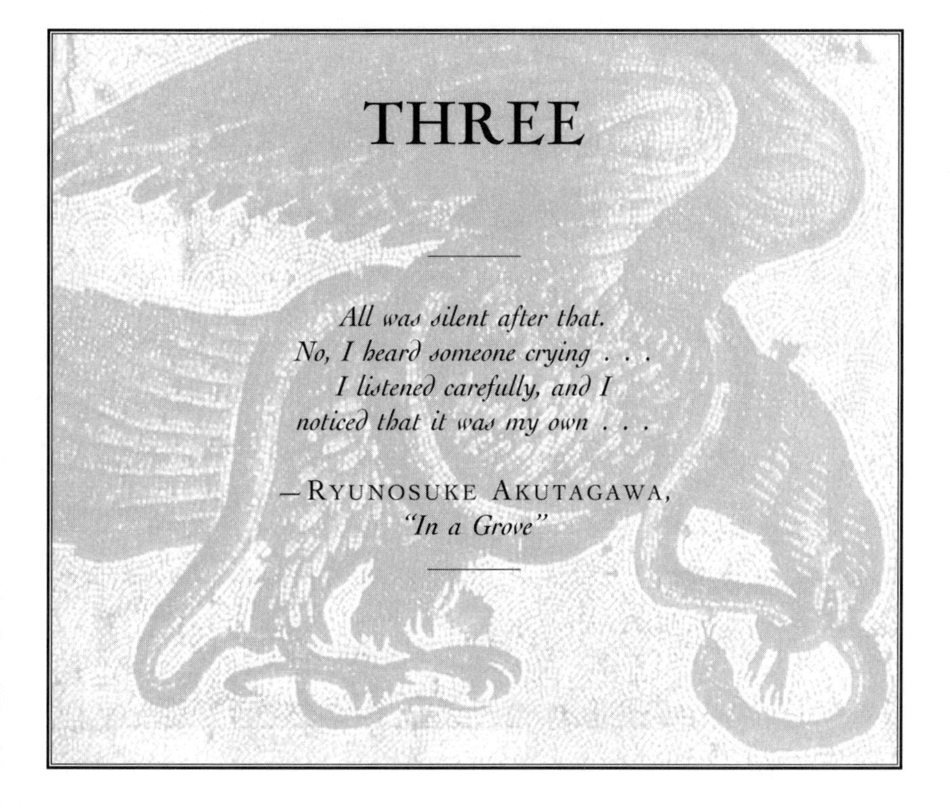

THREE

All was silent after that.
No, I heard someone crying . . .
I listened carefully, and I
noticed that it was my own . . .

—Ryunosuke Akutagawa,
"In a Grove"

18
Doesn't Anyone Hear Me?

The cabin shuddered slightly as we leveled off over the sapphire-blue Atlantic Ocean. Beth's words echoed in my head. "For my sake, for Chioke's . . . for the sake of our friends." I was terrified that I might be sentencing my comrades to death.

I replayed the last forty-eight hours of my escape in my head. I'd been wise to be distrustful of the Embassy and not approach the consul prior to his visit to Jonestown. There was no doubt in my mind he would have half-wittedly divulged my identity. The whole situation had felt surreal from the moment I told the consul of our plan to blackmail him, through the fiasco with my passport stamp and the missing $10 bill. The embassy officials seemed to me like unschooled impostors in a Grandmasters' chess tournament and each one of their moves had been absurdly orchestrated.

Dick McCoy had not taken my concerns seriously. Dan, too, had not grasped or considered the danger my life was in when he left me alone at the Tower Hotel. These two government officials, the people I had to depend on for my safety, who had to handle the repercussions of my defection in Jonestown, were completely oblivious to my warnings. Anxiously, I approached the consul, determined to get through to him. Dick McCoy had to know more . . . everything! I hadn't told him about the foreign bank accounts, that I would be arrested, that I was on the wanted list of the CIA.

The consul looked less powerful sitting in the cramped space of the plane. Just another traveler on my flight back to safety. I tapped his shoulder and asked if we could talk further. He stared at me blankly as I recounted everything I could remember of importance. I spoke of the smuggling of firearms into Guyana, the diversion of funds to foreign bank accounts, the millions of dollars in assets held by the Temple, the millions in cash buried in Jonestown with mothballs to keep the bills from disintegrating. I spoke of the total control Jim had over all his followers and how no one could get out while everyone wanted to.

When the consul furrowed his brow in disbelief and asked why someone wishing to leave could not escape through the jungle, I explained, for the second time, about the presence of armed guards, Jim's continual threats that the Guyanese would return any defectors, and the difficulty of escape through the tangled depths of the jungle. I advised him that even when someone from the American Embassy came to visit Jonestown to check up on the residents, there was not enough confidence in the ability of the official to take the resident out unharmed to warrant the risk.

I knew he didn't believe me when he asked, "If it was so bad, how come people came? Wasn't it of their own free will?"

I tried desperately to explain how all of us believed we were coming to a "Promised Land," a paradise of freedom. Not one person thought they would be entering an armed camp and be forced into hard labor.

I told him I thought someone needed to help and asked if he thought I should go to the press. Perhaps my warnings would encourage a reexamination of the Jonestown situation. McCoy insisted I should not talk to the press. Rather, he said, I should approach the Customs agency and the Bureau of Alcohol, Tobacco, and Firearms.

I wondered why he didn't offer to assist me in these efforts. I was inexperienced and didn't know who to call, and anyway, I explained to him, I would probably be arrested when we arrived in New York. He laughed.

"I've checked the Wanted List and your name's not on it."

Feeling ridiculous and ashamed, I returned to my seat. We arrived in New York at 11 P.M. Alone, I made my way to the hotel where Annalisa had made a reservation for me. I thought of Mama and our glass of wine at the restaurant. Suddenly I panicked and called Annalisa, whose number I remembered without difficulty now, to ask her to redirect my flight to Sacramento. I was certain the Temple would be lying in wait for me at the San Francisco airport. I also told her to call Larry immediately and tell him Jonestown was a prison camp, that he had to talk with me before he left. But I knew he'd probably already been told something that had thoroughly discredited me in his eyes. And I knew that I would have believed the same stories about Larry if our roles had been reversed.

Annalisa was superb. She left my original booking the same, under Deborah Layton Blakey, and booked me under Annie Moffitt, a childhood friend of mine, from New York to Sacramento. Still, within minutes of my arrival at her home in Davis, Pan Am called to ask if I had made it home safely. Obviously, airlines do not call to make sure that their passengers have arrived home safely and we realized the Temple was already looking for me. Annalisa, visibly shaken, immediately called our brother Tom, drove me back to the airport, hidden on her car's floor, and sent me off to Los Angeles and into the safe care of my big brother.

Tom had arranged for us both to stay at one of his friend's home in order to elude the Temple's detectives. A Harvard-trained archaeologist, Tom debriefed me on tape for three long days. He asked me questions about the Temple, how I joined, what I believed, and where I had traveled to. He had always sensed that the Temple was suspicious if not dangerous and kept my first words as documentation.

My second night in America, I had the first of many haunting dreams about my escape. I had been running away from Jonestown with hundreds of people hanging by their hands from my outstretched arms and Mama and Mary holding onto my neck. I must have cried out because when I opened my eyes Tom was sitting on the bed next to me, stroking my hair.

"You're home, Debsy . . . You're in America now," he whispered softly. The following morning he told me of a story he had read about a concentration camp survivor who had pinned an American flag over his bed, so that when he awoke from a nightmare, he'd instantly know he was safe. I wondered how long it would take me to stop having nightmares and feel safe. Little did I know it would only take a few more months before Jim was dead and I had no more reason to fear for my life.

On my third day in America I called John, the angry voice I had heard in the Jonestown radio room demanding to speak with his family. His parents had joined in Indianapolis when he was only eleven and his sister was six. I had always trusted him. When he left for law school, his first chance ever to be away from the Temple, he had gained the clarity to leave. John's defection had indelibly impressed upon Jim that no one, not even "almost blood" sons could remain loyal and resolute away from "Father's aura." John never gave up trying to get his family out.

I found his number through the operator. At first he was suspicious of me but said he was willing to fly to Los Angeles and talk to me. He would make an arrangement with Grace Stoen for his protection: If he did not call her every hour, she would contact the police. He told me of another member who had pretended to have escaped in order to infiltrate the Concerned Relatives as an informer for Jim.

I promised I was not sent to hurt him. Tom understood my need to speak to a former member, but he arranged to meet John at a place at the airport where he could first make sure that John had come alone. Everyone was afraid of everyone else . . . just as Jim had taught us.

That night, John became a beacon of light in the haze of my return to freedom. I felt drawn to his rational demeanor and his careful explanations about Jim and the Temple. He assured me that my fear of an FBI and CIA investigation of me was irrational. He wasn't mean and he seemed comfortable with his decision to leave the organization. I believed he was the only one who could truly understand the massive confusion I was feeling and I wanted to talk on and on with him about what he knew.

I remained in hiding but I was impatient to live on my own, make my own decisions, and be with people who had lived and seen much the same as I. Four days later, with hours of our taped discussions in his possession, I convinced Tom that I needed to return to San Francisco and though he was concerned, he acquiesced.

On the way to the airport I saw a police car driving alongside us and I panicked.

"Oh my God! Watch out, Tom . . . There's a police car!" I yelped.

"Debsy, honey, to me the sight of that car is reassuring."

In that moment I realized for the first time just how skewed my perception of reality was and I wondered how I was going to make it in the strange new world. Could I ever escape my deeply ingrained fears? Did I even know how?

Finally home in the Bay Area, my reunion with Papa was tearful and filled with joy. But as he cried and asked me questions about Mama and Larry, I could feel Jim's condemnations of him resonate within me. It had been a long time since I had considered him my father. It would take me many months to stop viewing him as "Old Man Layton" and trust him as I used to. Papa begged me to stay and live with him in our old house in Berkeley, but eager to begin a new and independent life in San Francisco, I declined.

The next thing I did was call Dick McCoy. It was May 17 and he was still in Washington, D.C. I urgently wanted to know whom he had informed, which agencies were now involved, and if he had sent my affidavit to the department heads at the State Department. But I could not get any answers from him. He tried to assure me that he had everything under control, and reiterated that I should not approach the press.

Fortunately, I had support from John and Grace and Tim Stoen. John and Grace had met me at the airport upon my return from my brother's in Los Angeles. Grace was suspicious of me at first, but once we began talking she saw that I was genuinely afraid. Grace and John became mentors, guides back into a world I had not visited since I was sixteen. I pelted them with a thousand questions: Had the wretched CIA questioned them? Did the evil FBI hound and pester them? Had the Temple put a rattlesnake in their mailbox, too?

Grace laughed and called Jim a "lying asshole." Like the sight of the police car in Los Angeles, Grace's words alarmed and terrified me. I caught my breath and stood perfectly still, shocked that she could be so irreverent. Father had ceaselessly warned us that something bad would happen to us if we spoke blasphemously of him. I expected lightning to strike us dead. But nothing happened. My coffee hadn't even spilled!

Grace proceeded to tell me just how many lies we'd been told. She started with her own son, John-John. "Tim is John's biological father," she said, then spoke in detail of Carolyn Layton's son, Kimo. Many of Father's clandestine missions had been visits to Carolyn's secret apartment in Berkeley to see her and their newborn son. He had explained Carolyn's year-long absence by saying that she had been arrested while on a mission to try to save the life of one of our members. He said she'd been tortured and raped in a Mexican jail, which spurred me to write her numerous heartfelt letters. When she came back after that year and I took care of Kimo, the product of her rape in Mexico, I never thought to question his blond hair and frightfully pale skin.

All those years I had mentally whipped myself for being selfish, for wishing I could have a relationship, dreaming of having a baby.

While I tortured myself, wrote myself up, admitted to being imperfect, and yearned to be like Father, Jones was sneaking off to movies. While the rest of us stayed up all night counseling troubled members, he was in Hawaii vacationing. I listened to Grace and John as they revealed one evil lie after another, and I was crushed by the sheer enormity of deceit that had been at the center of my existence for the past seven years.

By the end of May I had found a job on my own at a large stock brokerage firm in the financial district of San Francisco. My résumé stated, correctly, that I had been the financial secretary for the Disciples of Christ, the denomination that Peoples Temple was part of. I'd hoped by mentioning my schooling in England that they'd think I was smart. It was the first job I had ever had and I felt quite proud of my salary of $1,000 per month.

I was becoming acquainted with life outside the Temple but I still felt like an impostor. The ease with which my colleagues lived their lives often astounded me, so accustomed was I to living in fear. Here, no one I met was afraid of his or her neighbor. These people seemed to live each day as if they would always have another.

Most of my free time was spent worrying about my family and friends in Jonestown. On June 1, 1978, I received a letter from the Temple, addressed care of Annalisa. It had been mailed from Ukiah, California. The postage stamp glued to the letter warned:

Fear to do ill and you need fear naught else.

The unsigned letter conveyed a veiled threat:

> Debbie,
> You should know something that involves you personally. The Consul has told us that you approached him on the plane with an offer to go to the press, which he says he advised you against. Our opinion is that that doesn't sound like you. . . . The conspiracy goes on. . . . It is good to have something to stand for. There are people who care for you very much. You will always be welcome here, as long as you do not try to cause any destruction . . .

Why had McCoy jeopardized my life like that? What was his purpose in telling Jim I had offered to talk to officials and press? I had confided in him and I couldn't believe that he had betrayed my confidences to Jones.

I was confused and upset by McCoy's actions but was afraid to alienate him. He was now my only contact with Jonestown. Remembering his mention of an August Jonestown visit, I composed a letter to my mother and sent it to him asking him to please read it to her in private. I prayed that he would be more careful with the lives of those I had left behind than he had been with mine.

My dearest Mama,

I have asked Dick to read this letter to you as I was concerned that otherwise it would be given to the Clearing Committee and you would never receive it.

It took me a lot of time to figure out how to leave, but from the first day we both got into Jonestown I realized I was not cut out for that sort of life. By all means I had wanted you to come with me, yet I could not figure out how to do it. You mean so much to me and although they have told you horrible stories about my character and morals, I am doing very well. I have a respectable, well-paying job and have begun a new and structured life of my own.

Please believe and trust me—if you are willing to leave—go now with Dick. He can get you a new passport and your ticket is awaiting you in Georgetown. He assisted me in my departure and he will safeguard yours as well. Annalisa, Tom and I will help you when you return and you need not worry about your only possessions there. We can replace them here. It sounds frightening at first, as it is such a big move, but neither Jim nor the church will hurt you.

Things are not what Jim makes them to appear. . . . Of course nothing in the world is perfect or just, but at least here it is your own decisions and you are never threatened by death, mass suicide, the tortures of the box or the Learning Crew.

Lastly, there is no CIA plot either—You can even ask Dick McCoy.

I love you always and forever, *Debbie* ♥

I never received a reply from Dick and was never contacted by the embassy. I decided I could no longer remain silent with so many lives at stake. With Grace Stoen's assistance, I found an attorney and with her help, I wrote an eleven-page, thirty-seven-point affidavit entitled "The Threat and Possibility of Mass Suicide by Members of the Peoples Temple." It detailed the morbid conditions in

Jonestown and Jim's threat of a revolutionary suicide, most specifically in the following points:

> *1. The purpose of this affidavit is to call to the attention of the United States government the existence of a situation which threatens the lives of United States citizens in Jonestown, Guyana. . . .*
>
> *28. Visitors were infrequently permitted access to Jonestown. The entire community was required to put on a performance when a visitor arrived. Before the visitor arrived, Rev. Jones would instruct us on the image we were to project. The workday would be shortened. The food would be better. Sometimes there would be music and dancing. Aside from these performances, there was little joy or hope in any of our lives. An air of despondency prevailed.*
>
> *29. There was constant talk of death. In the early days of the Peoples Temple, general rhetoric about dying for principles was sometimes heard. In Jonestown, the concept of mass suicide for socialism arose. Because our lives were so wretched anyway and because we were so afraid to contradict Rev. Jones, the concept was not challenged. . . .*
>
> *31. At least once a week, Rev. Jones would declare a "white night," or state of emergency. The entire population of Jonestown would be awakened by blaring sirens. Designated persons, approximately fifty in number, would arm themselves with rifles, move from cabin to cabin, and make certain that all members were responding. A mass meeting would ensue. Frequently, during these crises, we would be told that the jungle was swarming with mercenaries and that death could be expected at any moment.*
>
> *32. During one "white night," we were informed that our situation had become hopeless and that the only course of action open to us was a mass suicide for the glory of socialism. We were told that we would be tortured by mercenaries if we were taken alive. Everyone, including the children, was told to line up. As we passed through the line, we were given a small glass of red liquid to drink. We were told that the liquid contained poison and that we would die within 45 minutes. We all did as we were told. When the time came when we should have dropped dead, Rev. Jones explained that the poison was not real and that we had just been through a loyalty test. He warned us that the time was not far off when it would become necessary for us to die by our own hands.*
>
> *33. Life at Jonestown was so miserable and the physical pain of exhaustion was so great that this event was not traumatic for me. I had become indifferent as to whether I lived or died. . . .*

36. I am grateful to the United States government and Richard McCoy and Daniel Weber; in particular, for the assistance they gave me. However, the efforts made to investigate conditions in Jonestown are inadequate for the following reasons. The infrequent visits are always announced and arranged. Acting in fear for their lives, Temple members respond as they are told. The members appear to speak freely to American representatives, but in fact they are drilled thoroughly prior to each visit on what questions to expect and how to respond. Members are afraid of retaliation if they speak their true feelings in public.

37. On behalf of the population of Jonestown, I urge that the United States Government take adequate steps to safeguard their rights. I believe that their lives are in danger. . . .

Deborah Layton Blakey

One month after my escape, on June 14, 1978, my attorney, Marny Ryan (no relation to Congressman Leo Ryan), and I completed the affidavit.

She mailed and telegramed copies of my allegations to a multitude of influential organizations and individuals including: the Associated Press Newswire; Cyrus Vance, Secretary of State; the heads of the other government and intelligence agencies, as well as to officials in three different divisions of the State Department: Douglas J. Bennett, Jr., Assistant Secretary for Congressional Relations; Ms. Elizabeth Powers, Special Consular Services, Department of State; Stephen A. Dobrenchuk, Chief, Emergency and Protection Service Division, Department of State

A strongly worded cover letter by my attorney, addressed personally, read:

I am enclosing an affidavit signed under penalty of perjury by Deborah [Layton] Blakey. Ms. Blakey recently escaped from the Peoples Temple and is extremely concerned for the welfare of not only John Victor Stoen, but also the remaining U.S. citizens in Jonestown.

She points out that while the State Department has made some contact with American citizens living in Jonestown, its investigation to uncover the actual conditions is inadequate. I continue to regard this matter as extremely important and again request your assistance in reaching some solution . . .

On that same day Marny Ryan sat with me as I recounted my story to the *San Francisco Chronicle*'s Marshall Kilduff and the *San Francisco Examiner*'s Tim Reiterman. Despite my fear, I had come to believe that without my going public there could be no hope or peace for my friends in the jungle. Only the *Chronicle* would print my allegations. Within hours, it was picked up by the Associated Press news service. I did not know that Congressman Leo Ryan would read the article and contact me a few months later.

JUNE 15, 1978
GRIM REPORT FROM JUNGLE

> The Peoples Temple jungle outpost in South America was portrayed yesterday as a remote realm where the church leader, the Rev. Jim Jones, orders public beatings, maintains a squad of 50 armed guards and has involved his 1100 followers in a threat of mass suicide . . .
>
> . . . [Layton] said the 1100 followers were told to drink a bitter brown liquid potion, after which they supposedly would fall asleep and then be shot by Jones' guards. The rehearsal went as far as having the community drink a phony potion before Jones called it off . . .
>
> . . . Peoples Temple officers in San Francisco last night relayed—via shortwave radio from Guyana—a refutation of the charges from two of the South American mission's residents, identified as Lisa and Larry Layton, the mother and brother of Deborah Layton.
>
> . . . "These lies are too ridiculous to refute," Lisa Layton said. ". . . We are treated beautifully here . . ."
>
> . . . Larry Layton said, "We are treated beautifully."

What else could they say? Jim had certainly summoned them into the radio room in a rage and instructed them on what to say.

I was petrified after the article appeared. Tim Reiterman had frightened me with his distant, perfunctory questioning. I knew he didn't believe me and I wondered if Jim had gotten to him. Marshall Kilduff on the other hand seemed genuinely concerned. He didn't act as if he had been raised with wet nurses and nannies as Jim had said.

What would Jim do when he saw this? Would he hurt Mama and Larry? I prayed he wouldn't send a hit man for me. My work colleagues had been protective and supportive after the article, but they could not insulate me outside of the office. I walked home via different routes and answered the phone by picking up the receiver and not speaking until I heard who was on the line.

Three days later I received another unsigned, typed letter addressed to me c/o my sister in Davis.

> Debbie,
> We know what you have done . . . about the money—that could have been understood and forgiven. But we don't understand what you are doing now. We wonder, is someone making you do these things, or are you possibly being set up, and you don't know about it?
>
> This is very hard for us to understand, why you would do this. And the people are having trouble understanding why you would do this to them. We would like an explanation as soon as possible. We don't understand why you have done these things to the ones who have loved you the most. We want to build trust. If somebody is trying to hold some lie over your head, let us know. We can help.
>
> You can still pick up the pieces with the various members of the press, and turn it around for good.

As the weeks passed, the letters ceased and life seemed to quiet down. My friends at work accepted that I was a strange celebrity, and never brushed me off. Much to my father's dismay, I moved in with John. John understood my fears and concerns. After all he had his mother, sister, stepfather, and adopted brother in Jonestown, too. I felt safe with him. I could talk about things with him no one else could understand. We grew closer.

My biggest puzzlement was adjusting to time alone. I was unaccustomed to having free time. Since boarding school, I'd constantly had someone telling me what to do, where to be, and how to think. I was not yet equipped to do it on my own. Now, for the first time I had time to question all I had been taught and to think about myself and life in new ways.

John and I lived in an apartment building in the run-down Tenderloin district of San Francisco. For now, I was comfortable in the studio. Someday I would be able to afford to live in a nice place. Papa had offered me money, but I had already taken too much from him and needed to learn to make it on my own. After all, that's why I was there.

Life seemed simple now. I no longer had to read through and decipher a thousand layers of deceit. Every morning, in a café near the office, several of my co-workers and I met and ordered a coffee drink called a "latte." For lunch, we walked to a Japanese restaurant on the edge of Chinatown and ordered a wonderful noodle dish called "udon." I felt extravagant eating at cafés and bistros. And then there were our two daily fifteen-minute coffee breaks. I'd watch in wonder as people pulled out books to read. I hadn't read a book for pleasure since boarding school!

Soon, I migrated onto the trading floor of a small yet prestigious investment bank where I would remain for the next eight years. Working closely with this young band of aggressive entrepreneurs, "evil capitalists" whom Father had condemned, my seven years of indoctrination slowly faded away.

A brand-new world opened its doors to me. I was very honest and told the personnel director about my history. He was kind and accepting about it, and I was relieved. In this fraternity of "evil capitalists," I found understanding and compassion. I was unlearning the falsehoods that Jim had so thoroughly ingrained in my vulnerable young mind. Little by little his brainwashing was losing its hold over me.

I was discovering many faults in how I viewed people. Ned Blackwood, one of the traders and a former Marine, became my mentor. It was his kindness that helped show me that there were good people outside of the Peoples Temple, that actions and deeds are what make a person. In the Temple I had been taught that all white men are bad, that wealth is antirevolutionary, and that all men are homosexual. I still didn't know any better. One day a rich stockbroker ordered lunch but left it in the kitchen, untouched. I looked around to make sure no one was watching, then took the sandwich out of the bag, set it on a napkin, took it back to my desk, and ate it. After all, I thought, he was rich and I was not. He could afford to buy another one. The following day the same very rich man stood at my desk, asking me for advice on one of his accounts. He casually laid his hand on my desk and I saw that it was manicured. I almost gasped. Just as Jim had warned, not only was he a capitalist but he was flaunting being gay! When he left my desk, I immediately went over to Ned on the trading desk.

"Ned, what a capitalist homo he is!" I could hardly contain my disbelief. "He's wearing clear nail polish!"

Ned stopped watching his screen, set down his phone, and looked inquisitively into my eyes.

"Where do you get these absurd beliefs? You say some of the oddest things. Yes, Debbie, he is wealthy. He is also a generous man and just because his hands have been manicured does not mean he's gay. I get mine done before a business trip, too. Now, about the sandwich I saw you take yesterday. . . . That was wrong."

"But, Ned, he can afford it."

"Yes, that's true. But, it isn't the point. That lunch was his, not yours, and he works incredibly hard for his money. He has the right to save his lunch, nibble at it, or toss it in the trash untouched. Only then, if you feel you deserve it, may you retrieve it from the garbage. But before then, you have no claims to his possessions. It is not your prerogative to determine how he should or shouldn't spend his money. You make enough money to purchase your own lunch, Debbie. You're twenty-five years old and making over thirty grand. I'd call that excellent. You're a sales assistant without a B.A. You're bright and a very quick study, but you have a lot to learn. What in the world did they teach you over there in England? It's almost as if you haven't really lived here. You don't know the television shows, you never seem to know who the sports teams belong to. . . . Sometimes I think there's a link missing. It's as if you're a wild child found in a jungle and are just now learning how the world works."

As I tried to acclimate to a free world, Leo Ryan was mounting a campaign against Peoples Temple. After the publication of my affidavit he had begun to receive more letters from the parents of members in Jonestown who had not heard from their loved ones in a long time. Grandparents were worried about their children and their grandchildren. Maria Katsaris's father, Steven, also contacted Ryan, asking for his help in bringing his daughter home. Ryan called and asked to meet with me.

I met Congressman Ryan, the Democratic representative from California's Twelfth District, on September 1, 1978, in San Francisco. I was anxious and shy. At first he acted as though he didn't believe me. But once I began my story, he admitted that he had several constituents whose children were in Jonestown and that my information corroborated theirs and confirmed his fears. He listened intently as I finished describing the conditions, the intimidation, the lack of food, and the weekly suicide drills we practiced in Jonestown.

"As a member of the House Committee on International Relations," he explained, "I am considering leading a congressional delegation to Guyana . . ."

I wondered what that meant and if it would drive Jim into a frenzy.

". . . and I want the State Department fully apprised of the appalling conditions in Jonestown, as your affidavit describes, where American citizens are being held against their will."

Maybe he would meet with Mama and convince her to come home, I thought.

After several hours of conversation, the congressman requested that I fly to Washington and repeat my story to a congressional committee. On November 9, I flew to Washington, D.C., with Grace Stoen and Maria's father, Steven Katsaris, to tell my story.

At last, someone had taken notice.

19
Descent into the Abyss

The air was chilly on the morning of November 13, 1978. The capital's autumn leaves of reds, yellows, orange, and purples swirled around me as I waited for my ride. What if they didn't believe me? Congressman Ryan had said that it was hard to believe. How was I going to convince the State Department?

A sleek black limousine pulled up slowly and stopped. The driver, an older gentleman with a dark olive complexion and wavy charcoal hair, walked around to open the door. I descended into the warm interior with soft and luxurious seats; a bright gold leaf blew in and settled on the armrest next to me. I felt like an impostor, an alien in a world I had once inhabited long, long ago. Although I was twenty-five, I still felt like a sixteen-year-old. My life had been on ice for nearly a decade.

The car turned and slowly pulled to a stop in front of a large building with colorful flags whipping about in the breeze. I waited where Congressman Ryan had suggested, just inside the doors. People were scurrying around me, down the stairs, in and out of the revolving door. Their casual air of freedom mesmerized me. What was it like never to have been weighed down with apocalyptic thoughts? Never to have been at the mercy of a tyrant? I envied their nonchalance and unshakable self-esteem.

I knew that my presence in D.C. would put me in potential danger. My thoughts traveled back to the first weeks after my escape, my fears of being followed, the phone calls at night with no one on the other end, my sense that my every move was being monitored.

Ryan's husky voice interrupted my brooding. "How was your trip?"

"Congressman . . . um . . . Leo. . . ."

"Are you worried about convincing these old farts?"

"Well . . ."

"Don't be. You'll do just fine."

How often I had heard those very same words from the officials at the embassy in Georgetown. He grabbed my shoulders and took my coat. We entered a dark hallway with a closed door every twenty paces, then turned down another hallway. Ryan waved to passers-by and stopped momentarily to chat with a couple of well-dressed women. Suddenly, a door opened and we entered an enormous wood-paneled conference room. A gigantic oval mahogany table occupied the center and about twenty maple-colored chairs were arranged around it.

Ryan positioned himself at the door to greet the distinguished officials he had summoned to attend my testimony. Gentlemen in pin-striped suits, pastel-colored shirts, and uniform white collars continued to file in. I felt homely and awkward in my dress and high heels. My stomach was churning and I prayed it wouldn't growl. I sat down, in an attempt to conceal my angst. The men took my lead, set their Styrofoam cups, yellow legal pads, pencils, and copies of my affidavit on the table, and sat down.

I could see from their furtive glances that many of them were dubious. I imagined they were relieved that *their* daughters would never get themselves into such a ludicrous situation. I caught someone's eye and smiled. But I felt defensive. I wanted them to listen and believe me. I wanted to scream that it could happen to anyone's child.

Ryan began to speak.

"I first heard about the incredible and courageous story of Deborah five months ago when she made public her disturbing affidavit chronicling her life in Peoples Temple and recently in Jonestown. This document, which each of you now has before you, was also hand-delivered to your offices several weeks ago. I hope you took the time to read it. This eleven-page document, 'Affidavit of Deborah Layton Blakey Re: the Threat and Possibility of Mass Suicide by Members of the Peoples Temple' dated June 1978, was sent to you, as officials of the State Department, to various members of Congress, and was reported in the news."

I surveyed the crowd apprehensively. They sat quietly, their eyes focused on Ryan and then me. I tried to sit higher up in the enormous chair. They listened politely and sipped their coffee.

"And now Deborah," Ryan reached his arm out to me and smiled benevolently, "will tell you the frightening details of life with the Reverend Jim Jones in Guyana. Please take notes."

I rose up. Everyone was quiet . . . waiting. The silence reverberated in my ears. The corner of my upper lip began to twitch. I wished I hadn't stood up. I began to talk, then sat back down on my leg to give me more height. My audience tilted their heads and scratched their temples in unison. I could tell from their puzzled looks and furrowed brows that they had not read my affidavit.

I spoke of my continued unsuccessful efforts to get word to my mother and brother in Guyana. The American Embassy was unhelpful, I told them, and why, after I had signed my testimony in the consul's office in Georgetown, hadn't an official immediately visited Jonestown? They had told me they would. Why, when they finally did condescend to visit the helpless inhabitants three months later, in August, hadn't I been apprised of my mother's and brother's condition? Had the visitors even been able to see them? Had they even tried?

I described how my brother had been taken as a hostage to Guyana the day I'd arrived in America, in an effort to ensure my silence. I described the wild paranoia that Jim had infused into every fiber of each and every inhabitant. And, finally, I warned them of everyone's mental instability. How I, too, had been crazed by misinformation, a lack of protein, a lack of sleep. I explained how I, like everyone else, had believed the American government was trying to invade the compound. We all believed we were the enemies of the United States Government.

"I was convinced that you, each one of you in this room, was conspiring to annihilate us. I heard what I believed to be your gunfire in the jungle."

The genteel men smiled dismissively. When I finished, their questions were tame, docile, and shamefully ignorant.

"Why did you join?"

"Were your parents supportive?"

"Why didn't you leave if you were unhappy?"

"Are you insinuating that the Reverend keeps the residents of Jonestown there against their will?"

I could tell they hadn't heard a single word I'd said. They looked impatient, as if their thoughts were already elsewhere. I imagined them contemplating their weekend plans—with whom they would have a round of golf, what movie they would see. They did not seem to be taking Congressman Ryan and me even the least bit seriously. How could I have failed to convey the gravity of this situation? Was it because most of the inhabitants were black that no one seemed to really care?

"Ya' done good!" Ryan smiled as we headed back down the maze of corridors. He patted his suit pocket. "I've got the letters your siblings wrote to your mom and brother right here. I promise I will read the letters to each of them individually, and let them know they have a prepaid ticket home. Are you sure you won't accompany us?"

"I . . . I can't . . . I'd be killed . . ." Or worse, I thought, drugged and imprisoned in Jonestown.

"Well . . . not to worry, Deborah. Everything is going to be just fine." He squeezed me with an enormous bear hug. "I'll call you the day I return."

It was impossible for those who had never known fear or stared into the face of darkness and death to conceive of my dilemma. It was impossible for them to know what all of us had been through and to imagine the dangers still lying ahead in the jungle.

Mama, I thought, I'm so sorry. I thought I would have had her home by now. I had tried to get messages to her. I was doing everything I could think of to get her back. Why wasn't I getting anywhere?

Ryan continued to hold my arm as he walked me to the rotunda. When I turned to hug him good-bye, I was startled by the sight of Teresa. She was entering the building with the Temple's attorney. I stiffened. Her terrified eyes met mine. I wanted to run over to her and apologize, say that I had always cared for her, that I was forced to report on her. But instead, I looked away. I felt filthy, like a snitch going to the other side. Why did she look so frightened? Surely I had not scared her. She must have known I was going to be here. What was Jim up to? Was she here to discredit me or to kill me? Or had she defected? Never, I thought . . . never, not Teresa!

As I drove off in the limousine, I felt unsure of what I had done, afraid of what would happen, and miserably aware that I had just upset the order of my new life, that the life I had run from was catching up with me again. I realized no one, not even Ryan, understood that lives were truly in danger. No one was capable of understanding how malevolent Jim Jones had become and what kind of power he had over the inhabitants of Jonestown. Ryan seemed to view his forthcoming trip like any other business jaunt. No one took the time to seriously ponder and evaluate the disturbing story I had told. Not even Ryan recognized the true danger his investigation was creating for himself, his entourage, and for the people in Jonestown. I could not figure out what else I could say to make them see the potential for catastrophe.

20
Hope Extinguished

November 18, 1978

A chestnut-brown cockroach sneaked out from under the hallway carpeting as my keys jingled in the lock. I walked into the kitchen and set down my groceries. I wondered how Ryan and his entourage of aides and newspaper reporters were doing. They'd been in Guyana for five days. They'd probably seen the dances, the entertaining skits. I wondered if Jim had had flowers brought in from the capital and planted them around the radio room and the Pavilion to impress everyone. Since my defection Jim had probably allotted more money for the construction of new cottages, more wooden walkways, and maybe even a guest cabin with conveniences like a sink, water, and a mosquito net.

And then the phone rang. A shrill voice shouted at me. I hardly recognized my sister.

"Slow down, Annalis . . ." My heart was pounding. I caught only tidbits. What was she saying?

"Ryan's been shot, his aide's been wounded, several cameramen have been hurt . . ."

"Where, Annalis? In the capital? Where?"

"News is skimpy . . . At an airstrip somewhere in the jungle. . . ."

"What? How?" My legs felt heavy and I slid down the wall to sit with my knees propped in front of me like a shield. "What about Mama?"

"Debs, get the hell out of there. No one is sure what happened. Maybe Mama is in the hospital. The reports say some people are in

Trinidad receiving medical care. Others are in the capital, but they don't know who . . ."

"Annalis."

"Leave! You're probably on a hit list! The instigator of a congressional invasion. I will meet you in an hour in town at that little fruit stand you like. A friend's offered her home. You'll be safe there. The Temple won't find you. Do not come here! They may have already started this way. I'll call John at the conference. I'll tell him not to go back to the house, but to come straight up here."

I grabbed my new flannel nightgown, toothbrush, pair of jeans, toilet bag, and rushed out to the car. Throwing my bundle into the backseat, I looked over my shoulder and locked the doors. With disbelief and fear pulsing through my veins, I drove over the Bay Bridge listening to the radio for more news.

What was happening down there? Leo Ryan shot? Had Jim finally panicked? But why? Weren't the mothers and children on a boat for Cuba? Hadn't the Russians accepted the money and finally granted asylum to the encampment? Maybe nothing had worked and now Father had declared war against everyone. I chewed the inside of my cheek. Had I been listed as "fair game"? Had Jim assigned someone to find me and take me out?

With one eye glued to the rearview mirror, I continued to switch radio stations. And then everything went silent. My hands trembled. My breathing was shallow and rapid. There was the thumping of feet, the smell of dirt scattering, the clouds of dust. Hushed, distraught voices whispered into my ear, an old, familiar voice rose above the vibrations, *"White Night, White Night."* Sweat broke out on my forehead. I stopped the car in the emergency lane. Where was Mama? It was happening again. I saw it, felt it, smelled it. I was being pulled back into the fear, the dread, the insanity.

I am here again.

Oh my God, help me. Help them . . . Someone stop this! I run across the walkway, away from the Pavilion, past the kitchen, down the footpath, looking for Mama. Up her stairs, onto her veranda, into her cottage. She is not here. Someone else's belongings have replaced hers. The purple, red, and orange serape is gone. Mama's sandals, her trunk, her clothes, gone. Mama?

I can hear Father's voice yelling over the loudspeakers, "Hurry, children, hurry to the Pavilion. The congressman has been killed. All is lost. We must die quickly. Die before they come in and kill us. Hurry, my darlings. Oh, how Father loves you . . ."

The voice on the radio filters through again. "We have just received news . . . Yes . . . It has just been confirmed that the entire community of almost a thousand . . ." No! No!!!

The words on the radio are telling me that my worst nightmare has come true. I can see it all in vivid detail in my mind. Father's loud voice, his words slurred, drugged. "Come, mothers, my sweet children, come quickly, before they do it for us." People standing close together, shivering uncontrollably, tears streaming down their brown cheeks, wondering why, why did it go so wrong? Babies in their arms, mothers with sons, daughters with fathers. Families forced apart by Father looking wildly for one another. Eyes searching the jungle for an escape route.

I am suddenly aware of a young mother. I cannot see her face clearly, but I can hear her thoughts. Who is she? Her voice is clear, she sounds familiar. She is trying to think within the chaos. She is trying to devise a plan in the midst of madness, a way to survive . . .

Should I run into the jungle with my baby? Could we survive in there? What if I am caught? Shot in the back? What if my baby is ripped from my arms as my wounded body writhes on the ground, as they drag him away from me, back into the death Pavilion? Could I stand hearing him scream for me, unable to comfort him as they hold him down and pour the pink poison down his throat? No! It's better to stay. I'll hold him, I'll comfort him. "Mommy's here, sweet-pea." I'll hum to him, tell him not to be afraid, "Mommy's with you." Yes! We'll die together, simultaneously, in an everlasting embrace that the world will see. The world will know how much I loved my baby. The world will know that the United States Government killed us.

Beth? Run! Run with Chioke . . .

Some won't swallow the poison, they're holding it in their mouths, preparing to secretly spit it out. But the cyanide is so terribly strong, it's being absorbed through the soft tissue in their mouths.

Panic, confusion, pain! Oh, the pain! Vomiting, cramps, dizziness. I am fading away. I am dying. God help us. Where did it all go . . . wrong?

I press my foot against the accelerator, rushing, aching, driving as fast as I can from a world where logic and reason no longer exist, where insanity has imploded upon itself.

Annalisa was waiting at the fruit stand. I followed her as she drove a long and circuitous route to a friend's house. Sick with fear and grief, I went into the bathroom and stared at my bedraggled reflection in the mirror. I did not look twenty-five. I did not look like my age. I was worn out and pale, too colorless to cast an image into the mirror. I leaned forward and stared into my lifeless eyes. I wondered when the tears would come, or if they ever would. In an attempt to create order, I unpacked my toilet bag, arranged my toothbrush and face cream neatly next to the salmon-hued sink, then rearranged them next to the rust-colored Indian vase. I shivered. I was cold. I could hear Annalisa in the kitchen. The news was murmuring from the television. The kettle reached a boil and suddenly went quiet as she removed it from the fire. I walked back into the bathroom and began to run a hot bath.

"Annalis . . . How's Papa?"

She appeared in the doorway with two steaming mugs.

"Tom's with him." She sat gloomily on the corner of the tub and handed me a cup.

The reports from Guyana said at least fifteen members were in the capital and had survived. One report stated that a woman named Sharon had slit the throats of her three children and then her own, in a bathroom at the organization's headquarters in Georgetown. Sharon's former husband had come to the capital with Leo Ryan and a group of the Concerned Relatives to visit the children whom he had been forbidden to see since Sharon had left America.

Jim had been right to trust Sharon. No one else in the capital had been allowed to have their family with them because it would make an escape more likely. But Sharon had been obedient to the very end.

I was sure Jim had Beth brought back into Jonestown after I left. She was probably not among the lucky few in the capital who had survived. And what about Mama and Larry?

My teeth began to chatter and I slid into the bath, the bubbles rushing up my back. What about Lee? Might he have fled into the forest when no one was watching? And what of Mary? Had she been in the kitchen when the sirens started? And where, oh where was Sweet Annie? Why couldn't I remember her face?

Annalisa and I sat in silence drinking Mama's German tea. This was the way she'd made it for us when we didn't feel good. The way Mutti had made it for her in Hamburg, sweetened with sugar and lightened with condensed milk. I thought how it must have been for Mama during the war, her parents hidden somewhere in Europe while she waited in America, praying and hoping for good news. She was twenty-five then. She had come here to start a new life, but she had been afraid. So many fears, so many secrets, so much shame. So many similarities between us.

Was everyone really gone? Jim . . . perished? Could he still hurt me? Or would he haunt me forever as he had always warned me he would? Oh God. How could I . . . how dare I . . . feel relief . . . ?

I heard the front door slam. John had made it.

After my bath, we sat in front of the television, flipping channels to get new information. Suddenly, I was assaulted by the image of a man I did not recognize but knew intimately. Larry, my brother, was being led someplace, accompanied by a herd of angry faces. The voice on the TV proudly announced it knew something I didn't. The voice was brimming with satisfaction. . . . "Larry Layton has just been arrested . . ."

I remained in Davis for several days waiting for news of Mama and more about Larry. Tiny morsels of information filtered up from South America, but never enough. Why hadn't they found Mama yet? Where could she be? I began to feel hopeful again. It seemed that no news was good news. Annalisa and I passed the time by taking walks in the orchards and biking to the fruit stand for hard, crisp, tangy apples.

On the morning of November 28, 1978, the telephone rang, then stopped and started again. It was the family code.

Tom was trying to steady his voice. "Debsy," he paused, "we just got a phone call, about Mama. . . . She died in Jonestown, perhaps a week before the massacre. Larry never left her side, not even for meals. He was with her till the end. Sweetie . . ." He cleared his throat. "She had one of us with her . . ." Tom was trying hard to sound brave, for me.

Two weeks after my useless visit to Washington, D.C., I packed my belongings again. I explained to Annalisa and Tom that I wanted to give Papa the news. It had to be me, the link between it all, the perpetrator, the deceiver. I had to be the one to tell him what had happened to his wife, to tell him his worst nightmares had come true.

I stood before Papa. His eyes downcast and dull, he seated himself on the couch Mama had reupholstered for his birthday. He looked up at me and patted the space next to him, inviting me to sit with him. I moved toward him, this man I had lied to, bad-mouthed, and taken money from to give to Father. The man whom I hadn't even called "Dad" since I joined the Temple.

"Dearest, come sit with me. Tell me what I dread." Then he sighed deeply, as if preparing for the coming onslaught of pain. His olive skin looked ashen and his soft blue eyes were turned away from mine. The evening wind had picked up and the fog was rolling in. The room grew chilly.

"Papa, I have good news and bad news," I began. "Mama did not die in the massacre." His eyes flickered with hope. "She passed away several days before." His face sank into deeper despair. I put my arms around his shoulders.

Papa fell forward, grasping his head with both hands and gasped in horror.

"Oh dear God, help us," he groaned through tears. "Where did I go wrong? Dear God, where did I go wrong?"

We sat for what seemed like forever. I held him and we cried. We grieved the loss of our innocence, our hopes and dreams. And as the enormity and magnitude of our reality dawned on us, we felt the weight of our regret.

We were unprepared for the self-righteous scrutiny of the media that would turn us into specimens of feverish interest. In a flash our family would no longer be just citizens, neighbors, or friends. No longer inconspicuous faces in the grocery store. We would be the objects of fascination for a prurient American public. We would symbolize what others were afraid to acknowledge and observe in themselves, and so they would soon condemn us.

During the next few days we continued to be inundated with more frightening news. Larry was alive and in a Guyanese dungeon.

He hadn't killed anybody, but he was charged with murder. We had to find and engage an attorney from 6,000 miles away. We needed to hire someone to prepare and bring food to him. Still no time to think, to reflect, to mourn Mama's death.

For weeks I was chauffeured by agents of the Federal Bureau of Investigation and the Secret Service to undisclosed locations for secret meetings. I was interrogated by Lawrence "Bonny" Mann, the Guyanese ambassador to the United States. I was deposed by U.S. Attorneys trying to recover the Temple's money from the Bahamas, Panama, and Europe. I met for hours with the House Committee on Foreign Affairs. I was subpoenaed to give sworn testimony before a federal grand jury. I was followed by news cameras, constantly questioned about Larry. Weary and filled with shame, I tried to explain that if I had been there, even though I wanted to leave, I, too, would have considered Congressman Ryan a threat. I would have viewed him as one of the evil mercenaries Father had warned us about. Yes, I would have gone to the airstrip and tried to shoot Ryan in an attempt to defend my comrades. Yes, when I lived in Jonestown I believed that anyone on the outside was the enemy.

Meanwhile, more news about Larry fired in at us. He was indicted for murder, he would be tried, and if found guilty, he would be hung from the neck until pronounced dead. I steeled myself for more bad news. I was growing exhausted, distrustful, and numb. And still I had not mourned Mama's passing.

While the world listened and watched in horror, my universe crumbled. My brother Larry, the sweet conscientious objector to the Vietnam War, was imprisoned. How could this be? I was just as guilty of conspiracy against the United States Government as he was. Why Larry and not me? Why my brother, out of all the innocent humans unwittingly caught in the ingenious machinations of a madman?

And as the months turned into years I made a pact with myself. I would never speak of it again. I would make it in this new world. I would make it on my own, by myself, and no one would ever know who I was . . .

I began to weave a cocoon of anonymity around myself. Like Mama, I, too, felt safer inside my protective shield. And from this place of safety I grew stronger while learning the ways of the "outside" world.

But I did not expect that my daughter would want to know, would need to know. For her, the losses from the Jonestown tragedy were manifold. She not only lost her grandmother, two aunts, and an unborn cousin, in many ways she also lost her uncle Larry, who remains in prison.

I once thought I could and should keep my daughter's legacy a secret from her. Just like my mother, who had lost her grandparents in Auschwitz and her mother by suicide, and who innocently believed that not telling her children would make our lives easier. But it didn't. Quite the contrary, in many ways, I suspect, the sense that I could never get answers from my mother contributed to my seeking out a person who promised to have all the answers.

When I began writing this book it was for my daughter, but as it grew I realized that I also had to tell this story for my mother, for her mother, and myself. I had to reveal the poisonous secrets handed down from mother to daughter. I felt compelled to come forward and confront my own guilt and shame in order to break the legacy of deception, of innocent, yet deadly deceit which had haunted my family for too long.

Mama died in Jonestown ten days before the massacre, with Larry never leaving her bedside. She died without pain medication because Jim had consumed it himself. For two months Larry watched our mother drift away from life without any relief from her agony until she finally succumbed to her lung cancer. She was buried somewhere in the jungle, near Lynetta Jones, but the location is unknown. I wish she were nearby, so that my daughter and I could visit her. She was sixty-three years old.

For years I would follow the backs of women who resembled my mother. I would walk for blocks trying to catch up with them, knowing that it was Mama, that she had survived and didn't want anyone to know. It is only now as I write this that I realize I can no longer turn away and close my eyes. It is time to finally mourn the loss of Mama.

I continue to dream of her and what pains me the most is that she will never know her granddaughter. She will never sit on my daughter's bed and read her to sleep . . .

Come away,
Child, and play

Light with the gnomies;
in a mound
Green and round
That's where their home is.

Honey sweet,
Curds to eat,
Cream and frumenty,
Shells and beads,
Poppy seeds,
You shall have plenty.

But as soon as I stooped in the dim moonlight
To put on my stocking and my shoe,
The sweet, sweet singing died sadly away,
And the light of the morning peeped through . . .

Epilogue

Looking back, there are a few things I have come to learn. People do not knowingly join "cults" that will ultimately destroy and kill them. People join self-help groups, churches, political movements, college campus dinner socials, and the like, in an effort to be a part of something larger than themselves. It is mostly the innocent and naïve who find themselves entrapped. In their openhearted endeavor to find meaning in their lives, they walk blindly into the promise of ultimate answers and a higher purpose. It is usually only gradually that a group turns into or reveals itself as a cult, becomes malignant, but by then it is often too late.

I hope my book will give my daughter some answers about how I got caught and how the Jonestown tragedy happened. I hope it will provide clues about the workings of a cult and shed light on the darkness of deceit. There are essential warning signs early on. Our alarm signals ought to go off as soon as someone tells us their way is the only right way.

When our own thoughts are forbidden, when our questions are not allowed and our doubts are punished, when contacts and friendships outside of the organization are censored, we are being abused for an end that never justifies its means. When our heart aches knowing we have made friendships and secret attachments that will be forever forbidden if we leave, we are in danger. When we consider staying in a group because we cannot bear the loss, disappointment, and sorrow our leaving will cause for ourselves and those we have come to love, we are in a cult.

If there is any lesson to be learned it is that an ideal can never be brought about by fear, abuse, and the threat of retribution. When family and friends are used as a weapon in order to force us to stay in an organization, something has gone terribly wrong. If I, as a young woman, had had someone explain to me what cults are and how indoctrination works, my story might not have been the same.

For each of my friends and comrades, and for my family, the story has turned out differently.

Stephan Jones, Jim's son and my Offering Room buddy, had been assigned to Georgetown along with two of his brothers, Jimmy Junior and Tim, on another endeavor to impress the Guyanese government. Although they survived and are alive today and doing well, they lost their entire family and everyone they had ever known.

Lee, my work crew leader, also lived, having been assigned as the chaperon and basketball coach for the last "presentation" games in Georgetown. He changed his name and lives with his family in California.

Shanda, my friend, who showed me the ropes when I arrived at the encampment, died in Jonestown. At the young age of nineteen, Jim had her interned in the medical unit and kept her comatose after she bravely refused to continue in her role as one of his concubines.

Robbi, my Offering Room comrade, who helped me with my workload when Mama was so ill, survived. After my escape I tried to reach her. I called the travel agent we had used to send people to Guyana, and explained to her what was happening in Jonestown. I had her call Robbi and pretend that Robbi needed to come in to correct a problem with the Temple's ticket billing, but the San Francisco Temple's staff were wary and refused to let Robbi go. Instead, she was immediately sent to Jonestown. She was one of the lucky few on assignment in Georgetown on November 18, but at the age of only nineteen, she lost her mother, father, seven siblings, and as many cousins.

Lew, Jim's eldest adopted son, his wife Beth, and their son Chioke died in Jonestown from cyanide poisoning. When their bodies were identified, Beth and Lew were holding each other and Chioke was lying between them. Lew and Beth were twenty-one years old.

Karen Layton, vivacious and in love with Larry, was five and a half months pregnant with their child when she died of poisoning in Jonestown. She was twenty-nine years old.

Gentle and kind *Mary,* the sorceress of delectable treats and Mama's gift-maker, died without her family, alongside the other 913 members. Mary was seventy-eight years old.

Annie, her sister Carolyn, Maria, John-John, and Kimo died in Jonestown, in Jim's house. Annie died last, after writing a letter to the world:

> . . . Where can I begin—Jonestown—the most peaceful, loving community that ever existed, JIM JONES—the one who made this para-

dise possible—much to the contrary of the lies about Jim Jones being a power-hungry, sadistic mean person who thought he was God—of all things.

I want you who read this to know Jim was the most honest, loving, caring, concerned person who I ever met and knew. His love for animals—each creature, poisonous snakes, tarantulas, none of them ever bit him because he was such a gentle person. He knew how mean the world was and he took any and every stray animal and took care of each one.

His love for humans was insurmountable and it was many of those whom he put his love and trust in that left him and spit in his face. Teresa, Debbie Blakey—they both wanted sex from him which he was too ill to give. Why should he have to give them sex?—And Tim and Grace—also include them. I should know.

I have spent these last few months taking care of Jim's health. However, it was difficult to take care of anything for him. He always would do for himself.

His hatred of racism, sexism, elitism, and mainly classism, is what prompted him to make a new world for the people—a paradise in the jungle. The children loved it. So did everyone else.

We died because you would not let us live . . .
—Annie—

Annie and Maria were twenty-four years old. Carolyn was thirty-one. John-John and Kimo were both under six.

It is believed that at Jim's request Annie shot him in the head in the Pavilion, then made her way down to their cottage and wrote this note. She was found with a gun in her hand, a bullet through her temple, and enough poison in her body to make sure she would die.

I find it interesting and sickening that Jim, the "great revolutionary" who espoused "death and sacrifice," was in the end too terrified to die by the agonizingly painful poison he so eagerly gave his disciples.

The saddest statement I can make about Annie's letter is that I could have written it myself had I been there. The letter shows so clearly the state of mind of a person who cannot for a moment think for herself. Sweet Annie was an innocent, who never gained back the ability to reason, who, over the seven years of her involvement, like me, could only deny reality and idealize the person who demanded, then took, her life. What she did made complete sense in light of her beliefs. It is so easy to become our surroundings, our environment. Without clarity, we are our own deceivers.

Sharon, Jim's lieutenant, was the only person in Georgetown who abided by the order from Jonestown for everyone in the capital to kill themselves. She was forty years old. Her intense loyalty and adamant refusal to let her pre-Temple husband, one of the Concerned Relatives, see their children led her to kill them first. She slit their throats with a knife. They ranged in age from eighteen to eight years old.

Teresa, my mentor, had been clever enough to work her way back into Jim's good graces after my damning report on her. She escaped Jonestown in October under the pretense of working with Jim's attorney on infiltrating the Concerned Relatives. I presume that was what she was doing in Washington when I saw her. She, too, did all she could to try and prevent the tragedy. I long ago heard she had a child, but I have never seen her since. I miss her and sincerely hope she is living well and in peace.

Leo Ryan was killed along with three newsmen and a female defector by a group of youths who came to the airstrip on a flatbed truck believing they were killing the mercenaries who were endangering the lives of their families and friends. When their "heroic duty" was accomplished, these young boys returned to Jonestown and took the poison with their families.

Mark Blakey had been assigned to the Temple's boat and was on the high seas during the demise of his world. I had our marriage annulled on my return to the United States, but he wrote me letters and kept in contact for several months afterward.

Dearest Debbie:

After you left Guyana I really hated you, not especially for leaving me, but if you had seen how your mum took it. She blamed herself and her health started to deteriorate. It was not until I got back to Guyana that I found out why you had left. I am sure we'll meet again someday. I know you did not like school in England, but those last two years of school were about the happiest time of my life. The early days of Jonestown were really exciting too, it's just a pity that you had not been here then.

Would you believe that the only reason I left Jonestown was that I thought we were really short of money and that the boat was a good money maker . . .

Although the atmosphere at Jonestown had changed a lot I never thought it would come to this. After the last crisis Jones said he would never do it, as he did not have the right to do it to the children . . . Then there was a long period of relative peace and all kinds of big plans to go to the Soviet Union. I really loved Jonestown because I built it and saw it all from when there was still bush there. It was not until Jones got there that things got bad. If he really wanted to do something for Socialism he could not have done anything worse.

Paula still feels very close to you . . . She said that she cried when you left and for that she was put under surveillance . . .

God, I wish the hell I had known what was going on . . . If a few people had gotten together who knew what was going on we could have done the bastard in . . .

Mark

After a while he returned home to Northumberland, where he now runs his family's farm.

Paula continued in her role as mistress to Ambassador Lawrence "Bonny" Mann and had his baby. But, tragically, two years later when he learned more of the circumstances in which he had been used by Jim and ultimately—so he believed—by Paula, he killed her, their child, and then committed suicide. They lived in Bethesda, Maryland, where he had continued to serve as the Guyanese ambassador to the United States. Paula was twenty-eight years old.

The only person held responsible for the insanity that befell the residents of Jonestown as well as the outsiders who had mistakenly believed they could come to Jonestown and help was my brother Larry Layton.

My brother Larry remains imprisoned to this day, the sole individual held accountable for the crimes of Jim Jones. He was implicated in the conspiracy to kill Congressman Ryan by virtue of the fact that he, along with hundreds of other Jonestown residents, signed a petition stating that they were opposed to his visit. On the day of the massacre, Larry was told that CIA infiltrators who had posed as loyal Temple members were "defecting" with Ryan in order to bring about the invasion of Jonestown. He was instructed to pose as a defector and then shoot the pilot of their plane once it was in the air in order to crash it. Larry consented, believing that by sacrificing his own life in this way, he would be saving the lives of 900 others. He was told this would give them time to get to Cuba. However, Jones had arranged for the actual assassination to take place before the planes took off. In the confusion, Larry shot and wounded two people, neither fatally.

Larry spent two years in a Guyanese dungeon before being tried and acquitted there. He was subsequently tried twice in the United States. His first trial ended in a hung jury voting 11–1 and 7–5 for acquittal, but the second trial resulted in conviction. Significantly, several prosecution witnesses, *including the two people he shot and injured,* begged for leniency for Larry, saying that he was not responsible for the insanity of the moment. So, too, did four of the jurors who had convicted him, as well as over fifty people who had been in Jonestown or who had lost loved ones there.

Federal Chief Judge Robert F. Peckham presided over both U.S. trials. In sentencing Larry, he took into consideration the compelling factors described above and his own conclusions that:

- Jim Jones was primarily responsible for the deaths and injuries that occurred:
- Larry's role in the conspiracy was less significant than that of a number of others—Larry did not participate in the shootings of the congressman, nor in the planning of the murders.

Judge Peckham recommended that Larry serve no more than five years from the date of sentencing. The federal probation officer who had extensively researched the circumstances of Larry's acts, interviewed dozens of people involved with the case, including psychiatrists and psychologists, and who wrote a lengthy presentencing report, also supported Chief Judge Peckham's recommendation.

In June 1991, Larry appeared before the Federal Parole Commission and was denied parole. He was sentenced to serve *another* fifteen years before he could be reconsidered for parole. In arriving at this weighty decision, two examiners spent no more than several *hours* over a two-day period reviewing his trial and prison records as well as over 450 pages of documentation submitted on Larry's behalf. During the subsequent hearing, the examiners repeatedly miscited the facts. Sadly, the considered judgement of a Chief Judge, the Honorable Robert F. Peckham, who spent sixteen months learning and deliberating the facts of the case, was dismissed. Larry's release is not scheduled to be *reviewed* again by the Federal Parole Commission until the year 2004.

Our papa turns eighty-four this year and will never again see his son a free man. Larry was thirty-one when he was arrested. He turns fifty-one this year.

After Jonestown's demise I met on numerous occasions with the Treasury Department, the Federal Bureau of Investigation, and the official, Robert Fabian, assigned to find the Temple funds Jim had stashed away in Switzerland, Barbados, Panama, and elsewhere.

With my help the money was recovered and subsequently depleted. First, the government was reimbursed for shipping the bodies back to America and the Temple's bills were paid off. Then, a monetary value was put on the lives of the deceased, and their relatives received a small compensation. John, for example, who lost his mother, sister, and adoptive father, received $14,000.

Because Mama had passed away before the massacre, there was no value attached to the loss of her life.

Acknowledgments

I am grateful to Renate Stendhal, without whose belief, guidance, and mentoring I would never have been able to complete this long and arduous project. An author, writing consultant, and friend, Renate urged me to go far deeper into the darkness than I thought I could. With the aid of her remarkable insight and honesty, I was willing to grapple with the demons of my nightmares, to take hold of the tormenting shame and guilt which had kept me silent for so long, and to step out from behind the shadows of Jonestown and stand tall in the light once more.

I am deeply grateful to Terrance Lim for not running away when he found out who I was, for believing in this book, supporting my decision to quit my job before I had even drafted a proposal, and for remaining my beacon of light as I descended into the shadows of my past. His belief spurred me on when the task felt overwhelming.

I would like to express deep gratitude to my literary agent, Amy Rennert, who believed in this book from our first conversation, helped shape the proposal and followed up with many long and encouraging phone conversations. I am beholden to my tireless editor at Anchor, Tina Pohlman, for her enthusiasm which gave my heart a lift, for her beautifully written missives filled with honest and insightful comments, and for our long Sunday conversations. I am also grateful to Martha Levin, former publisher at Anchor, without whose faith this story would never have made it into print. I am indebted to Phillip Ziegler for his counsel, his help in leading me into the past, and his giving me the strength to face the shame. He gave me my voice back and told me I had a story to tell.

I could not have written this book without the support of my family. I thank my father, Laurence Laird Layton, Ph.D., whose message, "think for yourself," I kept hidden in my secret compartment until I could finally hear it, for whom this tragedy will never end, who wept through each chapter and courageously read on; my brother Thomas N. Layton, Ph.D., professor, passionate family historian, and author himself (*The Voyage of the* Frolic: *New England Merchants and the Opium Trade*), for his enthusiasm for my project, his archive of family documents, encouraging phone calls, writer's block commiserating, and for having had the foresight to record my story immediately after my escape; my sister, Annalisa Layton Valentine, who has always been there for me, for her love and calm support when fielding my frightened calls from Guyana, for her invaluable help in editing critical portions of the manuscript, and her wonderful late night meals in front of her fire; my brother Laurence John "Larry" Layton, who called me every day from prison, who has given me the courage and unconditional love to write the story that devoured our youth, stole our mother, and continues to keep him behind bars. Larry remains an integral part of my life and over these many years has kept in touch with my daughter through the wonderful children's stories he writes for her. And especially, my daughter, Lauren Elizabeth, for remaining strong and brave as she learned the truth of my past, for her innate compassion, her love of history and the truth, and for her long list of suggestions for titles; my brother-in-law, Dr. Raymond Valentine, for his thoughtful suggestions and comments throughout; David Layton Valentine, my nephew, for his earnest reading of the manuscript and for not hanging up the phone when I was covertly calling his mother from Guyana when he was only four years old; Lori-Lisa Valentine, my niece, for her earthy spirit and support; Aunt Eva Philip Rosencranz, Mama's sister, who took me into her arms as one of her very own and mothered me when my daughter was born; Nance Rosencranz, my cousin, who took me in as well; and my mother's cousin Lisl Hirsch Burnham, who also has an escape story to tell.

I thank my dear friend Bridget V. Moar, whom I met during my metamorphosis at Montgomery Securities, who long ago began to instruct me on decorum, held my hand through each of my brother's trials, and, when I began to write, listened, advised me, and cried; Susan Feiga for her extraordinary friendship, her devoted support during Larry's trials, and for all the candles she has burned on my behalf; Brigitte Heftman and Dr. Erik Heftman, friends of my parents and gratefully now mine, too, who have read, listened to, enjoyed, and celebrated each new draft, and Sandye Lim, for her serene nonjudgmental ear, warmth, suggestions, and friendship.

I want to acknowledge the friends who encouraged this project, read drafts, and gave me their honest feedback: Will Weinstein, my boss on the trading floor of Genesis Merchant Group Securities, who has always believed in me, counseled, and taught me, and who has supported me in innumerable ways, and backed my decision to quit working for him and write my story; Chris Honoré, a writer, wonderful one-man support team, for invaluable suggestions throughout, for his encouraging calls and images of what *leaving* meant to him; Jim Randolph for sharing his feelings, wisdom, friendship, and his memories of my mother; Dr. Morris Weiss and Audrey Weiss for their insightful observations and for our rigorous discussions during dinners in Berkeley and Carmel; Theodore and Lillian Stewart for their friendship; Jan Hale for her writer's enthusiasm; Barbara Cohen and Georgia Cassel, who told me years ago that my past was something to be proud of; Dawn Margolin, for her aerobic counsel; M. J. Tocci and Dr. Jonathan Rest for their long-distance friendship, Jan Montgomery for her therapeutic phone calls and reassurance when I felt I was losing my way; Marya Grambs for her counsel, verve, and fascinating lunch discussions; Annie Stine for her last-minute assistance and wonderfully soothing voice; Virginia Raffi, for her many years of encouragement; Mark Witriol for his honest commentary; Jeannie Cahill for taking the time to ponder my questions; Beverly Shelton for her multiple readings; Yvonne Monteiro-Brown and Fran Sutherland for their friendship; and Mr. Fred Lincoln for telling me years ago that I could do anything I set my heart to.

I would like to give thanks to my *first* friends outside the Temple at the brokerage firm of Dean Witter Reynolds: David Cho for his unwavering belief, Sheryl Ishigaki for her love of life, and Mike Zima for his incredible humor; all three of you taught me well and I thank you all. Also to the many friends on the trading floor of Montgomery Securities. In particular, Thom Weisel for influencing me in ways he could not know and accepting me unconditionally; the late Ned Blackwood, whose life was taken too young, for taking me under his protective wing, and for my crash course on "This Other World: 101"; Ben Simon for his enduring kindness and delicious sandwich; Elaine and Ralph Blair for their chic camaraderie; James Stack for listening; and the late gifted and lovely Betsy Woods.

I am profoundly grateful to Loren Buddress, who granted me his honorable, moral, and heart-felt support in more ways than I can count or ever thank him for.

I wish Susie Smoke, my friend, photographer, and staunch supporter, were alive today to see me finally step out from the shadow of Jonestown. I miss her laugh, our spirited conversations, and her concern for my brother Larry.

I consider myself lucky to have had the opportunity to meet

Charles Krause, the Emmy Award–winning journalist, whose life was almost lost when he went to Jonestown on assignment for the *Washington Post.* Our paths crossed eighteen years later and I am grateful.

I am ever grateful to my friends John Clark and Grace Stoen, who became my mentors and friends after my escape, for opening my eyes. Both desperately tried to get their own families out from the clutches of Jim Jones, but lost their battles. John lost his mother, sister, stepfather, and stepbrother, and Grace her six year-old son, John-John.

I dearly thank Dr. Steven Katsaris, who didn't hang up when he heard my voice, for bravely reading my manuscript, and for his commentary. He too has suffered deeply with the loss of his daughter, Maria, and the injury of his son, Anthony, at the airstrip in Guyana. I thank Stephan Jones for his bravery, friendship, support, and willingness to share his thoughts, time, daughter, and family photographs with me; Dr. John and Barbara Moore, who lost their daughters Annie and Carolyn as well as their grandson Kimo; Dr. Rebecca Moore, Annie and Carolyn's sister, and her husband Fielding Mcgehee for their incredible strength, love, and passionate belief that Larry should be allowed to come home.

I remain deeply appreciative to Sheri Glucoft Wong for her guidance, and Dr. Philip Zimbardo and his Stanford psychology class on Mind Control. As I spoke to his class of 200 students, feeling embarrassed and ashamed of my part in this historical event, I was put at ease by their nonjudgmental and insightful questions.

Last, I wish I could thank in person the late Honorable Chief Judge Robert F. Peckham. I did not know him personally, but came to know him well while he sat in his black robes on the bench before me, judging my brother. He was firm and unrelenting in ferreting out truth from fiction, hype from fact, and ultimately fairness from political maneuverings. He believed Larry was a minor player in an enormous tragedy and never stopped trying to get Larry freed. The Honorable Robert Peckham died in 1993.

ABOUT THE AUTHOR

Deborah Layton was born in Tooele, Utah, in 1953. She grew up in Berkeley, California, and attended high school in Yorkshire, England. After her escape from Jonestown, Guyana, in May 1978, she worked as an assistant on the trading floor for an investment banking firm in San Francisco until she resigned in 1996 to begin writing *Seductive Poison.* Layton lives in Piedmont, California, where she is raising her daughter.